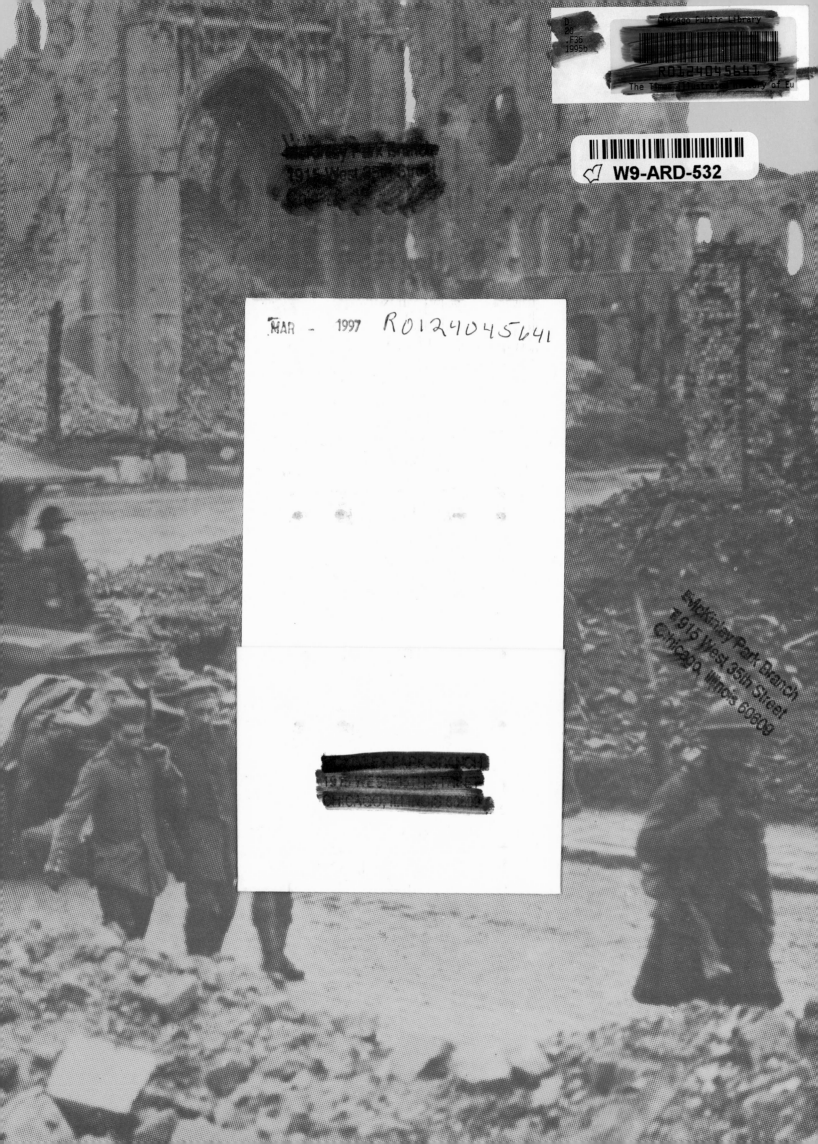

THE TIMES
ILLUSTRATED
HISTORY *of*
EUROPE

HISTORY

THE TIMES

of ILLUSTRATED EUROPE

Felipe Fernández-Armesto

TIMES BOOKS

TIMES BOOKS
77-85 Fulham Palace Road
London W6 8JB

First published by Times Books 1995
Copyright © Times Books 1995

Editorial direction:
Philip Parker
Cicely Oliver
Thomas Cussans

Cartographic direction:
Martin Brown
Neil Forrest
Annabel Newby

Design:
Ivan Dodd
Nik Keevil
Nick O'Toole

Picture research:
Anne-Marie Ehrlich

Index:
Janet Smy

Typesetting by Times Books

Colour separations by Colourscan, Singapore

Printed and bound in Hong Kong
by HarperCollins*Publishers*

British Library Cataloguing in Publication Data.
A catalogue record for this book is available
from the British Library.

ISBN 0 7230 0724 1

CONTENTS

Clay bronze-age votive object with swans and idols   Duljaja, Serbia

EMERGENCE

and ECLIPSE
ORIGINS *to* 1054

CHAPTER 1

OUT OF THE ICE
The non-completion of a continent

Spread of deciduous oak 11,000-5000 BC

5000 BC
5000 BC
North Sea
Baltic Sea
Atlantic Ocean
7500 BC
8500 BC
8500 BC
11000 BC
11000 BC
Mediterranean Sea

Faeroe Is

Tjikkiträsk
Lundfors

Föllinge
Bellsås

Ancylus Lake
Pulli
Zvejnieki

Skipshelleren
Tørkop
L. Vänern
Dvina
Hein 33
L. Vättern
Viste Cave

Skara Brae · Orkneys

Scotland
MacArthur Cave
North Sea
Dyrholm
Klosterlund   Ulkestrup
Ringkloster
Mullerup   Svaerdborg
Holmegård
Vistula
Janis Lawice

Mountsandel
Newferry   Larne
Dogger Bank
Duvensee   Hohen Viechein
Stellmoor
Oder
Witów
Star Carr
Leman and Ower   Pesse
Aberffraw   Deepcar
Zátyní   Konin
Orońsk
Soroki
British Ireland Isles
Havelte
Rhine
Ostrów
Carpathians
Peacock's Farm
Broxbourne
Thatcham   Farnham
Tašovice
Oakhanger   Iping Common

(English Channel)
Villeneuve-sur-Verberie
Fère-en-Tardenois
Lautereck
Sered
Coincy
Tannstock
Peres
Băile Herculane
La Adam
Oberlarg, Mannlefelsen   Birsmatten
Wetzikon
Cuina Turcului
Hœdic
Loire
Villars-sous-Dampjoux
Schötz
Vatte di Zambana
Betulov Spodmol
Lepenski Vir
R. Danube
Baulmes
Pointe de St-Gildas
Bellefonds
Ranggiloch
Romagnano
Grotta Azzurra   Kraške Spilje
Sous-Balme
di Samatorza
Po
Bay of Biscay
Col du Coq
Balkans
Rouffignac   Lascaux
Rhone
Adriatic Sea
Gramari
Apennines
Crvena Stijena
Sauveterre-la-Lémance
Montclus
Brassempouy
Gazel   Châteauneuf-lès-Martigues
Altamira
Le Mas-   Ponteau
d'Azil
Poyemau
La Crouzade
Corsica
Pyrenees   Le Tuc d'Audoubert
Cipolliane di Novaghie
Cogull
Aegean Sea
R. Douro
Ebro
Iberia
Perelló
R. Tagus
Cueva Remigia
Sardinia
Doña Clotilde
Balearic Is
Grotta della Madonna
Llatas
La Cocina
Mediterranean   Sea
Parpalló
Termini Imerese   Sicily
Guadalquivir

Hoyo de la Mina

Europe after the ice age, c. 10,000 BC
- Mesolithic settlement
- - - - modern coastline

- birch forest
- north mixed forest
- deciduous forest
- montane forest
- Mediterranean forest
- ice

BEFORE THIS, IT WAS NOT EUROPE, only the semblance of Europe, packed under the ice. At the coldest phase of the ice age, about 20,000 years ago, the covering was 1,500 metres thick over what is now Scotland and rather more over most of Scandinavia. It stretched almost as far south as the Black Sea, diagonally across the land, roughly from where the south-east corner of Britain now is. The Mediterranean basin was edged to the north by treeless tundra. The thaw which now began lasted for about five millennia but was followed by intense reglaciation until perhaps 12,000 years ago.

When the ice withdrew, something recognisably like the Europe we have today emerged. Two processes shaped the northern outlines of the continent from the Atlantic to the Baltic and the Arctic Ocean: ice disclosed vast shelves of land; and rising sea-levels covered a lot of it up again. Scandinavia really did rise from the ice, pushing it away like a giant heaving at bedclothes: the peninsula is still rising a little from the sea, year by year, at its northern end. At the same time, the melting ice flowed round new patterns of coastline. The English Channel was in place by about 10,000 BC, and the Baltic Sea – delayed by heaving landmasses – about 3,000 years later. The result could be characterised as a number of varied regions grouped around a vast bow-shaped lowland which stretches today from the Atlantic to the Urals with little interruption. To the south of this north European plain, the drainage areas of great river-systems are separated by the Russian uplands and the Carpathian mountains. The highlands that reach from these to the Massif Central fence off the Hungarian 'prairie' and the valleys of the upper Danube and Rhone, while the mountainous south, washed by the Mediterranean, is interrupted by only two broad valleys – those of the Po and Ebro. Lower, older ranges fringe the northwest, in Scandinavia, Britain and Ireland, where the mountainous edges are tattered by seas and gulfs.

Although the northern shore of the Mediterranean was barely modified in outline by the shift of the ice to the north, its climate warmed and dried, creating a new environment, while areas of the far north became habitable or penetrable for the first time in thousands of years. Though the climate of Europe has continued to fluctuate ever since, occasionally reclaiming the edges and uplands from unbearable cold, the dominant feature since the ice age has been stability. Compared with the relatively rapid turnover in extremes over the previous 10,000 years, the last 10,000 have been nearly static. By around 8,500 years ago, Europe can be said to have emerged out of the ice, with roughly the shape and more or less the range of climates which have been familiar ever since.

Even so, it was a rough-hewn, imperfect continent. The name 'Europe' has been a current geographical expression for at least two-and-a-half millennia and no agreed definition has yet been established. Paul Valéry's joke that it was really nothing more than a small 'promontory of Asia' has now become a commonplace. Whereas all other continents are obviously discrete, and Africa, Antarctica and the Americas all have sharp outlines which are immediately conspicuous on a map, Europe blends into Asia with no obvious discontinuities. The Urals are a ridgeless bump. The steppes which outflank them to the south reach to the Carpathians and Balkans. The Caucasus Mountains make a spectacular frontier zone but include no clear dividing line. There is no geographical logic in distinguishing Europe as a continent at all.

Thus 'Europe' is left as a term of convenience hard to match to any objective reality. Its landward extent can be made to vary according to the perspective of the beholder. Herodotus despised the Scythians, who, he claimed, never washed and drank their enemies' blood; so he fixed the frontier of Europe at the Don; Strabo, who thought of the Scythians as useful buffers for Rome, drew the line at the Dnieper. The elastic nature of Europe's landward frontiers has been illustrated in recent times by the temporarily successful attempt of Soviet geographers, for political reasons, to supplant the conspicuous Caucasus by the unhappily-named Manych Depression as the boundary in the southeast. People inside the European Union today have developed the misleading habit of speaking of Europe when they mean only themselves. Even on the seaward side, it is not clear which Atlantic islands to include in Europe, except by convention, and while the Canaries and Azores, for instance, get reckoned European for historical reasons, Iceland is sometimes left out of account.

While definitions have been framed to exclude particular regions and peoples, characterisations have been formulated which make some parts of Europe seem more European than others. In recent years, the debate in the United Kingdom over Britain's relationship to the rest of the European Union has often been expressed in terms of whether or to what extent the British are European. At least since the seventeenth century, there have been thinkers or jokers to aver that 'Africa begins at the Pyrenees'. Historians of Europe commonly give priority, in discussing ancient history, to the Mediterranean over the north and, in treating of modern times, pay more attention to the west than to the east. The very distinction between 'western' and 'eastern' is value-laden with the implication that 'western' is best and that

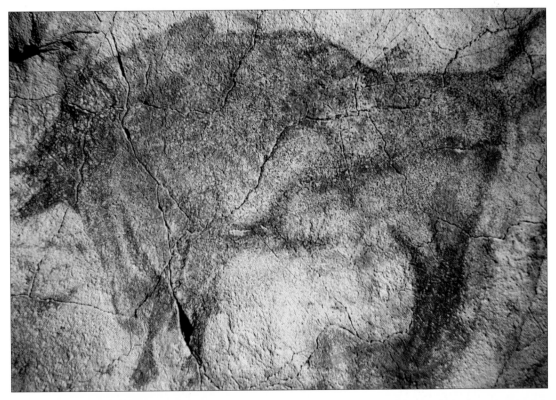

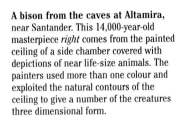

A bison from the caves at Altamira, near Santander. This 14,000-year-old masterpiece *right* comes from the painted ceiling of a side chamber covered with depictions of near life-size animals. The painters used more than one colour and exploited the natural contours of the ceiling to give a number of the creatures three dimensional form.

Europe after the ice age *map left*. The rapid warming of the climate after c. 8300 BC brought with it the northward spread of forest with the result that deciduous forests covered most of Europe by c. 5000 BC. Substantial areas of Europe were flooded as the sea level rose, and the land bridge joining Britain to the Continent was severed. The general warming opened areas of northern Europe to settlement which had been almost inaccessible in the harsh climate of the ice age.

whatever is to the speaker's east can safely be despised. In the vast lowland area where Europe shades into Asia, beholders further west can dismiss the inhabitants as 'Asiatic' – a term which, in the context, is always meant pejoratively. This is worse than a crime: it is a mistake. Europe, as understood in this book, has been made at least as much by east-west movements as by those originating in the west. The job of historians of Europe is not to tell the story of a region already defined, but rather to try to track a still-evolving concept.

Lacking obvious geographical unity, Europe might be thought to make a suitable unit of study on cultural or political grounds. But 'European culture' is as elusive a concept as the 'European continent' and has less obvious substance. As a cultural or political reality, Europe inspires hope unsupported by experience. Its potential citizens have fought from within over their rival perceptions of it. In these homelands of 'energetic mongrels' the idea that Europeans together form a distinctive 'race' would be laughable if its consequences had not been so evil in the past. It is sometimes thought that Europe is uniquely stamped with a cultural heritage combining the classical legacy with Christianity; but these have become world-wide influences. Europeans have done too much to spread them over the globe to claim proprietory rights convincingly. Christianity, in any case, is a tradition of extra-European origins which, since it was received amongst us, has done more to divide Europeans than to unite them. The confessional fault-lines have criss-crossed with others – linguistic, economic, ideological – and with powerfully divisive political frontiers. Students of modern history have sometimes claimed to detect a distinctively European 'scientific culture' or 'political culture' but, as we shall see, these notions have the attractions of a lifebuoy: they are useful to cling to only because they are empty.

For those enmeshed in its diversity, or caught in the cross-fire of its ethnic squabbles, Europe seems to defy coherent treatment. Except in resentment or envy, outsiders have rarely seen it whole. Repeatedly shaken, like the contents of a kaleidoscope, into different patterns and shapes, it has projected a bewildering variety of images. Flickering uncertainly in the beholder's eye, it seems, under critical scrutiny, to threaten to dissolve into parts or vanish into the *néant*. Yet its impact on the rest of the world has been solid enough and, like a pile of bones sanctified by devotion, Europe can be empowered by Europeans' willingness to believe in it. A sense of European identity is now becoming widespread – more so, perhaps, than ever before in history. Yet its ingredients remain unidentifiable and a European profile as hard to draw as ever.

If European identity ever does triumph above or alongside the divisions, it will be founded not on geography, race, culture or even common interest – which is too volatile a substance to bind for long – but on the slow, accelerating accumulation of common historical experiences which form the subject of this book. The first of those experiences was emergence out of the ice.

In the Europe which the ice left uncovered, there were environments people could exploit. Nature could be generous to settlers who followed in the lee of the glaciers. Even on the edge of icefields, life teems. While it was still under ice, the south of what is now Scotland might enjoy summer temperatures of up to nine degrees Celsius. Hunters who followed the icecap northwards shared the habitat of reindeer, elk, giant deer, red deer and seal. The far north of Scandinavia had already been repopulated more than 11,000 years ago and even apparently marginal uplands were colonised by about 7000 BC. Forests followed the retreat of the icecap northwards. Birch woodlands, with their appetite for cold, became widespread by about 11,000 years ago. The oak was about as widely distributed 7,000 years ago as it is today. For unadapted peoples, forests are a tougher environment than tundra and the flight northwards of hunters of reindeer explains the alacrity with which areas exposed by deglaciation were settled. On the other hand, the diversification of environments and species created opportunities which can be read in the well-worked middens of south-western France, with their increasing numbers of bones of deer and pig, elk and auroch.

Even in the glare from the ice, Europe looked like a promising part of the world. While most of the region was still icebound or tundra,

sublime works of art had been left by the cave-painters of Lascaux and Altamira or the modellers of the clay bison from Tuc d'Audubert or the sculptor of the long-necked woman of Brassempouy: these works have as much power to stir a response in a modern beholder as any more recent art and immediately establish our sense of kinship with predecessors of between 12,000 and 22,000 years ago. Compared with the environment they endured, the last 10,000 years have been easy. The departure of the ice left some of the best-equipped habitats for man on the planet: temperate climates, fertile soils, navigable rivers, ore-rich mountains.

Most of what is usually written about the lives led in the first few millennia after the emergence of Europe is based on assumptions about the uniformity of 'egalitarian' hunter-gatherer societies. But some real people of the time can be seen on wall-paintings in Spain: beating deer towards waiting bowmen, or fighting with bows under the leadership of plumed chieftains, or gripped in single combat with wild bulls, or gathering honey from swarming bees. In other parts of the continent, their bones lie in graves enriched with beads and blades and gifts of red ochre, sometimes still showing the wounds of their wars. At some sites – there is a remarkable display at Skateholm, now on the Baltic coast – their dogs lie nearby: burly, wolf-like hunters, buried with the spoils of their careers, including antlers and boars' tusks, sometimes with more signs of honour than attend human burials. These dogs were full members of societies in which status was determined by hunting prowess.

The variety of graves makes nonsense of the romantic image of savage freedom in societies of equals: sometimes shamans are differentiated by standing burial in vertical shafts; secular rank seems suggested by the bestowal on some dead of carved images of animals. In the village of Lepenski Vir in the Iron Gates of the Danube, where scaly fish-images, sculpted in stone, presided over the hearths of almost identical dwellings, the centremost of the thatched huts was

Fish-head sculptures, such as the example here *above right*, more than a foot high and engraved with scales, were kept close to the hearths of the mid-sixth millennium BC settlement of Lepenski Vir, overlooking the Danube, where the inhabitants of a couple of dozen huts hunted elks and auroch and caught carp and cuttlefish.

Mannerist elegance on the edge of the ice: a head carved about 22,000 years ago *above* and found at Brassempouy in the Landes, near the centre of a corner of Europe rich in the cave-art of the tundra huntsmen of the period.

The spread of agriculture in Europe *map right*. Whilst cultivated grasses, vegetables and livestock had to be introduced from the Near East, agricultural settlement did not expand into a cultural void: local initiatives, adaptations and advances must have been vital in harnessing the new opportunities offered by the progress of agriculture.

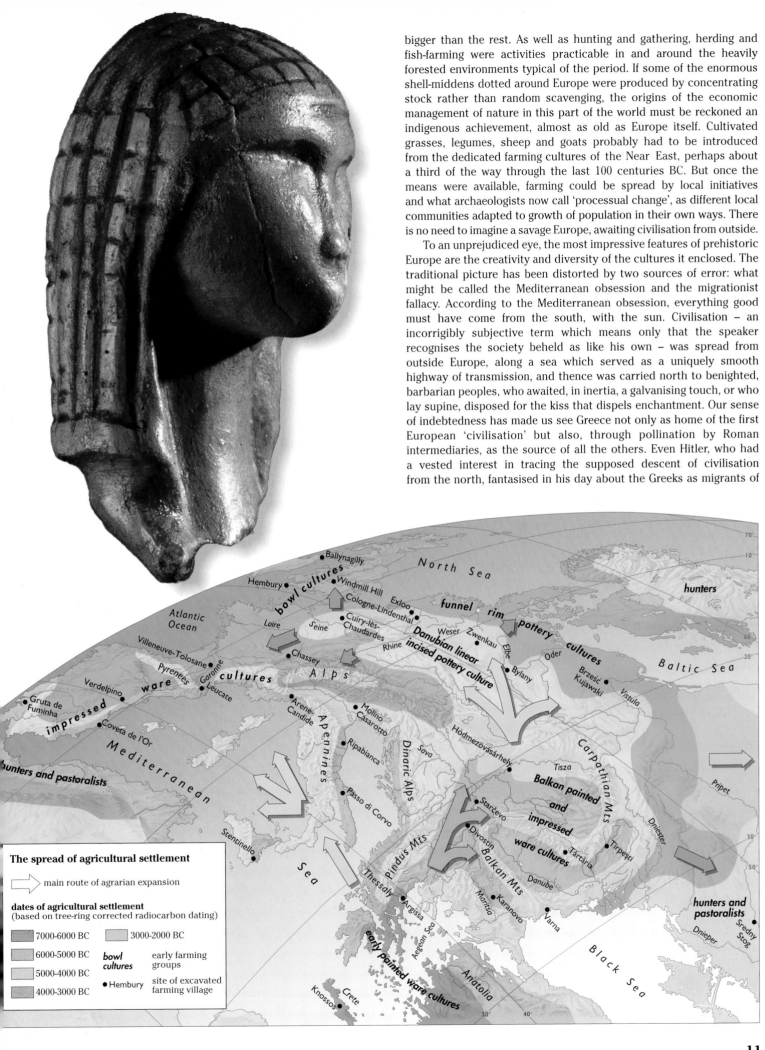

bigger than the rest. As well as hunting and gathering, herding and fish-farming were activities practicable in and around the heavily forested environments typical of the period. If some of the enormous shell-middens dotted around Europe were produced by concentrating stock rather than random scavenging, the origins of the economic management of nature in this part of the world must be reckoned an indigenous achievement, almost as old as Europe itself. Cultivated grasses, legumes, sheep and goats probably had to be introduced from the dedicated farming cultures of the Near East, perhaps about a third of the way through the last 100 centuries BC. But once the means were available, farming could be spread by local initiatives and what archaeologists now call 'processual change', as different local communities adapted to growth of population in their own ways. There is no need to imagine a savage Europe, awaiting civilisation from outside.

To an unprejudiced eye, the most impressive features of prehistoric Europe are the creativity and diversity of the cultures it enclosed. The traditional picture has been distorted by two sources of error: what might be called the Mediterranean obsession and the migrationist fallacy. According to the Mediterranean obsession, everything good must have come from the south, with the sun. Civilisation – an incorrigibly subjective term which means only that the speaker recognises the society beheld as like his own – was spread from outside Europe, along a sea which served as a uniquely smooth highway of transmission, and thence was carried north to benighted, barbarian peoples, who awaited, in inertia, a galvanising touch, or who lay supine, disposed for the kiss that dispels enchantment. Our sense of indebtedness has made us see Greece not only as home of the first European 'civilisation' but also, through pollination by Roman intermediaries, as the source of all the others. Even Hitler, who had a vested interest in tracing the supposed descent of civilisation from the north, fantasised in his day about the Greeks as migrants of

The spread of agricultural settlement

⇨ main route of agrarian expansion

dates of agricultural settlement
(based on tree-ring corrected radiocarbon dating)

- 7000-6000 BC
- 6000-5000 BC
- 5000-4000 BC
- 4000-3000 BC
- 3000-2000 BC

bowl cultures — early farming groups

● Hembury — site of excavated farming village

Germanic origins, who irradiated the world with high culture from their new home.

Yet the 'classical' value-kit we have got from Greece and Rome arose, by any standards, very late in the making of Europe – only from the late fifth century BC onwards. In the 4,000 years or so before that, numerous cultures of independent origins and splendid achievements had arisen, in patches and at intervals, all over Europe and inter-acted with each other. The most spectacular of them, by some standards, were certainly those that flourished in and around the Aegean Sea in the third and second millennia BC and part of the first: the elegant marble harpists of Karos do seem to strum in a new and glorious era. The scale and craftsmanship of the monuments of Minoan Crete and Mycenae seem to excel their rivals and the wealth that produced the luxury objects of their courtly centres might appear to beggar that of other parts of Europe. Yet many of their achievements were anticipated by events elsewhere; recent work on the chronology of the European bronze age exposes as a myth the influence formerly ascribed to them in spreading the amenities of a lavish life and a memorable burial to the northern and western edges of Europe. Nor can they be said to have formed part of the Greek tradition which subsequently contributed so much to the rest of Europe. To Plato and Aristotle, the Crete of King Minos was almost as remote as it is to us, dimly recalled in 1,000-year-old legends. Mycenae and late Minoan culture had, it is true, something in particular in common with the makers of the classical world: their peoples or, at least, their elites did speak a language recognisable as an early form of Greek; but they were also part of a lost world – separated from classical Greece by the 'Dark Ages' that followed the disappearance of monumental Mycenae, and shared among a great

array of European cultures or proto-civilisations of the bronze age.

The migrationist fallacy has been as powerful a force as the Mediterranean obsession in shaping our picture of the remote past. Our received wisdom about prehistoric Europe was formulated in the late nineteenth and early twentieth centuries when Europe was enjoying her own great imperial age. The experience of those times convinced self-appointed imperial master-races that civilisation was something which had to be spread from superior to inferior peoples. Its vectors were colonists, conquerors and missionaries. Left to themselves, barbarians would be mired in cultural immobility. The analogy with the origins of civilisation in Europe was hardly ever made explicit. The self-perception of the times was projected, almost without utterance, onto the depiction of the past. Stonehenge was regarded as a marvel beyond the capabilities of the people who really built it – just as to white beholders the ruins of Great Zimbabwe seemed to have been left by intruders, or the cities of the Maya to have been erected under guidance from afar. Early bronze-age Wessex, with its chieftainly

The origins of Stonehenge *below* greatly pre-date those of the 'Wessex culture' of rich burials which surround it, but it was a sacred site of such significance that it was tended and periodically modified for well over 1,000 years. The work involved in quarrying, transporting and erecting the stones make it one of the most astonishing monuments of stone-age Europe. The orientation of its entrance avenue towards sunrise at the summer solstice suggests its use as the centre of a cult of magic.

A bronze-age aristocrat bent over his beaker and bronze dagger-head *right* in a typical burial of the early second millennium near Stonehenge. In the foreground is a polished axehead belonging to the same 'Wessex culture'.

Harmony and elegance of life in an early bronze-age court in the eastern Mediterranean: a marble harpist *below right* from Karos in the Cycladic Islands, late third millennium BC.

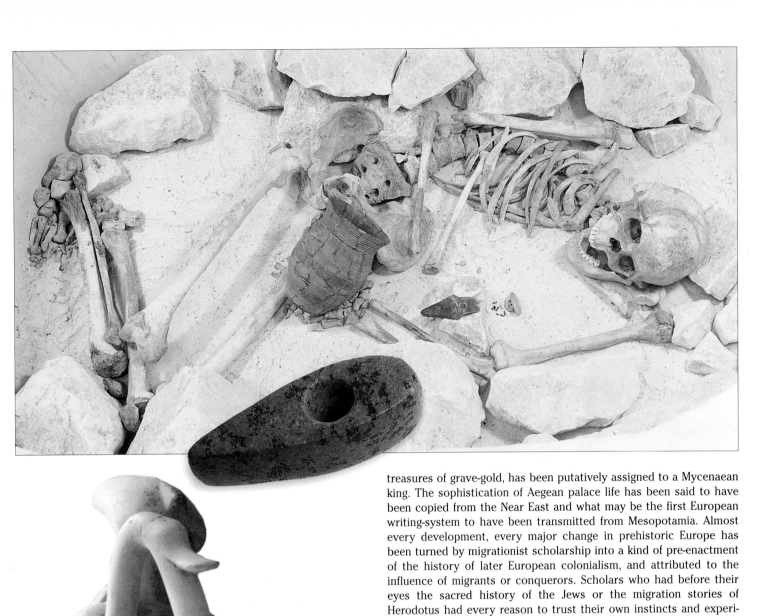

treasures of grave-gold, has been putatively assigned to a Mycenaean king. The sophistication of Aegean palace life has been said to have been copied from the Near East and what may be the first European writing-system to have been transmitted from Mesopotamia. Almost every development, every major change in prehistoric Europe has been turned by migrationist scholarship into a kind of pre-enactment of the history of later European colonialism, and attributed to the influence of migrants or conquerors. Scholars who had before their eyes the sacred history of the Jews or the migration stories of Herodotus had every reason to trust their own instincts and experience and to chart the progress of civilisation as movements on a map.

For instance, in the third millennium BC a new fashion in burials spread through western Europe, between Spain and Hungary, and became especially common in Britain: an individual grave was equipped with a kit of offerings, usually including a weapon and a beaker with a waisted shape. From the time such graves began to be discovered until the 1970s, they were generally supposed to be the marks of the passage of 'Beaker Folk'. The notion inspired elaborate, intriguing and, for a time, convincing fantasies. These complete imbibers were thought to be precursors of Spanish conquistadores, fanning out over Europe on horseback from a supposed homeland in Andalusia; or they were gypsy smiths or tinkers travelling back and forth in states of flux and reflux postulated to accommodate various sites' claims to priority. The artefacts that make up the 'Beaker culture' are now almost universally regarded as the products of social change occurring independently but in parallel among neighbouring peoples: as particular members of the group achieved special status, they were rewarded with individual graves and appropriate offerings at their deaths; the beakers – memorials of elite symposia or the drunken revels of a warrior class – were traded and copied from place to place without necessarily being accompanied by migrants.

The most tenacious migration myth, underpinned by an almost-compelling logic of its own, is that of the 'Indo-Europeans'. When the similarities in structure and vocabulary between European, Iranian and Indian languages were first systematically tabulated in the late eighteenth century, the assumption that all these tongues developed from a common *Ursprache* was irresistible. The speakers of 'Proto-Indo European' were imagined as a discrete people whose migrations and conquests spread their language from a putative homeland, which

In the fourth and third millennia BC, Malta housed the largest stone buildings known anywhere in the world, like the temple at Tarxien shown here *left*.

Beaker and urnfield burial sites *map right*. The widespread distribution of Beaker ware in copper-age burials is suggestive more of the long-distance trade contacts which had developed within Europe than of the hegemony of one particular group. By the eighth century BC, Beaker burials had been supplanted by cemeteries of urns containing cremations, which were the dominant burial rite from northern Spain to the fringes of the Steppes.

scholars have sought ever since, in a grail-quest that has led from the North Pole – seriously suggested by one school of thought – to the Himalayas. Yet this whole realm of scholarship is a tissue of inferences: there is no evidence that the *Ursprache* ever existed or that there was ever an *Urheimat* to enclose a father-race, nor is there any trace of the supposed migrations in the archaeological record.

The very notion of a single common tongue was an understandable assumption of scholars in the humanist tradition who treated whole languages as they did manuscripts, working back through the variants to a single source. The manuscript-analogy, however, may have been misleading. Languages, as far as we know, are always riven among dialects which shade into one another; they always interact with other languages at the margins to produce modifications and hybrids. One technique for identifying the *Urheimat* has been to treat the common terms for flora and fauna in languages of Indo-European descent as clues to the environment inhabited by the original speakers before their supposed migrations split them up. Yet the Proto-Indo-European vocabulary could have been composed from contributions from several different environments. Indeed, since it seems to have included words for plains and mountains, rivers and lakes, snow and ice, with names for plants and animals which have come to be applied to a bewildering range of species, the homeland, by the reasoning this method implies, must have been either very large or very diverse.

Similar attempts have been made to reconstruct the lives of the speakers of the postulated language. This is a hazardous proceeding and it is often pointed out that if we had to infer the culture of the original speakers of Latin from words which romance languages have in common, we should be bound to suppose, for instance, that they were Christians who drank coffee and smoked cigars. By inferences of this sort, disciplined by rational caution, speakers of the Indo-European *Ursprache* can plausibly be said to have had boats, wagons and dogs; they worshipped personifications of natural forces and sacrificed cattle; they divided work, prayer and war between groups of specialised function and – probably – differentiated status, led their brides home, pitied widows, fortified their settlements and farted. But even this limited range of features – with others which could reasonably be added – may not have characterised a single community but may rather have been combined from the experience of different groups. The notion of Proto-Indo-European developing in isolation, walled behind the gates of

Gog and Magog, or behind barriers of ice or mountains, has often been suggested, but is an obvious fantasy crushed out of minds bewildered by the intractability of the evidence.

Languages are not spread only by migrations and conquests. Low-level, small-scale settlement, trade, evangelisation and every sort of cultural contact may contribute to the same effect. Sometimes, what starts as a borrowed *lingua franca* displaces the indigenous tongue or modifies it so radically as to create a new language. Or again, a language adopted by an elite can spread through the whole of a society. Terms can be handed across frontiers, like the gifts the Hyperboreans were said to have sent to the shrine of Delian Apollo. In any case, some languages are classified as Indo-European on the basis of a thin trunk of terms and sprigs of grammar and accidence which could have been grafted on to a different sort of stem. It is easy to forget, in the swirl of debate about Indo-European origins, that 'Indo-European' is a term of classification, reflecting the perceptions of scholars rather than the reality of the way the language concerned, in any particular case, has evolved. To ascribe peculiar common ancestry to all speakers of Indo-European languages would be as foolish as to suppose that all the peoples who speak English today must have come from England or that all speakers of Swahili belong to a single ethnic group.

While treating 'Indo-European migrations' with reserve, we can, however, be sure that the transmission of influence which spread Indo-European languages over so much of Europe happened in general from east to west. The only surviving non-Indo-European language of western Europe, Euskara or Basque, shows no early traces of Indo-European influence: Basques only began to borrow words of Indo-European derivation when they came into contact with Latin. Nor – though this is a tentative judgement, given the state of the evidence – do the region's vanished non-Indo-European languages of which we have some knowledge, like the Etruscan and Iberian tongues, show signs of contact with Indo-European influences until well into the last millennium BC. Languages, however, now spoken at the opposite end of the continent, by peoples who live in Hungary, Finland, Estonia and between the Volga and the Urals, have loan words from Indo-European languages which were absorbed several millennia earlier. Though the migrations of some of these peoples cannot be reconstructed, it is at least certain that none of them has ever lived much to the west of their present areas of settlement. This conclusion is important because it identifies one of many vital sources of influence on the making of Europe in the east: for, although Indo-European speech is not a universal or defining feature of European culture, it is amazingly widely spread around Europe; indeed, European expansion has carried it across the globe and the Europe we know would be unthinkable without it.

Without need of the cultural snooker in which migrants cannon into static societies and impel them in promising directions, every kind of habitable European environment housed societies of enduring achievement before the period in which 'civilisation' is commonly said to have 'arrived'. Though they have all vanished, leaving bare hints of what they were like, those we know about were of prodigious longevity, enduring for centuries or even millennia. Some of their ruins are in surprising places, now thought of as marginal to Europe or even altogether outside it. The remains of the first large stone buildings known anywhere in the world are on Malta, where at least half a dozen 'temple' complexes were built in the fourth and third millennia BC. The Sumerians were building in brick at the time, and the early pyramids of Egypt are not known to be older. Cycladic civilisation was barely starting when that of Malta was almost finished. The Maltese temples are wrought of dressed limestone around trefoil courts, of which the biggest is 23 metres wide under a wall which still stands to a height of eight metres. Inside one, a colossal steatopygous goddess was

attended by 'sleeping beauties' – small female models scattered around her. There were altars and reliefs, carved in spirals or with deer and bulls, and communal burials, thousands-strong. Even in those days, Malta was a less than ideal environment, with soil poorer and drier than might be expected to sustain a society populous enough and leisured enough to build on a monumental scale. The public buildings absorbed almost all the available surplus energy though suitably dignified 'houses for the temple-builders' have recently begun to come to light. From early in the third millennium BC two houses have been excavated in Gozo, with floors of crushed limestone plaster over stone packing, mud brick walls and pillars which presumably supported the roofs. The floor plan of the bigger is of 40 square metres. The disparity in size raises presumptions about social differentiation: when we contemplate the cultural achievements of ancient peoples we have to slough off modern assumptions about the fertility of artistic freedom. The rise of 'civilisations' is linked to social inequalities, concentrations of wealth, tyrannies like that of Ozymandias and, usually, to what might be called 'state patronage' – the organisation of society from above to create enduring works.

Even before the start of monumental building in Malta, however, what can fairly be called a civilisation of independent origins arose in the shadow of the Carpathians; this was a 'civilisation' on a human

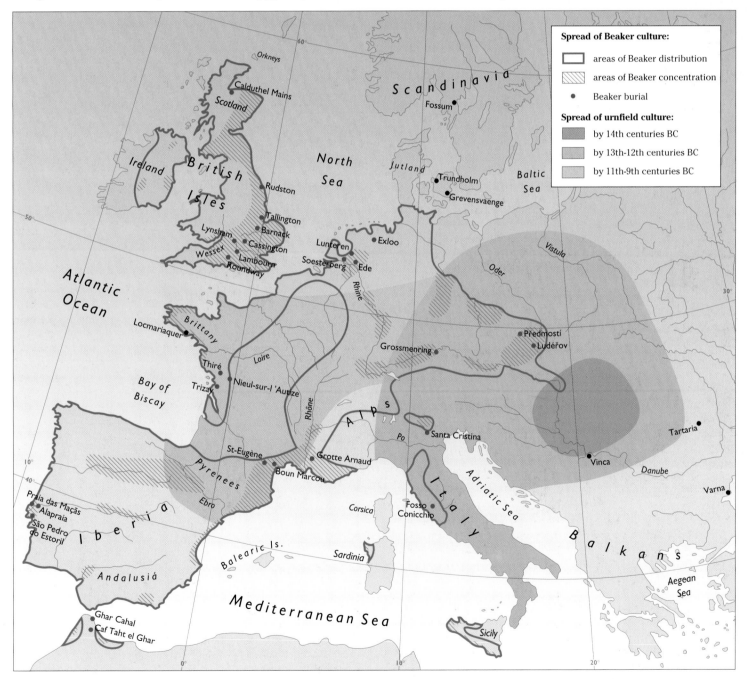

scale, in villages rather than cities, like the Mixtec world in Mesoamerica, expressed in lavish but diminutive art-works rather than huge edifices of stone. Some of its most impressive sites were in areas which would never again achieve such a high level of material culture relative to the rest of Europe. Here the use of copper started without any known outside influence on indigenous developments. Europe's oldest copper mine is at Rudna Glava, above the middle Danube; places like this were the sources of the transmutative magic which made smiths such potent figures of myth. Propitiatory offerings in fine pots were left in the mines. At Tisza in Hungary around the fifth millennium, cattle were domesticated, copper worked into beads and small tools and flint, obsidian, stone axes and fine pottery imported from uplands 100 miles away. At Vinca in Serbia, superb sculptures in clay were modelled in prodigious numbers in the fifth and fourth millennia, representing the finest, to modern tastes, of a huge variety of local styles characterising different sites all over the Balkan region. At Tartaria in Romania clay tablets incised with marks uncannily like writing have been unearthed: the impression of writing is so strong that the first scholars to examine them assumed that they revealed the spread of a writing-system of Mesopotamian influence; but these objects came from a context much older than the earliest indications of Sumerian writing.

In the Bulgaria of the fifth millennium, settlements were patterned like the Roman military camps of 5,000 years later: squared, trenched and palisaded with gateways exactly aligned at the points of the compass. From here exploration and adventure reached out to metal-rich hills. No place in prehistoric Europe gleams more astonishingly than Varna on the shore of the Black Sea. Nearly 2,000 years before the treasures of Ur or Troy were buried, a king was interred at Varna clutching a gold-handled axe, with his penis sheathed in gold. Nearly a thousand ornaments of gold were arrayed around him, including hundreds of studs or discs that must have spangled a dazzling cloak. This single grave contained one-and-a-half kilograms of fine gold. Other rich graves were symbolic burials of earthenware masks without human remains.

East of this region, the vast arc of European steppeland that curls

A stone-age Avernus: the underground mausolea of Brittany are the earliest structures of their kind and in some ways the most complex technically, frequently approached through long entrance-galleries, like that shown here *above* at Locmariaquer in a strip of uplands south of the River Arz.

The Vinca sculptures of the fifth millennium BC cover a wide range of types, but this one *above right* is typical: an anthropoid figure, bearing the stamp of power in eyes and attitude, elaborately helmed and dressed.

To judge from the great treasures of gold grave-goods, weapons and personal ornaments *right*, the richest place in the Europe of the fifth millennium BC was Varna, in what is now Bulgaria.

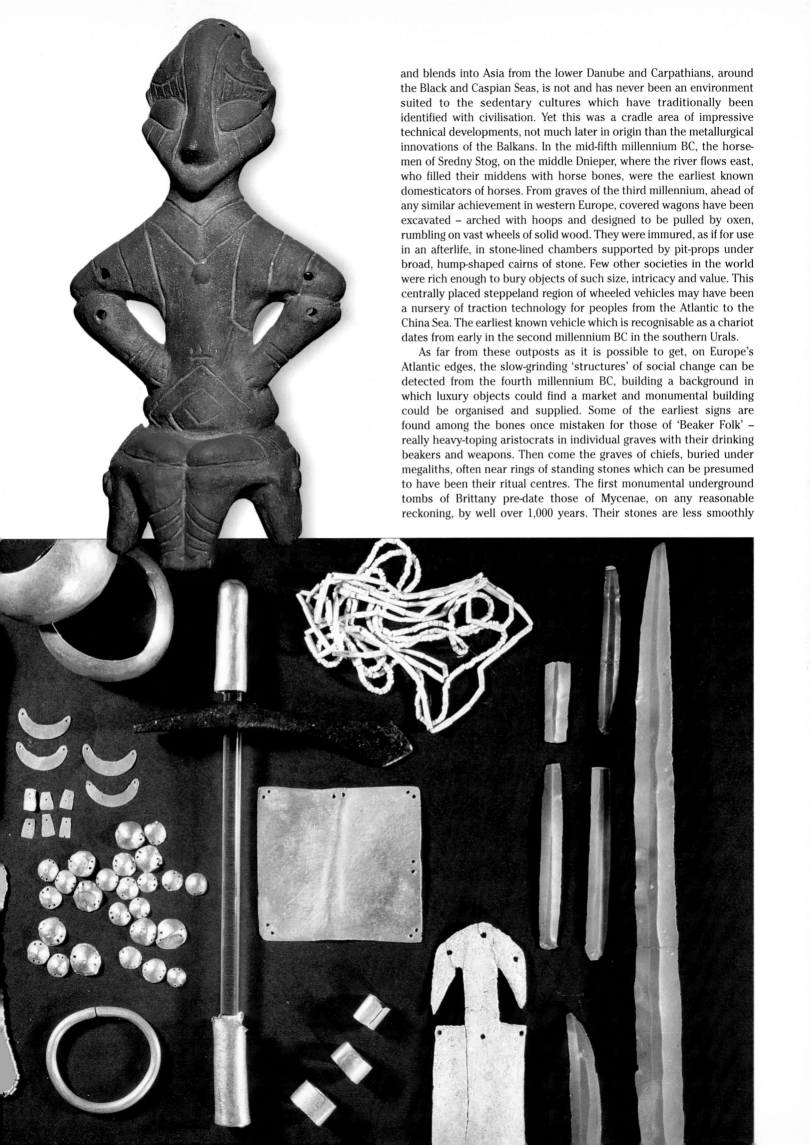

and blends into Asia from the lower Danube and Carpathians, around the Black and Caspian Seas, is not and has never been an environment suited to the sedentary cultures which have traditionally been identified with civilisation. Yet this was a cradle area of impressive technical developments, not much later in origin than the metallurgical innovations of the Balkans. In the mid-fifth millennium BC, the horsemen of Sredny Stog, on the middle Dnieper, where the river flows east, who filled their middens with horse bones, were the earliest known domesticators of horses. From graves of the third millennium, ahead of any similar achievement in western Europe, covered wagons have been excavated – arched with hoops and designed to be pulled by oxen, rumbling on vast wheels of solid wood. They were immured, as if for use in an afterlife, in stone-lined chambers supported by pit-props under broad, hump-shaped cairns of stone. Few other societies in the world were rich enough to bury objects of such size, intricacy and value. This centrally placed steppeland region of wheeled vehicles may have been a nursery of traction technology for peoples from the Atlantic to the China Sea. The earliest known vehicle which is recognisable as a chariot dates from early in the second millennium BC in the southern Urals.

As far from these outposts as it is possible to get, on Europe's Atlantic edges, the slow-grinding 'structures' of social change can be detected from the fourth millennium BC, building a background in which luxury objects could find a market and monumental building could be organised and supplied. Some of the earliest signs are found among the bones once mistaken for those of 'Beaker Folk' – really heavy-toping aristocrats in individual graves with their drinking beakers and weapons. Then come the graves of chiefs, buried under megaliths, often near rings of standing stones which can be presumed to have been their ritual centres. The first monumental underground tombs of Brittany pre-date those of Mycenae, on any reasonable reckoning, by well over 1,000 years. Their stones are less smoothly

dressed, but they anticipate the corbelled chambers and conical forms of the later mausolea. The most spectacular examples have long dry-stone galleries leading to the place of burial, buried under a mound and hinting at irrecoverable symbolism.

A dramatic approach to this world of chiefs is through what looks, at first glance, like one of its remotest outposts, in the Orkneys, settled about 3500 BC. An elaborate tomb at Meas Howe is close to a temple complex at Barnhouse, where the central building is filled with light at the summer solstice. The stone circles of Brodgar and Stengess hint on a smaller scale at the geomancy of Stonehenge. The expertly stone-built village of Skara Brae lies buried with hearths and fitted furniture still in place. It is tempting to imagine this as the farthest-flung colonial station of a megalithic metropolis in Wessex or Brittany, a sundowner-society in a cold climate, preserving the styles and habits of a distant home. Yet the dangers of facile assumptions about the direction of cultural transmissions in prehistoric Europe can at once be sensed if we invert the model: the real relationship could almost equally well be the other way round. The Orkneys might perhaps have been the Cycladic Islands or the Crete of the Atlantic, developing with little debt to the outside world and then colonising or influencing the

mainland. The Wessex culture that grew up around Stonehenge could be the colony which slowly and painfully came to exceed the Orkneian metropolis, as, say, the USA came to excel Great Britain.

Like the Orkneys, Scandinavia might be supposed, on the face of it, to have enclosed a particularly unfavourable environment in Europe's first few millennia: the cold north, where the ice still clung and crept and where the passage of the sun imposed demanding seasonal extremes. There was no tin here to support a bronze-age civilisation: craftsmen were reduced for hundreds of years to making slavish flint imitations of bronze daggers and axes, imported at great cost – in exchange, perhaps, for the amber so highly esteemed by Mediterranean peoples who had none of their own. Yet in the most favourable parts of the region, in what are now southern Sweden and Denmark, a brilliant and artistically inventive culture began to defy the environment early in the second millennium BC among a people understandably obsessed by the sun. The finest surviving artefact of the age is the mid-second millennium chariot of the sun, discovered in a bog at Trundholm in mercilessly preserving meres from which uncorrupted corpses of a few centuries later have been recovered, still hatted and with faces composed or contorted in death. From this

The Cyclades of the North? A standing stone in the Ring of Brodgar in the Orkneys *far left*.

The hearth, beds and cupboards of a house of the mid-third millennium BC are preserved within well-built stone walls at Skara Brae, Orkney *below far left*, where no perishable materials were available to the builders.

'Mercilessly preserving meres': the Trundholm Bog in Zealand has kept the features of some of its victims intact for nearly 2,000 years, such as this execution victim *above left* with the garrotte still round his neck.

Chariot of the Sun: a bronze horse of elegantly tapering lines draws a gold-plated disc nearly a foot wide *below*. One of the treasures yielded by the Trundholm Bog, mid-second millennium BC.

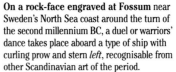

On a rock-face engraved at Fossum near Sweden's North Sea coast around the turn of the second millennium BC, a duel or warriors' dance takes place aboard a type of ship with curling prow and stern *left*, recognisable from other Scandinavian art of the period.

Scandinavian craftsmen of the second millennium BC worked imported bronze into the forms demanded by their own culture. A kneeling figurine *right* from Grevensvaenge in Zealand combines their two characteristic shapes: the sword-like bodies and the sinuous curl of the horns of their helmets.

The ruins of Knossos *below left* still look luxurious with their dressed stones, elegant colonnades and finely decorated pillars. The court of the Minotaur *below right*: the apartments of the palace are decorated with idealised scenes of the island's life, including war, trade and the balletic bull-leaping ritual which has become, for most people, the representative image of Minoan civilization.

natural archive and from grave-goods and rock-engravings, fragments of a picture of bronze-age Scandinavia can be pieced together: an inkling of the wealth which made it possible to import large amounts of metal; a glimpse of the appearance of the elite, in tasselled garments for the women and horned helmets for warriors; a sense of the importance in taste or worship of serpentine lines – copied, perhaps, from the curl of antlers – like those which form the curving prows of the many pictured ships or shape the six bronze trumpets, 3,000 years old, from a bog-cache in Brudevaelte in Jutland.

Because there were so many civilisations or proto-civilisations of independent origins in prehistoric Europe, it must not be supposed that they were isolated from one another or that exchanges like that of Baltic amber for Mycenaean bronze were freakish. On the contrary, almost as conspicuous a feature of the period as the richness of its cultures is the extent of some of its cultural 'horizons' – the spread, that is, over vast territories of particular styles or objects. 'Empires' of artefacts could cover enormous range. The spread of beakers as grave-gifts has been mentioned. The use of megaliths for stone-rings and tombs eventually became characteristic of a broad swatch of lands from Sweden to Spain, covering most of the Britain and Ireland. The cultural worlds of bronze-age Europe can be classified according to their various burial customs: whether in flat cemeteries or barrows, in chambers or shafts, in megalithic tombs or pits; yet in the last few centuries before the turn of the last millennium a new custom became widespread of cremating at least some of the dead and storing the ashes in pots in the ground or capacious urns. Though this was a culture-feature which was transmitted like a fashion from early sites between the Danube and Carpathians to a huge area from the Pripet marshes to the Pyrenees, its appeal is more likely to have depended on 'processual' changes in the societies which received it than on migrations from its place of origin.

The Cretan and Mycenaean civilisations which were once credited with so much influence on western and northern Europe were themselves, it is now generally agreed, the outcome of long-maturing regional 'processes' rather than implantations from abroad. Their characteristic monuments are the 'palaces' like that of Knossos, where Arthur Evans uncovered 'the labyrinth of the Minotaur' in 1901 or the sumptuous shaft- or hive-shaped mainland graves, such as the one where Schliemann in 1876 'looked on the face of Agammemnon'. Knossos covers 13,000 square metres and the 'labyrinth' was an immense area of storage for clay jars, two metres high and, in some cases, still in place, filled with wine, oil and grain. Stone chests lined with lead were the strongboxes of a 'central bank' for the organised

From early in the second millennium BC, Crete played host to the highly developed Minoan culture, whose rulers built impressive palaces such as that at Knossos. By the 15th century BC, however, the Cretan palaces were destroyed, by natural disasters or invasion. Until the 12th century BC, the Aegean was dominated by a culture from the Greek mainland, that of the Mycenaeans *map right*.

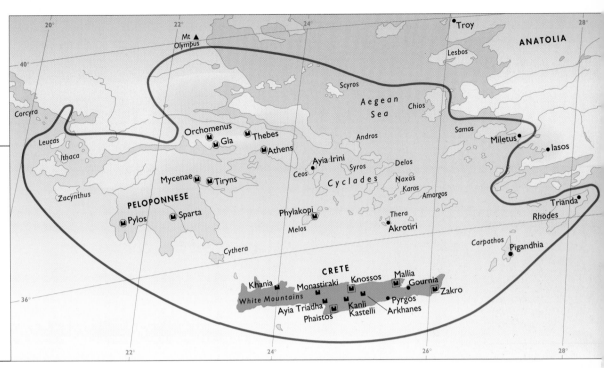

The Aegean, 2500-1200 BC

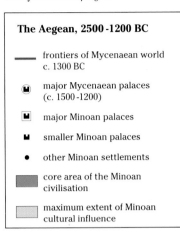

— frontiers of Mycenaean world c. 1300 BC

▣ major Mycenaean palaces (c. 1500-1200)

▣ major Minoan palaces

▪ smaller Minoan palaces

• other Minoan settlements

▨ core area of the Minoan civilisation

▨ maximum extent of Minoan cultural influence

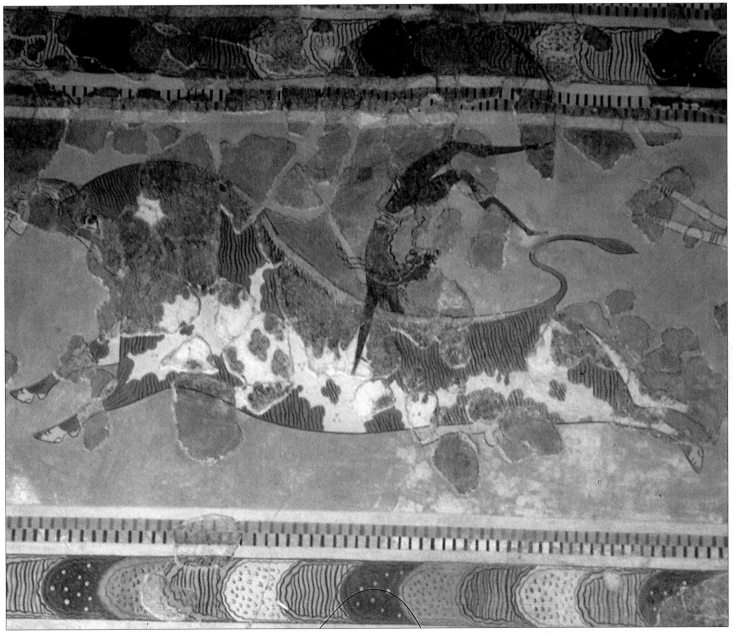

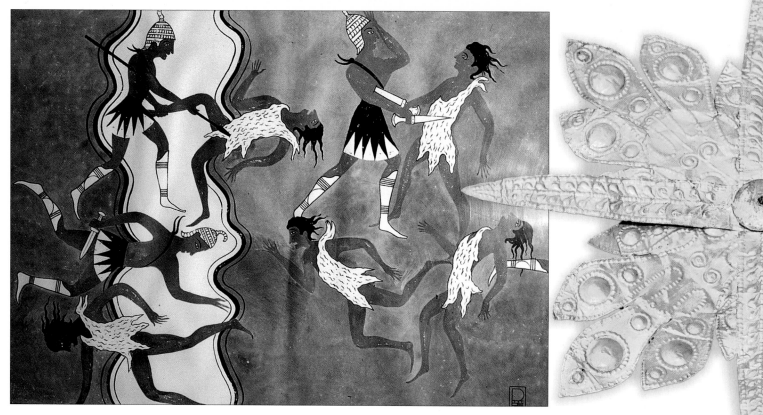

redistribution of produce or perhaps for state-controlled trade. Yet this and buildings like it were genuinely palaces – dwellings of an elite who lived in luxury. The noble floors were reached by majestic stairwells, supported on squat columns with capitals like fat pumpkins. These pillars, and those which supported the principal chambers, were lacquered in red, and the wall paintings – with scenes of bull-leaping and Egyptian monkeys and fleets of oared and sailed ships, plunging through seas alive with dolphins – featured a wonderful cerulean blue.

Lesser dwellings, grouped in genuine towns, were tiny imitations of the palace; many had columns, balconies and upper storey galleries. The specialist products for the rich upper levels of society survive in fairly large numbers, including colourful potters' art, thin as porcelain, and elaborate stone vases, ground with emery into seductively sinuous shapes. Yet at lower levels few people lived beyond their early forties – a smaller proportion, indeed, than in most Mesolithic sites, by the same methods of measurement. And if the purpose of the state was to recycle food, its efficiency was limited: exhumed remains show that the common people of Minoan Crete lived near the margin of malnutrition. The environment was capriciously destructive. On the nearby island of Thera, which was blown apart by a volcanic eruption of disputed date around the middle of the second millennium BC, the lavish city of Akrotiri was buried in volcanic ash under layers of bare pumice. Knossos, and similar palace-complexes around the coasts of Crete at Phaistos, Mallia and Zakro, were all rebuilt once or twice on an increasingly generous scale, after presumed destruction by unknown causes which seem in some cases to have included earthquakes. Some of the features of the 'second palace period' suggest another hazard: internal warfare. Knossos's role as a model could be explained as the result of a political takeover; some of the elite of the east and south of the island seem to have moved to villas near Knossos at about the time the palaces were rebuilt.

By the time of the last destruction of Knossos, generally dated at around 1400 BC, the fate of Crete seems to have become closely entangled with that of the so-called 'Mycenaean' civilisation of the Peloponnese, where a number of states were ruled by kings whose characteristic activities were warfare and the hunting of lions. Their courts were centred in palace-storehouses of a kind apparently similar in function to those of Crete, like that at Pylos, where a long series of clay tablets discloses the vital and tiresome routines of a numerous official hierarchy: levying taxes, exacting the social

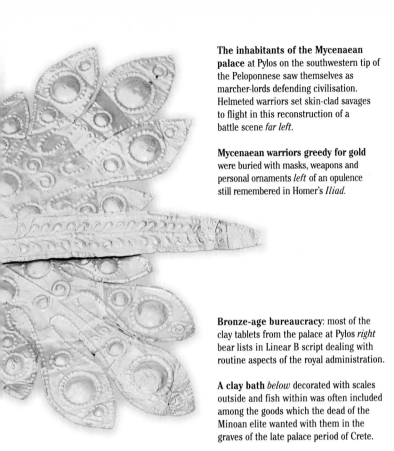

The inhabitants of the Mycenaean palace at Pylos on the southwestern tip of the Peloponnese saw themselves as marcher-lords defending civilisation. Helmeted warriors set skin-clad savages to flight in this reconstruction of a battle scene *far left*.

Mycenaean warriors greedy for gold were buried with masks, weapons and personal ornaments *left* of an opulence still remembered in Homer's *Iliad*.

Bronze-age bureaucracy: most of the clay tablets from the palace at Pylos *right* bear lists in Linear B script dealing with routine aspects of the royal administration.

A clay bath *below* decorated with scales outside and fish within was often included among the goods which the dead of the Minoan elite wanted with them in the graves of the late palace period of Crete.

obligations of a landowner-class, mobilising resources for public works and garnering valuable raw materials for a system of manufacture and trade: bronzeware and perfumed oils made in the palace of Pylos were exported to Egypt, the Hittite empire and northern Europe.

The duties of the bureaucrats presumably included equipping their rulers for the warfare which was evidently endemic to Mycenaean society. Unlike Cretan sites, those of the mainland in this period are heavily and cleverly fortified. As well as fighting each other, the kingdoms felt the threat of the barbarian hinterland which may in the end have overwhelmed them. Warriors painted on the walls of Pylos, in the boars' head helmets also worn on Crete and Thera, are shown in battle with skin-clad savages. Stunned by earthquakes, strained by war, Mycenaean cities followed those of Crete into abandonment and oblivion by the last century of the second millennium BC. It is surprising, perhaps, that fragile economies, sustained by bureaucratic redistributive methods, should have managed to go on feeding the cities and supporting the elite culture for so long.

The bronze age empires broke up and some of the continuities that had marked the progress of European civilisations since the retreat of the ice were severed by unknown catastrophes. The centralised economies controlled from palace labyrinths vanished. The patterns of trade were disrupted. Settlements and monuments were abandoned. This was not an unravelling peculiar to the Aegean: the bronze-age civilisation of Hittite Anatolia collapsed; Egypt was almost overwhelmed by invasions; the people of Nubia vanished from the records. This 'general crisis' was followed by 'dark ages' of varying duration.

Less centralised cultures, however, are sometimes immune to the sudden catastrophes that can make a civilisation vanish when its nerve centre is under attack. The 'dark age' of the eastern Mediterranean was an age of progress in much of the rest of Europe: progress in metallurgy, in particular, towards the hotter furnaces in which iron could be forged; progress in the extraction of salt and glass and the widening circles of trade such products encouraged; progress in the diversification of crops, as millet and rye became supplements to traditional staples in central and northern Europe respectively. The construction of splendour and prosperity continued in the last millennium before our era, sometimes in areas not far removed from the great civilised or civilising centres of the bronze age, in a relatively unsung Europe beyond Greece and Rome.

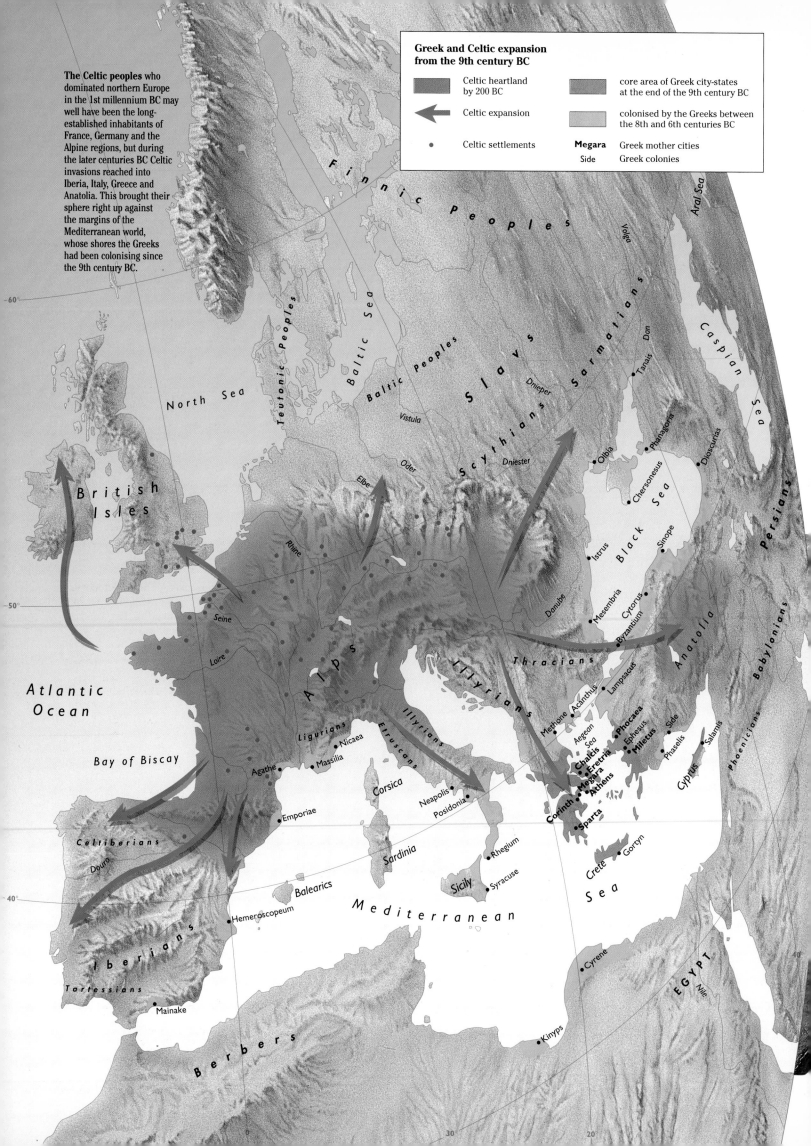

The Celtic peoples who dominated northern Europe in the 1st millennium BC may well have been the long-established inhabitants of France, Germany and the Alpine regions, but during the later centuries BC Celtic invasions reached into Iberia, Italy, Greece and Anatolia. This brought their sphere right up against the margins of the Mediterranean world, whose shores the Greeks had been colonising since the 9th century BC.

Greek and Celtic expansion from the 9th century BC

Celtic heartland by 200 BC

Celtic expansion

Celtic settlements

core area of Greek city-states at the end of the 9th century BC

colonised by the Greeks between the 8th and 6th centuries BC

Megara Greek mother cities
Side Greek colonies

Finnic Peoples

Teutonic Peoples

North Sea

Baltic Sea

Baltic Peoples

Slavs

Scythians

Sarmatians

Volga

Don

Tanais

Dnieper

Aral Sea

Caspian Sea

Vistula

Olbia

Phanagoria

Dioscurias

Oder

Elbe

Dniester

Chersonesus

British Isles

Rhine

Istrus

Black Sea

Sinope

Persians

Seine

Danube

Mesembria

Cytorus

Byzantium

Anatolia

Atlantic Ocean

Loire

Alps

Illyrians

Thracians

Babylonians

Bay of Biscay

Ligurians

Nicaea

Etruscans

Illyrians

Methone

Acanthus

Lampsacus

Phocaea

Ephesus

Side

Aegean Sea

Chalcis

Eretria

Miletus

Phaselis

Salamis

Agathe

Massilia

Megara

Athens

Cyprus

Phoenicians

Emporiae

Corsica

Neapolis

Posidonia

Corinth

Sparta

Celtiberians

Sardinia

Rhegium

Syracuse

Crete

Gortyn

Douro

Balearics

Sicily

Sea

Hemeroscopeum

Mediterranean

Iberians

Cyrene

EGYPT

Tartessians

Nile

Mainake

Berbers

Kinyps

CHAPTER 2

EUROPE WITHOUT 'EUROPE'
The continent in antiquity beyond Greece and Rome

The Bassae frieze *below* in the British Museum depicts Theseus's defeat of Amazon invaders when he was king of Athens. His capture of and marriage to their queen, Hippolyta, represented the domestication of unnatural savagery.

WHEN THE JESUIT missionary Matteo Ricci introduced Christian cartography to China in the late sixteenth century, he complained that in Chinese world maps the Middle Kingdom filled almost the available space. 'With this image of the bigness of their country and the smallness of the rest of the world, they were proud, and it appeared to them that the rest of the world was barbarian and uncouth in comparison.'

Most cultures are similarly egocentric. Most languages, indeed, have no word for human being except that used to denote their own speakers. In dismissing the barbarian world outside their borders as inferior, ancient Greek and Roman scrutineers were not being exceptionally myopic: they were indulging a widespread vice. In legend and art, the oddities of foreigners became exaggerated. In extreme cases, they were turned into monsters, like some of the adversaries of Hercules, or mutations, like the Amazons who grapple with Greeks in the Bassae frieze. Sometimes they were seen in moralists' mirrors, which reflected back magnified images of the beholders' own virtues and vices; at others they were glimpsed with the warped and fantastic vision of dreams.

Between them, the Greeks and Romans – who became collaborators in a single empire – established a near-monopoly of the written

sources of the pre-Christian history of Europe. Their values and perspectives have informed almost every account of the subject ever since. Those they classified as barbarous have remained, until recently, on the edges of maps which have their spiritual meridians through Rome and Athens, or in the silence of a history too hard to write. From about a third of the way through the last millennium before Christ, the history of Greece and Rome takes over from the history of Europe in the textbooks.

Yet most of the people who lived in ancient Europe – at least, in what is now called 'Europe', at a time when the concept was in its infancy – were outside the reach, and many outside the notice, of the Greeks and Romans, while others, who were absorbed in the expanding Roman empire or lived on its frontiers, virtually vanished as their cultures became 'romanised'. We have to shift the meridians to take them into the map, re-work the sources to fit them into the picture.

Like those cunning computer buffs who can retrieve deleted files, historians and archaeologists have worked apparent miracles in recent years in drawing from the shadows peoples previously concealed by the penumbra of Greece and Rome. Scholars were once happy to connive in the Graeco-Roman view because they believed that the Greeks and Romans were the most 'important' peoples of European antiquity – indeed, most scholars in the west would formerly have said, of all the peoples there have ever been in the world. They therefore seemed to deserve most study. Today, the rise of cultural relativism has made such a sweeping judgement hard to accept without qualification. Enhanced sensitivity to the claims of each human culture to be judged on its own terms makes us more alert to beauties and skills previously overlooked or undervalued. And while the enormous influence, the 'heritage', of Greece and Rome in the modern world justify particular attention to their history, it seems likely, as a matter of common sense, that some of what they assimilated and passed on must have originated elsewhere.

These are relatively new insights. In the cases of some peoples, they can be followed up with the benefit of old evidence: the spadework and groundwork of nineteenth- or early twentieth-century nationalists who began to assemble materials for studying those they identified as their ancestors. Nationalism has already become a doctrine proscribed by political correctness and even cultural relativism seems to be slipping out of fashion. Between them, however, these two -isms have made it ever easier to write the history of ancient Europe beyond Greece and Rome.

Around the Mediterranean peninsulas in which the Greeks and Romans had their heartlands there lay a thick crust of peoples whose potential for creating civilisation in terms we recognise – with a large surplus of resources, monumental cities, a literate culture and a vibrant art – was not far behind that of their peninsular neighbours, even, in some respects, on a par.

The Thracians, for example, according to Herodotus, were the most numerous of peoples after the Indians and only their disunity preserved others from their mastery. Their lands between the Dniester and the Aegean – though they have been invaded many times from most directions – are well fortified with mountains and cradled, at the time, cultural continuities of remarkable longevity, which lasted from before the Bronze Age until the coming of the Slavs. Thracian identity – if the term is not too strong – was kindled in rites of fire commemorated in the spiralling incisions which swirled on their hearths for millennia. A fine bronze-age example from Sigishoara imitates a shimmering sun. A horseback hero dominated their art: defaced images trampled into the ground at early Christian shrines leave no doubt of his divine status. In surviving examples we can see him hunting with hounds, wrestling with a three-headed monster from the east, mastering wild animals, severing an enemy's head, drinking, feasting and perhaps – on a sumptuous series of repoussé plaques of the fourth century BC, in silver-gilt, from northern Bulgaria – engendering the race. The Thracians' history has to be felt and inferred, for even at their most cultured they were never very literate. Their written materials have perished – like the mushroom on which the last Thracian ruler wrote a message to a Roman emperor – and the only surviving inscription, in Greek letters, is undeciphered.

Thracian (and pre- or proto-Thracian) kings were figures of magnificence and sometimes of power and mystery. One, buried in northern Serbia in the second millennium BC, exhibited limbs ringed in gold with the spirals of the fiery sun or bulging with the curls of stylised horns. Others intimidated the Argonauts in the legend of Jason – like the blind prophet-king Phineus who controlled passage through the Bosporus. King Rhesus supplied Troy with white horses. In the 5th century BC Thrace had an imperial age when a series of energetic rulers – flesh-and-blood figures, known from Greek sources unshaded by myth – imposed periods of unity and threatened expansion. The climax was perhaps represented by Sitalkes, who invaded Macedonia in 429 with an army said to number 150,000. His failure marks a new period, when Thracian states played a passive role, squirming to survive alongside mightier neighbours. The attempt by Seuthes III in the late fourth century to recreate, after Macedonian conquest, the glories of the era of Sitalkes left the modest ruins of Seuthopolis – a palace-city of five hectares, mostly of mud brick and painted stucco, now flooded by the Georgi Dimitrov dam.

The last great Thracian realm was Dacia, founded in the first century BC by Burebista, who elected himself king, imposed unity by banning tribal coinage and, according to Strabo, 'raised the people to such a height through training, sobriety and obedience to his commands that within a few years he had established a great empire.' The emphasis on sobriety suggests a proverbial Thracian failing: brandished goblets were a motif of their art from the bronze age and Burebista's vital ally was said to be the wizard Decenus, who persuaded them to chop down their vines. Dacia was a military state, a stronghold-kingdom, 'glued,' Romans said, 'to its mountains.' It bristled with stone forts, many containing royal apartments to house restless warrior-kings, and with pillared sanctuaries open to the sun. It deployed mounted archers in scale armour and wild mercenaries, half-naked and armed with studded clubs. The ruling class had the reputation of men of action – 'impatient of speech and tense as racehorses,' a Greek who knew them said. Their deadly womenfolk tortured prisoners – flaying them with

In a gravestone from Plovdiv *above*, the Thracian horseman wrests his quarry from a lion's maw. Though he is also depicted fighting and feasting, the hero appears most often as a huntsman – lord and exploiter of the natural world. Reliefs of this kind are so common and so nearly identical that one might almost speak of mass production.

In a series of repoussé plaques *left* in silver-gilt from Letnitsa in northern Bulgaria, the Thracian hero is shown inside an edging of stylised horns. In most of the scenes he is a warrior, among the severed heads of men and horses, otherwise interpreted as symbols of wealth and power. At bottom right he holds a cup aloft while leading a bear.

In one of the reliefs *above right* – photographed from a flat cast in the National Museum of Bucharest – which envelop his column in a continuous spiral, Trajan supervises the defence of a Roman camp, fortified with square blocks like those still visible at the sites of Roman fortifications on the Dacian frontier. Slingers have prominent place in the Dacian attack.

staves, clawing them with fingernails, singeing them with torches.

After Burebista there was no ruler strong enough to threaten Rome until Decebalus in the late first century AD. The causes of the war are obscure: a trial of strength between neighbours who were too strong for each other's security; a conflagration sparked by envy, Roman for Dacian gold, Dacian for Roman manufactures. Decebalus's blitzkrieg of AD 85 intimidated Rome into a humiliating peace, but one conspicuous Roman virtue was patience in preparing vengeance. The end of Dacia in campaigns of AD 101 to 106 is told in carvings in marble on Trajan's column.

They are more than triumphant propaganda: tributes to a worthy enemy who contended with men and gods and would not surrender; scenes of the disasters of war, in which flocks are slaughtered, trees stunted, refugees driven from burning towns. Humanity is celebrated on both sides: Trajan recoils from the severed heads his soldiers offer him; a Dacian greybeard dabs his eye with his cloak over the corpse of a tousle-haired young soldier. In one of the final scenes, Decebalus slits his own throat with a curved dagger, sinking to the ground as the Romans close in.

Thracian culture, transformed by centuries of Romanisation and Christianisation, was finally buried under layers of Slav immigration – though a trace of the Thracian hero may have lingered in the cults of mounted saints. The Thracians' neighbours to the west, the group of peoples known to Greek and Roman writers as Illyrians, perhaps survive to this day, if the Albanians are justified in reckoning themselves their descendants.

They had the good fortune to be rediscovered by Arthur Evans. Before he became the renowned excavator of Knossos, the budding antiquarian had a varied youth as a sensational journalist in the Balkans, hunted by Turks and imprisoned by Austrians. He broke – and perhaps exaggerated – the news of the 'Bulgarian atrocities' of 1878, which helped to precipitate a Balkan war and almost to unseat a British government. His passionate devotion to Illyrian antiquities and assiduous promotion of Illyrian studies were inspired in part by his liberal temper, revolted at the repression of ancient identities by despotic empires. But the colours with which enthusiasm tints scholarship are rarely true and the conviction that the Illyrians existed, and were once important, and even – as some archaeologists of the late nineteenth century thought – occupied a great swathe of southern and central Europe as the 'original' pre-Celtic population, did not help say who they were. They are still best defined negatively, as people who lived between the Thracians, Greeks and Celts without belonging to any of them. Their unity was perceived probably only from outside and their potential for collective action was even less than that of the Thracians'.

Their world in the middle of the last millennium before Christ was of rich principalities, whose rulers and notables were buried with varied gold- and silver-hoards and sacrifices of oxen and wild boar. The easeful life of an Illyrian court is depicted on the most famous object known to have been left by them: an urn found at Vace in Slovenia, on which, as well as parading warriors, hawking-parties can be seen and deer-hunts. Dignitaries in phrygian caps display their authority with a double-headed sceptre or play on pipes and are fed by long-haired houris. Their love of food and drink was notorious. A commonplace-story in antiquity was about the cunning of strategists who defeated their foes by letting them capture sumptuous foods laced with powerful laxatives: it acquired credibility when ascribed by Theopompus to the Illyrians. King Agron died of celebratory over-indulgence when he heard of his troops' victory over the Aetolians in about 231 BC.

In the two centuries which led to their submission to Rome, the Illyrians' history parallelled the Thracians'. Some of them challenged Macedonia with initial success early in the fourth century – inviting Macedonian vengeance with results similar to those which befell

Iberian civilisation in southern Spain was preceded by the rich bronze-age culture of El Argar, which produced lavish artefacts, like the gilt sword hilt and finely incised blade, *right centre*.

The Dama de Elche *left* represents the peak of a copious Iberian tradition of female figures splendidly attired and sculpted in hieratic poses, at various levels of quality and to a great range of different scales. The standing type represented *near right* generally stands on a pedestal and holds a libation vessel. A number of them have been found at Cerro de los Santos (Montalegre), giving rise to the presumption that they represent priestesses of a shrine at the spot. The Dama de Elche is the chef d'oeuvre of ancient Iberijan art and, even by Greek standards, one of the outstanding sculptures of antiquity, combining exceptionally sensitive portraiture with technically consummate workmanship.

The gleam of gold from the Thymiateria of Lebrija *far right* in the Archaeological Museum of Madrid suggests the opulence of royal or religious cults among the ancient Iberians. These objects are unparalleled elsewhere and their function is hard to imagine: they seem ill-suited to burn lights or incense.

Thrace. Early in the third century BC a powerful kingdom re-emerged: not struggling with memories like the Thrace of Seuthes but dauntingly rich, with a copious silver coinage and a fleet of hundreds of sail. The wars between Rome and Macedon created an opportunity: one could be played off against the other. But the Illyrians ended with the reputation of 'enemies of all alike'. Gentius, their last king, was overthrown in a Roman campaign of only 30 days in 167 BC. The booty was said to include 27 pounds of gold, 120,000 Illyrian silver coins, 220 warships and twenty million sesterces' worth of other goods.

An even more desirable – and more actively coveted – world of wealth lay at the western end of the Mediterranean. By Greek traders in the middle of the last millennium before Christ, 'the god of riches was thought to dwell in the entrails of Spain.' This message is implicitly confirmed today by the 'Iberian' room of the Archaeological Museum in Madrid, in which rich and strange objects from widely separated places, mainly from coastal areas and the lower reaches of rivers, are gathered in a glittering and startling array. The room is dominated, as one approaches from the lobby, by the golden 'candlesticks' of Lebrija, a strictly unprecedented treasure from the lower Guadalquivir – the very region, beyond the Pillars of Hercules, where Herodotus's Phoenicians raised their smoke and Arnold's Tyrian undid his bales. These long and delicate thymiateria of fine gold are each reinforced by 44 regular, round mouldings, like gentle corrugations or the folds of a concertina. The little concave finials, which can hardly have borne much in the way of incense or light beyond their own natural gleam, are echoed towards the bottom of the stems by matching plates which project to form a gripping-space. Below the lowest of the concertina-folds, the broad bases, finely moulded, taper sinuously to where they join the upright stalks in well proportioned, chubby, oblate-spheroid knobs, fashioned in the same gold. Their workmanship and survival seem equally miraculous.

The impression of a rich and original civilisation is driven home by the nearby treasures from Aliseda in the relatively low-lying lands of Extremadura, north of the Guadalquivir valley. The centrepiece of this further collection of fine gold is a belt decorated with repoussé scenes of a hero in combat with a lion. A jewel-hoard from Javea, in the south-east corner of Spain, from the region which has yielded the finest 'Iberian' sculpture, shows that high standards of gold-craft were found far afield.

Equally impressive of the wealth and power of the coastal and lowland elites for whom these jewels were hoarded are the surviving examples of sculpture and monumental art. Some of the best can be examined in the same room of the same museum. The huge funerary monument from Pozo Moro, in the far west, has been adventurously reconstructed: in its present form, the tall, elegant, tapering shape is unparalleled – albeit vaguely oriental in flavour – but its daunting dimensions are not in doubt, nor are the quality of its big guardian lions, or the sophistication of its friezes, which depict a banquet of cosmic monsters – one with two heads, one with forked tongue – feeding on boar. In another scene, a hero challenges a fire-breathing monster. Extremadura, where this presumed tomb was built, became, in modern Spain, the epitome of a harsh environment and a poor population – the nursery of conquistadores hardened by deprivation. Yet in pre-Roman times it sustained a polity with the resources to build on a large scale and the power to inspire heroic and terrible images of authority.

On the other side of the peninsula, on the east coast, a different sort of art of comparable quality – quality comparable, indeed, with that of other Mediterranean civilisations of antiquity – was produced by the makers of the most famous artefact in the Madrid museum, the imposing sculptured female known, from her place of discovery as the Dama de Elche. She has been so often described and so often illustrated that her impact is dulled by familiarity. Only her bust survives but her general similarity to a rather cruder sculpture found in a grave at Baza, north of Almería, in 1971, suggests that she was originally enthroned and housed in a tomb, where the hollow in her back concealed, perhaps, some propitiatory offering or the ashes or bones of a human fellow-occupant. Her luxurious dress, her elaborate coiffure, her capacious headdress and her enormous jewels, which bulge like Hollywood costume-pieces, leave no doubt of the loftiness of her status or of the wealth of the society which produced her. That is consistent with all we know about life in the southern and eastern coastal civilisations of pre-Roman Iberia and comes as no surprise. Too impressive, however, for bland absorption is the startling realism with which her face is carved and the enigmatic subtlety of her expression. Within the canon of a predictable aesthetic – perfection of proportion, regularity of form, rigour of symmetry – the artist captured profound emotional tension in the clear and proud, but slightly downcast eyes, under their delicately creased lids, and the sensuously curved but mutely parted, almost tremulous lips. The skilful realism of 'Iberian' art at it height is excelled in no other example, but often approached – particularly, for instance, in a small terracotta in the Museum of Alicante, from near the site of the Dama de Elche: this weeping figure is not only extraordinarily expressive, but also extraordinarily lively in posture and gesture, as she bends forward, streaking her tearful face with outstretched fingers.

That the world of the Dama de Elche was widely spread around the coastal regions is shown by the crudely matching lady from Baza. In the far north of the peninsula the coastlands were capable of sustaining a similarly impressive urban civilisation, which produced the Tivissa dish, chased in silver with scenes of the boar-hunt and of winged and centaur-like creatures. This same region, generally regarded as the poor relation of the richer south-east and south, also has the finest surviving example of a pre-Roman city at Ullastret, near Empúries – conveniently located for tourists who want to inspect it together with the Massiliot and Roman ruins at the nearby site. Its four square kilometres are surrounded – except on the east, where cliffs protect – by the ruins of a wall of dressed stone, with towers at intervals of about 30 metres. Of the four gates, the chief is protected by curious defences: on one side, a round tower juts from inside a pentagonal redoubt; on the other, the curtain wall is jerked back in a dog-leg to overawe the entrance passage.

All the glamorous artefacts of 'Iberian' workmanship that can be reliably dated are from after the orientalising phase of the seventh century BC in the cultures of the central Mediterranean, and it seems consistent with common sense to extend the reach of this process as far as south-west Spain, where Phoenician traders were active at the time and where fine imports of eastern Mediterranean origin have been unearthed alongside the original creations of native craftsmen. Indeed, according to a Greek tradition, the Phoenician colony of Gadir was established before the beginning of the first millennium BC and there were Greek colonies on the east coast by the seventh century of the same era.

In part, at least, of the future ambit of 'Iberian' civilisation, the incoming orientals found a dazzling realm already in place. Herodotus gives, in different places, rival versions of its discovery by Greek merchants; both leave open the possibility that Phoenician influence had already wrought what the Greek newcomers found. The second account gives the location of this realm of 'Tartessos' on the Atlantic shore of lower Andalusia:

A ship from Samos, whose captain was Coleos, was sailing for Egypt but... they were blown by the east wind beyond the Pillars of Hercules and by divine providence reached Tartessos. This market was at that time still unexploited. Therefore when they returned to their own country the men of Samos made more profit from their wares than any Greeks we know of, save Sostratos of Aegina – for there is none to compete with him.

Herodotus's other version is richer in historical context and circumstantial detail:

The Phocaeans were the earliest of the Greeks to make long sea-voyages; it was they who discovered the Adriatic Sea and the Tyrrhenian and Iberia and Tartessos, not sailing in round freight-ships but in 50-oared vessels. When they came to Tartessos, they made friends with the king of the Tartessians, who was called Arganthonios. He ruled Tartessos for 80 years and lived for 120 years. The Phocaeans so won this man's friendship that he first entreated them to leave Ionia and settle in his country where they would; and when he could not persuade them and heard from them how the power of the Persians was increasing, he gave them money to build a wall around their city. Without stint he gave it.

In other words, Phocaean relations with Tartessos were well established by the mid sixth century BC – roughly a generation after the settlement of Greek colonies in Catalonia. Tartessian subsidies were aired as a legendary explanation, perhaps, of the strength of the famous wall that withstood the siege by Cyrus in 546. The king's eagerness to attract a Greek colony to his shores hints at a desire to

On plates from the Tivissa treasure, *left, below and right,* the Iberian cult of the boar hunt is suggested by the snarling maws of boar and hound. The earthenware drinking vessels from the previous millennium *bottom* look crude by comparison, but were delicately made at El Oficio (Antas, Almería) where the art of the bronze-age culture of El Argar flourished.

play off Phoenician monopolists or to strengthen his defences against a Phoenician or inland threat. Arganthonios is more likely to be a title than a personal name: in a Celtic tongue it might mean 'ruler of the land of silver' and the incredible longevity ascribed to an individual would make sense if applied to the duration of a particular dynasty or political system. A fragmentary exclamation ascribed to Anacreon – 'I would not ... rule Tartessos for a hundred and fifty years' – suggests that the wealth and political stability of this kingdom were proverbial among the Greeks.

The riches of Tartessos are entirely convincing, in view of the opulent material culture that a mining economy sustained in the region in pre-Roman times, where the banks of the Rio Tinto are blotched from the flow of copper-bearing ores. Some students have been tempted to isolate the Turdetani, located by Roman writers around the lower Guadalquivir and Rio Tinto, from 'Iberian' civilisation and to class these diggers of deep underground galleries, drained by Archimedes' screw, as the heirs and perhaps descendants of the Tartessians, certainly as practitioners of the same miners' arts. Both cultures occupied a substantial part of the Iberian pyrite belt, an area of about 250 km by about 35 km in southern Portugal and south-western Spain, rich in iron, copper, silver and gold. Pre-Roman silver slag deposits found at ancient Rio Tinto mining sites, and the presumed antiquity of the fortifications which surround a mining centre at Tejada Vieja, a short way inland between Huelva and Seville, where a productive mint was at work in the third century BC, suggest the kind of economy that might have sustained Tartessos. It is tempting to picture the splendour of its kings with the help, say, of the grave-toy chariot of the Huelva Museum – a splendid, sinuously moulded confection, with wheel-caps in the form of quizzically peering cats' heads.

No attempt so far to link parts of surviving treasure-hoards to Tartessian origins has proved convincing but in Greek esteem – as has often been said – Tartessos was an El Dorado. Its richness and remoteness made it a fantasy-land, where Hercules tamed the flocks of Geryon and intervened miraculously to defend his Gaditan temple in a naval battle against King Theron. Although it is reasonable to suppose that Tartessos could have enjoyed only a limited development without Mediterranean trading partners – and the transition from the savage pastoral realm of Geryon to that of the equally mythical Theron, sophisticated and maritime, may be taken as an image of its progress – indigenous cultures, given the resources, were naturally capable of spontaneous economic growth; Tartessos might have had a bronze-age origin, like the shadowy civilisation of El Argar, which flourished in south-east Spain, in the region of Almería, for most of the second millennium BC until users of iron destroyed or displaced it.

Whatever it may have owed to an indigenous past, the 'Iberian' high culture of the coasts and lowlands in the fifth and fourth centuries BC, when its remains begin to make it clearly visible to us, can only be understood in the context of longstanding oriental influence, Mediterranean-wide trade, and the presence of Greek and Phoenician colonies stretching from Greek Emporion and Rhode in the north-east, through Cartagena ('New Carthage') in the south-east to Gadir in the south-west. The trading links forged along routes joined by these colonies led from the Mediterranean to the Atlantic and opened the prospect of trade with ancient maritime commercial partners of the Atlantic communities of the Iberian peninsula in the far north, in western Britain and Gaul. Thus in ancient times was inaugurated a role which the coasts of Spain played throughout the age of sail, as staging-posts in the creation of a common western economy – and, to some extent, a common western culture – helping goods, people and ideas to cross the sharply divisive watershed of the Straits of Hercules. It is hard to imagine, from deep inside the steam age, how inhibiting was the strength of current that penned sail-ships and oared ships inside the Mediterranean, where access was 'closed' by 'a rapacious wave' and where Hercules had erected his pillars as a warning against the monster-haunted seas beyond, 'towards the darkness'. Readers of this phrase of Pindar's have often interpreted the text as relating to the 'closure' of the straits by war; but the current of some eight knots seems adequate to account for the strait's general reputation.

The picture conjured up by the ruins, fragments and legends of Iberians and Tartessians – a rich way of life, lived in well built cities, on shores lapped by waters that bore Mediterranean craft – contrasts vividly with the other face of pre-Roman Spain, the Spain of the uplands and tablelands where people scratched at relatively infertile soils or gained by preying on neighbours or selling their prowess in war. The contrast between the two Spains of antiquity – between the thrifty, hardy heart of the peninsula and its high-spending, high-living edges – encouraged observers and historians to distinguish two races: one in the 'Iberian' coastlands and lowlands, and another, 'Celtic' or 'Celtiberian' on the tablelands. The peoples the Romans called 'Celtiberians' occupied a zone of acculturation between the civilisations of the Mediterranean rim and the vast arc of Celtic-speaking peoples who dwelt mainly to the north, occupying continuously a huge area from the Atlantic to the Carpathians.

The jealousy in which the 'Iberian' rim of Spain was beheld from the 'Celtiberian' interior might account for the destruction of Ullastret by raiders at around the turn of the fourth and fifth centuries BC, and for the string of forts that screened Upper Andalusia in the same period, blocking access from the meseta of New Castile like a Great Wall of China of southern Spain. The underprivileged interior provided the 'billy-goat-bearded' mercenaries who fought for Aristarchus in 411 BC or supplied Syracuse with shock-troops or bred the warriors who fought against Sparta in 369 and for Carthage from 342. Their evil-smelling woollen mantles were woven at a vast cultural distance from the rich purple capes of the Guadalquivir valley, which were esteemed

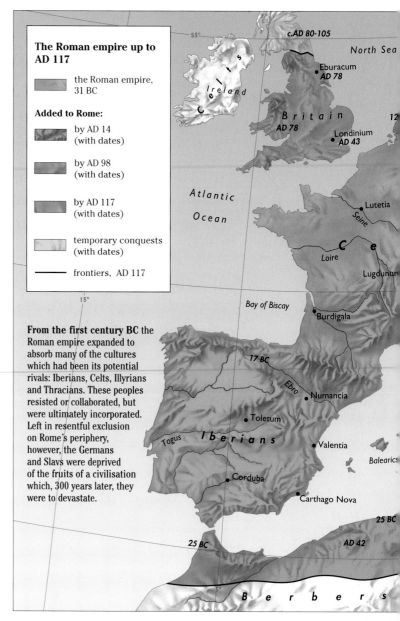

The Roman empire up to AD 117

- the Roman empire, 31 BC

Added to Rome:

- by AD 14 (with dates)
- by AD 98 (with dates)
- by AD 117 (with dates)
- temporary conquests (with dates)
- ——— frontiers, AD 117

From the first century BC the Roman empire expanded to absorb many of the cultures which had been its potential rivals: Iberians, Celts, Illyrians and Thracians. These peoples resisted or collaborated, but were ultimately incorporated. Left in resentful exclusion on Rome's periphery, however, the Germans and Slavs were deprived of the fruits of a civilisation which, 300 years later, they were to devastate.

in Rome. While sybarites in Setefilla, near Seville, dined on banquets of dolphins' flesh, the people of the wind-swept rock-cities of the upper Duero filled their middens with the husks of wheat.

The hard, poor life of the upland peoples can be appreciated at Duero-region ruins, like those of Numancia (which resisted the legions of Scipio Æmilianus in a year-long siege) or the comfortless shell of nearby Tiermes. In contrast to the gold of the south, the mineral wealth of Numancia lay in iron from the Sierra del Moncayo, which can be seen from the settlement's commanding site. By the general standards of inland Spain in pre-Roman times, this made Numancia quite a metropolis, covering a site 200 metres by 400 and arranged in neat, rationally disposed streets of up to seven metres wide. The Romans' booty, from one terrible campaign, was said to be 3,000 oxhides and 800 horses. But the dwellings of the town were of mud and thatch on rubble podiums and not even chiefly residences were distinguished by ornament or scale. The environment was unfriendly. The winter cold killed off besieging Romans' Numidian mercenaries and elephants. The colonists the Romans settled were driven away by the extremes of climate and the labour required to survive. Only inhabitants 'of a spirit resigned to death and a body inured to abstinence and fatigue' could endure.

Numancia was the Asterix-village or perhaps, to judge by its fate, the Masada of Spain. It resisted antiquarians as firmly as it had repelled the Romans. Its location was a mystery in the middle ages. A chronicler of the late tenth century identified it with Zamora. The resources of Renaissance humanism, manipulated by Antonio de Nebrija at the beginning of the sixteenth century, were needed to track it down. The

romance of the story of its conquest had made it a compelling antiquarian goal. In the 20 years from 153 BC, eight consuls had been defeated in attempts to seize it. According to Appian, Rome turned to Cornelius Scipio 'as the only man who could defeat the Numantians.' When he arrived in 134 he prepared his campaign by galvanising an army enfeebled by soft living. He expelled merchants from the camp and, reputedly, 2,000 prostitutes of both sexes, while outlawing depilatory instruments and beds. Even then his forces were not hardy enough to storm the place. He surrounded it with six camps and cut off its supplies by viciously intimidating neighbouring communities. Only the despairing collective suicide of the defenders brought the siege to an end in 133.

Tiermes, though less celebrated than Numancia, was even more tenacious in resistance and even less agreeable to live in. Here Quintus Pompeius was bloodily rebuffed in 142 BC. Titus Didius's conquest of the town in 97 was of short-lived effect. And, once re-occupied by the expelled inhabitants, the town remained effectively independent until Pompey the Great crushed resistance to Rome throughout the Castilian meseta in the aftermath of Sertorius's rebellion. For most of this heroic age, the defenders lived in caves in an acropolis of natural rock, sometimes adding rudimentary structures to the cave-mouth, to enhance their 'lifestyles' – like the conservatory extensions of the modern bourgeoisie. The settlement's water supply was borne from springs in the Sierra de Pela through a tunnel carved under the acropolis in the living rock, of nearly a metre wide and up to 2.32 metres high. Ferocity, hardiness and poverty seem connected in the lives of these indomitable troglodytes. Their easy-going neighbours, the Vaccei, who were celebrated

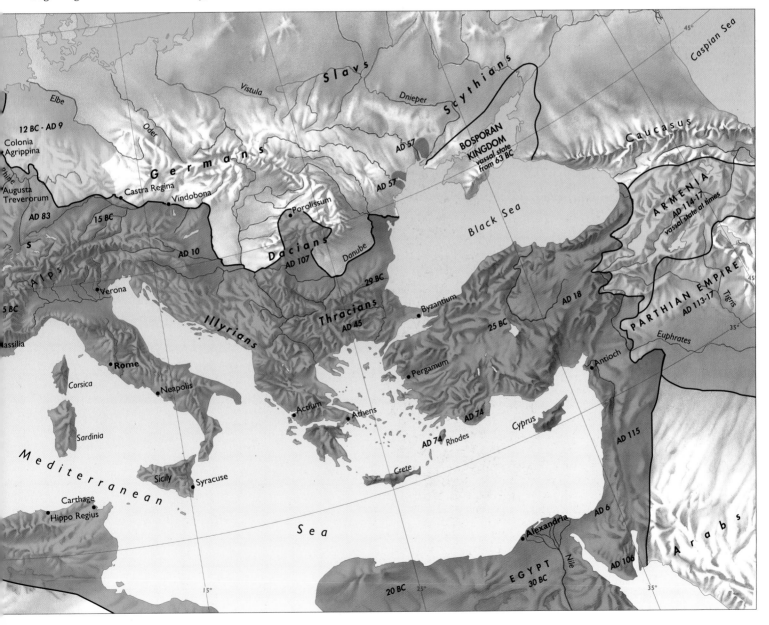

agriculturists and manufactured exportable quantities of sheep's wool cloaks, were happy to accept the expensive convenience of Roman peace.

This range of their reactions to Roman imperialism – from canny collaboration to resistance to the bitter end – was also evinced by the Celts of Gaul and central Europe. Of all their neighbours, apart from the Persians, the Greeks and Romans paid most attention to the Celts, whom they knew as enemies, trading partners and, ultimately, as co-operators in an empire which came to include most of the Celtic lands. Even before the visual evidence is added, we can get a vivid picture of how the Celts appeared to the many classical writers who referred to them. First, and most remarkably, they were an astonishingly homogeneous group of peoples, considering the vast extent of the territory they occupied. Their cultures were recognisably of a piece, their languages obviously akin and their name for themselves was uniform. Alongside huge regional variations, their looks were distinctive, with warriors' bleached and shaggy hair and bodies stained blue for battle. They were feared – and some of the stories about them ripple with Greek and Roman gooseflesh: they hunted human heads, for instance and hung them on their saddle gear. They practised human sacrifice, stitching victims for burning inside huge wicker images of gods.

Their bravery was proverbial – undaunted 'by earthquakes or waves'. Their impetuosity was the subject of contempt: they were easily beaten in battle because of it; they were rash enough to take up arms against the sea. Their drunkenness was a matter of awe and profit: for Italian merchants, the Gallic love of wine was their 'treasure-trove'. The importance of drinking-rituals in Celtic culture is borne out by grave finds, like the famously sumptuous grave of a rich, 35 year-old hostess at Vix, buried with an enormous Greek wine-vessel of fabulous workmanship – so large that it had to be imported in sections and assembled on arrival – and an array of cups.

The way they were depicted in art helps to show how they filled stereotyped roles in Roman minds. In a frieze of the third century BC from Civitalba, where Gaulish raiders were too well known, naked warriors flee, dropping their booty as they run. The splendidly sculpted Gauls made by order of Attalus at Pergamum die defiantly under Greek hooves or slaughter themselves and their wives in defeat. In marbles which survive in early copies in Venice and Rome, they are

The splendour of the Vix Krater *above* shows how heavily the Celtic elite was prepared to spend on imported Greek urns and cups for drinking-parties.

A sculpted marble *below* derived from the bronzes of Pergamum shows the Greek image of a doomed but defiant people. In the seventeenth century the Dying Gaul became one of the most esteemed sculptures of antiquity, representing an heroic ideal without the compromise of realism.

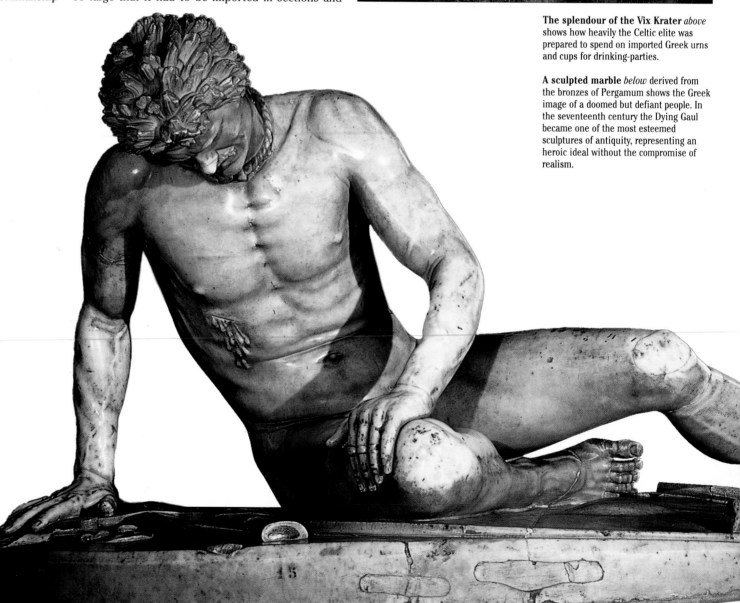

shown dead or dying or falling to the ground, but never resigned, wearing in defeat the disdainful expressions which infuriated Pausanias. The image in the art fits the image in legend: the Celts were seen as a doom-fraught people of visceral pessimism – the most famous story about them to this day, thanks to Goscinny and Uderzo, is that they feared the sky would fall on their heads; yet they were unwilling or unable to make practical compromises. 'Vae Victis!' – woe to the vanquished – exclaimed a Gaulish chief who raided Rome in 390 BC. They abandoned pragmatism to nature's victors.

In antiquity the ultimate test of civilisation was invincibility: 'natural slaves' condemned to servitude by inferiority included, for example, the captives in battle of men of greater prowess. In Greek and Roman eyes, the Celts' indigenous culture therefore got a low rating. Yet, by a less severe test, they had a civilisation of glitter and promise. The professional learned class, the druids, was said to be suspicious of writing its wisdom down, out of the understandable secrecy of a hieratic elite; but enough inscriptions have survived, in the Etruscan, Greek, Iberian and, ultimately, Roman alphabets to show a willingness to experiment in literacy. Writing was used to record laws – another indicator, by Aristotle's criteria, of the difference between civilisation and savagery – and administrative data: Caesar was able to calculate the number of men he faced by means of captured census returns.

Statistical sophistication was founded on more theoretical mathematics. Fragments of a divinatory calendar buried at Coligny – though probably of a late date, when Roman influence was strong – show mastery of semi-lunar timekeeping, involving centuries of records of celestial movements. This justifies Caesar's esteem for the druids' astronomy. Urbanisation – which Romans identified with civilisation – was patchy: when the British chief Caractacus was borne in triumph to Rome he is supposed to have marvelled that the creators of such an environment could covet his people's hovels. Yet the towns that emerged on Celtic lands before the Romans invaded had two defining features of civilisation: fresh water supplies and sanitary drainage. Even while towns were few, sparse and, by Roman standards, gimcrack, by the time of the first Transalpine war, early in the last quarter of the second century BC, the Celts of Gaul had a society the Romans recognised as like their own: no longer stuck in tribal structures but richly differentiated, with individuals ranked by wealth, prowess and ancestry as well as by status in a kinship-system. Nobility was measured in livestock, not land; peasant-tenancies with great lords were for the rent of cattle, paid in calves, pigs and grain.

The economy was restrained by the way wealth drained out of it. Those most unproductive of consumers, the dead, gobbled up vast sums in grave goods. Celtic princes' insatiable taste for high-cost imports from the Mediterranean world imposed a permanent trade deficit which had to be made up in gold. From the late fourth century BC luxury imports were too precious to bury with the dead. Though the more or less progressive adulteration of Celtic gold artifacts with copper may owe something to aesthetics – the red glow of gold alloyed with copper has a gaudy appeal – it is likely to have been the result of a slowly-tightening squeeze on bullion supplies. The prestige of wine-bibbing from Greek situlae could only be enjoyed at a price. The Celts' invasions of Mediterranean lands had been substitutes for trade: in a story told by Pliny, Gaulish conquerors had first crossed the Alps, seduced by the souvenirs – a dried fig and grapes, wine and oil –

The druids' divinatory calendar *right* from Coligny is the oldest surviving document in a Celtic language. Its 16 columns cover a five-year cycle of 62 lunar and two intercalary months, divided into propitious and unpropitious periods. Though late enough to reflect Roman influence – in particular in the use of the Roman alphabet – it illustrates the sophistication of the Celtic mathematics reported by Caesar.

brought home by 'a Helvetian, Helicus, who resided in Rome and worked as an artisan.'

In Roman eyes, the story of Celtic warfare was of heroic defeats, but images of a society organised for war crowd Celtic art. These armies had their successes, albeit mostly against each other. The most famous surviving Celtic artefact, the cauldron of Gundestrup, meticulously illustrates a cosmic drama – a great array of divine myths; equally conspicuous are its parades of soldiery: cavalry with crested helmets and spears are the 'knights' whom Caesar described and who brought their retainers to the field in discharge of a social obligation; infantry march with greaves and long shields, or trumpeters with tall, serpentine tubae. While such parade-scenes may have been conventional borrowings from Greek models – a similar parade is featured, for example, on the sides of the wine-jar in the Vix burial – they sometimes occur with convincingly realistic touches: the Arnoaldi situla in Bologna, for instance, incised perhaps in the fifth century BC with marching footsoldiers and rearing charioteers, shows warriors in typically Etruscan dress alongside unmistakable Celts, as if to celebrate one of the alliances or mercenary contracts attested in written sources at the same period. To judge from the contents of a tomb in München-Obermenzig, armies went into battle with surgeons at hand: the warrior buried there had a trepanning saw and surgical probes as well as weapons.

The wars in which so many Celtic principalities were overthrown by Rome were the result of a clash of rival imperialisms. Celtic expansion had a fitful history: a phase around the middle of the millennium spread colonists and, perhaps, mercenaries, from a heartland between the upper Rhone and upper Elbe, where almost all the princely graves of the sixth century BC are concentrated. A great migration in the early fourth century turned Italy north of the Rubicon into 'Cisalpine Gaul'. In a final great offensive in the late fourth and early third centuries BC, Delphi was sacked, the Balkans crossed and a Celtic kingdom established in Galatia. For a century and a half after the expulsion of the invader from Greece in the 270s, Celtic warriors figured only as mercenaries and allies in other protagonists' campaigns. In 125 BC, Rome's allied city of Massilia

The Gundestrup cauldron *above* of about 100 BC – a splendid piece of repoussé work – was discovered in a Danish bog in 1891. The extensive iconographic programme depicts rituals and myths as well as a procession of 'knights' with boar's-head crests, on the inner rim of the bowl. The cauldron's style shows Thracian influence, though the subject-matter is undeniably Celtic.

(present-day Marseilles) had to be defended from a federation of Celtic tribes. The series of Roman conquests which followed almost succeeded in creating what the Celts of Gaul had never seemed able to achieve on their own: an effective, united and imperial state. The regal image of Vercingetorix, who launched late but almost-successful resistance against Caesar in the middle of the last century of the millennium, stares from the last coinage of independent Gaul.

By then, Romanisation had already started – not only among the Celts of Italy, Spain and southern Gaul who had lived under Roman rule for generations, but also beyond the frontier among those who looked to Rome for trade, patronage and an example of fine living. A syncretic art of wonderful originality was among the results. Heads remained objects of religious devotion and aesthetic attraction, but the magnificent brutality of native traditions surrendered to a classicising tendency. In 1969, Kenneth Clark tried to define civilisation by making a notorious comparison between an African mask, which once belonged to Roger Fry, and the Apollo of the Belvedere – both representing spirit messengers from other worlds, of fear and darkness, light and confidence respectively. He could have made the same comparison between Gaulish bronze heads of the first century BC, without leaving the museum of St Germain-en-Laye. Alternatively, the distinctive look of romanised Gaulish art which is not yet fully Roman can be represented by the delicate looks and gestures, the sinuous allure of the dancing Venus-figures, made early in the period of Roman rule and buried at Neuvy-en-Sullias.

An Etruscan situla of sheet bronze *far left* from the late sixth or early fifth century BC, shows the cultural continuities – manifest in the dress, furniture and music depicted as well as in the artists' style and technique – between the Po Valley, where this example comes from, and the Illyrian lands of the strikingly similar Vace situla.

The bronze dancers of Neuvy-en Sullias *left* have been dismissed as crudely provincial work but their animated modelling and expressive gestures seem the effects of masterful simplicity, influenced by metropolitan models.

The hieratic stare of this idol *right* is typical of earlier divine sculptures by Celtic artists, but in this example of the first century BC from Bouray-sur-Joine, the contrivedly ugly, almost simian look, calculated to inspire terror, has been eliminated, apparently by the influence of Roman portrayals of Apollo.

'A man of boundless energy, ': Caesar recognised Vercingetorix, whose name adorns the last independent coinage of Gaul, *above right*, as a kindred spirit.

Despite the ferocity of the gorgon's head breastplate from a southern Russian barrow burial *below left*, most surviving Scythian art of the mid-first millennium BC shows peaceful scenes. On the gold cup from a large stone-vaulted tomb at Kul Oba near Kerch in the Bosporan kingdom *left*, the comradeship of the camp is featured, as one soldier binds another's leg. A wonderfully rich silver-gilt amphora from Chertomlyk *right* is decorated with scenes of the capture and breaking-in of wild horses: in the detail shown here, a typical episode of domestic life, in which a servant unhobbles his master's horse is juxtaposed with griffins devouring a stag. The Medusa-image was popular with Scythians under Greek influence: this example, from a burial under the huge earthworks of Elizavetinskaya, comes from an area where Greek merchant-colonists and Scythian aristocrats lived side-by-side on the island known in antiquity as Alopecia. As well as decoration for armour, the same motif supplied many small gold plaques for personal use.

In images from Roman funerary art, the Germans are depicted as fiercesome opponents, war-like and bearded, as in this sarcophagus from Rome, *above far left*. After Roman legions campaigned as far as the Elbe in the early first century AD, crushing defeats at German hands pushed them back to the Rhine from where Rome uneasily faced the German world for four centuries.

Because of their potential for civilisation, the Celts were deemed worthy of Roman conquest: they could be absorbed in the empire without compromise of standards. The Germans, whose lands lay beyond them to the north-east, and who were not even noticed in classical sources until late in the fourth century BC, were regarded as too barbaric for absorption. Caesar looked on the Rhine as a practical frontier between civilisation and savagery; in the first years of the Christian era, when Roman relations with German-speaking peoples beyond the frontier were developing fast, the general Velleius, who fought against some of them, dismissed them as 'wild creatures', resembling men only in outward appearance and power of speech. They could learn neither laws, in his opinion, nor civilised arts. After a brief flurry of conquering ambition in Rome, the Germans were left to their own devices. This was probably a mistake. If the Roman world had absorbed all the sedentary peoples on its frontiers, it might, like that of China at the other end of the Eurasian steppe, have survived for millennia as the guardian and common heritage of a sort of co-operative of settled peoples against the nomads outside. Instead, almost all the speakers of Germanic languages were left in resentful exclusion, to revenge themselves in due course with effects, destructive or, as historians now prefer to say, 'transforming', to be reviewed in the next chapter.

Beyond the Germans there were farmers or foresters whose profile in the Graeco-Roman world was vague or fabulous. The Venedi, whose name, at least, survived in the form 'Wends' in medieval Slavic and Scandinavian states, were known as sword-wielders and builders who fought on foot. The Neuri – sometimes said to have been predecessors of the Slavs – were thought of as wanderers, driven from their homelands by plagues of snakes, and as werewolves, whose collective metamorphosis could be predicted from the phases of the moon. Far better known, because they were close neighbours, at some points, of the Greeks and Romans, were the nomads of the European steppe: the Scythians and Sarmatians.

The temptation to treat them as 'Asiatic' peoples who do not belong, except as interlopers, in a European history, should be resisted as the prompting of prejudice. The assumption that only sedentary peoples can fully be part of Europe is based on a value judgement hard to support objectively. A substantial strip of what is now considered Europe is steppeland – stretching from Asia across the lower reaches of all the rivers that flow into the Caspian and Black Seas and the Sea of Azov, from the Ural to the Danube – and a pastoral economy and nomadic way of life belong as well at the European as at the Asian end of it. In one mood, Greek writers sensed that the peoples they called Scythians and Sarmatians belonged to an alien world, wild and menacing. Herodotus, who found them intensely interesting, reported the dream-like findings of Aristeas of Proconnesus, who 'possessed by Phoebus' undertook a mysterious journey into the world beyond the Don, from which he returned to tell the tale only from beyond the grave.

At another level, the nomads were familiar partners of regular trade: depicted by Greek craftsmen in everyday scenes, milking ewes or stitching their mantles of unshorn sheepskin. These images were produced under the patronage of Scythian princes and are echoed in their own goldsmith-work, like the spherical gold cup from a royal tomb at Kul-Oba, between the Sea of Azov and the Black Sea, where bearded warriors in tunics and leggings are shown at peace or at least in the intervals of war: dressing one another's wounds, fixing their teeth, mending their bowstrings and telling campfire tales. Their reputation was as huntsmen first and warriors second – distracted even on the battlefield by a running hare. This was evidently their self-perception, too, for the hare-course was a favourite theme of their art, on a terracotta figure, for instance, from Kerch in the Crimea, where the hooded hunter joins his dog in the chase.

These lands beyond the direct control or knowledge of Greece and Rome were the shadowlands of Europe – marchlands, patrolled by the imaginations of the literate peoples to the south. The concept of 'Europe' was a Greek invention, which barely penetrated the territories of excluded peoples. Strabo, who tended to equate Europe with the extent of Roman influence, made the Don the dividing line which separated it from Asia. Yet Greek and Celtic trade-goods filled princely graves in the Volga valley in the second half of the last millennium BC. In and around the Crimea, the Scythians had access to the heritage of the Greek emporia of the Bosporan kingdom. Here was the 'Scythian Neapolis', a courtly centre covering 40 acres within a stone wall: the Scythians' greatest town – perhaps their only town, since the settlements deeper inside Scythian territory may have belonged to other peoples, Finnic perhaps, tolerated for their fiscal potential. Metropolitan fashion could be felt in the steppes. The Sarmatian queen of the first century AD, who stares, in Greek attire and coiffure, from the centre of a jewelled diadem found at Khokhlac-Novocherkassk, between the Dnieper and the Don, looks as if she fancied herself as Athene. Above her head elaborately wrought deer feed on golden fig-leaves – or perhaps, in the steppeland tradition, they are antler-crowned horses: the rigs for such a disguise are known in a mixture of felt, copper and gilded horsehair from Siberian graves of the fifth century BC.

Alongside the neighbours they affected to despise so much, the Greeks begin to look less 'special' than they have been painted. A few years ago, the Greek tourist board filled pages of glossy magazines in Britain with pictures of nubile tourists cavorting amid doric ruins under the slogan, 'You were born in Greece.' Considered objectively, this message might have been obscure, but no one who saw it is likely to have mistaken its meaning: it was an appeal to modern Europeans' common belief that the civilisation to which they belong began in Greece, from where crucial features of it – including assumptions about art, science, philosophy and politics – have been transmitted across the centuries with continuity often imperilled but never dissolved. This faith in the specialness of Greece inspired the volunteers who fought for Greek independence in the nineteenth century and impelled decision-makers in the European Community to take Greece in as a member when her adhesion to the Treaty of Rome could be justified neither by her backward economy nor her immature political system. Reason is supposed to be one of the faculties the ancient Greeks taught us to prize; yet sentimental philhellenism makes people act irrationally. To see Europe as the Graeco-Roman world thinly spread is obviously wrong: it ignores the contributions of peoples from beyond Greece and Rome, like the Germans, and even from outside Europe, like the Jews. It also ignores the contribution the classical legacy made to other cultures – especially to Islam, and to parts of the world later impregnated with classical influence by European colonists. Aristotle had as much influence on the Muslim philosopher-scientist Avicenna as on the Christian theologian Aquinas, and Latin has lasted longer on the curriculum in Malawi than Milan.

We should be wary of enshrining the Greeks in their 'special' status without critical reflection. So much of what has always been said about them needs, or is now undergoing, radical revision. Today, when we look at the *ostraka* and jurors' tokens that once seemed fragments from the very foundations of democracy, we see only evidence of a harsh and rigidly stratified political system. When we contemplate a classical building or statue, we no longer see it as a chaste specimen of the taste which the 'classicism' of intervening centuries has shared, but we have been taught to clothe it in the strident, gaudy colours with which it would have been decorated in its day. When we think about the inhabitants of Olympus, we see them no longer as personifications of virtues and vices, but capricious manipulators of demonic nature in a world regulated – in the imagination of most Greeks who had to contend with it – not by reason but, if at all, by mysteries and weird and bloody propitiatory rites. We are more inclined to find our information about the Greeks' moral code in the street-wisdom of Aristophanes than the school-wisdom of Socrates.

Nevertheless, there is a sense in which the influence of ancient Greece has genuinely helped to make us in modern Europe what we are. When William Guthrie was a boy, made to read Plato and Aristotle at school, he found the former's language beautiful but opaque, the latter's intelligible with startling clarity. At first, he thought it was because Aristotle was a

In Greek communities, votes in favour of exile or 'ostracism' were recorded on fragments of broken pottery or oyster-shell called *ostraka*. Byzantine monks later re-cycled them for keeping records, short texts and personal documents of every kind, as in this example *above* from Herodium, the sumptuous city founded by Herod the Great.

Although her taste was predominantly of Greek inspiration, among the regalia of the Sarmatian queen buried at Khoklac-Novocherkassk in the first century AD was a gold coronet or collar in the Scythian tradition *above right*, ringed with fantastically entwined beasts. Her grave goods included a dozen other large objects – bracelets, boxes, jugs and a perfume bottle – as well as the diadem described in the text, and hundreds of gold spangles sewn onto her apparel.

The Acropolis of Athens *bottom* was adorned with its buildings in the late fifth century BC, early in a long period of extraordinary cultural productivity. Throughout the 430s, the effective patron of the work was Pericles *right*, who manipulated Athenian democracy to establish his personal rule.

'modern' thinker, ahead of his time, who 'thought like us'. Only gradually did he realise that the truth was the exact opposite: it is we who think like Aristotle, whose formula for thinking in logical stages has continued to characterise the 'western' mind ever since and to inform our methods of distinguishing true statements from false ones. Much of the rest of Greek literature and art has had a similar impact. Because it has survived in large quantities or, when not directly available, has been transmitted through copies of art-works or, in the case of writings, through translations or intermediate texts, its images, concepts and values resonate in the traditions of the peoples, including, particularly and prominently, European peoples, who received them.

The Greeks were not just another European people among many. What was significant about them was what was exceptional and often marginalised: Socrates was condemned to suicide; Pythagoras was probably killed by rioting specimens of 'common man'. Sophocles had to defend himself against a charge of insanity by a public reading of his great play about exile. Plato abandoned politics in disgust. Diogenes withdrew to a barrel, Aristotle, at one time, to a cave. But, from among the Greeks, enough output survived from exceptional minds and talents to be, in sum, uniquely significant.

All their neighbours envied the Greeks enough to imitate them. Whereas the Scythians' legacy was limited to a few art-forms transmitted to the Goths and Celts, and the Thracians' culture disappeared entirely, except, perhaps, for echoes in those icons of mounted saints; whereas the Illyrians, Etruscans and Iberians left nothing which lasted except in ruined or buried form; whereas the Celts survived only on the Atlantic fringes of Europe and left – in relation to their former vast dominion – astonishingly little influence behind them as they were pushed out of the way; in contrast to all these examples of mutability, the Greeks, almost alone, with the Romans who borrowed from them and passed on so much, achieved a kind of cultural immortality.

CHAPTER 3

FROM 'EUROPE' TO CHRISTENDOM
The formation and distortion of a concept of Europe

IN **ABOUT 500 BC** a tyrant of Miletus displayed to a ruler of Sparta a bronze tablet engraved with a map of the world. Clues to what it might have looked like have to be raked from fragments of text in medieval Byzantine manuscripts, but because the proposal which accompanied it was for a joint invasion of the Persian empire, the world was probably depicted in two roughly equal parts: a distended Europe at the top, like a protruding upper lip; and Asia and Africa crammed together into the lower half. Thus Asia was reduced to the proportions of a manageable conquest, Europe elevated to an exaggerated size and a superior position.

The meaning of 'Europe' has continued to be adapted ever since to the convenience of the moment. In the absence of a satisfactory geographical definition, its limits have been expanded or contracted according to the perspective and prejudices of the beholder. Such a vague term, with so little objective justification, might never have survived had not its Greek origins made it respectable and its elasticity made it exploitable: cartographers' projections have been devised to reinforce cultural assumptions or justify short-term policies;

politicians' definitions have been formulated to exclude unwanted peoples or to overtrump international rivalries. The process of defining 'Europe' is still going on today, with motives as self-interested as ever.

The origins of the term baffled even the ancient Greeks, who were responsible for embedding it in our vocabulary. In the late fifth century BC Herodotus was unable to explain 'why the earth, which is one' should have been divided into continents nor 'whence people got the names they gave them'. 'Europe' first occurred among surviving texts as the name of one of the divisions of Greece in an eighth-century BC hymn to Apollo. In the sixth century its usage expanded to cover Greece's vast European hinterland. When next mentioned in an extant work, by Pindar in the early fifth century, its western limits were fixed beyond Cadiz. Herodotus put the eastern frontier on the lower Danube, while deferring the problem of the northern limit to future exploration. With a growing conviction of the vastness of the world, lands beyond the Danube were incorporated until by the beginning of the Christian era Strabo regarded the river as more or less bisecting the continent. At the same time, Europe's relative size diminished: Strabo's Asia was

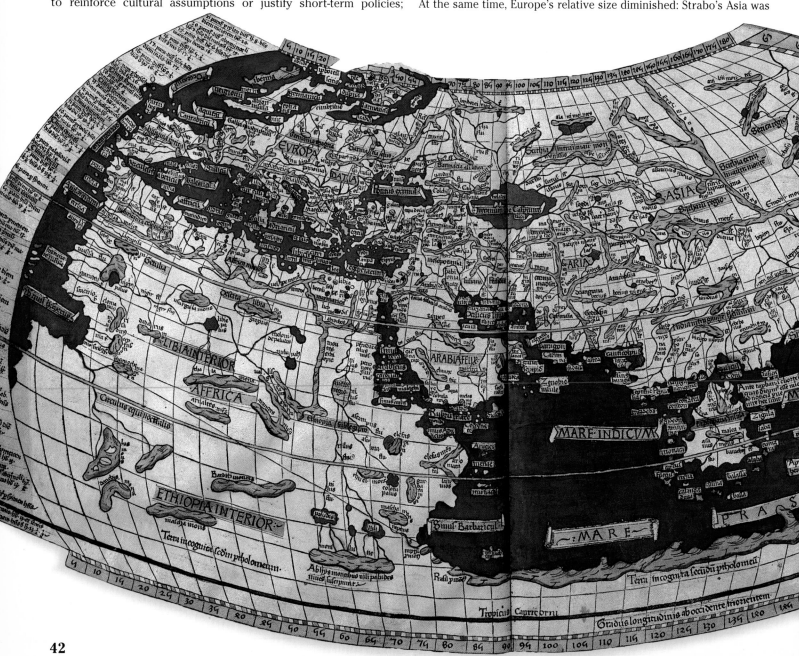

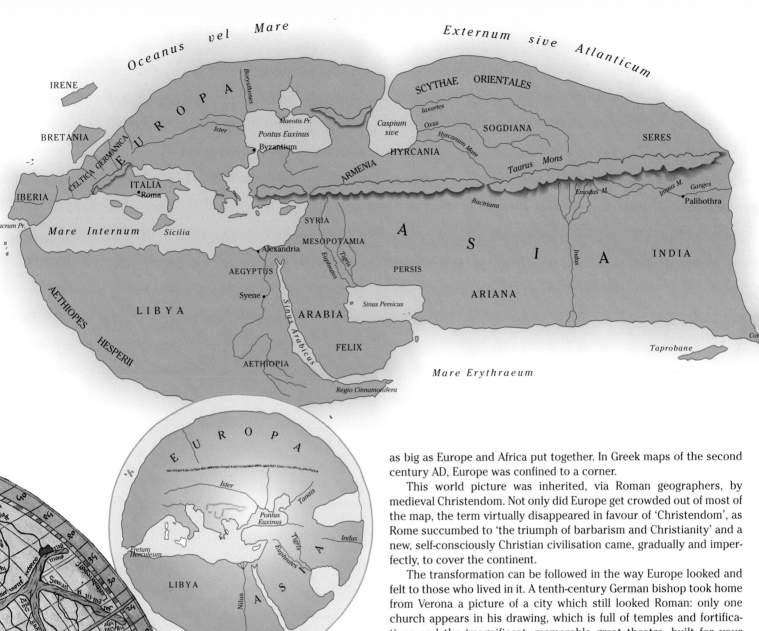

as big as Europe and Africa put together. In Greek maps of the second century AD, Europe was confined to a corner.

This world picture was inherited, via Roman geographers, by medieval Christendom. Not only did Europe get crowded out of most of the map, the term virtually disappeared in favour of 'Christendom', as Rome succumbed to 'the triumph of barbarism and Christianity' and a new, self-consciously Christian civilisation came, gradually and imperfectly, to cover the continent.

The transformation can be followed in the way Europe looked and felt to those who lived in it. A tenth-century German bishop took home from Verona a picture of a city which still looked Roman: only one church appears in his drawing, which is full of temples and fortifications and the 'magnificent, memorable great theatre, built for your splendour, Verona.' A poem written in the city's praise in the eighth century devotes its first 24 lines to the buildings erected in honour of Roman gods. Yet even as it was praised, this past was partly repudiated. 'Look,' said the poet, 'how fine was the building of evil men, who did not know the law of God and worshipped ancient idols of wood and stone.' The true greatness of Verona consisted, he felt, in the relics of her three dozen saints, which made her 'singularly rich among the hundred cities of Italy' and lined her parapets with 'most holy guardians to defend her.' Instead of the civic patriotism of antiquity, Verona had adopted Christian self-consciousness as the basis of her identity. This was a transformation recorded in many cities by Prudentius as early as the late fourth century: according to his methodical ranking, Rome was rated above other cities because of her muster of martyrs.

Verona was typical of the re-forging of consciousness as 'Europe' turned into Christendom: the lessons of Rome were remembered like those of an old school whose pupils have outgrown it but remain under its lingering enchantment. Wherever Roman vestiges were visible or wherever their lack was felt, pride in the Roman past could never be entirely expunged. Christendom got ideas and elites from outside the Roman empire and eventually grew to fill wider frontiers, but it retained a sense of being the creation and heir of Rome. The Roman empire remained the model and inspiration of medieval Christian empire-builders. Strabo exaggerated when he said that 'most of Europe' was under the influence of Rome: ironically, it became true later, when, to outward appearances, the Roman empire had vanished.

In Asterix's village, only magic could stop the Romans. In the real Roman world, the magic all seemed to be on the other side. One of the

The world map as conceived at Miletus in about 500 BC with Europe dominating the composition *above*. In the conception of Eratosthenes about 200 years later *top*, Europe had shrunk to occupy less than a quarter of the surface of the habitable world. Ptolemy's attempt to map the world from Alexandria in the mid-second century AD still concentrated on Europe, for which he made ten maps, compared with four and 12 for Africa and Asia respectively. In his conception *left*, however, the extent of Europe had shrunk even further to fill only about a sixth of the available space. His maps did not survive: this illustration shows a reconstruction of the late fifteenth century.

Constantine adorned his new city
of Constantinople with spoils from around
the Roman world. One of the most spectacular
remains of the city he founded is the
Hippodrome *right* which boasts the column
of serpents and the obelisk of Theodosius.
When the column of Constantine *above*
was erected in AD 330 at the centre of the
Forum, the relics buried at its base included
the Palladium of Troy, Aeneas's own
supposed icon of Athena, the sun-rays of
Apollo's crown, the nails of Christ's passion
and fragments of the True Cross. A statue
of Constantine stood at the top.

Conimbriga *above far right,* near
modern Coimbra, on the Atlantic coast of
Portugal, was as remote from Rome as any
western colony of its day; yet the
metropolitan affectations of its citizens
inspired them to re-design their settlement
in direct imitation of Rome.

Individual careers linked remote
points around the Roman world: a
funerary stela of the first century AD *far
right* in Cologne represents the civilised
garrison-life of a soldier born in Andalusia.

great unsolved riddles of history is how a small city-state of obscure origins and limited manpower conquered the Mediterranean, extended its frontiers to the Atlantic and the North Sea and transformed almost every culture it touched. We have embarrassingly large numbers of explanations of the empire's 'decline and fall' – over two hundred different theories by a recent count, including excessive asceticism and excessive hedonism, centralisation and decentralisation, Christianity and polytheism, superstition and rationalism, urbanisation and civic decline. But bigger mysteries are why the empire lasted so long and how it happened at all.

In part, Roman imperialism worked because it struck the kind of balance between unity and diversity for which the European Union is struggling today. This was a collaborative empire, like Britain's, one of its later imitators, which encompassed both emirs in Nigeria and Maharajahs in India without undertaking the trouble of displacing them altogether. Roman methods were part-predatory, part-placatory. The predatory character can be sensed today in the middle of Istanbul, at the highest point of the city, under the roar of traffic, amid billowing exhaust-fumes and flurries of dust. Here, charred, broken and half-buried, spoils of the ancient world still adorn the site of Constantine's forum: the serpent-throne of the Delphic oracle, obelisks of pharaonic Egypt, a column carved with a hippodrome-scene are almost all that is left of the ornaments of three continents, scooped together in the early fourth century AD to build an imperial capital from scratch.

Yet this was an empire that gave as well as took. While encompassing a huge diversity of peoples and environments, it was able to re-fashion some of its parts in a common image. The result, rough-hewn and imperfect, was a single Roman world.

All over the rim of the empire, the Romans founded cities in the image of Rome. The biggest basilica was in distant London, the widest street in a vanished city of south-west Spain. Colonists on the Atlantic shore of Portugal, where the salt spray corroded the mosaics, demolished their town centre in the first century AD in order to rebuild it to resemble Rome's. In Italica, Rome's first overseas colony, founded near modern Seville to accommodate Scipio's veterans during the Second Punic War, metropolitan glamour is still represented among the ruins: by the gigantic amphitheatre, the liveliness of the sculptures of artists from Rome, the traces of luxury-filled shops and, most vividly of all, the scenes of priapic debauchery which decorate a bathroom floor. The amenities of civilised Mediterranean life – villas, wine, olive oil, mosaics – were exported to the provinces or forced into home-growth in unlikely climates. Envoys from federates on the shores of the Atlantic and the Black Sea hung offerings in the temple of Jupiter on the Capitol.

Some of the cities housed colonies – usually of retired soldiers, who, Latin-speaking and schooled in a universal allegiance, helped to spread a common culture. On his funerary stela in Cologne a retired veteran of Astigi (modern Êcija in Andalusia) is depicted, exuding all the classic confidence of a Roman citizen, reclining, attended by his wife and son, with food and wine arrayed before him on an elegant claw-foot tripod table. Romans like him spread an instantly recognisable 'classical' style all over their world. Its surviving fragments – sewers in Spain, pediments in Pannonia, sarcophagi in Syria – make us think it was a monolithic structure, as strong and uniform as its stone buildings. In reality, it could work only as a variegated state – an immense federation of cities and peoples or, rather, a number of such federations, sometimes rather loosely articulated. Even when the institutions were most unified, there were at least two empires: one, Roman-Celtic, in the west; another, Roman-Greek, in the east.

Everywhere the Romans ruled with the collaboration – sometimes enforced – of established elites: magistrates of existing civic communities, chieftains of thousands of 'tribes', distinguished by Roman geographers and endowed with varying degrees of autonomy by Roman officials. Iberian officials with barbarous names followed Roman law in making adjudications which they ordered to be carved in bronze. Hebrew exarchs and Germanic war-chiefs retained their authority under licence from the empire. When imperial authority collapsed in the west some of the chieftaincies briefly flourished as the realms of kinglets – like the shadowy Vortigern or perhaps 'King Arthur' in

Britain. Most disappeared, sunk in new 'hyphenated identities' as Gallo-Romans, Romano-British and so on. Greeks, Celts and other smaller peoples – Iberians, Ligurians, even Jews like St Paul – could enjoy the status of Roman citizens, which in the third century was extended to all the inhabitants of the empire.

Inside this vast arena of political co-operation between constituent elites, the Roman empire operated a system for the enrichment of its inhabitants. Economic historians have, perhaps, been crudely obsessed with long-range trade. In the case of the Roman empire, however, the commercial stimulation of the *pax Romana* and the multiplication of wealth by virtue of the extension of trading patterns seem genuinely to have been vital in creating unprecedented prosperity in the parts of the world Rome ruled. This was both an effect of the empire and a cause of its durability. In the first century AD, merchants from a clan in the Duero valley were buried in what is now Hungary; Greek potters made amphorae in which wine was shipped from Andalusia to Provence. Because the Roman empire represented an extension of a Mediterranean civilisation beyond the basin of that sea, Mediterranean products were among the most widely exported. In one of his vulgar schemes for making money, Petronius's satirical creation, Trimalchio, lost thirty million sesterces in the shipwreck of a single wine shipment and more than made it up on the next. But as industrial production became geographically specialised, commercial relationships criss-crossed the entire empire. In Spain, at Roses in the north-east and Bolonia in the south-west, the huge evaporators of garum factories survive, where the empire's favourite fish sauce was made from the blood and entrails of tunny and mackerel. North-east Gaul was a centre of cloth manufacture: the lives of the merchants are engraved on a mausoleum at Igel on the frontier of Germany and Luxembourg. They conveyed huge bales of finished cloth by road and river and sold it in elegant shops, banqueting on the profits they made at feasts displayed to emphasise their superior status over their farming neighbours.

The statue which stands on the summit of the Capitol in Rome shows the Emperor Marcus Aurelius, who died in AD 180, victoriously horsed, baton in hand. No image of command has ever been so influential or so often copied for portraits of other rulers. It expresses, for most people, the triumphant serenity of the Roman empire at its height, spreading its peace through strength over an unprecedented swathe of the western world. Yet the reign of Marcus Aurelius has also been traditionally regarded as the far edge of the high plateau of Roman achievement, after which decline set in, punctuated only by the lower peaks of ever more desperate recoveries.

Even after a long period of rarely interrupted success for Roman arms and Roman methods of control of subject-peoples, the empire bequeathed by Marcus Aurelius was not much bigger than that founded by the first emperor, Augustus, around the beginning of the Christian era. Except in Britain, the gains since Augustus's day had the nature of frontier adjustments, between the Rhine and the Danube, in Dacia and – beyond Europe – on the eastern front. Augustus had established not only frontiers of surprising sustainability but also a remarkably enduring system of government. He founded an hereditary monarchy without offending the republican traditions of the Roman elite, calling himself by the neutral title of *'princeps'* and using or abusing republican rhetoric to justify his personal power. But even in his own day, the idea of an autocratic magistracy became irremediably compromised by associations with monarchical traditions. The emperor's office – made sacred by fusion with the role of 'Supreme Priest' of the Roman civic religion – was made even more numinous by the apotheosis of dead rulers and the worship of living ones. The power of the traditional republican institutions – the senate and the elective magistracies – was progressively weakened or by-passed. The system had some advantages: unified command, strong leadership and popular appeal. But it carried with it a disadvantage that might prove fatal: in the absence of an enforceable method of deciding the succession, armies had effectively usurped a constitutional role in making and unmaking emperors. No means of forestalling the consequent dangers of fragmentation and civil war was ever devised.

The mausoleum of a merchant-family in Luxembourg *left*, first century AD, with reliefs showing scenes of trade in grain.

An imperial cameo of Augustus *above,* crowned with victory and carrying an eagle wand, preserved as a result of being set in a medieval cross.

The statue of Marcus Aurelius on the Capitol *right*, where the temples were shrines to the guardian deities of Roman power, embodies the virtues of stoicism and material strength: the hand points to a far horizon; the horse stamps in a conventional gesture of hegemony.

By the time of Marcus Aurelius two further dangers could be discerned for the future. First, Christianity was ever making new converts and penetrating ever higher levels of society. From the perspective of most of the traditional elite, this was a development incompatible with the survival of the state, since – to the pious – Rome's greatness was at the disposal of the gods, while – to the practical – Roman political unity depended on adherence to the state religion and worship of the divine emperor. Second, the subject peoples within the empire and the barbarians on its borders were growing increasingly covetous of the

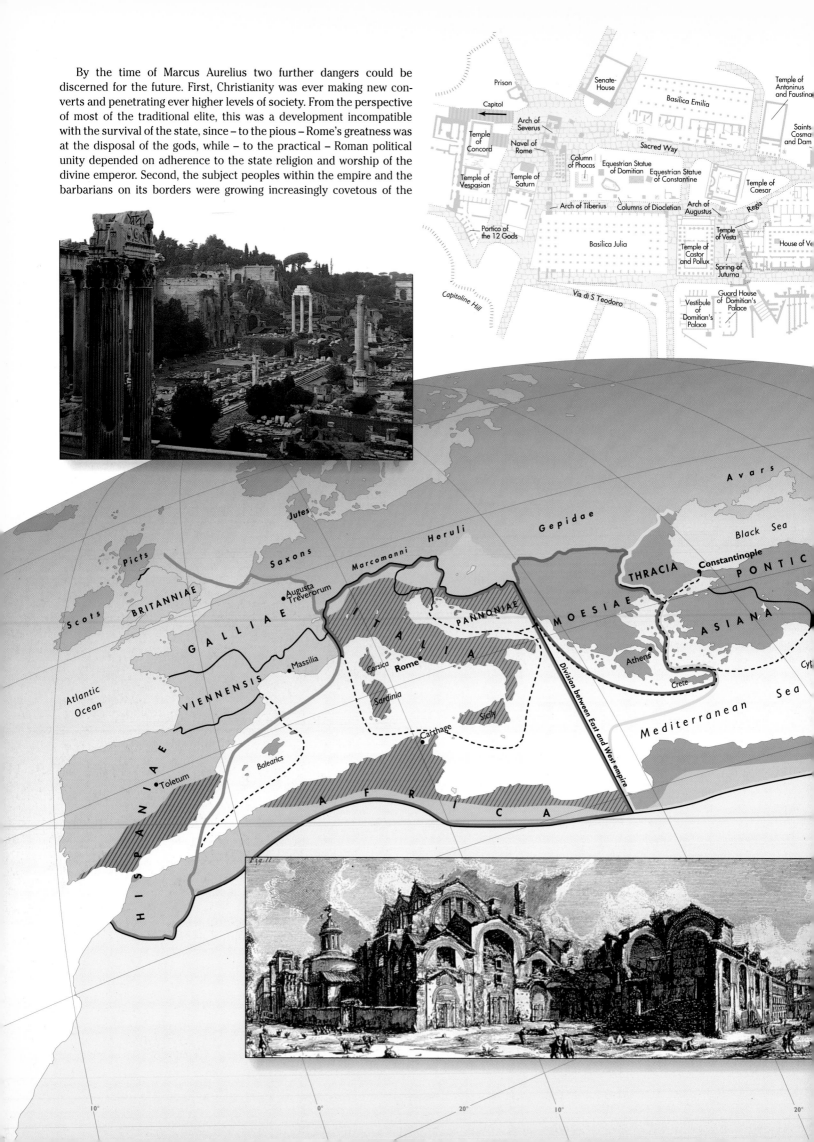

Prison
Senate-House
Basilica Emilia
Temple of Antoninus and Faustina
Capitol
Arch of Severus
Saints Cosma and Dam
Temple of Concord
Navel of Rome
Column of Phocas
Sacred Way
Equestrian Statue of Domitian
Equestrian Statue of Constantine
Temple of Caesar
Temple of Vespasian
Temple of Saturn
Arch of Tiberius
Columns of Diocletian
Arch of Augustus
Regia
Temple of Vesta
House of Ve
Portico of the 12 Gods
Basilica Julia
Temple of Castor and Pollux
Spring of Juturna
Capitoline Hill
Via di S Teodoro
Vestibule of Domitian's Palace
Guard House of Domitian's Palace

Avars
Jutes
Black Sea
Heruli
Gepidae
Saxons
Marcomanni
Constantinople
Picts
PONTIC
THRACIA
BRITANNIAE
MOESIAE
Scots
Augusta Treverorum
PANNONIAE
ASIANA
GALLIAE
ITALIA
Atlantic Ocean
Massilia
Corsica
Rome
VIENNENSIS
Sardinia
Athens
Cyp
Sicily
Crete
Division between East and West empire
Carthage
HISPANIAE
Balearics
Mediterranean Sea
Toletum
AFRICA

10°   0°   20°   10°   20°

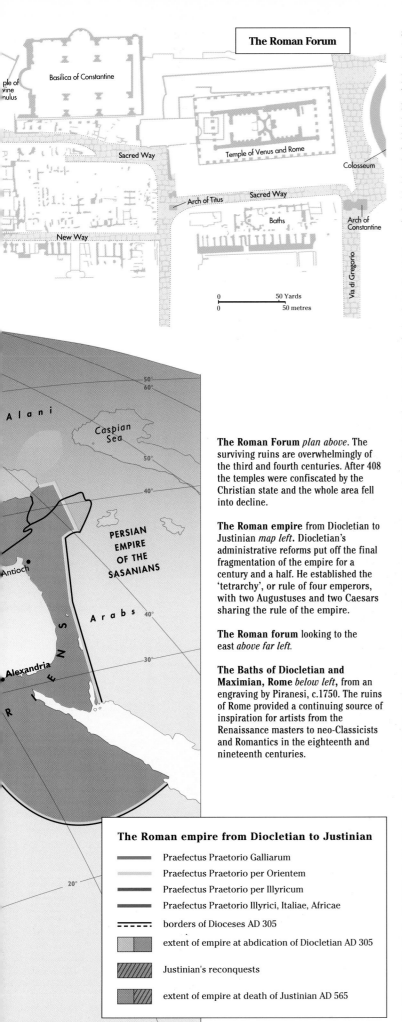

The Roman Forum

Basilica of Constantine

ple of
vine
nulus

Temple of Venus and Rome

Sacred Way

Colosseum

Arch of Titus — Sacred Way

Baths

Arch of Constantine

New Way

Via di Gregorio

0   50 Yards
0   50 metres

The Roman Forum *plan above.* The surviving ruins are overwhelmingly of the third and fourth centuries. After 408 the temples were confiscated by the Christian state and the whole area fell into decline.

The Roman empire from Diocletian to Justinian *map left*. Diocletian's administrative reforms put off the final fragmentation of the empire for a century and a half. He established the 'tetrarchy', or rule of four emperors, with two Augustuses and two Caesars sharing the rule of the empire.

The Roman forum looking to the east *above far left*.

The Baths of Diocletian and Maximian, Rome *below left*, from an engraving by Piranesi, c.1750. The ruins of Rome provided a continuing source of inspiration for artists from the Renaissance masters to neo-Classicists and Romantics in the eighteenth and nineteenth centuries.

Alani

Caspian Sea

PERSIAN EMPIRE OF THE SASANIANS

Antioch

Arabs

Alexandria

The Roman empire from Diocletian to Justinian

————	Praefectus Praetorio Galliarum
————	Praefectus Praetorio per Orientem
————	Praefectus Praetorio per Illyricum
————	Praefectus Praetorio Illyrici, Italiae, Africae
------	borders of Dioceses AD 305
▨	extent of empire at abdication of Diocletian AD 305
▨	Justinian's reconquests
▨	extent of empire at death of Justinian AD 565

status of Roman citizenship and the wealth of the Roman world. The 'prosperity gap' between Rome and most of her neighbours was like that between 'North and South', on a global level, today – inspiring fear in the prosperous and envy in the poor. Marcus Aurelius himself anticipated two ways in which the empire was to cope with these pressures for the next two or three centuries. He embraced stoicism as his personal philosophy and became, indeed, a source of some of the best-known maxims of the stoical tradition. He was therefore a patron and practitioner of the culture, based on stoicism, in which Christians and pagans became reconciled and which made it possible for Christianity to replace the old religion at an official level. Moreover, he sensed the need to divide the unwieldy responsibilities of governing the vast empire, admitting his adoptive brother to the rank of co-emperor in what was to be a recurrent formula for saving the state from crisis.

The political fortunes of the empire can be read in the stones of the Forum – not from inscriptions, but from the configurations of the ruins. It is amazing that they are there at all. Nowhere else – at least, in the centre of no other thriving capital – could such venerable remains have been so cruelly depleted without being callously re-developed. In 408 the temples were confiscated by a Christian state and left to rot. From 459 the spoliation of the site was legitimised. Yet though the buildings were pillaged and cannibalised, the site was protected – perhaps by some faint delicacy of feeling but more thoroughly by the new direction taken by the development of the city. The Vatican – a humble by-way at its foundation – became a powerfully magnetic pole of late antique and medieval Rome, which dragged urban expansion, such as it was, away to the west. So the ruins of the Forum stayed, bared to the sight, to arouse the patrician sensibilities of Renaissance popes, inspire the antiquarian taste of Renaissance scholars, admonish the Enlightenment and enchant Romantics. The Rome they evoke is, however, not genuinely the classical city of the Republic and early patriciate. The ruins of what we can see now are overwhelmingly of the late third and early fourth centuries. They belong to an extraordinary, concentrated, late burst of public building and civic patronage, after a long period of the erosion of civic spirit in which buildings erected for common good and use had gradually declined in number. Outside the Forum, the walls of Aurelian and the baths of Diocletian are conspicuous monuments of this era but it is inside the numinous circuit – now hideously fenced, like a football ground against latter-day barbarians – where the evidence is most impressive.

As you walk from the foot of the Capitol, the chaste cube-like brick structure with the pedimented facade was once the new Senate-House of Diocletian. It has long since been stripped of its marble and of its doors, which now adorn the church of Santa Maria Maggiore. Diocletian rebuilt it in 284, after the original was destroyed by fire, as a gesture of confidence in a patriciate he was thought to despise and a capital he was suspected of abandoning. Next to it is the Basilica Emilia, the only monument of the Forum from republican times. Opposite are the Basilica Julia, restored in the same era, and the five columns erected to Diocletian and his caesars. A few paces to the east is the curiously curved, colonnaded facade of the Temple of Divine Romulus, abutting the east end of what is now the church of Sts Cosmas and Damian, an addition of the same reign.

Maxentius's reign – from 306 to 312 – brought even more spectacular efforts to bear on the enhancement of the Forum than his predecessor's. Maxentius remodelled Hadrian's Temple of Venus and of Rome at the east end and built the crushingly enormous new basilica, whose groin-vaulted nave and huge niches dwarf their surroundings. This, the greatest monument of the Forum, was almost the last. Constantine put his own statue inside it – a cheap way of taking credit for the work of his predecessor. By repudiating the pagan gods and founding a new capital in the east, he doomed the city of Rome to decline and the Forum to stagnation. Symbolically, his triumphal arch seals the view to the east. From a distance it looks impressive enough, a proud reversion to imperial tradition; but by comparison with the earlier arches, it is a shoddy piece of work, with inappropriate friezes re-cycled from earlier buildings. After his time only the column of Phocas was added – a sentimental sentinel, watching over the Forum's ageing wreckage.

Diocletian had already anticipated some features of Constantine's revolution. The steadfast clasps exchanged by tetrarchs in war gear outside St Mark's treasury in Venice are gestures of contrived solidarity, betraying doubts of the prospects for imperial unity once the administration had been divided. Diocletian's 'mania' – denounced as such by a fellow-caesar – for his eastern administrative centre at Nicomedia pre-figures Constantine's foundation of a new Rome at Constantinople. Yet Diocletian's last act was an affirmation of the sort of 'antique virtues' which were commended by philosophers and occasionally embodied by dictators in republican times. Like Cincinnatus returning to the plough or Sulla surrendering power, he retired to plant cabbages in Split. Above all he reaffirmed the empire's nearest approximation to a ruling ideology – a religion of civic rituals and emperor-worship – by persecuting Christians. Christian writers revelled in it and inflated or invented an army of martyrs – defiant virgins, recalcitrant soldiers, indomitable priests and deacons. The persecution did not work, and was probably less intense than Christian legends alleged. But it did mark the beginnings of a decisive shift: by the end of the century, pagans would be the victims of milder persecution by Christians.

Constantine's reign was like a trench across the course of Roman history, diverting it into new channels. Like so many future invaders and tourists, he came from the north and was seduced by the feel and flavour of Mediterranean culture. The standard tale of the beginning of his conversion to Christianity is not incredible. Approaching the decisive battle of his bid for the throne at Milvian Bridge, he saw a vision of a cross in the sky – perhaps like the cruciform clouds Edward Whymper saw on his way down from the first ascent of the Matterhorn. The priorities reflected in the message, 'In this sign, conquer,' seem to have been Constantine's own: he was looking for a Lord of hosts rather than a God of love.

If the document is genuine, an alternative account of the conversion may be Constantine's own: it is a standard story of revelation imparted by grace: 'I did not think that a power above could see any thoughts which I harboured in the secret places of my heart ... but Almighty God, sitting on high, has granted what I did not deserve.' Despite the emperor's new convictions, emperorship was an essentially pagan office, incorporating priesthood, conferring deification, and it could not be suddenly purged of its traditional character. Official religion - continued. Panegyrists classified Constantine's victims in battle as divine sacrifices and his birth as a gift of the gods. One constructed a framework of paganism over which the emperor's Christianity could fit: 'You have secret communion with the Divine Mind, which, delegating our care to lesser gods, deigns to reveal itself to you alone.' In Spain, bishops allowed Christians to hold official priesthoods, provided they celebrated with games rather than sacrifices. Constantine banned the placing of his statues in pagan temples but continued to personify the Unconquered Sun – perhaps because prophecies of Christ were conventionally attributed to Apollo, or because Christ appeared clad

Medallions of Constantine *bottom left*, led by victory and attended by a chariot-team.

Early fourth-century Tetrarchs in battle-dress *below*, outside the treasury of St Mark's, Venice, embracing in a gesture of solidarity.

The apotheosis of a fourth-century emperor *right*. While a deity in a chariot- looks on, the new deity is raised aloft by genii under an awning adorned with signs of the sun and the zodiac.

The Battle of Milvian Bridge *far right*. The emperor Constantine's rise to power was closely identified with his adherence to Christianity – he fought at Milvian Bridge in the name of the Christian God against the usurper Maxentius. His victory is celebrated on the Arch of Constantine.

as the sun in Christian iconography: a solar Christ, for instance, drives a chariot in a third-century mosaic under St Peter's basilica.

Constantine's was the religion of a pragmatist. Like the other Christian monarchs of his day – Tiridates in Armenia and Aeizanas in Abyssinia – he used the church to promote social peace and, as if instinctively, to serve his own power. Addressing bishops, he showed mastery of their own sacred texts and rhetoric, calling himself their 'fellow-servant' and 'true servant of God' and even 'the equal of the apostles.' He was abrupt with contentious theology. The controversy of the day over the relative ranks of the persons of the trinity he dismissed as 'the frivolity of an idle hour.' 'You should not have raised such questions,' he told squabbling bishops, 'or, once raised, have left them unanswered.' He presided over the Council of Nicaea in person and the form of words which was found to express the relationship of the Father and the Son was ascribed to his invention. Emperors might still be honoured and portrayed as gods: a particularly sumptuous and exotic ivory of the late fourth century in the British Museum shows winged genii bearing an emperor up to his ancestors by way of the signs of the zodiac. Imperial apotheosis, however, could now be redefined in Christian terms as a divine vicariate on earth and, in deserving cases, sanctity after death: in coins issued by his sons, Constantine is guided into heaven on a chariot, like Elijah's, by the hand of God.

For Christians, imperial patronage was an extraordinary windfall. Despite the slow accumulation of converts among the socially respectable and intellectually reputable, theirs had remained essentially 'a religion of slaves and women', one of many oriental mystery-cults which occasionally transcend in appeal the cultures in which they start. Christianity still bore the marks of its origins as a Jewish heresy, founded by a rabbi whose birth and death were, in the world's eyes, equally disreputable and whose messianic claims were commonplace enough to be easily rejected as delusive. Its scriptures were, by the standards of the schools, so badly written as to embarrass all educated Christians.

Now, according to Eusebius, who had chronicled the persecutions of previous reigns, 'it felt as if we were imagining a picture of the kingdom of Christ and that what was happening was no reality but a dream.' In Constantine, Origen's prophecy seemed to be about to be fulfilled, and Christianity to be spread throughout a united world by a Christian emperor. There were subsidies for the church, exemptions from fiscal and military obligations for the clergy, jobs in the state service for Christians, and the assurance, from the emperor's own hand, that the worship of Christians benefited the empire.

Constantine's reformation would have been impossible if paganism and Christianity had not already modified each other, made mutual compromises and established common ground. The conflict of paganism and Christianity showed signs of bitterness. Sopatros, an eminent pagan philosopher in Constantine's service, was beheaded after denunciation by a Christian for having magically 'fettered the winds' that brought grain-ships to Constantinople. When paganism returned to imperial favour in the reign of Julian, some mobs took the chance of revenge on churches that had displaced temples: stuffing disembowelled nuns with barley and feeding them to pigs was said to be a common manifestation of popular outrage.

Insults, however, were more usual weapons in this war. Rutilius Namatianus, the pagan Gaulish aristocratic whose visit to Rome near the end of the fourth century was a sort of secular pilgrimage, denounced the dirty habits and obscure rites of monks; the elegant senator Symmachus and St Ambrose, bishop of Milan, exchanged ironic compliments on each other's rhetorical skill during the debate which surrounded the dethronement of the goddess of victory from the Senate-House in 382. Insults could be matched by action: in a typical incident, a Christian senator in 375-6, who might have been expected to mark his prefecture of Rome by building a civic monument or amenity, instead destroyed a pagan shrine. On the whole, however, paganism could be defeated, once emperors were Christians, by being starved of patronage, despoiled of religious endowments and expelled from official

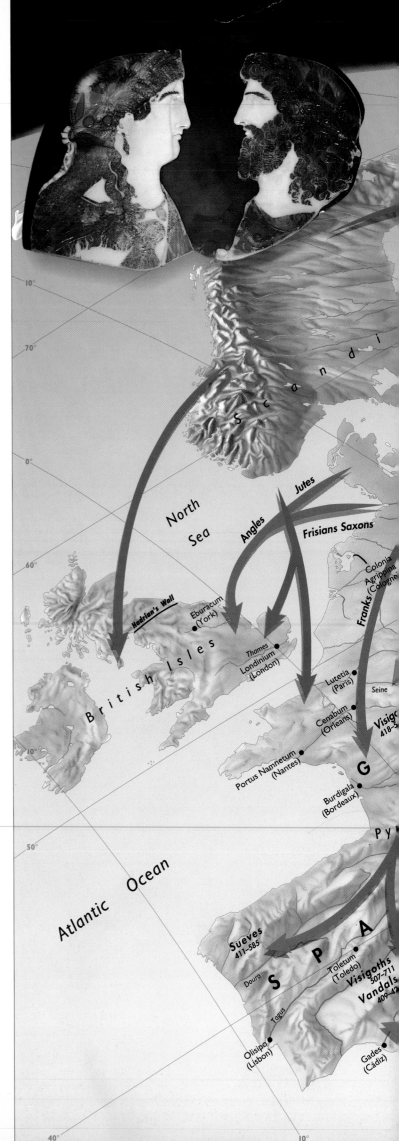

A Roman emperor and empress as pagan gods *right*. This sardonyx cameo probably depicts emperor Julian the Apostate, who sought to re-establish paganism within the empire.

Scenes of pagan funeral banquets and Christian love-feasts are effectively indistinguishable on catacomb walls, *bottom right*.

The barbarian invasions of Europe *map right*. From the end of the fourth century a series of devastating invasions by Huns, Goths and Vandals overwhelmed the western Roman empire. Even after the fall of Rome in AD 476, Lombard, Scandinavian, Moorish and Magyars invaders swept across the continent.

rites; and the conflict of principles could be waged across dinner tables or in tracts written in a common language of philosophical tradition.

For paganism and Christianity shared a common culture: stoic in demeanour, philanthropic in morality, Augustan in taste, Hellenising in discourse, proudly old-fashioned in its educational programme. Even after his apostasy, the emperor Julian wore the tousled beard of a Christian holy man. He advised pagan priests to beat the Christians by imitation: by benevolence to strangers, care of graves and holiness of life. St Jerome experienced a conventional angelic warning against reading the classics, but went on writing imitations of Virgil. Though Jerome exercised commendable restraint in translating the Bible into a demotic sort of Latin, most of the Christian Roman gentlemen who put their religion into writing made it their business to improve on the evangelists' rustic styles. In the art of the catacombs, the pagan and Christian messages are expressed in similar imagery: the pagan Vibia is led by an angel to a heavenly banquet, companionably spread like the Christian love-feasts depicted on neighbouring tombs. The evangelists are shown with the same equipment and in the same postures as pagan philosophers.

The rise of the Church, from persecution to predominance, was completed in 395, when the emperor Theodosius proclaimed Christianity the official religion of the empire and reduced pagan traditions to the underprivileged status formerly imposed on Christians. Considered from one point of view, this was an aspect of the diversification of the imperial elite: Christian bishops became servants of the state; the old patriciate was displaced by a new meritocracy; barbarian technicians were increasingly appointed to military commands; and in many parts of the empire and especially in Italy, Gaul and Asia Minor, the senatorial aristocracy began to withdraw from civic life and political responsibility, retiring to the management of their estates. Some historians have seen the retreat from this tradition of *noblesse oblige* as the critical event in the unmaking of the ancient world but the Christian empire was still recognisably the Roman empire. The barbarians represented a much bigger threat to historical continuity.

On the borders of the empire – especially the European borders with Germanic peoples – the growing clamour of the barbarians was not only for admission as temporary mercenaries in Roman service or as raiders on their own account, but as permanent settlers and sharers in imperial prosperity. The vast length of the frontiers could not be policed with entire effectiveness and the trickle of immigrant communities could not be completely staunched. Raids en masse were almost as hard to cope with for the over-stretched imperial authorities. Those of the mid-third century, which devastated much of Gaul and penetrated Italy, had coincided with internal political crisis and almost dissolved the empire. Not until the late fourth century, however, did the struggle to exclude mass migrations of barbarians become hopeless.

Rome had built European civilisation from south to north and from west to east and, indeed, in the perceptions of modern Europeans, those have been the predominant directional forces in the making of European history; now, however, the Germanic migrations were re-infusing influences from the east, reminiscent of the direction taken by earlier makers of Europe – the 'Indo-Europeans' and the Celts. The migrations are easily masked by arrows on a map; the human stories of suffering and sundering are harder to reconstruct . The earliest surviving poem in what is recognisably German is the *Hildebrandslied*, the story of an Ostrogothic family, split between the war-bands of rival chiefs in the chaos of the fifth century. Hildebrand's wife was left 'in misery' with the baby who was to grow into his battlefield adversary. The father's overtures, backed with a present of 'twisted torcs, set with

Huns

Moors

Germanic peoples

Scandinavians

Slavs

Magyars

Roman empire AD 395

Slavs

Baltic Sea

Crimea

Black Sea

Slavs 500

Vistula

Constantinople

Elbe

Slavs 625

Huns c.451

Vindobona (Vienna)

Lombards 568-732

Huns c.451

Morava

MACEDONIA

Naissus

Pergamum

Rhine

Danube

Aegean

Augusta Treverorum (Trier)

Ravenna

Adriatic   Sea

GREECE

Athens

Lugdunum (Lyon)

Verona

ITALY

Visigoths 410

Sparta

Ostrogoths 489-552

Sea

Burgundians 443-534

Rome

Neapolis (Naples)

Crete

Corsica

Messana (Messina)

Tolosa (Toulouse)

Sardinia

Sicily

Mediterranean   Sea

nees

N

Balearics

Carthage

Corduba (Córdoba)

Carthago Nova (Cartagena)

gold besants, which the King of the Huns had given him', were rejected as a trick by the boy, who had no inkling that Hildebrand still lived. Only the first few lines survive of the terrible denouement, in which father and son fight to the death.

Most of the peoples who were forced into this sort of trauma were not nomadic by nature. Some barbarian bands were drawn into the Roman empire; most were driven. Those drawn were usually relatively small, highly mobile war-parties, composed of men detached from their places in traditional kinship-structures by loyalty bought by a ring-giver – a war-lord whose wealth was booty or the wages of mercenary-service. In every barbarian treasure-hoard, the trinkets and tokens of warband-service are buried: rings and armbands set with bezels or onyx or inscribed with reminders of loyalty; a gold ring in the Cesena treasure bulges with a garnet in expectation of a kiss.

The social disruption which produced these bandit hordes was caused by the proximity of Rome and the concentrations of movable wealth, in the form of gold and jewels, which could be built up by individuals in cross-border contacts by protection-money, ransom and extortion. In most cases, however, this social instability was the consequence of migration rather than its cause and the forces which impelled refugee-peoples into the Roman empire were hunger and the convulsive, pressing turbulence of change in the Asian steppes.

The Ostrogoths, the easternmost of the recorded Germans, had ploughed furrows across the steppe on the banks of the Don since about the end of the second century AD. Though war bands split off and invaded the Roman world, the Ostrogothic state remained intact until it was destroyed by invaders from the east on its vulnerable steppeland flank in 376. No one knows what released the Huns from their steppes north of the Aral Sea for this sudden and unstoppable expansion. Ammianus Marcellinus tried asking them 'where they were

born and whence they came – and they cannot tell you.' Fear of them glistens between the lines of every early account: fear of their monstrous appearance, which Roman writers suspected must be produced by deliberate self-deformation; fear of their symbiotic relationship with their horses, which made their mounted archery deadly; fear of their merciless treatment of their victims, which cowed their enemies into despair. After a series of bloody defeats, the Ostrogothic army was forced over the Dnestr into the territory of the Visigoths who, unable to oppose the Huns, were forced to seek refuge in the Roman empire. The Ostrogoths were not nomads by tradition or inclination, but, displaced from their lands they were, according to their earliest historian, Jordanes, 'driven to wander in a prolonged search for lands to cultivate.' Cannoning like snooker balls, Germanic peoples ricocheted into the Roman empire. As Rome tried to defend the empire from within by settling German war-bands along its roads, these troublesome saviours began to transform the empire.

The Visigoths were the first people to be admitted en bloc. In about 275, when the Romans finally abandoned trans-Danubian Dacia, they were settled in the vacated territory. After border trouble in the 320s they were granted federate status but by the late 360s relations had deteriorated and the Visigoths' privileges in imperial trade were being withdrawn. Long experience of life as the Romans' neighbours had profoundly influenced their culture. They had been converted to a heretical form of Christianity (St Jerome had Visigothic correspondents whose Latin he corrected). In 376, when the invasion of the Huns obliged them to beg refuge of the Romans, a reputed 200,000 were allowed over the Danube. But the Romans then left them to starve, provoking a terrible revenge which culminated in the Visigoths' victory at Adrianople in 378. This battle destroyed the Roman reputation for invincibility and set an irresistible example to other tribes. Henceforth,

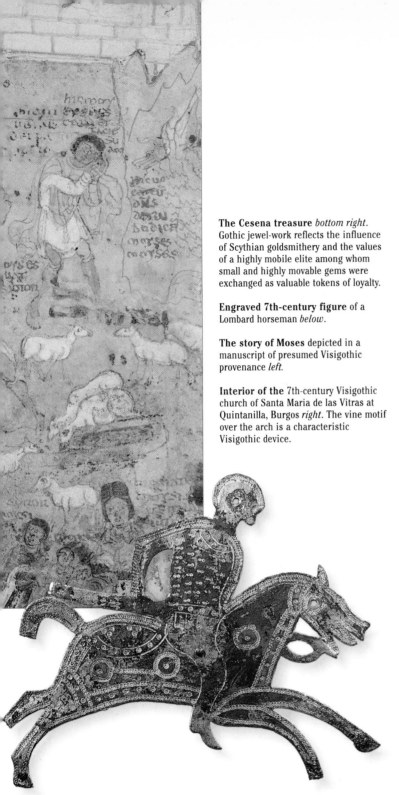

The Cesena treasure *bottom right*. Gothic jewel-work reflects the influence of Scythian goldsmithery and the values of a highly mobile elite among whom small and highly movable gems were exchanged as valuable tokens of loyalty.

Engraved 7th-century figure of a Lombard horseman *below*.

The story of Moses depicted in a manuscript of presumed Visigothic provenance *left*.

Interior of the 7th-century Visigothic church of Santa Maria de las Vitras at Quintanilla, Burgos *right*. The vine motif over the arch is a characteristic Visigothic device.

the empire could not guarantee to manage the barbarian war-bands whom it was forced to admit in increasing numbers. The pattern of Roman relations with the Visigoths became normal: there were periods of tense collaboration, but neither party could ever fully trust the other and from 395 to 418 the Visigoths undertook a destructive migration across the empire, terrorising the areas they traversed. In 410 they sacked Rome itself, inspiring apocalyptic speculations among shocked subjects of the empire, before settling as the paid 'guests' and, in effect, the masters of the local population in southern Gaul and northern Spain. Their art shows both their amenability to Roman influence and their adherence to barbaric traditions. Their magnificent gold-work is reminiscent of the Scythians', especially the belt-buckles of jewelled eagles' heads which were one of their specialities, and their finest bibles were artistically unprecedented, written in silver ink on purple vellum. But the vine-tendrils on their rood-screens and their horseshoe-shaped arches are unmistakable signs of their seduction by the south.

The coming of the Huns wrought equally impressive changes beyond the Roman frontier. Rome's had for so long been the only great

state in Europe that the emergence of a rival empire in the fifth century seems an anomaly which was unsurprisingly brief. Yet the Hunnic empire, albeit short-lived, did demonstrate the potential for state-formation on a grand scale outside Roman Europe. Despite their legendary ferocity in battle and their reputation for enduring hunger and thirst 'from the cradle', as Ammianus Marcellinus said, the Huns were unable to pose a serious threat to the Roman empire or construct a large state of their own while their primitive, pastoral economy rendered political integration impossible and united military action impracticable. By the early fifth century, however, infusions of booty and fiscal exactions from subject-peoples were transforming the economic base of Hunnic society. The conquest of the Ostrogoths by the Huns in 376 presupposed an unprecedented concentration of force. By about 420 a permanent Hunnic confederacy was in being, which was further enriched in tribute, booty and land by supplying mercenaries to Rome and extorting 'protection money.' Under the rule of Attila, from the mid-430s, this system came under intolerable strain as the Huns' ambitions were fed by success and by the revenues of an empire which stretched from the Baltic to the Black Sea and the Caspian. In 445 Attila murdered his co-ruler, Bleda. In 447, needing a continuous intake of plunder to sustain his warriors, he invaded the eastern Roman empire, at a time when an unusual combination of natural disasters – plague, famine and earthquakes – sapped resistance. In 450 he launched a similar invasion of the western empire, on the unconvincing pretext that he intended to punish the Visigoths on the empire's behalf; though frustrated in Gaul by the united resistance of Romans and barbarians, he turned on Italy in 452. He seems to have fancied himself as the puppet-master of the whole Roman world, but the empire was spared by his sudden death – drenched, it was said, from a burst blood-vessel, during a wedding night of excess – before the start of the campaign season of 453. Divided among his sons, the Hunnic state – softened by the luxury of booty and stymied by its size – lasted only a dozen more years before

being torn apart by internecine strife and swept aside by another Asiatic nomad-horde, the Avars.

With hindsight, the Roman empire in the west is seen to have been fundamentally transformed with the foundation of Germanic kingdoms inside the Roman frontier in the fifth century. At the time, writers of history and prophecy, peering through the twilight of the empire, could not believe it was over. Rome was the last of the world-monarchies foretold in scripture. Its end would mean the end of history. Everyone, including the barbarian kings, therefore connived in pretending that the empire had survived. Most of the Germanic kingdoms were founded by relatively small bands, accommodated within the empire as uneasy allies, entrusted with tasks of imperial defence, quartered in rural garrisons at the expense of their host-communities and only gradually taking over the cities and usurping or accepting authority over the non-Germanic populations. The empire had successfully absorbed non-Roman peoples at intervals in the past. The Germanic settlers were all, in varying degrees, susceptible to Romanisation, and their kings, in most cases, were prepared to show some measure of deference to imperial institutions. The Visigothic leader Athawulf, outraged by Roman perfidy, vowed 'to extirpate the Roman name' but ended by marrying into the imperial family and collaborating with Rome. The kings of the Burgundians were effectively isolated from Roman influence and inaccessible to Roman revenge, but they continued a sycophantic correspondence with Constantinople for as long as their state survived. The Franks adorned their kings with emblems of Roman governors and consuls and applied to the emperor for gifts of relics. Even the Germanic settlers of Britain, most of whom had virtually no contact with the Roman empire, evinced in their poetry nostalgia for the rule of Roman 'giants'.

Though there was no emperor in Rome after 476, the empire did not come to an abrupt end but entered a long period of decline. Theodoric the Ostrogoth, who ruled Italy without having to tolerate the nuisance of a resident emperor, seems to have had a conscious vision

of a culturally hybrid state. His pedimented palace is depicted in a mosaic on a church wall in his courtly centre at Ravenna, with a throne room of gold, curtained like a sanctuary and lit with hanging lamps. His tomb evokes the tumulus of a Germanic king but is also in the eclectic style favoured by the late Roman aristocracy for funerary monuments: a sepulchral caprice, like the pyramid of Gaius Cestius or the tomb of Caecilia Metella. No barbarians were proof against acculturation. Vandals, whose name has become a by-word for mindless destruction, had themselves portrayed in mosaics. The marauding ways of the Suevi shocked their early victims; but they soon settled down into the kind of sumptuous palaces of Roman workmanship still just discernible in a pair of gleaming marble columns which survive in a church-front in Ourense.

Nevertheless, with the foundation of barbarian kingdoms inside the territory of the western Roman empire, Europe was beginning to take on the configurations it was to display in medieval and modern times. In place of a single empire, reaching out from the Mediterranean, a series of effectively sovereign states took shape, founded, in most cases, by barbarian invaders. The cultural heritage of Europe was complete when Germanic traditions were fused with the Graeco-Roman and Judaeo-Christian legacies which moulded the civilisation of the late empire. Germanic invaders arrived as pagans or Arians: conversion to Catholicism – or rather the adoption of Catholic forms of official ritual – was a rough standard of measurement of Romanisation. Some rulers, like those of the Franks and Suevi, made a rapid transition from paganism. Clovis, the Frankish chief who conquered most of Gaul in the 480s, gave up the persuasive claim of descent from a sea-god for the advantage of allegiance to a God who could deliver victory and equip him with literate administrators. Others made a shakier change, like Redwald of East Anglia, who added an altar of Christ to his sacred grove. Some clung for generations to the Arian heresy, perhaps as a badge of identity or perhaps because, until the late sixth century, when mutual persecution and religious strife supervened, Arian-Catholic co-existence was normal: the court of Theodoric, with its twin baptisteries, Arian and Catholic, was exemplary in toleration. In Britain kingdoms evangelised from Ireland and Scotland retained their own rites and methods of Easter computation until the late seventh century. By then, however, all the courts of the barbarian west were ruled by Catholics of the Roman allegiance. The support of the church was expensive – but it was obviously worth adding to any king's network of lordship and gift-exchange the generous celestial patrons at the clergy's command. The value can be measured, for instance, by the weight of gold and jewels in the votive crown which the seventh-century Visigothic king Reccesvinth hung between the Corinthian capitals of the chancel-arch in the sanctuary of his royal basilica at Baños. In return for such sumptuous gifts, matched by comparable generosity in land, he got – quite apart from spiritual benefits – an array of worldly advantages: the prayers of the religious; the services of a clerical bureaucracy; and the power of the relics of an army of martyrs.

Imperial dissolution was speeded up in the sixth century by the emperor Justinian's attempts to stop it. Justinian aimed to be a restorer but was more suited to be a revolutionary – 'a born meddler and disturber', as Procopius called him. He had the ill-disciplined energy of all insomniacs as he paced the palace corridors at night, 'like a ghost', as courtiers said. Like Lloyd George, he was 'a dynamic force' and 'a very terrible thing'; but he was more dangerous still: an intellectual who thought big thoughts and had a cosmic sense of his own destiny. He had himself depicted, in the great statue Procopius described, toting a globe in one hand and spreading the other towards the rising sun. His projects included importing silk from China and allying with the Arabs and Ethiopians against Persia. He built the biggest church in the world and when it fell down built it again.

A peasant's son who chose as his consort an actress of dissolute reputation, he was above all a snoot-cocker, who defiantly alienated every powerful interest. At a time when the army made and unmade emperors, he was the most unmilitary of rulers: his service in the palace guard in his youth was like Prince Edward's in the marines – hurriedly

ended and buried under aesthetic preferences. At a time when the church legitimised authority, he abused his role as the guardian of orthodoxy by dabbling in heresy: his wife protected Monophysites and probably shared their faith, while his own theological ponderings eventually took him into the heresy of Docetism – according to which Christ did not truly suffer on the cross. At a time when the monarchy needed its traditional supporters, his fiscal policies made the rich howl with anguish, while jobs went to a new aristocracy of service and mighty subjects tumbled to his arbitrarily wielded weapon of disgrace. He was a great lawgiver who had himself depicted as Moses and yet broke all the rules himself. Paradox enlivened his character and diminished his achievement. The reconquests made from the barbarians in his reign, which he urged on, at crippling cost and with fanatical perseverance, reunited the Mediterranean world: his buildings stretched from Morocco to the Persian frontier. But the reunited world was also transformed, doom-fraught, impoverished and vulnerable to the next wave of barbarian invasions. It was also a hag-ridden world, in which bishops and holy men took over the functions of vanishing public authorities and relics of saints kept demonic powers at bay. Early in the seventh century, the learned Visigothic king Sisebut interrupted his verse treatise on the lunar eclipse to assure his readers that it was a vulgar error to suppose this effect was procured by a hag jiggling a mirror.

Justinian outlived his friends as well as his enemies and died lonely and embittered. The loss which mattered most was that of the wife he married in defiance of her own past and the world's opinion. He relied on her strength and intellect: she was the counsellor of every policy and the troubleshooter of every crisis. By the time the famous mosaic portrait of her was unveiled in the sanctum of San Vitale at Ravenna, she was probably already dead. Though her stature was understandably exaggerated by the artist, the rest of Procopius's description of her is recognisable: the lovely face, the pallid complexion, the eyes grim and tense. She wears jewels of triumph and a cloak embroidered with the images of the magi – those embodiments of kingship and wisdom combined. Majestically isolated, unnaturally elevated, she stares from under a lonely aedicule, between parted veils of death.

The impression Justinian made on the barbarian west quickly faded. The next invaders of Italy, the Lombards, created a kingdom at a much greater emotional distance from the Roman heritage than that of the Ostrogoths had been. They entered the peninsula in 568, just in time to gather the spoils of the wars in which Romans and Visigoths had exhausted each other. A plaque of gilded copper, made to adorn a helmet or crown, shows how, by the beginning of the next century, the court of king Agilulf had soaked up some of the genius of the place. He sits enthroned in the centre of the composition, a figure of commanding sanctity in the chlamys of a priest or emperor, gesturing in blessing; on either hand he is guarded by nobles whose horsehair plumes swirl in the wind; beyond them, winged figures brandish the drinking-horns of a traditional Germanic court along with placards marked 'Victory' of the kind paraded in Roman triumphs. His sumptuous cross – all Christian barbarian kings had something similar – is a wand of victory, a 'sign in which to conquer.'

The Church, which has often been credited with destroying the civilisation of classical antiquity, was left as the great upholder of Roman standards of learning, art and government. This is not surprising in the case of the patrician-bishops, whose family traditions represented continuity with antiquity: men like Pope Gregory the Great, who organised the defence of Rome against the Lombards, launched missions of spiritual reconquest to lost provinces and re-imposed on the western empire a kind of unity by the sheer range and volume of his correspondence; or like Isidore of Seville, the most intellectually distinguished of a brood of saints, who distilled the learning of the classics and passed it on to future generations in encyclopaedic form; or like Martin of Braga, who dedicated to a Suevic king a treatise on virtue, based on a lost work of Seneca. To be Roman, these men had only to be themselves. It was harder to domesticate the church's own barbarians, the anti-social ascetics and hermits, the retiring cenobites, whose response to the problems of the world was to withdraw from them or rail at them from their caves.

In turning the ascetic tradition from a neutral or negative force into a powerful agent and servant of civilisation a decisive – or, at least, a representative role – is traditionally given to St Benedict. This great maker of Christendom has been proclaimed by a recent pope as the patron saint of Europe. The only certain date in his life is 542, when the Ostrogothic king Totila visited him at his monastery of Monte Cassino.

A thirteenth-century fresco *left* depicts the donation of bread to the Benedictine monks at the cave-mouth of Subiaco.

Carved dragon head *above* from the Viking ship burial at Oseberg *c.* AD 850. Monster-head prows such as this became one of the symbols of the Scandinavian invaders whose raiding-parties struck across Europe from the late-eighth century.

Gregory the Great wrote the earliest surviving life of him nearly 50 years after his death and clouded the verifiable facts with miracles. Still, Benedict is a lively and approachable figure, discernible through the impression he made on disciples and between the lines of his great gift to mankind: the monastic rule which bears his name.

He was well born in the Sabine hills and well educated in Rome. St Gregory claimed that he did not complete his studies but abandoned the city in disgust, 'with the knowledge of ignorance and the wisdom of the unlearned.' This can be dismissed as pious rhetoric: an ascetic was supposed to prefer the folly of God to the wisdom of men, to affect simplicity and to shun luxuries like learning, which can be bought with wealth. In reality, Benedict's prose is full of echoes of the law-schools and his rule full of respect for erudition. He shared the bookish taste of his younger contemporary Abbess Radegund of Ste-Croix in Poitiers, who sent to Constantinople for a portable reading-desk which still survives.

His early preparation was conventional: he set up as a recluse in a cave – perhaps symbolically sited by the ruins of one of Nero's palaces at Subiaco. Food was lowered to him by another anchorite while he disciplined the lusts of the flesh in a convenient thorn-bush. In one of the earliest surviving illustrations of his life, in an eleventh-century manuscript from Monte Cassino, the cave-mouth is shown jagged and streaked with blood. Unwisely, he submitted to the importunities of a group of monks who wanted him to lead them: they proved selfish and strife-torn and he was lucky to escape from them unpoisoned. The saints he was devoted to show the kind of life he already wanted monks to lead. When he established his own community at Monte Cassino on land given by an admirer, he re-dedicated the pagan shrine of Jupiter on the spot to St Martin, the patron of poverty who gave his cloak to a beggar, while another, smaller shrine of Apollo became the chapel of St John the Baptist, the voice crying in the wilderness. The practice of charity in refuge from the world's ways was his starting-point for the re-creation of something like heaven on earth.

His book of rules for monks was one of many: indeed, it borrowed freely from others and almost the whole of it was filleted out of a rather rambling earlier rule. But its superiority and universality were recognised almost at once and there has hardly been a monastic movement or revival ever since that has not been based on or deeply influenced by it. After Benedict's experiences with unsatisfactory anchorites it is not surprising to find that his emphasis is on a quest for salvation in common and his aspiration is the subordination of all individual wilfulness. Extremes of mortification and the silly tradition of holy philistinism are abjured in favour of steady spiritual progress, manual labour and study and prayer in private and in common. Gregory the Great showed how well he had interpreted Benedict's spirit when he dictated the last line of the master's life: 'I must stop talking now for a while, so that by silence I may repair my strength and be able to narrate the miracles of others.' Benedict had sought a way of making paradise immediate. He had found a means of making civilisation survive.

The barbarian invasions were not yet over. In his shrine at Arkona the four-headed deity of the Slavs was perhaps already developing the thirst for wine for which he later became notorious. During the seventh and eighth century, in an expansion almost undocumented and never explained, Slavs spread over most of eastern Europe from the Baltic to the Peloponnese. In the late seventh century the Bulgars, another invader-people from the steppes, crossed the Danube and set up as the elite of a state which stretched almost under the walls of Constantinople. In the early eighth century, Muslims from North Africa, supplemented by a few co-religionists from Syria, began to settle in patches the northern shores of the western Mediterranean and created an enormous emirate covering most of Spain, planting 'a palm tree in a western land, far from the homes of palm trees.' In Scandinavia, warriors who fought on sleds with monster-head prows and wore helmet-masks that hid every flicker of human weakness, were preparing to plunder the rest of the world of its wealth: towards the end of the eighth century, Viking raids began.

These were formidable enemies – as were the Magyars in the tenth century, the last steppeland invaders to get as far as Germany and Italy – and Christendom lost territory to all of them, at least for a time. All of them inhibited the revival of long-range trade, interrupted the rhythms of life, destroyed the basic 'plant' of civilisation – monasteries, libraries and towns – and scattered feelings of security. Still, they were all absorbed or deflected in the end. In spite of them – even, in some ways, under their stimulus – Christendom began in the eighth century to outgrow, in Europe, the frontiers of the Roman empire and to approach the limits of Europe as they are understood today.

CHAPTER 4

THE SLIDING HORIZON

Christendom stretched and cracked

ONLY THE ABBOT and one young lad, who already knew how to read and chant, survived the terrible plague of 685. The rest of the monastic community at Jarrow in Northumbria was wiped out. The boy, who must have been about thirteen at the time, evidently had no administrative gifts. Despite the chance of advancement conferred by the obliteration of his seniors, he never held any important office. The young Bede did, however, have other gifts – scholarly and literary – and he went on to supply medieval learning with some of its brightest ornaments.

Bede's Northumbria was cold, unhealthy and – viewed from the perspective of the great Mediterranean centres of the civilisation to which he was heir – a dauntingly remote place. Here was no vital tradition of classicism or Christianity. The Roman empire had withered from the place three and a half centuries earlier. Bede's own grandfather was probably a worshipper of Odin and Thor. The memorials of Roman times, which Bede visited when young, were the rugged remains of a military frontier on Hadrian's wall; the works of art available for him to see depicted barbarism held at bay at lance-point, like the Pict expiring under hammering hooves on the Bridgeness slab. When, at the age of seven, he was handed over for his education to the abbot of Wearmouth,

The main thrust of Christian expansion into Europe was north and east from the line of the Rhine and the Danube. In both directions the Frankish church took the lead. Meanwhile, Rome and Constantinople competed for the allegiance of the Balkans

The spread of Christendom, from the 8th to the 12th centuries

→ main route of mission

✝● metropolitan see

◉ bishopric

⊕ monastery/hermitage

▨ Frankish realm 714

▭ furthest extent of Frankish empire 814

The **Bridgeness slab** *below*, despite the victorious Roman image, conveys a reminder of the insecurity of the Northumbrian frontier.

'**The fish-flood lifted the bones** onto the mainland.' : the inscription on the front panel of the Franks Casket *bottom* explains how the material of which it was made came to hand in seventh-century Northumbria. On the left the magic smith Wayland fashions goblets from his enemies' skulls, while plotting the violation of a princess seen entering with her maid. His brother strangles birds to make wings from their feathers for Wayland's planned escape. Incongruously, to the right, the Magi worship Christ.

the little monastery was even younger than he was. The new foundation helped to make this a frontier of settlement, while the monastery library, which was set up by one of the most ardent bibliophiles of the day, made it a frontier of learning. It seems incredible that shafts of a dark-age enlightenment should have radiated from here. Yet Bede's output alone, his 35 works of history, grammar, biblical commentary, theology, science – even without the evidence which survives of heroic feats of art and learning in other monasteries in the area at the same time – would mark eighth-century Northumbria as a seed-plot of European civilisation.

Bede, who dreamed of Rome and doodled in Greek, was typical of his fellow-monks in his passion for antiquity and the Mediterranean. Though the Bible came increasingly to fill his mental horizon as he grew older, his early works quote Virgil, Ovid, Livy and Cicero. In 716, when his friend the old abbot, then 74 years old, set off for Rome in the hope of dying there, the monks parted from the pilgrim with emotions aroused at the thought of this renewal of contact with their intellectual and spiritual home. Their attitude to Latin and Greek was mature enough to tolerate freedom in vernacular culture: Bede was praised for his skill in Anglo-Saxon poetry and when he died he was at work on translations into Old English of St John's Gospel and the works of Isidore of Seville. The same sort of array of traditions was carved in whalebone on the Franks Casket in the generation before Bede's birth: the story of Wayland the Smith is depicted alongside the birth of Christ and the suckling of Romulus and Remus. Bede's was a civilisation in touch with its own heritage, aware of every strand in its thread.

His absorption of classical and biblical traditions was enlivened by the responses of a critical mind. His historical writings were painstakingly documented and verified. He contemplated the universe in as much confidence of its order and intelligibility as any eighteenth-century *philosophe*. He corrected contemporary misconceptions on tides and devoted a great deal of space to a comparison of Hebrew, Roman and Egyptian methods of recording the passage of time. His novel ideas on the computation of the age of the world inspired a joking accusation of heresy at a tipsy feast – one of the small ways in which the aristocratic members of Anglo-Saxon religious communities kept up treasured aspects of their secular way of life.

Northumbria was remote but not alone. At intervals along the eroded edges of the former Roman world, the classical and Christian inspiration of civilisation showed amazing habits of persistence and powers of recovery. In Dacia, pockets of Latin-speakers survived by withdrawing to the uplands as Slav migrants swirled round them. In Asturias – to the Romans, a wild frontier which they hardly bothered to colonise – refugees from Islam collected libraries good enough to make a commentary on the Apocalypse, written there by Beatus of Liébana in the late eighth century, one of the most esteemed and often-copied works on the subject for hundreds of years. Here in the ninth century Roman diptychs were preserved and imitated to decorate the door-jambs of a royal church.

Beyond Rome's farthest north and west there were even monastic exiles – like St Columba, longing to compose his hymns 'on a rocky promontory, looking on the coiling surface of the sea' – who took memories of antiquity into places in Scotland and Ireland where the legions had never been. In 675 in Iona, Bishop Arculf told Abbot Adamnan how the founder of Constantinople had been inspired by a dream and led by a heavenly guide. A similar – perhaps even more purposeful, certainly more dangerous – enterprise flickered in Germany, where St Boniface travelled from Exeter in 719 to share the gospel with his fellow-Saxons. This was a supremely important moment in the making of Europe: an attempt to spread the Roman legacy outside the old frontiers and, in effect, to extend the reach of a common European culture beyond the limits to which Roman power had taken it. Boniface was martyred in 744, after sending home for copies of the works of Bede. The task he had begun was taken up 30 years later, by other means, from inside the most dynamic spot or salient on the frontier of Christendom: the northern corner of the kingdom of the Franks.

Here in the late eighth century a single generation produced two figures whose legendary proportions rival Arthur's or Alexander's. Roland fell to a Basque ambush while commanding the rearguard of a Frankish army in 778 and became the hero of a literary tradition similar in length and variety to that generated by the memory of El Cid. The echoes of his horn called generations of knights to their obligations in the late middle ages; the refrain of the poet of his deeds, 'Infidels are wrong and Christians are right', remains the best one-line guide to popular medieval ethics. His lord, the Frankish king who came to be known as Charlemagne, was, in life, the most successful war-leader in the west since Attila and, after his death, a once-and-future monarch of miraculous, and in some respects magical, reputation. In the eleventh century he was a saint and crusader, painted in his chariot on an apocryphal journey to Jerusalem. From the twelfth, his rebirth was awaited as the 'Last World Emperor' whose cosmic battle with Antichrist would herald the end of the world. The real story of Charlemagne was only a little less fantastic. Stepping to sole power in Francia over the corpse of a brother he probably murdered, Charlemagne commanded a bigger army and ruled a richer land than any monarch in western Europe since the disintegration of the Roman empire. Though he claimed to enjoy readings from St Augustine, he was a violent illiterate whose court resembled a brothel. Two events, however, transformed him from a Germanic war-chief into the self-styled renovator of Rome. His first journey to Italy in 774 opened his eyes to the splendour of the ruins of antiquity and enabled him to gather the scholars, books and examples that would furnish the raw material of a 'Carolingian Renaissance'. A few years later, in the 790s, he began to be able to afford unprecedented ambitions thanks to his conquest of the Avars: he captured their 'ring' of wagons and, secreted within it, the fabulous but long-inert dragon's hoard of treasure which those Asiatic raiders had accumulated over many generations.

Taking advantage of the doubtful legitimacy of the Empress Irene in Constantinople, he proclaimed himself the divinely elected successor of the ancient Roman emperors and was crowned emperor by the pope in Rome on Christmas Day, 800. At first, perhaps, this change of status counted for little in practice; some at least of the Frankish warrior-aristocracy were hostile or indifferent to this alien intrusion. It became increasingly apparent, however, that Charlemagne fancied himself in his new role. He affected what he thought was Augustus's taste in footwear. He appeared on his coins in a laurel crown. His seals were stamped with slogans of imperial revival. His panegyrists at court, who

A **circus-scene** of lion-tamer and acrobat from a Roman consular diptych inspired the decoration of a door-jamb *left* from the church of San Miguel de Lillo, at the Asturian kings' ninth-century summer resort of Naranco. The rope-carved pilasters *right* decorated a doorway in the summer palace of King Ramiro I (842-50), where emblems copied from Sassanid tableware lined the audience hall.

For Frederick Barbarossa, who endowed the tomb at Aachen with a shrine *right* which is a masterpiece of romanesque jewelsmithery in gold, enamels and gems, Charlemagne was a saint and a personal patron, able to confer political legitimacy and martial success.

must have known what he wanted to hear, likened him to Constantine and Justinian, and even to pagan emperors. The manuscript-painters, scribes and ivory-workers of his palace school modelled their work on fragments centuries old. Charlemagne even decreed that priests should imitate what was thought to be classical pronunciation of Latin when reading their offices, and when the Byzantine court presented to St Denis a work attributed to Dionysius the Areopagite – a mystical treatise which helped to inspire western mysticism from then on – it was even possible for scholars in Charlemagne's entourage to translate it from Greek, albeit not very well.

The most spectacular projection of his self-image was the chapel of his palace at Aachen. It was designed after the church of San Vitale at Ravenna – the most emphatically imperial model which could be found, where the large mosaic portraits of Justinian and Theodora spangled the sanctuary (*see* page 58). Marble columns were brought ready-made to Aachen from Ravenna and Rome. The chapel's octagonal nave implicitly associated it with Byzantine tradition, as did the provision for a gallery for the emperor's devotions. At this level Charlemagne's throne looked down on the altar of Mary and faced the altar of Christ.

In one sense, Charlemagne did more than just 'restore' the empire. He added to it territories which Roman arms never reached. Even before he came to the throne the Frankish kingdom had incorporated German peoples who lived beyond the margin of the old empire, especially in Frisia and Thuringia; and Charlemagne began his wars against the Saxons as an unreconstructed Frankish king with, as yet, no imperial pretensions. His conquest of Saxony, however, – a bloody war of attrition and atrocities, which took 18 years of campaigns to complete – was genuinely a new departure: the first annexation of a large new province in Europe by a self-consciously 'Roman' empire since the days of Trajan. Not since the reign of Augustus had imperial armies seen the Elbe. More significant yet was the enduring nature of this conquest. Charlemagne tried to civilise the Saxons by massacres and forced conversions. In the long run, it worked. Saxony, wrested – said Charlemagne's servant and first biographer – from worshippers of 'devils', became the exercise yard of Christendom, the nursery of 'Roman' consciousness, the crèche of a Renaissance and the point of departure of further expansion eastward.

What Francia was to the Carolingian Renaissance, Saxony would be to the next great revival of classical art and learning in the tenth century. Here Rosvita of Gandersheim wrote her extraordinary comedies in praise of chastity in the style of Plautus and Terence; here Bernward of Hildesheim brought the classical taste he learned in Rome, commissioning a column to display the life of Christ in imitation of those of Trajan and Marcus Aurelius; here Gerbert of Aurillac 'sweated' over the arcane mathematical learning which he had picked up in Spain. Here Gerbert's pupil, the emperor Otto III, who was crowned in time for the new millennium, brought his Greek wife. Meanwhile,

Saxony was converted from an insecure frontier into an imperial heartland. First incorporated into Christendom in the ninth century, Magdeburg became in the tenth an opulent city, where imperial power was concentrated and expressed in lavish works of art. A panel from the ivory frontal of the cathedral altar reveals a vital moment in the transformation. Christ blesses the church humbly presented by Otto I,

Bernward, bishop of Hildesheim, Otto III's court chaplain, was an enthusiastically classicising patron of the Ottonian Renaissance, whose column *right*, cast in bronze with scenes of the life of Christ, was evidently inspired by the imperial columns (like Trajan's, *see* page 27) carved with emperor's deeds, which he saw on a pilgrimage to Rome.

Though the thirteenth-century illustrator of Charlemagne's deeds puts the warriors into the armour of his own day *below*, he captures a faithful memory of a highly mobile army, well equipped with heavy paraphernalia for sieges.

In leaves from Otto III's gospel-book *above left and right,* made in the sumptuous mosaic scriptorium of Reichenau, Rome leads Gaul, Germany and the Slav world in presenting gifts at Otto's throne, where he towers over lay and spiritual coadjutors.

Otto I *below right,* helped by St Maurice and St Innocent, presents his foundation at Magdeburg under the gaze of the denizens of heaven.

allegories of Germany, Gaul and the Slav lands humbly bearing their tribute towards him: but they were led by Rome. Still, the Ottonians' Roman obsessions masked the long-term realities of the politics of Christendom: Europe was becoming, like south-east Asia, home to a 'state-system' – an arena of competing territorial states. Despite the frequent assertion of universal pretensions, the Ottonians' was essentially a German state, covering much of the same ground as modern Germany.

On Christendom's other exposed flanks in Europe, similar expansion made stuttering progress over a similar period. In 980 the story of the

which – beginning in 937, until his death in 974 – the emperor raised 'of wonderful magnitude' and filled with imported relics and pillars of marble. Otto's patron, St Maurice, who with St Innocent was the co-dedicatee of the church, supports Otto's figure, tiny under his crown, as he approaches the cosmic throne, while St Peter and other denizens of heaven look on with features animated by interest.

Otto made a big emotional investment in the title of emperor, which had been transmitted to him, or, rather, wrested by him, from the heirs of Charlemagne. As he understood it the empire was 'holy' – co-terminous with Christendom – and the office of emperor was a sort of Christian palatinate. His Magdeburg was like the Trier of the old empire: a frontier capital. Like a shop window of Christendom it was arrayed to entice and fascinate the pagans beyond the Elbe. He had his own barbarians to turn back. Indeed, his imperial status was defined by his relationship with them: between the 890s and the 950s, 30 raids deep into Christendom – as far as Pavia and Aquitaine – are recorded by the nomadic Magyars. Beyond their lands of choice in the Hungarian plain, which suited their way of life, they were not interested in permanent conquests – only in the looted treasure that could pay for their cavalry's keep. Yet their formidable record and habits of casual ravage inhibited security and development in the west until Otto wiped out their warriors and hanged their leaders in 955.

Acclaimed on the battlefield and crowned by the pope, Otto had established a reputation as a protector of Europe. The 'Roman' status of his empire mattered to him: Abbot Adso, the prophet of Châlons-sur-Marne, who had been the guru of Charlemagne's dynasty when Otto was young, had declared that the world would survive until all its kingdoms had seceded from the 'empire of Romans and Christians'. When Otto's grandson, Otto III, looked back at the reflection of himself that stared, throned in power, from a leaf of his gospel-book, he could see lavish

miracle at Chonae first appeared in a Byzantine compendium: the escape of the Roman empire from destruction at barbarian hands seems echoed in this story of how the Archangel Michael diverted the river that had been turned to threaten his church by evil pagans. By then, Bulgars, Arabs and Slavs had all been seen off under the walls of Constantinople and a Byzantine 'commonwealth' of Christian states was being built up – a diplomatic ring of outer defences. In 864, the decision of the Bulgar Tsar Boris to accept Christianity and impose it on his people was that rare sort of event – a change so richly charged with consequences that it deserves to be called a turning-point. It did not relieve pressure on Byzantium: on the contrary, the Bulgarians rapidly became like the Franks, rival claimants to the mantle of Rome, under a Tsar who called himself 'Emperor of all the Greeks and Bulgars'. By the end of the tenth century the courtly centre of the Bulgars at Ochrida in present-day Macedonia – where parts of the walls still enclose fragments of the churches of the time – was said by some visitors to rival Constantinople in splendour. Yet if the Bulgar empire was a threat to Byzantium, it was a bulwark for Christendom. No more steppeland invaders crossed the Danube. The Magyars and pagan Slavs were held at bay or, in the case of the Serbs, reduced to submission. When Byzantium reconquered great Bulgaria – almost at a blow – in the second decade of the eleventh century, a Balkan peace was already in place.

Christendom's other vulnerable frontiers were at the far end of the Mediterranean, in Spain, and along the Viking routes in the north. Whereas barbarian invaders from the north and east had all proved more or less seducible by the usefulness of Christianity and the glamour of Rome, Islam, which had supplanted the Roman empire in Africa and Spain, seemed proof against acculturation. This was a religion which provided secular rulers with advantages similar to those offered by the church, and which had its own ideal of a universal state – the Caliphate, the rule over the faithful of the spiritual heirs of the Prophet Muhammad – which owed little or nothing to the Roman example. On this frontier, the barbarians could not be converted or domesticated. They had to be fought.

The limits of Islamic conquest in Europe were set, however, not by the tenacity of Christian resistance but by the limitations of Muslim manpower and the distribution of environments suitable to support their way of life. According to a famous joke of Gibbon's, but for the outcome of the battle of Poitiers in 732, when a Frankish army turned back Muslim raiders on the Loire, 'another 1000 miles would have carried the invaders to Poland and Scotland' and 'the pulpits of Oxford might demonstrate to a circumcised people the sanctity and truth of the Quran'. There was never any real chance of that. Muslim settlement of Spain had been limited to the parts where they could practise their traditional economy: the river-valleys, the warm south and the Mediterranean seaboard for the Arabs, the pastoral uplands of the south

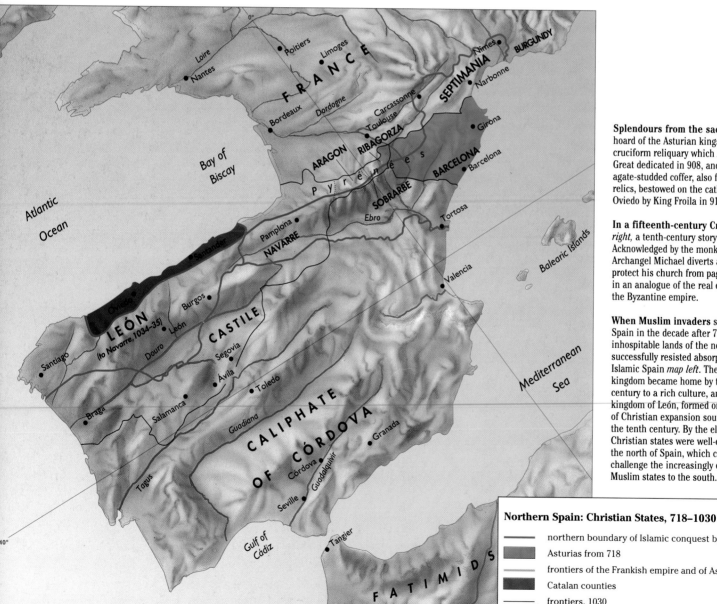

Splendours from the sacred treasure-hoard of the Asturian kings *right*: the cruciform reliquary which Alfonso the Great dedicated in 908, and the agate-studded coffer, also for secreting relics, bestowed on the cathedral of Oviedo by King Froila in 910.

In a fifteenth-century Cretan icon *far right*, a tenth-century story is recalled. Acknowledged by the monk Archippos, the Archangel Michael diverts a river to protect his church from pagan invaders, in an analogue of the real experience of the Byzantine empire.

When Muslim invaders swept through Spain in the decade after 711, the inhospitable lands of the north successfully resisted absorption into Islamic Spain *map left*. The Asturian kingdom became home by the ninth century to a rich culture, and, as the kingdom of León, formed one of the nuclei of Christian expansion southwards from the tenth century. By the eleventh century, Christian states were well-established in the north of Spain, which could effectively challenge the increasingly enfeebled Muslim states to the south.

Northern Spain: Christian States, 718–1030

——— northern boundary of Islamic conquest by c.740

▓▓ Asturias from 718

——— frontiers of the Frankish empire and of Asturias in 814

▓▓ Catalan counties

——— frontiers, 1030

and centre for the Berbers. The political frontier was pushed into the Duero valley only in order to safeguard the flank of the long, exposed road from Córdova to Saragossa via Toledo which was the axis of communication between the great centres of al-Andalus. Neither the will nor the resources were available to conquer the rest of the peninsula.

Though often depicted as cowering in the shadow of Islam, the frontier states on this flank of Christendom were by no means contemptible. Despite its small size and isolated position, Asturias was home in the ninth century to a rich kingdom and a sumptuous court. Part of the glamorous treasury or, rather, the sacred armoury of her kings can still be seen in Oviedo Cathedral — reliquaries of gold and ivory and lapis lazuli, housing even more precious scraps of wood and bone that could have a magical effect on the battlefield. On a hill above the town, Ramiro I could look out on his kingdom from the elegant tribuna of his summer palace, equipped with hypocaust and bath-house, or receive ambassadors in a hall decorated with reliefs moulded after Sassanian silver-work that must have been inherited from the Roman past. By the end of the century the kingdom ruled from here had broken out from behind the barrier of the Cantabrian mountains to Burgos and León. Exploitation of the shrine attributed to St James the Great at Compostela gave this realm an advantage over other Christian states in Spain – in pilgrim wealth, monastic colonisation and the chances of recruiting knightly manpower; but a frontier position generally was good for state-building. From 910 a kingdom is

continuously, if sparsely, documented with its centre at Pamplona. Further east, before his death in 898, Wilfred the Hairy, claiming a hairy man's birthright, conquered, with his brothers' help, almost all the Frankish counties south of the Pyrenees. Laborious settlement of underpopulated areas is the subject of all the documents that survive from his time. Clerical adulation for donors of church lands was usually expressed in highly coloured language; yet the terms in which a synod at Barcelona recalled Wilfred's generosity a few years later particularly captures the churches' sense of obligation to him. 'Moved with pity for that land, the Lord made arise the most noble prince Wilfred and his brothers, who, filling men of diverse provenance and lineage with pious love, managed to return the famous church with its dependencies to its former state.' Here, and in the recollected facts recorded in later charters, are hints of Wilfred's success in attracting population to the lands of the march. Wilfred's story was typical of the edges of the Christendom of his day. In lands reclaimed from pagan conquest on the northern frontier, in England, Alfred the Great was securing a similar reputation as a state-builder by lavish generosity towards the custodians of the historical record. By 924 Alfred's heirs had completed their reconquista of northern and eastern England from the Danes.

Christians in tenth-century England continued to feel beleaguered, however, by the Viking menace. And in Spain, despite the patient work of building up the frontier, the enormous power of Muslim Córdova remained daunting. The story of 'Moorish' Spain is often treated as an

exotic subject, abandoned to orientalists and confined to a non-European history. But when it slipped outside Christendom, al-Andalus did not cease to be part of Europe. The conquerors of 711 were among the last barbarian invaders of a still recognisably Roman world. They changed it more than their predecessors, the Visigoths, had: they rejected its inherited values more thoroughly and introduced influences from further afield; but the continuities which underlay those changes were more substantial than is commonly supposed. Irrigation, for example, which is often regarded as one of the defining innovations of Islamic civilisation in Spain, was developed from Visigothic practices. The horseshoe arch was a Visigothic or indigenous invention. The Great Mosque of Córdova was housed in what was probably an old Roman warehouse. The native population was not displaced – except patchily and late – and much of it remained Christian for a long time: in the *qadi*'s court in eighth-century Córdova many litigants did not know whether to classify themselves as Christians or Muslims, and at the level of popular religion the difference was probably small. Throughout the middle ages, border shrines retained their sanctity for those living on both sides; allusions to substantial Christian minorities in the Muslim territories disappear from the record only in the late twelfth century. In the sumptuous ivories of tenth-century Córdova, crowded with lovers and huntsmen, figural representation broke Quranic taboos with enthusiasm.

Still, the frontier of Christendom in Spain remained, in the perception of its people, vulnerable until the early eleventh century. Sampiro, teacher and chronicler at the court of León, recalled towards the end of his life the raids of 987-90, which drove him from his home and destroyed the wealth he had built up by inheritance and painstaking labour. An illuminator of the *Commentary on the Apocalypse* of Beatus chose to model his representation of Babylon on Córdova, gleefully swathed in flames. In 1002, the death of the wide-raiding vizir, Almanzor, was the removal of a scourge and, in a sense, of a mask: the empire of Córdova, which had looked so solid and formidable from a distance, appeared riven with rivalries and riddled with rot. The weakness Almanzor's energy had concealed was revealed in 1008, when his younger son mounted an inexpert putsch and condemned the state to internecine strife. Within two years, a raid on Córdova by a large expedition of Catalan knights dramatically illustrated how the roles of victim and prey had been reversed. Contemporaries hailed it as a revolution which 'gave tranquillity to the Christians. And they went out and travelled around the marchlands wherever they wished and they rebuilt many fortifications and castles which had formerly been destroyed by the power of the infidels.' This was a sanguine assessment: the Catalan raiders were mercenaries, called in to al-Andalus by one of the contending parties in the domestic squabbles of the decaying empire. The raid was most important for its effect on Christian morale. Meanwhile, the Córdovan state was enfeebled by seraglio-politics at the centre, eroded by usurpations at the edges. In the 1030s it dissolved among small, competing successor-states, which the Christian realms could challenge effectively.

Europe was being built outwards, as it were, by the extension or restoration of the frontier of Christendom. At the same time, a secular political tradition was being spread even further afield. A letter from Novgorod is said to have reached a Viking prince in 862. 'Our land,' it read, 'is great and rich. But there is no order in it. Come and rule over us.' In response, he founded the state which eventually became Russia. The story may have got over-simplified in the record, but it shows how territorial statehood was exported, far beyond the limits of the old Roman empire, to relatively immature political worlds in northern and eastern Europe. Some of the cultural legacy of the Romans was carried along with it, helping to integrate once-remote areas into an emerging 'European' culture.

In 811, for instance, after a victory over a Byzantine army, a Bulgar khan began to call himself 'Caesar'. Then in 846, among the Bulgars' neighbours to the north-west, Frankish ideas of leadership were imposed on the Slav state which had succeeded the Avar 'empire' north of the Danube. The kingdom founded there by Mojmir I was probably ruled in conscious imitation of an earlier Moravian state – the 'empire' of Samo, who exploited an interlude in Avar domination from the 620s to the 650s

The Great Mosque of Córdova *right* has become a symbol of the inventiveness of Moorish arts, but the space and structure were probably adapted from an old Roman warehouse and the columns and capitals of the early phases of construction were cannibalised from Roman and Visigothic buildings. The purpose-built columns and arches added in the late tenth century in the section shown here are indebted to indigenous tradition.

The courtly life of Córdova is portrayed on a pavilion-shaped casket *below right*, made to be filled with fragrances and carved in ivory with lavish scenes of leisured luxury, like the huntsmen, lutanist and attendants with fans and unguents shown here. It was presented, according to the inscription, by the Caliph al-Hakam to his younger brother in 967.

The Leonese illuminator of this eleventh-century copy of the *Commentary on the Apocalypse* by Beatus of Liébana *below far right* imagined Babylon burning at the onset of the Day of Judgement in the image of Córdova.

The remotest outpost of Latin Christendom was Brattahlid in Greenland *below*, founded by Erik the Red in 968, where his wife, Thjohild, built the first church around the turn of the millennium. The settlement grew to number 190 farms, 12 parish churches, a cathedral, a monastery and a nunnery.

– but the Franks intervened to elevate the rebellious prince Ratislav. This did not guarantee compliance: in due course, they had to depose, blind and banish him to a monastery. It did, however, ensure Moravia's cultural re-orientation towards the Roman church and western influence.

State-building initiatives usually came from dark-age strongmen; but, almost everywhere, the follow-through depended on the church. Tribal hegemonies could only be turned into territorial states by communications and administration. Because the church virtually monopolised literacy or – in the case of the Glagolitic and Cyrillic alphabets – actually invented it, the range of statehood was spread by missionaries. By legitimising strong-arm rule and by sanctifying weak authority, the church could also make enormous contributions to political stability. An amazing generation of evangelisation in the late tenth and early eleventh centuries equipped the rulers of Denmark, Poland, Russia, Hungary and Norway with the administrative and propaganda resources available to their brother-kings inside the shell of the old Roman empire. In the eleventh century, it was possible for royal spouses to be exchanged between England and Hungary or Russia and France. The Europe we know was taking shape.

The incorporation of the Scandinavian world was a great prize because of the dynamism and destructiveness of the Vikings. Now the dynamism could be harnessed for Christendom, and the destructiveness tempered or re-directed at external enemies. Viking destroyers had put out the light of the Northumbrian renaissance, extinguished the great age of Celtic monasticism, mulcted the wealth of Anglo-Saxon England and distracted and arrested the Frankish empire. Now their colonies became outposts of Christendom and recruiting grounds of crusades. In 999, the Icelanders decided to make their island Christian. Shortly afterwards, the wife of Erik the Red raised the turf walls of the first church at Brattahlid in Greenland. Normandy and, to a lesser extent, Orkney, were Viking foundations that became nurseries of crusaders.

For the future of Europe, however, the most important convert of the period was probably Volodomir, ruler of Kiev. The blood of this prince, like the culture of his country, was a mixture of Viking and Slav, pagan on both sides. In 1988, to commemorate 1000 years of Russian Christianity, statues and plaques in Volodomir's honour, erected by subscriptions of orthodox congregations, appeared all over the western world, confirming his image as a Christian and his status as a saint. But like many great saints he sinned with gusto in his life, keeping a seraglio reputedly of 800 girls, coining proverbs in praise of drunkenness and leaving a reputation in German annals as 'fornicator immensus et crudelis'. The traditional story of his emissaries' quest for the perfect religion emphasises the seductive beauties of orthodoxy:

The Bulgars bow down and sit, look hither and thither, like men possessed, but there is no joy among them, but only sorrow and a dreadful stench. Their religion is not good. Then we went to the Germans, and we saw them celebrating many services in their churches, but we saw no beauty there. Then we went to the Greeks, and they led us to the place where they worship their God: and we knew not whether we were in heaven or on earth: for on earth there is no such vision or beauty and we do not know how to describe it. We only know that there God dwells among men.

In fact, Volodomir's conversion was the bride-price of the Byzantine princess whose hand in marriage he extorted from Constantinople by threat of force. The faith he opportunistically espoused he then rigorously enforced. Its reception was oiled by the use of the vernacular liturgy. His wife was a unique prize – a princess 'born in the purple', such as Byzantine law and custom forbade to barbarian suitors. Only a short while before, the emperor Constantine Porphyrogenitus had banned 'monstrous demands' for a marriage alliance with 'shifty and dishonourable tribes of the north … For just as each animal mates with its own species, so it is right that each nation also should marry and cohabit not with those of other race and tongue but of the same tribe and speech.' The marriage proposals brought from the court of Otto I had been rejected as 'a thing unheard of'. For Volodomir, elevation by affinity to the imperial house was therefore a prize well worth the sacrifice of his pagan gods. When his reluctant bride arrived, under the

The power of pagan animal imagery to awe and terrify persisted long in Scandinavia, as in this carved wooden horse collar of the early fourteenth century *right*.

A tenth-century Danish jewelsmith's mould *left*, used for making both Thor's hammer and Christ's cross.

The larger of the Jelling stones *below* records the piety, filial and Christian, of King Harald Bluetooth, while the smaller – bearing the first record of the name of Denmark – is a monument erected towards the middle of the tenth century by his pagan father, Gorm, to his queen.

inducement of bloody threats, he solemnly dethroned the occupants of his sacred grove of idols. The thunder-god, Perun, with his golden, silver-moustachioed head, was lashed to a horse's tail and beaten with sticks on his Calvary to a river-bed grave.

Christ was a king and the extension of his kingdom depended on the collaboration of his fellow-monarchs. Missionaries who ventured unprotected among unconverted Slavs and Scandinavians usually ended up martyred. Individual conversions were, from the missionaries' point of view, uneconomical of time and effort and, from the perspective of the convert's salvation, often insecure and tentative. The result might be a hybrid religion like that of Helgi the Lean in Iceland, who 'believed in Christ' and yet made vows to Thor in extremities, or like that catered for by makers of metal tokens in tenth-century Denmark, who used the same moulds for Thor's hammer and Christ's cross. Kings could not improve the purity of their subjects' religion, but they could harry pagans and proscribe their cults. When it arrived in frontier courts, Christianity commonly brought not peace but a sword. Pagan elites could have enormous vested interests in the old religion. Chiefs claimed kinship or friendship with the gods. Priests creamed off the perquisites of cults, like the libations of precious wine, the levels of which were solemnly measured at intervals by the guardians of the shrine of the many-headed supreme deity of the Rugians at Arkona. They had to be prised out of positions of profit and power.

Pagan religions were entrenched, in some places, by the psychological power of terror. The Caliph's ambassador, Ibn Fadlan, who witnessed a human sacrifice among the Rus in 969, was profoundly impressed by the horror of it. The slave-girl chosen for immolation with her master sang songs of farewell over her last beakers of liquor before ritual copulation with her executioners. An old woman, called 'the Angel of Death', then wound a cord round her neck and handed the slack to men standing on either side. Warriors beat their shields to drown the victim's screams. While the cord was tightened, the Angel of Death plunged a dagger repeatedly in and out of the girl's breast. The pyre, built on a ship, was then lighted and the fire fed until it was consumed to ashes. 'After this, on the spot where the ship had lain when they dragged it from the river, they built something that looked like a round mound. In the middle of it they set up a big post of birch wood, on which they wrote the name of the dead man and of the king of the Rus. Then they went their way.'

The human and vulnerable God of the Christians could not compete in terror with many-headed monster-gods without the help of earthly strong-men. Much of what remains of King Harald Bluetooth's Denmark could belong to a pagan past: the ring-shaped forts, the burial mounds of his parents. Between the royal graves, however, he erected the largest carved stone in Scandinavia, engraved with an image of Christ crucified and the inscription, 'King Harald ordered these monuments to be made in memory of his father Gorm and his mother Thyre: that Harald who won the whole of Denmark and Norway for himself and who made the Danes Christian.' The priority given to his warfare and the emphasis given to the royal initiative in spreading the faith suggest the political context of Christian evangelisation. In Norway, the success of the church was so dependent on the arms of King Olaf Haraldson that he was canonised within a year of his death in battle in 1030. In Poland, too, Christianity was a royal option: the makers of the bronze doors of Gniezno Cathedral recalled King Boleslav in the 990s, distributing blessings and assisting at baptisms while his swordbearer stood by. The baptism of King Simeon of Hungary in 1000 represented the domestication of the Magyars in the service of Christendom. All these states were rewarded for embracing the church by the consequences their kings looked for: enhanced fiscal efficiency, improved military effectiveness and wider sway. Neighbours who, for the time being, clung to their pagan identity – like the Serbs, Finns and Lithuanians – forfeited power.

Stretched by these successes, Christendom cracked under the strain. As differences grew over rites, doctrines, language and discipline between the sees of Constantinople and Rome, conversion to Christianity tended to divide European peoples from one another. Thus in the ninth century, Moravia was converted to the Roman

On the doors of Gniezno Cathedral *above*, Boleslav I of Poland (992-1025) is depicted in a quasi-saintly role spreading Christianity, with tonsured hair, the clippings of which were sent in submission to Rome.

The bronze from Eyrarland in Iceland *below* probably depicts Thor, thunderbolt-wielder and protector of the Norse gods, clutching a curious anthropomorphic weapon or implement.

allegiance and the Latin liturgy by St Methodius's mission from Rome, while a Slavonic rite was implanted in Bulgaria by disciples of his brother, St Cyril, from Constantinople. Byzantine diplomacy, which tended to make conversion the spiritual obverse of a political relationship, ensured that the eastern Slavs would be orthodox; German crusades and Polish missions ensured that their western brethren would adhere to Rome. Europe became split between rival civilisations. Underlying the theological bitterness were deep cultural incompatibilities.

Even at the height of Roman power, the eastern part of the empire had been predominantly Greek-speaking. By the time of the crusades the use of Latin had died out even for the ceremonial and legal purposes for which it had once been favoured. The Byzantine empire – as historians call the eastern empire in its later phases – was therefore cut off from the basis of western Christendom's unity: the use of Latin as the language of learning, liturgy and international communication. Moreover, while the west had become an 'empire of barbarians', the east had absorbed its invaders or kept them at bay. When envoys presented credentials from the 'august Emperor' Otto I at Constantinople in 968, the Byzantine officials were scandalised at 'the audacity of it! To style a poor barbarian creature "Emperor of the Romans"!'

Nothing, however, divided the two Christendoms of east and west like religion. Again, this was in part a matter of language, for Greek tongues could utter theological subtleties inexpressible in Latin. Untranslatability was at the basis of mutual misunderstanding. Dogmas which started the same in east and west turned out differently in Latin and Greek. But religion is more a matter of practice than of dogma, and of behaviour than belief. The differences between the Catholic and Orthodox traditions accumulated over centuries of relative mutual isolation. The process began, or became continuous, as early as the mid-sixth century, when the eastern churches resisted or rejected the universal primacy of the pope. Allegiance to Rome gave the west a basis of common doctrine and common liturgical practice, which gradually took shape until, by the time of the crusades, Rome had established herself as the arbiter of doctrinal questions, the fount of patronage and the source of liturgical usage from the Atlantic to the Bug and the Carpathians. The western church still enclosed tremendous diversity, but it was recognisably a single communion.

Meanwhile, particular doctrinal differences had driven wedges of controversy between east and west: some dogmatic squabbles had come and gone or had been amicably resolved. In 794, however, for reasons that probably had less to do with Christianity than with the political relationship between the empire of Byzantium and the kingdom of the Franks, a western synod had arbitrarily altered the wording of the creed. To this day the western churches – including those now reformed and without allegiance to Rome – profess their belief that 'the Holy Spirit proceeds from the Father and the Son' while the easterners omit mention of the Son and limit to the Father the explicit source of this heavenly emanation. No one knows quite what either formula means, or what precisely is the difference between them. Yet that difference, impossible to define, has been deadly in effect. During the 1200 years when the formula of 794 has been accepted in the west, every attempt to effect a rapprochement between the eastern and western churches, has foundered on these profound shallows. The westerners acted with unchristian arrogance in presuming to modify the creed without the consensus of their brethren, just as the Church of England errs today in seeking to legitimise the ordination of women without the agreement of the Roman and Orthodox communions. But such errors are always easier to make than unmake.

The split between the eastern and western churches became definitive in 1054. Yet never, since the fall of the Roman empire in the west, had the need for collaboration between Rome and Constantinople been more obviously in the interests of both. In the upper arm of a Byzantine cross of the period, in the Dumbarton Oaks Museum, an image of the emperor's namesake, Constantine the Great, makes the point by bowing before an icon of Saints Peter and Paul, proffered or brandished by a pope. Pope and emperor both wanted to draw or drive

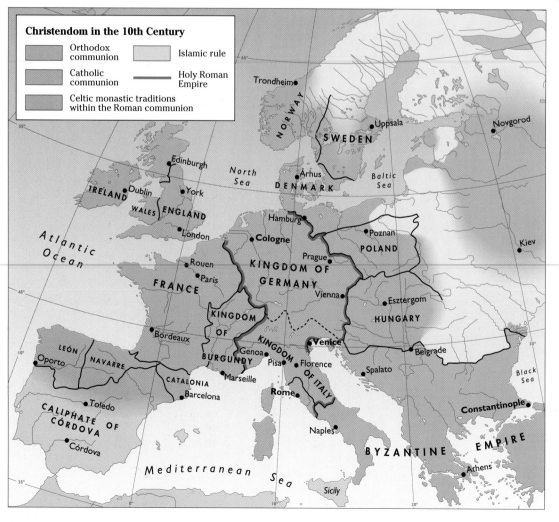

Christendom in the 10th Century

- Orthodox communion
- Catholic communion
- Celtic monastic traditions within the Roman communion
- Islamic rule
- Holy Roman Empire

Although by the eleventh century Christendom seemed to be making gains at the expense of the Muslims and pagans who had previously threatened to engulf her, the church remained divided between eastern and western communions *map left*. Bitter competition for the allegiance of the Balkans was exacerbated by theological differences. In 1054 a formal schism occurred, with the excommunication of the orthodox patriarch by a papal legate.

Norman invaders from Italy: the emperor, in order to retain his remaining lands in the peninsula; the pope, to preserve his political independence. Their military alliance had been enthusiastically contracted but inefficiently applied. On 17th June 1053, a Norman army cut the pope's German guard to pieces and, imploring his forgiveness on bended knees, carried the holy father off as a captive. In the long run, the papacy would win the Normans round and turn them into the pontiff's swordbearers. The captive pope's immediate policy, however, was 'to remain faithful to our mission to deliver Christendom' and to maintain the Byzantine alliance until 'this enemy nation is expelled from the church of Christ and Christendom is avenged'.

In Constantinople, the patriarch Michael Cerularius was equally determined that the alliance should founder, not for the Normans' sake but for his own and that of his see. Rome's claim to universal primacy threatened the authority of other patriarchs. Rome's increasing fastidiousness in matters of doctrinal formulation and liturgical practice threatened the traditions of the eastern churches. If the emperor became dependent on a western military alliance, the church of Constantinople would be compelled to conform to the dictates of Rome – as indeed would happen later in the middle ages, when, under the influence of the Turkish peril, the orthodox were driven to submission by despair. The patriarch forestalled any such development by initiating a vulgar exchange of abuse with Latin prelates. In a letter from his mouthpiece, the primate of Bulgaria, Latin practice was denounced as tainted by Jewish influence. He wrote to the pope, urging goodwill but omitting some of the usual titles of courtesy; and when papal legates arrived in Constantinople he refused to receive them or even to acknowledge their presence. He accompanied this campaign of provocations by forcibly closing the Latin churches in Constantinople.

Pope Leo, teaching himself Greek in the grip of a mortal sickness, was, like most of his line, too confident to barter the rights – as he conceived them – of the church for a worldly advantage. He was resolved to face death standing crutchless on his principles. He responded to the patriarch's insults in kind and sent to Constantinople a mission that was in no mind to compromise. Its leader, Cardinal Humbert, was renowned for his theological subtlety, diplomatic skills and noble principles. All these qualities seemed to desert him in Constantinople. His strategy was to appeal to the emperor over the patriarch's head; but, although the emperor enjoyed greater influence over the church in his realms than any ruler in the west, he could not coerce the patriarch and the legate's policy was doomed. Humbert offended the politicians by his indifference and the churchmen by his arrogance. He denounced a disputatious but moderate monk as a 'pestiferous pimp' better suited to a brothel than a monastery. He put the emperor, who was anxious to be conciliatory, into an impossible position by raising the irresoluble question of the procession of the Holy Spirit. After three months of waiting in vain for a dialogue with the patriarch, he lost his temper and slapped a bull of excommunication on the high altar of Hagia Sophia 'upon Michael, neophyte and false patriarch, now for his abominable crimes notorious'. It was too late. In Rome, death had overtaken Humbert's master, comforted by heavenly visions. The legation to Constantinople had therefore outlived the source of its authority. Humbert's bull, moreover, was flawed. Many of the charges it levelled against the Greeks – practising castration, rebaptising Latins, marrying priests, excommunicating the beardless and distorting the creed – were either false or wrongly formulated. At the time, it was generally supposed that it would soon be rescinded or forgotten. In fact, relations between the eastern and western churches never recovered and intercommunion has never been fully or enduringly re-established. The great schism left a cultural fault-line across Europe.

Secular society, too, tended to get wrenched in the east out of the western mould. The territorial state has rarely fitted for long into eastern Europe's geography. In Europe beyond the Danube, cut into and crossed by invaders' corridors, the flat, open expanses, the good communications and dispersed populations contribute to an environment in which states can form with ease, thrive with effort and survive only with luck. The region favours vast, fragile empires, vulnerable to external attack and internal rebellion. In the present millennium, they have come and gone with bewildering rapidity. In the first generation or so of the period, Greater Poland had frontiers on the North Sea and the Danube, the Pripet Marshes and the Bohemian Forest. Similar, volcanic hegemonies were established by the Mongols in the thirteenth century, Poland-Lithuania in the fourteenth and, on either side of the Dnieper, Poland and Muscovy in the fifteenth. After a period of relative stability for most of the modern era, when the area was disputed between the Habsburg, Ottoman and Russian empires, with German and Swedish states playing some part, the region has reverted to its former habits in the twentieth century, with the sudden rise and demise of the Third Reich and the Soviet Empire. Even in the period of greatest political stability, the region, as we shall see, has housed societies organised in profoundly different ways from their western neighbours.

As well as by religious schism and political divergence, the unity of expanding Christendom was impaired by heresy. If popular heresy existed in the west before the eleventh century, it was beneath the notice of the church. With the turn of the millennium, however, it began to be perceived as a threat. In about 1000 a peasant called Leutard from a village in Châlons had a vision in which bees – a traditional symbol of sexless reproduction – entered his body through his penis and drove him to renounce his wife, shatter the images in the local church and preach universal celibacy: he attracted a following among his own class which survived his death, albeit not for very long. In 1015, the first burning of heretics since the death of Priscillian in 383 was kindled at Orléans, even though the victims formed an esoteric group not known to have infected ordinary Christians. At Limoges in the 1020s the keepers of the shrine of St Martial became worried about the defection of devotees to a fierce band of mysterious unofficial ascetics. From then on, popular heresies were a continuous and, on the whole, a growing feature of western European history.

Two long, slow changes seem to underlie this phenomenon. First, this was a kind of ugliness in the beholder's eye: imperfections in lay religion detected by fastidious clerical scrutiny. By the late eleventh century a movement of Christian renewal and evangelising fervour, inspired by a pope and known to historians as the Gregorian reform was demanding exacting new standards both of clerical behaviour and lay awareness of the faith. The mood of clerical self-criticism, rooted in popular wisdom, voiced in many texts, is made palpable in one of the grotesques carved on the facade of Verona Cathedral: a wolf in a monk's habit alludes to the rhyme about a priest's efforts to instruct the creature:

However good the master who would make the wolf a priest,
He'll find him still the same grey, evil, grim and profane beast.

At the same time, the evangelical fervour of the clergy was lowering its sights to include the previously under-evangelised peasantry. This was the result, in part, of a long accumulation of dissatisfaction with the depth of penetration of popular consciousness by earlier apostolates. Among its effects was a new or increased stress on the theme of self-abasement in hagiographical literature: by doing menial jobs, the saint could – in today's jargon – 'relate' to the lowly, like the Count of Poitiers who, having renounced the world for the cloister in about 990, was set first to keep the hens, then the sheep, then the pigs, and was astonished at his own delight in each successive task.

On the other hand, the rise of popular dissent bears some of the signs of a revolution born of prosperity. Lay people were themselves stepping up the demands they made of their clergy. The really popular heresies of the eleventh and twelfth centuries were those ministered to by men of ferocious sanctity, like the Waldensian preachers and the Cathar 'perfect'. At the same time, the unaccustomed security of life, the opportunities to gather uninterrupted harvests, the conferment of leisure by increased yields from the soil all bought for ordinary people in the 'high middle ages' a luxury their 'dark age' predecessors had lacked: time to think about the Christian mysteries and desire to get involved in them. At a relatively high level of society and education, the church could satisfy these stirrings by providing pilgrim-rites, private prayers, devotional reading-matter and, ultimately, orders of chivalry. Spiritually minded peasants, like Leutard's enthusiasts, could not be accommodated so easily.

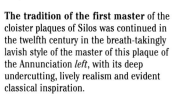

The tradition of the first master of the cloister plaques of Silos was continued in the twelfth century in the breath-takingly lavish style of the master of this plaque of the Annunciation *left*, with its deep undercutting, lively realism and evident classical inspiration.

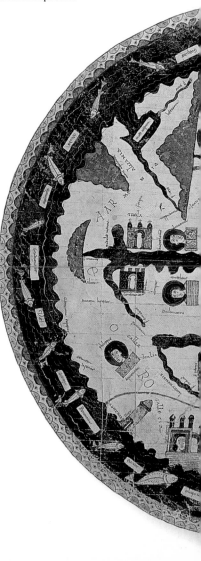

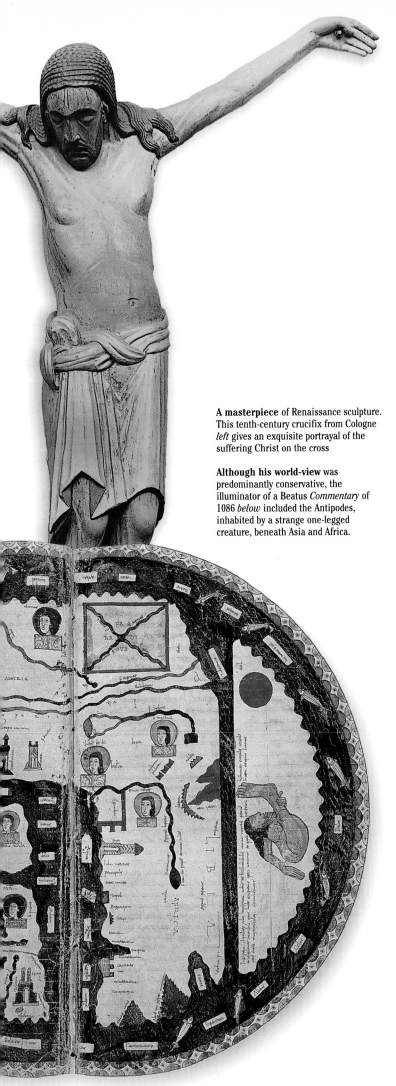

A masterpiece of Renaissance sculpture. This tenth-century crucifix from Cologne *left* gives an exquisite portrayal of the suffering Christ on the cross

Although his world-view was predominantly conservative, the illuminator of a Beatus *Commentary* of 1086 *below* included the Antipodes, inhabited by a strange one-legged creature, beneath Asia and Africa.

The art of the west in the eleventh and twelfth centuries reveals a sort of cult of the common man. Peasants and artisans were spread around church portals, close to inhabitants of heaven, engaged in the productive economic activities that paid for these monuments. Here were arrayed the members of a peaceful and orderly society, with everyone in his place and doing well out of it. The way artists showed God, our Lady and the saints was affected by the new mood. Most people nowadays unfairly associate Romanesque and pre-Romanesque art with a cold and distant style of celestial portraiture: with hieratically-staring virgins and kingly, judgemental Christs. Yet really the humanisation of heaven is the essence of Romanesque painters' and sculptors' inspiration: the evocation of poignant emotions, the recourse to low-life models as parables for the kingdom of heaven. Early in the eleventh century, the painter of the gospel-book of Abbess Hitda of Meschede was working in a studio where rigid conventions were enforced; yet he was able to paint a scene like that of Christ asleep in a storm on the sea of Galilee in which the very vessel seems to leap into life and the anxiety of the apostles to leaden their brows. The Christ of Archbishop Gero in Cologne dates from before the end of the tenth century, but no Renaissance master ever modelled the human body with a nicer combination of realism and restraint or chiselled the face of the suffering Christ with more exquisite agony: drawn lips, taut cheeks, nerveless lids and a trickle of blood at the brow. About 100 years later, the master of the first cloister plaques of the monastery of Silos, when he depicted the encounter at Emmaus, shared our Lord's own gift for sketching heaven in a scene of everyday life.

The state of Christendom in the eleventh century was riven with paradox: it was still expanding but its unity was cracked. It was full of confidence, tempered by dissatisfaction with the pace of evangelisation, and anxiety at the spread of heresy. It was prosperous by the standards of the recent past but still poor by comparison with Islam. Even as it expanded into new territories, Christendom seemed to shrink into a small corner of a world map that was growing, in the perceptions of the well informed, faster still. Europe had emerged into eclipse.

A Muslim geographer like al-Ishtakhri, contemplating the world from Persia in 950 might hardly notice Europe at all: in his map, it is squeezed almost out of the picture, dangling feebly off the edge of the known world. Meanwhile, the Christian who looked out at the world in his imagination probably saw something like the version mapped by the illuminators of the *Commentary on the Apocalypse* of Beatus. An example in the library of the cathedral of Burgo de Osma is dated 1086 but is highly conservative: even the calligraphy is carefully copied in an antique style. Asia takes up most of the space, Africa most of the rest. Europe consists mainly of three peninsulas – Spain, Italy and Greece, jutting into the Mediterranean – with a thin strip of hinterland above them. Against this background, the crusades seem like an explosion of claustrophobic frustrations: indeed, Pope Urban VI summoned crusaders to the first such expedition in 1095 by warning them,

The world is not evenly divided. Of its three parts, our enemies hold Asia as their hereditary home – a part of the world which our forefathers rightly considered equal to the other two put together. ... Africa too, the second part of the world, has been held by our enemies for 200 years and more. ... Thirdly there is Europe, the remaining region of the world. Of this region we Christians inhabit only a small part, for who will give the name of Christians to those barbarians who live in the remote islands and seek their living on the icy ocean as if they were whales?

Adam of Bremen, writing in the 1070s, with privileged access to knowledge of the Slav, Scandinavian and Baltic worlds, pictured Europe beyond Christendom as inhabited by green men who lived 100 years, cannibals and Amazons who bore dog-headed children. Inside Christian Europe, and on its edges, were unexplored recesses, unassimilated peoples, unexploited lands, untamed forests and unfrequented mountain ranges. To an objective scrutineer, European states can hardly have looked like future world powers, nor would the continent have seemed the home of a world-shaping 'miracle' of hegemony. Even during the next few centuries of unconscious preparation for world-wide exploration and expansion, it remained an unpredictable consummation.

The five eldest children of Charles I Sir Anthony Van Dyck 1637

REVIVAL

and RISE
1054-1815

CHAPTER 5

FITS AND STARTS

Medieval Christendoms and the rest of the world

IN 1051 A MESSENGER TRAVELLED north from the Pyrenean monastery of Canigou bearing news of the death of Count Wilfred of Cerdanya. All the way to Maastricht he found the local speech intelligible. If he had crossed the Channel to England he would still have been able to find communities of Romance-speaking monks with whom to converse. Beyond, in the lands of Germanic speech, Latin would have served as a means of communication with his fellow-churchmen. Anyone moving through this world, as scholar, pilgrim, messenger, merchant or as a clergymen on his way to take up a job, would have a strong sense of belonging to a single civilisation. In some respects, the same feelings of belonging extended even beyond the range of the Latin church, to embrace the Byzantine 'commonwealth' which formed another, uneasily fraternal Christendom.

Looking at Europe from the inside at about the turn of the millennium, Radulf Glaber expected the Latin church to be extended over the world 'as Christ and Peter once trod the sea.' Objectively considered, that would have seemed an optimistic forecast. A cosmic observer, privileged to look down on the world of 1000 years ago from a commanding height, would have seen a number of civilisations, most of them separated from one another by vast distances and poor communications. Asked to predict which of them would be most likely to dominate the others and become the springboard of world-wide empires, the observer, unless also endowed with foresight, would have been most unlikely to nominate any part of Christendom.

By comparison with China, for instance, Europe would have seemed under-populated and technically backward. Contrary to Gibbon's famous assertion, China had long enclosed 'the fairest part of the world and the most civilised portion of mankind'. Most technological advances of a critical sort for rates of production in agriculture or industry, for effectiveness in warfare, for efficiency in the use of power, for recording and transmitting information and for carrying and extending trade by sea had originated in China, and would continue to do so at least until the sixteenth century. From an astral height, Europe's main seaway, the Mediterranean, would have looked almost landlocked, its western bottleneck virtually stoppered by the current racing between the Pillars of Hercules. From the eleventh century to the fifteenth, judged in global perspective, Europe's relative position seemed to get even worse. The divergence of eastern and western Christendoms became unbridgeable. Despite the early successes of crusaders, most of the direct military encounters between Christendom and Islam in the period ended to the latter's advantage. The gaps in wealth and technology between Europe and superior civilisations to the east remained, in most respects, unclosed. On the other hand, with hindsight, some potential for future expansion can be seen to have accumulated, uncertainly, in fits and starts and patches, over a very long period of time, in the Europe of the high and late middle ages.

European maritime technology – a prerequisite of the prosperity borne by long-range trade and of the reach of most long-range imperialism – was especially primitive by the non-European standards at the start of the period. Most ship types available in Europe were unsuitable for ocean voyaging, compared with the junks of China or the plank-sewn craft of the Arabian seas and the Indian Ocean. Advice from a treatise of about 1190 represents an early stage of the reception in Europe of the navigator's most rudimentary tool. When the moon and stars are enveloped in darkness, Guyot de Provins explained, all the sailor need do is place, inside a straw floating in a basin of water, a pin well rubbed 'with an ugly brown stone that draws iron unto itself', for the point of this floating needle will always turn to the north. As far as is known, there were as yet no maritime charts in the west: indeed, the earliest certain reference to such a device dates only from 1270 and

throughout the period cartographic techniques in general were vastly inferior to those of the Chinese.

The exception was the shipping of Scandinavia. In the folk-memory of the Icelandic people, all their colonisations were heroic products of stormy seas and stormier societies: like the first sighting of Greenland, ascribed to Gunnbjorn Ulf-Krakason in the early tenth century, driven west by a freak wind, or the colonisation of the same island by Erik the Red, expelled for murderous feuding in 982, or the first sighting of the New World by Bjarni Herjolfsson in 986, when he was trying to follow his lost father to Greenland and overshot his mark. In reality, nothing was more natural than that Norse navigation should span the north Atlantic, where a series of currents, winds and island-hops links Norway with Newfoundland. The last stage of the crossing, from Greenland to America, is a short haul, current-assisted as far as Newfoundland. But on the return voyage, bound for Iceland, with the prevailing westerlies, long stretches of open-sea navigation had to be risked.

The true heroism of the Viking navigators was their willingness to follow the winds and currents: to cross the monster-filled seas depicted, for instance, in the stunning embroidery-work of the early twelfth-century 'Creation' hanging of Girona. Generally, in the history of exploration

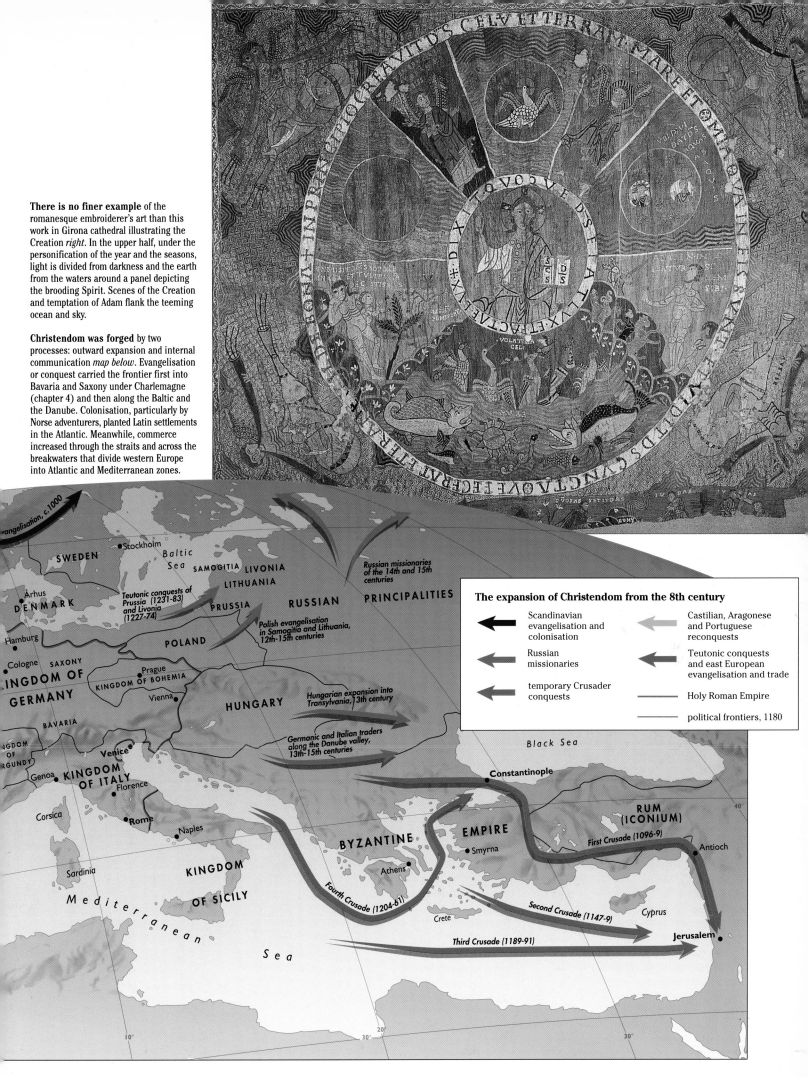

There is no finer example of the romanesque embroiderer's art than this work in Girona cathedral illustrating the Creation *right*. In the upper half, under the personification of the year and the seasons, light is divided from darkness and the earth from the waters around a panel depicting the brooding Spirit. Scenes of the Creation and temptation of Adam flank the teeming ocean and sky.

Christendom was forged by two processes: outward expansion and internal communication *map below*. Evangelisation or conquest carried the frontier first into Bavaria and Saxony under Charlemagne (chapter 4) and then along the Baltic and the Danube. Colonisation, particularly by Norse adventurers, planted Latin settlements in the Atlantic. Meanwhile, commerce increased through the straits and across the breakwaters that divide western Europe into Atlantic and Mediterranean zones.

The expansion of Christendom from the 8th century

- Scandinavian evangelisation and colonisation
- Russian missionaries
- temporary Crusader conquests
- Castilian, Aragonese and Portuguese reconquests
- Teutonic conquests and east European evangelisation and trade
- Holy Roman Empire
- political frontiers, 1180

would-be discoverers have preferred to sail against the elements because they were more concerned to cling to a way home than to find new destinations. The Norse in the Atlantic, like their Polynesian counterparts in the Pacific, soared above such inhibitions. Their ability to find havens and cross open sea without charts or technical aids to navigation seems miraculous to sailors dependent on the compass. But these practised seamen, whose powers of observation were uncorrupted by advanced technology, could make a rough judgement of their latitude, relative to a well-known point, by scanning the height of the sun or the Pole Star with the naked eye. When it was cloudy or foggy, all they could do was to sail on by guesswork until the sky cleared. Like the Polynesians, and some modern Atlantic fishermen, the settlers who followed Leif Eiriksson to Newfoundland during a series of voyages in the early eleventh century may also have been guided by familiar swells. When they approached land, they read the cloudscape or followed the flight of homing birds – like the legendary discoverers of Iceland in the ninth century, who carried ravens which they released at intervals.

Their ships were not the slinky 'serpent-ships' used by Viking raiders, nor the 'gold-mouthed, splendid beasts of the mast' sung of by Norse poets, but broad, deep vessels of a kind unearthed by archaeologists at Skuldelev in 1962. Their keels and ribs were of oak and the overlapping planks of the outer shell were pine, fastened with snugly-expanding pegs of lindenwood. Other fixings were by iron rivets, made, perhaps, by the solemn, bearded smith who works with bellows, hammer and tongs in a twelfth-century carving at Hylestad. The gaps between the planks were stopped with animal hair skeins soaked in pine pitch. The central mast had a square sail of coarse woollen cloth (useful only with a following wind), which rested on great T-shaped crutches when furled, with perhaps a small extra sail for manoeuvrability. There were just a few oar-holes fore and aft for working inshore. Rudderless, the ships were steered by a pole dangled over the starboard side towards the stern. Lacking a full upper deck for drainage, they had to be almost constantly bailed with wooden buckets. Stores – salted provisions, sour milk and beer – were stowed in an open hold amidships in skins or casks which could not be kept dry. No cooking could be done on board, but the excavated ships were provided with huge cauldrons for use on shore when possible – a hint of the longings with which sea-voyages were endured. As to 'your enquiry what people go to seek in Greenland and why they fare thither through such great perils', the answer, according to a Norwegian book of 1240, is 'in man's threefold nature. One motive is fame, another curiosity and the third lust for gain.'

The Vikings were pirates but piracy, considered from one point of view, is a primitive form of exchange which can develop into commerce as the pirate-peoples build up sufficient resources. It can work rather like 'aid' today, which is a transfer of resources, free or on easy terms, made in the hope of triggering economic development from which the donor-state can profit. The first empire-builders of medieval Genoa preyed on Moorish shipping; those of early modern England on the Spanish main. Similarly, spectacular trading initiatives and fruitful colonial ventures were launched from Viking havens. The Rus – eastward-exploring Vikings – made the Volga Europe's longest corridor of trade in the tenth century. The Iceland colony, which was a Viking-Celtic joint-enterprise, remained a magnet for ocean-going shipping and was, until the development of the Canaries and Azores in the fourteenth and fifteenth centuries, the only oceanic destination of trade from any part of Europe. The colony in Normandy, though authentically 'Norse' settlers were never more than a small minority there, inherited some Viking talents and retained a social system with Scandinavian habits, sending out younger sons to make their way in the world. The age of Viking raids was succeeded by that of Norman conquests, which established Norman dynasties in England, southern Italy, Sicily and Antioch.

The Viking experience demonstrated facts of enormous significance for the future of Europe's place in the world. To come from behind was no disadvantage in the medieval space-race and a place on the margins of civilisation was a good spot from which to start. For the success of commercial and imperial initiatives, motivation was more important

than technical prowess. Poverty could be a source of compulsion, wealth of complacency. When global empires were eventually launched from European bases, it was again peripheral and poor communities, in Spain, Portugal and the Netherlands, that led the way. In every case, an appropriate social system and scale of values counted for more than the ample means available to Asian powers.

Internal expansion came first: incorporation of the interior and threshold, the secret recesses, the unfrequented edges, the mountains and forests, the marshlands and marchlands. In the twelfth century the riverbankers of Latin Christendom conquered the wild wood. Unable to sleep 'on a certain night' in 1122, Abbot Suger of Saint-Denis rose to search the forest for twelve trees mighty enough to frame the new sanctuary he was planning for his abbey church, to be full of light and to 'elevate dull minds to the truth'. The foresters smiled at him and wondered if the abbot was 'quite ignorant of the fact that nothing of the kind could be found in the entire region'; but he found what he needed 'with the courage of faith'. It was a representative incident in a vast project for the domestication of little-explored, under-exploited environments. Gothic architecture, erected by means which economised on wood, was a style adapted to shrinking forests. The Cistercians, the most dynamic religious order of the century, disputed Suger's views on

aesthetics but favoured monuments on the same vast scale. They razed woodlands and drove flocks and ox-teams into the wildernesses where now, all too often, the vast abbeys lie ruined in their turn.

The peoples brought by this process into the candle-glow of scholarship had, for the writers who contemplated them, a variety of uses. Adam, bishop of Bremen, wielded his image of the pagan Prussians as a weapon with which to belabour the moral shortcomings of his fellow-Christians: without the advantage of access to the gospel, they shared their goods and despised gold and silver 'as dung'. For the Emperor Barbarossa's encomiast, Gunther of Pairis in Alsace, the Poles were just the opposite: savages despite their Christianity, with their wolves' voices and unkempt hair. Perhaps the Polish elite who, notwithstanding their impeccable Slav credentials, fostered a myth of their descent from Sarmatian nomad-warriors, brought such misjudgements on their own heads. For the pilgrim-guide writer known as 'Aiméry Picaud', the mountains and forests that had to be crossed by pilgrims to Compostela housed misplaced exotics, whose unnatural lusts – sodomy and bestiality – licensed pornography: a mule was as good as a woman for the Basques' perverted purposes, he thought, and 'a Basque is even said to fit a chastity belt to his own mare or mule, to prevent anyone else getting at them.'

Yet among the distractions of these partial purposes, medieval ethnography was able to achieve some real 'fieldwork' and to construct some realistic images of marginal peoples and their societies. Before looking outward, through the windows opened by colonial and commercial expansion towards Asia and Africa, scholars turned to contemplate alien faces in a mirror of their own, among dwellers in the frontiers and fastnesses of their own world. The most representative enquirer, perhaps, was Gerald of Wales, whose journeys through Wales and Ireland really were projects of self-encounter, as this Normanised, Anglicised scholar searched out his Celtic roots, denounced by his enemies 'as a Frenchman to the Welsh and to the French as a Welshman'. His preferred habitat was comfortable, scholarly and urbane. Transferred from the fleshpots to the frontier, Gerald beheld the wilderness of his birth with the nostalgia of a returnee and the discomfort of a misfit.

Gerald inherited a dilemma from classical tradition. He could never rid his mind of the conviction that sedentarism was civility and transhumance was savagery. Yet he was also susceptible to the myth of Arcady and inclined to see his fellow-Celts as revelling in a rustic idyll, with sidelines in brigandage and rapine. He condemned the Welsh as incestuous and promiscuous, the Irish – conveniently for their would-be conquerors in England – as wild infidels. Irish barbarity was typified by two hairy, naked savages fished up in a coracle by an English ship off the Connaught coast and astonished by the sight of bread. On the other hand, the Welsh had the conventional virtues of a shepherd-race, among whom 'no one is a beggar, for everyone's household is common to all.' Genuinely torn between conflicting perceptions of his subject-matter, Gerald evolved a model of social development of great sophistication. 'The Irish,' he wrote, 'are a wild race of the woods ... getting their living from animals alone and living like animals; a people who have not abandoned the first mode of living – the pastoral life.' The Irish proved peculiarly intractable, but, in general, Latin Christendom's internal and frontier barbarians became integrated with their neighbours. Hungary, which Otto of Freising in the mid-twelfth century thought

The ribs of a Viking trading-vessel *left,* broader and deeper-draughted than the famous long-ships, found at Skuldelev by Roskilde Fjord in 1962.

Viking technology: in a cycle of carvings depicting the legend of Sigurd the Volsung *below left*, Regin the Smith forges the sword with which he himself will be killed. Sigurd, helmeted, breaks it when he tests it on the anvil.

The spread of Norman conquest is marked by the castles which housed the colonial military elite. The first, outer walls of stone at Rochester *bottom left* were built in the 1080s by Bishop Gundulf, followed by the keep, shown here, from 1127.

The ruins of Melrose Abbey *below* in the Scottish borders reflect a relatively flamboyant phase of Cistercian art, with window tracery from a later fourteenth-century rebuilding. When building first began, the style, though characteristically monumental, was gaunt and undecorated, reflecting Cistercian austerity.

too good for the Hungarians, became in the fifteenth a cradle-land of the Renaissance, where King Matthias Corvinus built a palace in imitation of Pliny's villa. Basque lineages, so despised by Aiméry Picaud, supplied a new aristocracy to the rest of Spain in the fourteenth century. The Wendish lands repulsed the crusaders of 1147 but submitted to monastic colonists over the next half-century by a not altogether peaceful process: Absalon of Roskilde, patron of Cistercians, who died in 1192, was remembered in the next century as 'half prelate and half pirate'. Dwellers in remote or inhospitable areas never escaped urban contempt, and rarely met the doctrinal standards of zealous evangelists, but the quest for the barbarian was increasingly turned outwards to the world beyond the boundaries of Christendom. On the frontiers, restrictive inheritance customs released or drove excluded sons from their patrimonial lands into marches of conquest and settlement.

Behind the expanding frontier, modest technical revolutions were increasing productivity: large ploughs with curved blades bit deeper into the land; more efficient mills, more exact metallurgy and new products, especially in arms and glassware, extended the range of business and the flow of wealth. The population of western Europe may have doubled while these changes took effect, between the early eleventh and mid-thirteenth centuries. The range of commerce broadened as new trade-routes enmeshed Atlantic and Mediterranean seaboards in a single economy. Naturally, western Europe has two economies – a Mediterranean and a northern – separated by a narrow strait with widely different sailing conditions along the two seaboards and a chain of breakwaters which determines the flow of rivers and, therefore, the directions of exchange. For much of Europe's history, communication between these two zones was not easy. Limited access through the Toulouse gap, the Rhone corridor and the Alpine passes kept restricted forms of commerce alive, even in periods when commercial navigation from sea to sea was abandoned. In the thirteenth century, Mediterranean craft – mainly from Genoa, Majorca and Catalonia – resumed large-scale ventures along Atlantic coasts.

They faced enormous problems of acclimatisation and adaptation. The Strait of Gibraltar had to be forced against the current. Heavy seas beyond threatened ships low in the gunwales; Finisterre was their 'cape of no return', beyond which lay a long excursion out to sea around or across the Bay of Biscay. Galleys, which carried much of the trade, depended on huge inputs of victuals and water from on shore. All in all, the journey called for great sang-froid and was in its way almost as bold a venture as the Portuguese swoop out into the south Atlantic, 200 years later, in search of the westerly trade winds. The rewards were worthwhile. The Zaccaria family of Genoa tried to corner the English alum market. The Frescobaldi of Florence got their talons on a significant share of English wool. Bruges, where, in the late middle ages, merchant-houses from 'all the nations of the world' were said to be represented, became an emporium for the exchange of goods between the Mediterranean and the Baltic.

Jaume of Aragon and Catalonia considered his conquest of Majorca in 1229, depicted in paintings on the walls of the Saló del Tinell of the royal palace in Barcelona *above* to be 'the best deed man has done for 100 years'. Central position and command of sea-lanes made it the most important emporium of the western Mediterranean.

Hamburg's image of itself, illuminating the city charter of 1497 *above right*, is of a harbour full of commerce, paved quays with stacks of goods, rich citizenry and a turreted skyline. Though it was transformed from a group of merchants into a league of cities – defensive as well as commercial – in the third quarter of the fourteenth century, the Hanse continued to be characterised by a spirit of collaboration between traders in different centres which contributed to the success of each of the member communities.

The Justitzpalatz in Bruges *right* exemplifies the medieval splendours of a city which acted as one of the principal trading centres of the Hanseatic League, a commercial pre-eminence it only lost in the later fifteenth century as the estuary of the Zwin silted up.

The Hanseatic League *map left,* led by Lübeck in the Baltic, promoted trading privileges and monopolies for its member towns. From its beginnings in the twelfth century, the League grew to 70 members and around 200 associated cities. The cities were ideally placed for access to markets where Mediterranean produce and commercial interests met those of the Baltic and the North Sea.

Hanseatic trade routes

- Hanseatic League town
- ▲ main trading outpost
- △ trading outpost

—— Hanseatic trade route

— frontiers, 1382

Meanwhile, the northern seas were being unified in a similar way by German merchants whose shipping and caravans linked London and Bruges with Lübeck and Novgorod. Lübeck, founded in 1143, was the pioneer-city of what became the Hanseatic League – a string of colonies along the North Sea from Riga, definitively set up in 1201, to Danzig founded in 1238 and Memel, Elbing and Königsberg, all foundations of the 1250s. The league eventually became about 70 towns strong and had nearly 200 others associated with it. Exchange across vast distances made geographical specialisation and genuine industrialisation possible. All the industries served, for instance, by the trade of Genoa depended on geographical specialisation. Textiles depended on concentrating wools and dyestuffs from widely separated places of origin; food processing on the meeting of fresh foodstuffs with salt. The gold industry of Genoa itself, which turned raw gold into coins, leaf and thread, relied on supplies of African gold to Italian technicians; shipbuilding demanded a similar marriage of raw materials with technical expertise, and matching of wood, iron, sailcloth and pitch. Majorca, because it was a great emporium, could become a land of medieval *Wirtschaftswunder*, with a cloth industry documented from 1303, an arms industry that shipped literally thousands of crossbows to Flanders and England in the 1380s and a high reputation in the manufacture of the modest miracles of medieval technology which made long-range seafaring possible: the compass, the maritime chart and the cog – the sea-going cargo-vessel.

Expansion was more than conquest and the extension of trade: it was a process of the export of culture. The self-conscious town remained, as it had been in antiquity, a defining feature of the civilisation. Even the oldest-established cities might experience a renewal of civic spirit. As Isidore of Seville said, 'Walls make a city, but a civic community is built of people, not of stones.' The commune of Verona is shown in the tympanum of the cathedral in its moment of creation, as traditionally conceived: the patron saint, Zeno, 'with a serene heart, grants to the people a standard worthy of defence'. On the facade of the church of Santa Anastasia, he presents the assembled citizens to the Holy Trinity.

At times of assembly, in sight of these designs, civic identity was symbolised and reinforced. In Milan, the assembly point was in front of the church of Sant' Ambrogio, decorated with a similar scene of St Ambrose conjuring the commune into being. In reality, the commune – the citizens considered collectively – became an institution of civic government in the tenth century in some precocious cases, but in most only in the very late eleventh or early twelfth centuries. In what seems to have been a conscious reaching-back to an antique model, many Italian cities acquired 'consuls' in this period. By the mid-twelfth century Otto of Freising regarded autonomous city-governments as typical of northern Italy. Instead of deferring to some great protector – bishop or nobleman or abbot – cities became their own 'lords' and even extended their jurisdiction into the countryside: 'scarcely any noble or great man can be found in all the surrounding territory who does not acknowledge the authority of his city.' In effect, some cities were independent republics, forming alliances in defiance or despite of their supposed lords; others bade unsuccessfully for the same status. Twice in the 1140s and '50s Rome itself expelled the pope and proclaimed its independence.

Though independent city-states remained rare or short-lived outside Italy, urban awareness grew, as the number and dimensions of towns grew, all over Europe, and was exported to the new areas of frontier settlement. Planned towns like Elbing in Prussia were laid out with the measuring-rod and peopled by wagon-train, bringing the human flotsam of recruitment campaigns in the Rhineland and northern France. They bear the gridplan-brand of the colonial city throughout history: the same rectilinear image is stamped on the faces of Lima and Melbourne. In Spain, the progress of settlement on the frontier with Islam was marked by the granting of charters to tiny new towns: these usually gave the inhabitants' representatives some share in administrative and judicial power. At the other end of Christendom, Novgorod and Pskov occupied a similar position on the Finnish mark, contending against a hostile climate beyond the edge of the grainlands on which the citizens relied for sustenance. They were more often beleaguered by famine than by human enemies. Even today, the walls of Novgorod seem to stare bleakly over a defenceless wilderness.

The Veroli casket *below* shows a flash of classical paganism in the inspiration of Byzantine ivory-workers during an eleventh-century 'renaissance', with a lubricious Europe, a frolicsome Hercules and centaurs playing for a maenads' dance.

Control, however, of porterage-routes to the Volga made it rich. It never had more than a few thousand inhabitants yet its progress is chronicled in its monuments: the Kremlin walls and five-domed cathedral in the 1040s; in the early twelfth century a series of princely foundations, marking an era of power-sharing between the territorial prince and the town aristocracy; and in 1207 the merchants' church of St Paraskeva in the market-place. From 1136, communalism had been dominant in Novgorod and the citizens' principle was, 'If the prince is no good, throw him into the mud!' At the opposite end of Christendom, the citizens of Santiago de Compostela had a similar attitude: they tried to burn their prelate in his palace, along with the queen, in 1117. From the 1140s the aldermen of London were entitled to be called 'barons'; the celestial patrons who decorate their early seals – St Paul and St Thomas Becket – were both defiers of princes.

All towns of the time were small by modern standards. As few as 2,000 citizens could make a 'town' if it had walls and a charter and some sort of civic consciousness. Thirty-thousand inhabitants made a metropolis. Most towns were courts or forts or markets. Production was typically something that happened in the countryside. But the towns of the eleventh and twelfth centuries did restore to European life something of the flavour of antiquity: they became concentrations of wealth and power, with enough civilised amenities to attract aristocrats to live in them at least some of the time.

In the art, literature and scholarship of the age a strong sense of continuity with ancient civilisation shines through. The church of San Miniato, which overlooks Florence, looked so convincingly classical that Renaissance admirers mistook it for a genuinely ancient building. The sculptor of an eleventh-century capital at Frómista was either copying a classical Laocoon or inspired by Pliny's description of one. On the twelfth-century tomb of St Vincent at Avila, Jews try to steal the saint's body in a scene redolent of the tensions of the urban life of the time – but the modelling of the figures shows knowledge of classical tradition. The ideas of Suger on the aesthetic of light were derived from what he thought was a Greek text from the time of St Paul's visit to the Areopagus. The medieval English historian Geoffrey of Monmouth traced the 'British' monarchy back to one of the sons of Priam. The cathedral of Novgorod was hazily modelled on that of Constantinople. Abelard's lectures in Paris introduced the logic of Aristotle permanently into the western tradition. Poets in Bath and Benedictbeuern experimented with the prosody of Virgil and the style of Catullus. A 'renaissance' of classical pagan aesthetics also happened in Byzantium: on the Veroli casket, Europa, feted by satyrs and centaurs, pouts prettily at her pursuers in perpetuation of ancient taste. In Byzantine scholarship of the late twelfth century, nothing commanded more prestige than classical research. Michael Choniates, bishop of Athens, was delighted to have the Parthenon to preach in and the *Hecale* of Callimachus to read for pleasure. Eustathius, bishop of Thessalonica, compiled commentaries on Pindar and Homer and searched old manuscripts to improve the text of Sophocles' *Antigone*.

Despite this common interest in the legacy of the ancient world, the experience of Latin and orthodox Christendom – or, to put it another way, of western and eastern Europe – diverged alarmingly in the thirteenth century. For the west, despite the Islamic reconquest of crusader colonies in the Levant, it was a period of unprecedented expansion within Europe; orthodox Christendom, meanwhile, contracted and seemed threatened in its very survival. The most spectacular territorial gains were made by the Christian states of Spain in the Iberian peninsula and the western Mediterranean. In one of the most active and sustained periods of the so-called 'reconquest' of the peninsula, between the 1220s and the 1260s, the kingdoms of Valencia and Murcia constituted a substantial 'Mediterranean front', subjugated largely by Aragonese and Catalan forces.

Conquests by Castile and Portugal, however, in the south-west, in Andalusia, Extremadura, the Alentejo and the Algarve, belong to a different, Atlantic world. Their coasts were washed by the Atlantic and into the Atlantic their rivers drained. They were or became, for the most part, lands empty or emptied of the indigenous population; at least, the natives tended to be depleted or displaced. They were a seedplot of a colonial people and, in some respects, a nursery of colonial experience. They resembled the future lands of Atlantic colonisation, but were radically unlike those of the Mediterranean, where native labour forces and indigenous economic systems were essential to colonial life. The difference would be appreciated by any film-goer or aficionado of historical romance: the Mediterranean conquests were a sort of Raj, in which the indigenous economy and society were not displaced, except in scattered pockets, but overlain by a thin colonial elite. The Atlantic lands enclosed a sort of wild west, of sparse settlements, tough frontiersmen and vast ranches.

The tenor of life there is hard to capture. For the Arab eulogists of the high middle ages, Andalusia had been a paradise, a garden of earthly delights. If, leaving aside the well-known poets, we turn to Ibn al-Awwam, the twelfth-century agronomist, we seem transported into a world of epicene contentment, in which he mingles aromatic vinegars, concocts foie gras and happily devises recipes for compotes to please his sybaritic king. Though the climate continues to be praised,

When the cathedral of Holy Wisdom *above far left* was rebuilt in stone after a fire in Novgorod in 1042, the architects came from Constantinople, though a further source of influence was rivalry with its counterpart in Kiev, which it was designed to excel in splendour.

The relics of St Vincent came to Avila as part of a distribution of sacred gifts – an attempt to spread and secure political authority. The work on his tomb *above left* is one of the most animated and realistic of romanesque sculptures.

Christians and Jews play board games by a pavilion in a garden in a thirteenth-century Spanish manuscript *far left.* In 'reconquered' Spain, the garden image was inherited from Muslim Andalusian writers.

Though San Miniato al Monte *below* was built shortly after 1018, its harmonious and balanced facade convinced Renaissance architects that it was a genuine model of classical Roman workmanship.

Christian Andalusia never speaks to us with that lush, rich voice. In some respects, it was a land of opportunity, where the great bulk of the urban citizenry enjoyed the status of direct vassals of the king and where wages were high and land prices low. But the opportunities were hard to exploit and the conditions of life variable. It was difficult to make the most of Andalusia's rich soil, with the hazards of the frontier, shortage of labour and the relentless progress of aristocratic tenure imposing pastoralism on much of the country. Olive oil, the liquid gold of Moorish Andalusia, though prized by Genoese merchants, was little esteemed by the conquerors, who preferred lard. As under Islam, it remained an urban world, with big towns lapped, like oases, by under-populated hinterlands. The resultant high demands on the productivity of the countryside led to frequent breakdowns of supply. Remote communities strove, with the self-consciousness of an urban culture, to preserve the amenities of civilised life. Among the settlers of Vejer there were two priests, a miller, two gardeners, a tiler, a blacksmith, a shoemaker, a butcher and no fewer than three surgeon-barbers – though presumably they must have plied some other trade as well. Almost within bow-shot of the Islamic frontier, you could go, shriven and shod, to the hairdresser's.

On Latin Christendom's eastern front, similar successes, extending the frontier deep into formerly pagan worlds in Livonia, Estonia, Prussia and Finland, were registered from Scandinavia by the conventional feudal and mercenary armies of kings or from Germany by warriors whose way of life combined high secular and religious ideals. Military orders like the Sword-Brothers and the Teutonic knights led a life of monastic rigour and discipline, espoused an aristocratic ethos of prowess and valour and practised a battlefield-culture of holy war which justified terror and massacre, along with martyrdom, by appealing to one of Christ's most haplessly chosen commands: 'Compel them to come in.'

Here savagery was turned to the service of civilisation. The *Rhyming Chronicle* of the conquest of Livonia recounts with equal pleasure the immolation of native villages and the piety of forcible converts. The Swedes who conquered the Tavastians of Finland in 1249 aimed, according to their own rhymed account of their deeds, 'to bring destruction and little cheer' but also congratulated themselves as harbingers of truth and peace: the long-term effects are implicitly praised in the charming woodcuts of Olaus Magnus's history of the north, in which Finnish wild men ski to mass. An even more sanitised version of the crusading past in the north was engraved on the shrine of St Henry of Finland at Nousiainien, where the Finnish and Swedish knights of a legendary twelfth-century encounter are shown as indistinguishably helmed and mailed: the Swedes themselves were said to have wept over the potential converts slain on the field. In the 1220s, a Danish garrison at Jerwia was destroyed by allegedly cannibal enemies,

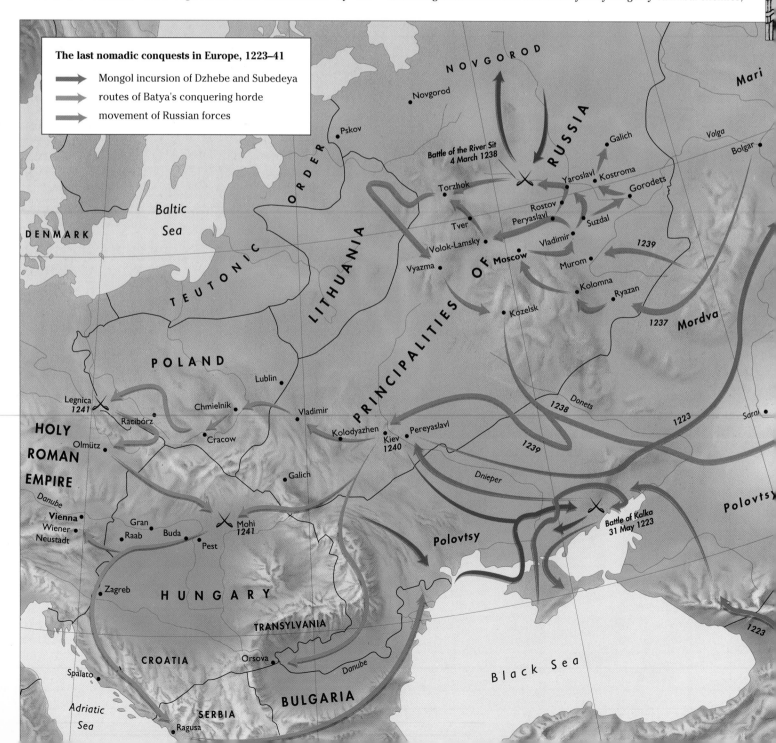

The last nomadic conquests in Europe, 1223–41

→ Mongol incursion of Dzhebe and Subedeya

→ routes of Batya's conquering horde

→ movement of Russian forces

but in the same decade the Danes built Reval, with eight churches, two chapels, a leper-house a hospital and a guild-house, creating in a cold climate a parody of the urban world which the Spanish reconquest was constructing at the sun-blessed end of Latin Christendom.

While Latin Christendom grew in the thirteenth century, eastern Christendom was hard put to survive. The twelfth-century crusades, which ought to have united Byzantines and westerners against a common foe, only deepened the breach through the disillusionment provoked by failed alliances and the contempt bred by increased familiarity. The crusading hosts that arrived in the east in 1097 were partly a popular rabble, whom the Byzantines admired for their piety but resented for their poverty, and partly a formidable army which was welcomed for its usefulness but feared for its indiscipline. According to Anna Comnena, an imperial princess and blue-stocking who chronicled the period in Homeric style, they were 'a race under the spells of Dionysos and Eros' among whom those who 'undertook this journey only to worship at the Holy Sepulchre' were outnumbered by predatory enemies whose 'object was to dethrone the emperor and capture the capital'. In the very long run, after more than a century, her words proved prophetic. The tense co-operation between Byzantines and crusaders, which characterised the First Crusade, broke down in the second and third. The crusaders blamed 'Greek treachery' for their failures; the Byzantines emerged fortified in their conviction of superiority over barbarian impiety and greed. The Fourth Crusade, launched in 1202 as a pilgrimage under arms for the recapture of Jerusalem, ended shedding Christian blood on the ramparts and streets of Constantinople. The long-term consequences can be sampled on the outside of St Mark's cathedral in Venice, studded and dotted with the spoils of Constantinople and adorned with the riches of an empire which Venice acquired at Byzantine expense. The great bronze horses above the west doors stamp and snort in victory. Below, a Hercules looted from Byzantium carries off, in his turn, the Erymanthean boar and the hind of Ceryneia. Hitherto Byzantine art had been imitated in the west. Now, it was appropriated.

The damage and losses were never entirely made good. While Constantinople was in the hands of Latin conquerors – as it was, with much of the rest of the empire, from 1204 to 1261 – the northern lands of the Orthodox commonwealth were cut off and almost obliterated by the last nomad invasion of Europe from Asia: the coming of the Mongols. For eight centuries, the broad corridor of the Eurasian steppe had admitted hordes of nomad warriors into Europe. Between the fifth and tenth centuries the Huns, Avars, Magyars and Bulgars had penetrated into the west to varying depths, but all had ultimately been defeated and settled or destroyed. More recently, Pechenegs, Cumans and Turks had battered and eroded the defences of Byzantium. Despite this long experience, when the Mongols descended, their victims did not know what to make of them.

The first Latins who heard about them – crusaders in their camp at Damietta in 1221 – assumed, because of their depredations against Muslims, that the Mongols must be Christians. Information from those with direct experience might have disabused them, but the warnings of Queen Russudan of Armenia, who reported them as 'evil folk' who 'inflict many disasters', mouldered unheeded in the papal archives. Guiragos, an Armenian monk who despised the queen as 'an amorous and shameful woman, like Semiramis,' recognised agents of a vengeful Providence in 'precursors of Antichrist ... of hideous aspect and without pity in their bowels ... who rush with joy to carnage as if to a wedding-feast or orgy.'

When the Mongols struck Russia two years later, the blow was entirely unanticipated: 'no man knew from whence they came or whither they departed.' They were treated by annalists almost as if they were a natural phenomenon, like a briefly destructive bout of freak weather or flood or a visitation of plague. Some Russian rulers even rejoiced at the greater destruction visited on their hated Cuman neighbours. But the first Mongol invasion of Russia proved to be no more than a reconnaissance. When the nomads returned in earnest in 1237 their campaign lasted for three years. They devastated and depopulated much of the land of south and north-east Russia and

King Eric of Sweden's arrival on crusade, accompanied by Bishop Henry, on the shores of the pagan Finns, as imagined by the fifteenth-century engraver of a plaque *above* adorning the shrine of St Henry at Nousiainien. In retrospect, the Finns are made to seem as urbane as their conquerors.

The engravings accompanying Bishop Olaus Magnus's sixteenth-century compendium are a vital source of the history of northern European peoples: the scene of a Finnish family skiing to mass *below* expresses the bishop's satisfaction at the domestication of a once savage frontier.

Mongol invaders used traditional steppeland routes and, where the soil was firm enough to support cavalry, explored most of the plains of eastern Europe *map left*. It would be rash, however, to suppose that their conquests had reached the limits imposed by geography when succession disputes caused them to withdraw their armies eastward in 1241. Western Europe had proved vulnerable to horseborne conquerors from the east many times before.

ransomed or looted towns. They only turned back, without being checked by opposition, when their vanguards were deep inside Poland and Hungary.

Refugees spread horror-stories across Europe, gathered by an incredulous annalist in Cologne. 'No little fear', he wrote, 'of that barbarous race invaded even very distant lands – not only France but even Burgundy and Spain, where the name of the Mongols was previously unknown. Of the origins, habits and way of life of the aforesaid barbarian race, we hear many things which are incredible and which we forbear to write down here, because we are not altogether sure of them until the unadorned truth reaches us.' Meanwhile the rumours circulated in the west: Mongols looked like monkeys, barked like dogs, ate raw flesh, drank their horses' urine, knew no laws and showed no mercy.

Yet within Russia, the Mongols came rather to exploit than destroy. According to one chronicler, they spared the peasants to ensure continuity of production. Ryazan, a principality on the Volga, south-east of Moscow, seems to have borne the brunt of the invasion and suffered the least discriminating pillage; yet there, if the local chronicle can be believed, 'The pious Grand Prince Ingvary Ingvarevitch sat on his father's throne and renewed the land and built churches and monasteries and consoled newcomers and gathered together the people. And there was joy among the Christians whom God had saved from the godless and impious Khan.' Many cities escaped lightly by surrendering soon and Novgorod, which might have been a coveted prize, was by-passed altogether. The rumours which had reached western travellers, like the pope's envoy John of Piano Carpini, who heard that in Kiev only 200 houses were left standing, and that the fields were strewn 'with countless heads and bones of the dead' – seem, like much wartime reportage – to have been exaggerated by sensationalism.

After their thirteenth-century apogee and nadir, the relative positions of western and eastern Christendom were reversed. A series of setbacks muffled western initiative in the fourteenth century. In 1303

a pope's health was wrecked by the terminal shock of irreverent French knights who invaded his bedchamber: the unity of Latin Christendom never looked quite so impressive again, as western churches became increasingly 'national' in character and personnel. Between 1304 and 1307 a Franciscan zealot improbably called Fra Dolcino proclaimed a millenarian republic of the foes of Antichrist in an Alpine valley: it was one of a convulsive series of social rebellions and radical religious spasms. Between 1315 and 1317, the dead of an exceptionally lethal sequence of winters of famine and floods were mourned from the Elbe to the Loire: it was the centrepiece of a climatic change now called the 'little ice age', which marginalised some areas of settlement and emptied others; the front of Christendom gradually withdrew, into the fifteenth century, from their outposts in Greenland and the Baltic while in the heartlands hitherto became untenable. The Icelandic annals recorded the islanders' venture to Markland in 1347. The following year, the Black Death began to scythe through western Europe: a visitation of plague of unprecedented range and fatality spreading north from the Mediterranean reach Scotland and Scandinavia by 1350. Some villages in Provence lost four-fifths of their population; half the villages of Sicily were abandoned, as were a quarter of those around Rome. Mortality was more modest elsewhere, but significant, especially among the young, wherever the plague struck.

The impersonal enemies – plague, famine and cold – were supplemented by human foes. In 1354 a violent earthquake demolished the walls of Gallipoli: Turks were waiting to take over the ruins, inaugurating a history of European anxiety about the defensibility of the eastern Mediterranean frontier which would last, with fluctuations, for over 200 years. In 1396, an attempted counter-attack at Nicopolis on the Danube was so heavily defeated that people in Latin Christendom refused to believe the news: a miniaturist of Froissart's *History* showed the duke of Burgundy ransoming his captured heir from the sultan, with his attendants strained and buckled by the weight of the bags of gold. Meanwhile, in the north-east, pagan Lithuanians eroded the conquests

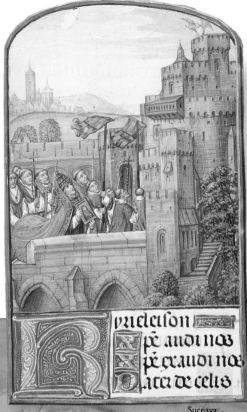

The expansion of the Ottoman Turks into Europe

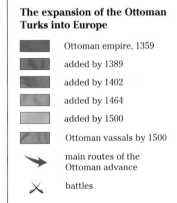

- Ottoman empire, 1359
- added by 1389
- added by 1402
- added by 1464
- added by 1500
- Ottoman vassals by 1500
- → main routes of the Ottoman advance
- ✕ battles

Turkish raiders first devastated, then occupied large tracts of the Byzantine empire in Asia Minor from the mid-thirteenth century, crossing over into Europe from the mid-fourteenth. This 16th-century fresco *left* depicts the results of one such raid in 1352: the monks of the monastery of Saint Simon are martyred by the turbanned invaders. The expansion of the Ottoman Turks into the Balkans *map right* would take them as far as the gates of Vienna by the early sixteenth century.

In their despairing hope for del'verance from the scourge of the plague, medieval illuminators looked to the iconography of an earlier age. Here, in a medieval Book of Hours *above right*, the sixth-century Pope Gregory I is seen leading a procession interceding for the deliverance of Rome from the terrible blight.

Vienna

Danube

Suceava

Dniester

HUNGARY

MOLDAVIA

Prut

Venice

Sava

Kilia

BOSNIA

Bosna Saray (Sarajevo)

Belgrade

Semendire 1444

Tergoviste

WALLACHIA

Danube

HERZEGOVINA

SERBIA

Nish

Vidin

Silistre

Adriatic

Sea

RAGUSA

MONTENEGRO

Cattaro

KOSOVO POLJE

Sofia

Nicopolis

BULGARIA

Varna 1444

Black Sea

ALBANIA

Üsküb

RUMELIA

Edirne (Adrianople)

Durazzo

Ochrida

Selanik (Salonica) 1453

Istanbul (Constantinople) 1453

V E N E T I A N

Yanya (Janina)

Corfu

THESSALY

Gelibolu (Gallipoli)

Ankara 1402

EPIRUS

Aegean Sea

Anatolia

Cephalonia

Patras

Euboea

(to Chios)

Izmir

Zante

MOREA

Athens

to Genoa

R E P U B L I C

DUCHY OF NAXOS (to Venice)

KNIGHTS OF ST JOHN

Modon

Rhodes

Crete

Mediterranean Sea

Cyprus

Venetian 1489

Ottoman tributary 1517

of the Teutonic Order along the Baltic, though the losses were made good for Christendom, if not for the Germans, by the gradual diffusion of the Catholic faith, under Polish influence, into Lithuania. When the Greenland colony was finally extinguished in the fifteenth century, it was by mysterious raiders of savage ferocity known as Skraelingar. Like so many other imperial checks – to Rome in the last Punic War, to the Ottomans by Timur, to Britain in the American War of Independence – the check suffered by European expansion in the Holy Land in the twelfth century seems, in retrospect, more like a respite than a repulse, a starting-point of further greatness, a pause for the re-winding of springs. The fourteenth-century experience – in which Latin Christendom's expansion slowed and sloughed – had few such redeeming features. Its incapacitating legacy made western Europe in the fifteenth century the least promising of the world's civilisations and among the worst equipped to profit from the world's 'age of expansion'. The late medieval west was a civilisation in contraction or stagnation.

Decline or eclipse also afflicted Byzantium. The expansion into Europe of the most dynamic power of the late middle ages, the Ottoman Turks, was largely at Byzantine expense; yet, paradoxically, eastern Christendom as a whole experienced its greatest-ever growth, even as its old heartlands were gobbled up by these invaders. The shrinkage and, in the mid-fifteenth century, the disappearance of Byzantium was more than made up for by the phenomenon of Muscovy, building a Russian empire more dynamic and, in its way, more enduring than any of the western empires which, from today's perspective, seem to have dominated recent history. In the 100 years from 1362, Muscovy developed from a poor, despised, small and upstart principality, under the tutelage of Mongol masters, into a substantial state covering a swathe of territory from the northern Dvina to near the source of the Don, dominating the upper and middle reaches of the Volga. In 1478 the conquest of Novgorod – a northern polis with a tradition of independence and a hinterland-empire in the Venetian style – secured frontiers on the Pechora and Lake Ladoga. In 1480 Mongol sovereignty was repudiated and Moscow was proclaimed

the Third Rome, recovering the baton, and perhaps the sceptre, dropped from the dead hand of Byzantium.

Muscovy had proved that, deftly handled, Mongol hegemony could be manipulated to advantage. By acknowledging Tatar overlordship, Alexander Nevsky, prince of Novgorod in the mid-thirteenth century, was able to establish an undying reputation as a Russian national hero: submission to the Mongols enabled him to fight off German and Swedish incursions. His son David was the effective founder of Muscovy, proclaiming Moscow's independence of the centres which had formerly ruled it. His grandson became known as Ivan the Moneybag from the wealth he accumulated as a farmer of Tatar taxes. With the title of 'Grand Prince' and the possession of the metropolitan see, Moscow from his time (1329-53) was able to bid for imperial pre-eminence over other Christian states. Despite a premature challenge to Tatar supremacy in 1378-82, Moscow's privileged relationship with the overlords survived more or less unbroken until 1480 when Ivan the Great, having engorged most of Russia's other surviving Christian principalities, was ready to

repudiate it. He married a Byzantine princess, incorporated a double-headed eagle into his arms, forged a genealogy which traced the house of Alexander Nevsky back to the Roman Caesars, and contemptuously dismissed the Habsburg emperor's offer to invest him as king. 'We have been sovereign in our land from our earliest forefathers,' he replied, 'and we hold our sovereignty from God.'

There were – or might have been – other contenders for the role of the Third Rome. In the middle of the thirteenth century, the recently Christianised Serbian kingdom already housed some of the most purely classical paintings of the middle ages on the walls of the royal monasteries of Sopocani and Mileseva; about a century later the Serbian monarch Stefan Dusan dreamed of beating the Turks to the conquest of Constantinople and described himself with pride – if a little exaggeration – as 'lord of almost the whole of the Roman empire'. His younger contemporary, the Bulgar Tsar John Alexander, claimed lordship over 'all the Bulgarians and Greeks' and had himself painted in boots of imperial scarlet and a halo of gold. Where a Byzantine

On a leaf of this Slavonic gospel-book *left,* the mid-fourteenth-century Bulgar Tsar John Alexander wears imperial garb, crowns, boots, sashes and cuffs in allusion to the Tsar's claim to have replaced Byzantium.

The monastery of Sopocani, founded by King Stefan Uros I, houses frescoes, including this one of the Virgin Mary *above,* which, together with those of other royal monasteries of mid-thirteenth-century Serbia, form a series of some of the most astonishingly pure works of classical inspiration from the middle ages. The workmanship and sources of this sophisticated art are unknown, but the court of Stefan Uros drew on a range of cosmopolitan connections: he had a Venetian mother and a French wife.

The geography of eastern Europe, with its vast plains and long navigable rivers, where troops and messengers can move easily, favours big, short-lived empires, often created by invaders from outside. Muscovy became the kernel of an exceptionally durable imperial state, *map right,* partly, perhaps, as a result of slow building outwards from a central position.

The growth of Muscovy to 1505

- ▮ Muscovite territory at the end of 13th century
- ▮ acquisitions to 1462
- ▮ acquisitions under Ivan III 1462-1505
- — boundary of Russian territories in 1462

chronicler had hailed Constantinople as the New Rome, a translator at John Alexander's court substituted the name of the Bulgar capital of Trnovo and called it 'the new Constantinople'.

But these bids were premature: the proto-empires of the Serbs and Bulgarians were themselves to be swallowed up by the same Turkish expansion that expunged Byzantium. They were colours in the kaleidoscope of European dynastic empires that was shaken and re-shaken, while a new dominant pattern – a new political culture – gradually emerged: the unity of Christendom was compromised by nothing so much as by the strength of its component states. Their strength should be understood not in relation to their own subjects – for states all over the world were weak in practice, by modern standards, in that respect – but in relation to each other and to the church, which claimed a higher allegiance. By the late middle ages, no part of the world except south-east Asia had a state system as richly variegated as that of western Europe. The sometime unity of Islam had crumbled by the start of the present millennium, but the Ottoman Turks were at work, restoring a large measure of it. China seemed to seek, as

if by some mysterious natural process, through all its divisions, a unity which the Ming began to restore in the late fourteenth century. Even the volatile Indian sub-continent enclosed a dominant state, the Sultanate of Delhi. In contrast to these imperial worlds, Europe outside Ottoman control was an exceptional arena of discrete territorial states.

They had their own languages – no longer mutually intelligible across vast frontiers as they had been to the messenger from Canigou of 1051 – and their own enmities. 'Who will understand the different languages?' wrote Pope Pius II in the mid-fifteenth century, 'Who will rule the diverse customs? Who will reconcile the English with the French or join the Genoese with the Aragonese or make the Germans agreeable to the Hungarians or Bohemians?' They had their own native clergies and, increasingly, their own universities in which to train them. Some of them even had, or threatened to have, their own churches in opposition to the universalist claims of Rome: the Bosnian church seceded for a while in the fourteenth century, that of Bohemia in the fifteenth; the English state was almost captured by heretics keen to abjure Roman allegiance in the late fourteenth and early fifteenth centuries.

Meanwhile, what had been dynastic conflicts became national wars, animated by chauvinism. The rallying of France to the House of Valois in the last phases of the Hundred Years' War has in part the character of a national self-discovery – as well as of a social revolution which propelled a peasant-girl and low-born 'scorchers' to the command of armies. The Kingdom of Bohemia, depicted in the maps of Nicholas of Cusa as defiantly ringed by mountains, expelled its Germans in a wave of Czech nationalism and in 1421 the diet denounced the ruler of Germany as 'the enemy of all who speak the Czech tongue'. Even the Holy Roman Empire, which had always represented a universalist ideal, came in the fifteenth century to look increasingly like a German nation-state, represented by the Bavarian humanist Aventinus as a community of great antiquity and unbroken continuity.

This ought to be a matter of surprise. Everyone at the time who thought about it, and who recorded his opinion, recalled admiringly the unity imposed by Rome and felt a reluctance to shelve the pretence that the Roman empire still existed. In a sense, it did still exist. The styles of 'King of the Romans' and 'Holy Roman Emperor' belonged to the elective head of the loosely agglomerated states of Germany and of some neighbouring territories. Whenever the holder of such titles had enough clout of his own – enough *Hausmacht,* inherited along with his particular dynastic territories – optimists surfaced to acclaim the potential restoration of the empire of Augustus or Constantine or, at least, of Charlemagne.

In 1220, for instance, Frederick II, the 'wonder' and 'transformer' of the world, was crowned emperor in an atmosphere alive with millenarian prophecy. For a brief spell early in the fourteenth century, when the Emperor Henry of Luxemburg was marching on Italy, Dante envisaged an era of universal peace, justice and happiness under imperial rule. In the early sixteenth century, when the Emperor Charles V united in his person more power, dynastic and elective, than any of his predecessors since Charlemagne, an Extremaduran conquistador, an Italian cardinal and Spanish and Belgian courtiers echoed this sort of language without embarrassment. In the intervening periods, imperial resources could hardly justify such pretensions. The grandiloquence was unbacked by grist. Territorial princes, however, remained wary of imperial potential. When the Emperor Sigismund V visited Henry V of England, his ship was met by a knight who waded out with the tide to demand his prior renunciation of any superior rights over the kingdom. A long tradition of eschatological prophecy fed hopes of the re-unification of Christendom by a 'Last World Emperor' whose cosmic battle with Antichrist would usher in the millennium. Holy Roman Emperors – even feeble ones – tended to attract the expression, at least, of such expectations, but they were commonly aroused in the entourages of French and Aragonese kings, too.

Under the spectral shadow of Rome, and the remote goad of the apocalypse, the chief executives of western states got on with their own business and concentrated sovereign power within their frontiers. Fourteenth-century Castilian kings, and a sixteenth-century English one, called their kingdoms 'empires'. Evolved in the fourteenth century, applied in the fifteenth, the doctrine that the kings of France were 'emperors in their own realm' spread and enhanced the self-perception of most western monarchs. Ideological strategies devised by propagandists to enhance the image of kings included the notion that the French king's office was miraculous, endowed by God with 'such a virtue and power that you perform miracles in your own lifetime', and the formula, tediously repeated in the fifteenth century, that the authority of the king of Castile was 'sovereign and absolute'.

Territorial sovereignty became entrenched as the functions of the state changed. Traditionally, the business of government was jurisdiction and law was a body of wisdom handed down from the past, not a continuous area of innovation. On the tomb of the great early fourteenth-century teacher of law, Cino da Pistoia, access to this numinous wisdom seems to magnify the towering figure of the professor, as he rests his hand over a pillar of justice, or to invest him with charisma, while attentive students lap at his words. As states grew in size and complexity, and as their technical resources expanded, the range of their stewardship extended – over the vast vistas of common life and public welfare displayed in Ambrogio Lorenzetti's panorama of good government on the walls of the Signorie of Siena. Husbandship of the commonwealth in all its aspects became the goal of kings who had the example of Joinville's St Louis before their eyes, servant of his people, a layman of unrivalled holiness: his *Life* was the ultimate mirror for princes, more influential on late medieval European government than any work explicitly of political theory. Accompanying the enlarged vision of the scope of the state, and perhaps in partial consequence, laws and administrative regulations multiplied.

Statute-making therefore gradually came to replace jurisdiction as the principal job – indeed, eventually, the defining characteristic – of

Joinville's enthusiasm for St Louis stopped short of approving or accompanying the 'ill-advised' crusade to Tunis in 1270, on which the king met his death; here his departure is depicted *above*, ten years after the event, as a symbolic navigation in saintly company. In reality, the king was 'so weak that he could not bear to be drawn in a coach or to ride' and Joinville claimed that he had to carry him to the point of embarkation in his arms.

The growing range of the responsibility of the state for every aspect of its people's lives appears in the panoramic landscapes and cityscapes of Ambrogio Lorenzetti's programme of the effects of good and bad government painted onto the walls of the Signorie of Siena *left*.

The towering intellect of the law professor of Bologna University, Guitone Sinibaldi, known as Cino da Pistoia, who died in 1337, is symbolically represented on his tomb *below*.

Jacques Coeur's house *below left* evokes reputedly the biggest commercial fortune of the late middle ages – wealth so vast as to arouse royal cupidity and provoke its owner's judicial murder.

Icons of kingship in genuine likeness: on what was probably his travelling altarpiece *left*, Richard II of England, who was born on the feast of Epiphany, is presented to Christ by John the Baptist, his personal patron, and to two royal predecessors, Edmund the Martyr and Edward the Confessor. The angels wear the king's livery-badge. The image of the king enthroned in the choirstalls of Westminster Abbey *below*, payment for which was recorded in 1395, raises the monarch above faction and close to God.

sovereign authorities. Law-making bodies – kings and representative assemblies – could begin to monopolise sovereignty, which had formerly been shared with rival sources of jurisdiction within the realm, with feudal suzerains outside it whose jurisdiction overlapped and, above all, with popes who performed a supra-national role as a court of final appeal in cases belonging to their sphere. In 1476, the monarchs of Spain began to use the printing press to circulate their huge legislative and administrative output. At the height of legislative activity in the England of Henry VIII, eight sessions of parliament in eight years produced the unprecedented total of 333 new statutes. Growth in the complexity of administration kept pace with the inflation of legislation as technology enhanced the reach and power of government to communicate and enforce its commands. From the fourteenth century, the use of paper slashed the cost and boosted the turnover of chanceries. In the mid-fifteenth century, carrier-pigeons, post riders and printing presses speeded the generation and flow of words. Royal commands could now be broadcast with a lavish hand. Missives from princes were like the relics of saints – bearing with them a mysterious fragment of the royal persona, a kind of proxy, a hint of a monarch's presence. 'When a letter comes from a king,' as Bernardino of Siena averred in a sermon, 'how sweet it is to go and hear it read.' When letters arrived from the king of Castile, the officials who received them would kiss them, place them on their heads in token of submission and read them aloud to the people in a prominent public place – on the steps of a church or at the door of a town hall.

Images of rulers, like all art, became increasingly lively and realistic: the earliest recognisable French portrait is of King John the Good, done in the mid-fourteenth century. At the same time, painters contrived to invest the portraits with more numinous distance, more awesome majesty than the idealised types previously favoured: John, for instance, is shown in profile, as if in a classical medallion, against a field of gold like an icon. In the 1430s, Charles VII of France had himself painted, in his own unmistakable features, as St Louis and as the first of the Magi. But the fashion for individual portraits of majesty had already been attained its greatest splendour when it reached the court of Richard II in England in the last quarter of the previous century. In his choir-stall at Westminster Abbey his portrait permanently sat, as if perpetuating his presence, staring hieratically from amid a shimmer of gold leaf. In the famous travelling altar known as the Wilton Diptych, the king kneels before the Virgin, attended by angels who wear his livery badge: the gesture he flutters in her direction has been variously interpreted, but he seems really to be opening his hands to receive the Christ-child whom the Virgin appears to be about to hand to him, as if in a eucharistic allusion appropriate to this kind of furniture and to the court of a king anxious to advertise the closeness of his relationship to God. In Richard's case, this sort of propaganda failed: he was deposed and murdered. The new style of 'sovereign' kingship cut across some old traditions which remained powerful.

In particular, despite the growth of bureaucracies and the importance, in some realms, of institutions representative of various estates, it was still necessary for princes to remember that they were lords among lords, united with their peers in knightly companionage. The most successful royal images remained those unabstracted from an earthly context, in which kings appeared in war, joust, hunt or feast, surrounded by their magnates as natural companions and counsellors.

In thirteenth-century theory, the close collaboration between kings and nobles was expressed in the language of the rediscovered *Politics* of Aristotle as the virtue of 'polity' – the mixture of the advantages of monarchical and aristocratic government – or as the outward form of the 'community of the realm' of which king and other lords were both part: 'head and members of one body politic'. In some 'polities', such as the crown of Aragon or the Holy Roman Empire, subordinate lords or 'princes' claimed to hold their lordships, like the monarch, directly from God. The model, however, which probably made most sense to most people – especially to the laymen of little learning who held most lordships – derived from romances of chivalry, the universally popular station-bookstall pulp-fiction of the age, which provided its heroes and role-models. In metrical versions of their lives, heroes of the kingship

of a pre-chivalric age, including Alexander, Arthur, Pericles and Brutus of Troy, were transformed into exemplars of a chivalric set of values. Even the bible was ransacked for recruits to this essentially secular array of ideals. King David and Judas Maccabeus were ascribed to the ranks of the *Nine Preux* of exemplary chevaliers. Maccabeus appeared in illuminations and wall-paintings as an exponent of the art of jousting. Edward I of England had himself represented as the new Maccabeus on the walls of his state bedchamber, alongside personifications of knightly virtues, such as Equanimity conquering Anger and Largesse slaying Covetousness. Edward III had Arthur's Round Table reproduced at Windsor – the palpable form of the equality of a band of knights. Rituals of jousts and vows and conferment of knightly accolades became the foci of political display in almost every princely and ducal court. The most famous such occasion has also been the most derided – the day of the 'Vow of the Pheasant' at Lille on 17th February 1454, when Philip the Good of Burgundy, who presided over the most sumptuous court, with the most inventive splendours, exacted a crusading oath from banqueters. According to a participant, 'there was a chapel on the table, with a choir in it, a pasty full of flute-players, and a turret from which came the sound of an organ and other music'. Wine sprayed from the breast of the figure of a naked girl, guarded by a lion; the duke was served by representations of an elephant and a two-headed horse ridden by trumpeters. 'Next came a white stag ridden by a young boy who sang marvellously, while the stag accompanied him with the tenor part and next an elephant ... carrying a castle in which sat Holy Church, who made piteous complaint on behalf of Christians persecuted by the Turks.' Yet this was no empty display of conspicuous consumption but a ritual theatre in which the ostentation was meant to strengthen, not undermine, the solemnity of the vow.

Chivalry was a powerful force. It could not, perhaps, make men good, as it was intended to do. It could, however, in contemporary opinions, win wars and mould political relationships. In the 1480s, the monarchs of Castile conquered the Kingdom of Granada by treating the war as a chivalric escapade, 'a beautiful war', in the words of the Venetian ambassador, in which 'all were competing in the conquest of fame ... There was not a lord present who was not enamoured of some one of the ladies of the Queen, and these ladies were not only witnesses to what was done upon the field, but often handed the sallying warriors their weapons, granting them at the same time some favour, together with a request that they show by their deeds how

great was the power of their love ... wherefore one can say that this war was won by love.' The conventional relationship of knight and lady was used in the same reign to smooth over the relationships of a king and queen who had rival claims to supreme political authority. For the queen, chivalric relationships informed the world she imagined as well as the world she knew, and she died with prayers to the Archangel Michael as 'prince of the chivalry of the angels'.

Chivalry could also impel overseas expansion. Lining the walls of the abbey church of Pomposa, almost overlooking the Adriatic, are paintings of the legend of St Eustace, the Roman *eques* or knight supposed to have been converted to Christianity while hunting by a vision of the Cross between the antlers of a stag. His faith was tested by separation from his family in a shipwreck, followed by a long seaborne search, amid many calamities and afflictions. Reunited at last, after humanly unbearable sufferings, they were all martyred together by roasting in a bronze bull. The dramatic possibilities of this story made it a favourite with romanticisers and it hard to say whether some of the many works written in the Eustace tradition belong more properly to the genre of hagiography or that of chivalric romance. Though its relationship to the Eustace tradition is disputed among scholars, a fourteenth-century Spanish work, the *Historia del cavallero Zifar*, tells a similar tale of the hero's search for his lost wife and sons. The transformation of the Roman archetype from knight to saint and back to knight reminds us of the double lives of some of the heroes of early European maritime expansion: of Henry the Navigator, for instance, the explorer's patron who took pride in his chastity and his hair shirt, or of Columbus himself, who affected almost simultaneously the roles of 'a captain of cavaliers and conquests' and of a prophetic, almost priestly figure, clad in a friar's habit.

Of all the protagonists of this type of fiction, the most popular was Amadis of Gaul. Though the original version of his story ended with his tragic death, mistakenly inflicted in a joust by his own son, the best-known text transformed him into a once-and-future hero, like Arthur, Alexander and Charlemagne. Amadis is the personification of every chivalric virtue – a sort of Lancelot with the human weaknesses left out. He does not have to embark on seaborne adventures to find a wife – his Oriana is a princess of the court he serves; but he does have to undertake an Odyssey and endure a demanding series of them before he can be united with her. In a sense, the sea is his proper element, for he was cast adrift at birth to spare his royal but unwed parents from the

shame of an illegitimate child. A great part of his adventures takes the form of island-hopping between isles whose names are strongly reminiscent of the Atlantic toponymy of contemporary charts, where he struggles with enchantment or contends with monsters.

The sea was also an important part of the background of a particular tradition within the Arthurian cycles of tales, which were universally known and loved in late medieval Latin Christendom. A lost but much-mentioned version, well known in the fifteenth century, dealt with Arthur's supposed seaborne adventures and attributed to him the conquests of six western islands as well as of Iceland, Greenland, Norway, Lapland, Russia and the North Pole. The last claim is not as outlandish as it sounds: the belief that a clear-water route led to the Pole was common at the time and a fourteenth-century English friar claimed to have been there at least five times. In a Spanish text of a little before 1476, it was suggested that the enchanted isle where Arthur's body lay might be the island of Brasil, frequently included in maps and actively sought, towards the end of the century, by explorers. As a sense of maritime space opened up on late medieval maps, the chivalric imagination worked to fill it and to inspire its exploration.

Chivalry was probably the main ingredient in Europe's unique culture of expansion which made Christendom's a more dynamic society, more energetic and far-going in exploration and out-thrust than better-equipped neighbours to the east, like Islam and China. Ideology has often been said to have supplied the deficiency of resources: the ideology of crusade or of Reconquest. But ideology commonly influences rhetoric more than deeds and the trend of modern research has been to limit or even eliminate the importance of these traditionally over-emphasised themes. Ethos is more powerful than ideology in shaping behaviour because it supplies individuals with standards by which to adjust and appraise their actions. Not only was chivalry the great unifying aristocratic ethos of the western middle ages, it has continued as a powerful and enduring spur to western actions and self-perceptions ever since. In the nineteenth century, it could still cram Victorian gentlemen creaking into their reproduction armour. In the twentieth, it could still compensate the 'knights of the air' of the Battle of Britain for their generally modest social origins. In the late middle ages it was still strong enough to inspire the vanguard of Europe's overseas expansion, as characters in search of the denouement of their own romance reached out, in projects of commerce or colonisation, without loss of face or caste.

97

London
Court of Henry VIII.
Humanism: visits of Erasmus, 1505-11, to the circle of Thomas More. Eustache Chapuys, Imperial ambassador in London, 1529-44, brings wide range of humanist contacts from Turin.

Florentine sculptor Torrigiano visits England, c. 1511-20. His pupils del Nunziato and Penni naturalised in England, 1537.

Sir Thomas Wyatt travels to Rome in 1527; brings back Italian verse forms Hans Holbein, humanist and portrait painter, visits England 1526-28 and 1532-43; decisively influences English portrait styles.

Renaissance architecture introduced through patronage of Cardinal Wolsey from c. 1529. Nonsuch Palace, begun in 1538, sees introduction of further Italian architectural influences, mediated via Loire.

Brussels
Court of Mary of Hungary.
After Ottoman rout of Hungarians at Mohács in 1526, Mary brings tradition of court of Matthias Corvinus to Brussels: patronises painters and humanists from Basle and Florence. From the 1540s, she forms a large collection of paintings by Titian.

Nuremberg
Civic authorities patronise arts. Dürer travels to Italy c. 1494-5 and to Venice 1505-6. Influenced by engraving, especially of the work of Mantegna in Mantua.
2 Dürer visits the middle Rhine c. 1493
3 Dürer works as an engraver c. 1493
4 Dürer visits the Netherlands 1520-1

Cracow
16th-century court of Sigismund I and II. Marriage of Sigismund 1 to Bona Sforza, 1518 reinforces links with Italy, initiated with the travels of Florentines Berecci and Della Lore to Cracow in 1507, where they begin work on Wawel Castle (completed 1536). Contacts with Italy reinforced by Jagiellonian University: Copernicus studies in Padua.
1 Vilnius becomes site of court of Sigismund II to 1548

Regensburg
Civic and imperial patronage of humanists. German scholar Aventinus has humanist contacts with Milan, Florence and Rome.

Northern Habsburg courtly centres
Prague Court of Anne, wife of Ferdinand I. Letohrádek Palace begun 1538.

Vienna Court of Ferdinand I. Collection of antiquities assembled, especially Roman coins. Scholarship patronised.

Innsbruck 34 Roman busts made or collected for mausoleum of Maximilian I by Jörg Kölderer, c.1540.

Fontainebleau
Court of Francis I.
During Francis's Italian campaign in 1515 he sees "all the best works in Italy"; acquires services of Leonardo and Andrea del Sarto. In Rome, he acquires cast of Laocöon and large collection of casts and bronzes of classical statuary. Francis patronises Florentine artists, e.g. Rosso (1530), Primaticcio (1532) and Cellini (1540). In 1541, Venetian architect Serlio recruited to work at Fontainebleau.

Basle
Humanist printers patronised. Holbein visits Lombardy c.1520? Correspondence of Erasmus and other Basle humanists with Venice, Florence and Rome; trade in engravings.
5 Visits of Erasmus to Brussels and London.

Augsburg
Fugger family patronise arts. 1505, Hans Burgkmair visits Venice and Milan; 1515, Herman and Peter Vischer visit Rome. Stefan Loscher, decorator of Fugger chapel, studies in Italy. Indirect Italian influences on painters Altdorfer and Holbein arrive via engravings; direct Italian influences become strong only with arrival of painter Leoni in 1548.

Toledo
Influence of Andrea Navaggiero, Venetian ambassador 1522-8. Italian verse-forms introduced (1520s) by Boscà and De la Vega (latter exiled to Naples, 1532-6). Classicising Hospital de Tavera built by de Covarrubias, 1541.

Lisbon
Sá de Miranda returns from Italy (1526) with Italian verse forms.

Seville
Classical influences mediated via Toledo and Granada: e.g. classicising tomb of Cardinal Mendoza (1510) and Town Hall by Riaño (1527).

Granada
Close contacts with Italy reflected in classicising buildings: cathedral by de Siloe (1528) and palace of Charles V by Pedro Machuca (1531).

DENMARK
North Sea
LITHUANIA
Vilnius
MOLDAVIA
ENGLAND
Oxford
London
Bruges
Antwerp
Cologne
Brussels
Louvain
Rhine
HOLY
Prague
ROMAN
Elbe
Cracow
Regensburg
Nuremberg
Vienna
Strasbourg
Augsburg
Colmar
Freiburg
EMPIRE
Salzburg
Basle
Innsbruck
Paris
Fontainebleau
Seine
Blois
Loire
50°
FRANCE
Venice
Padua
VENETIAN REPUBLIC
Verona
Milan
Mantua
Ferrara
Lombardy
Parma
Bologna
Turin
PAPAL
Siena
Urbino
Tuscany
Umbria
STATES
Adriatic
Florence
Sea
Rome
Naples
NAPLES
OTTOMAN EMPIRE
Sardinia
Atlantic
Ocean
Bay of Biscay
Ebro
ARAGON
Douro
SPAIN
Balearics
Mediterranean
Sea
Sicily
40°
Toledo
Tagus
PORTUGAL
Lisbon
CASTILE
Seville
Granada

The spread of Renaissance influence from Italy before c.1540

Italian centres of Renaissance influence
- Lombard
- Tuscan and Umbrian
- Venetian
- Neapolitan
- Papal States and Ferrara
- Habsburg courtly centre

Influences on non-Italian centres of Renaissance diffusion
Granada
- Lombard
- Tuscan and Umbrian
- Venetian
- Papal States and Ferrara
- Neapolitan
1 diffusion of Renaissance ideas to other centres in Europe

CHAPTER 6

FROM CHRISTENDOM TO EUROPE

The redefinition of Europe from the Renaissance to the Enlightenment

'I MUST BEGIN WITH EUROPE,' wrote Strabo, 'because it is both varied in form and admirably adapted by nature for the development of excellence in men and governments.' Between the fifteenth century and the eighteenth, that ancient confidence in the reality, cohesion and superiority of Europe was recovered by Europeans. The divisions of Europe did not heal. In some ways, the clashes of religion and the recoil of diverging social trends made them more numerous and worse. Yet the sense of belonging to a European community and sharing a Europe-wide culture became typical of an influential elite. The uniformity of enlightened taste in the eighteenth century made it possible to glide between widely separated frontiers with little more cultural dislocation than a modern traveller feels in a succession of airport lounges. Gibbon – Strabo's devoted reader who made his stepmother send him his copy to study while he was at a militia camp – was mid-way through his *History of the Decline and Fall of the Roman Empire* when he formulated a European idea: 'it is the duty of a patriot to prefer and promote the exclusive interest of his native country: but a philosopher may be permitted to enlarge his views, and to consider Europe as one great republic, whose various inhabitants have attained almost to the same level of politeness and cultivation.'

Like Strabo's, his belief in this common European culture was inseparable from a conviction of European superiority, 'distinguished' – in Gibbon's words – 'above the rest of mankind'. The re-emergence of a concept of Europe was fraught with menace for the world. In the Académie Royale des Sciences in Paris, where in the late seventeenth century Cassini's grand project took shape for an accurate map of the world, compiled from world-wide readings of longitude and latitude, Louis XIV could play a Jove-like role, nodding at a planet spread before him. In increasing self-esteem, Europeans beheld undaunted their unfolding 'great map of mankind'.

It did not happen easily. Like so many ancient notions forgotten or neglected in medieval Christendom, the concept of 'Europe' was rediscovered by late-medieval and early-modern humanists: students, that is, of a 'humane' and predominantly secular curriculum of grammar, rhetoric, poetry, history and moral philosophy, imbibed from classical texts. The use of the term had never entirely died out, but it got an enormous boost from re-discovered texts of Ptolemy and Strabo in the early fifteenth century. 'Europe' was a small item in a vast warehouse of revived terms which helped to stock a revolution in values: the classics as well as – even, in some respects, instead of – Christianity came to inform common ideas of morality, politics and taste. At first a specialised training, an 'alternative' curriculum offered in a few French and north Italian schools to pupils not intended for commerce or the church, humanism became Europe's great seminary

The world at his feet: one of Louis XIV's visits to the Académie Royale des Sciences, engraved by Sébastien Leclerc *right*. The king keenly followed the progress of Jean-Dominique Cassini's project for mapping the world on a grid of lines of longitude and latitude, from readings provided by explorers, merchants and colonial officials.

The spread of the Renaissance from Italy *map left*. The travels of artists and humanist scholars were instrumental in diffusing Italian Renaissance ideas. Royal patronage, such as that of the Habsburg courts and Francis I of France, gave powerful backing to their spread.

of values and most prestigious form of learning. The conquest of Europe by humanism was never complete and took a long time. It was a change so gradual that it is impossible to date with precision its beginning or end, or any decisive moment within it; but a few footprints of increasing depth can be detected along the way in the late middle ages. In the last third of the thirteenth century, Brunetto Latini, who had learned respect for classical models of literature from French writers, introduced the works of Cicero to students of oratory in his native Florence. In Padua and Arezzo, where Petrarch was born in 1304, the lawyers' curriculum began to include the study of classical types of successful rhetoric. Petrarch and Boccaccio, the most admired writers of the mid-fourteenth century, were saturated in pagan literature: Petrarch had a Greek Plato and Boccaccio commissioned a translation of Homer from the original. Humanism appealed to the mobile social world of late medieval Italy, full of rich parvenus disposed to patronise such new trends in moral philosophy as might compensate for their lack of ancient rank. It suited the competitive world of city-state politics in which republicans could exult in the legacy of classical republicanism, while despots mobilised expert rhetoricians for their own propaganda. Popes promoted it in Avignon and Rome, Visconti strong-men in Milan and Pavia, Aragonese kings in Naples and patricians and publishers in Venice.

Florence was an arena of two kinds of fertile rivalry: at the end of the fourteenth century, Milan was attempting to conquer Florence and Florence in its turn to subdue Siena. Meanwhile, within each city, institutions, families and factions contended to accumulate clients and control the state. The Medici established an ascendancy in Florence – but it was always precarious and had to be won and defended against the rivalry of families whose badges and monuments decorate areas and quarters of the city to this day: the name of the Ruccellai blazes from Santa Maria Novella, the emblems of the Albrizzi decorate street corners in their own quarter and the Pazzi Chapel represents an attempt to outdo the Medici in the erection of a family pantheon in classicising taste. Florentine palaces, like those of other urban elites of the period,

are virtual fortresses. At San Gimignano, the 15 towers – survivors of a sometime 72 – glare at one another across the streets. Internecine hatreds had to be deferred, however, when huge projects of civic self-glorification were undertaken in rivalry with other towns. Siena had, in Il Mangia, a tower far higher than any in Florence; but Florence, thanks to Brunelleschi's engineering genius, was eventually able to acquire a cathedral dome more capacious than Siena's. Princes, warlords and merchants invested in art not only for sound commercial reasons but also to display their largesse, show their taste, court popularity and win votes. The rhetoric of humanists could sway masses in vast public spaces designed for civic action, like Florence's Piazza della Signoria;

The Piazza della Signoria of Florence *below* provided a space for the civic rituals of a fiercely republican community, decorated with symbols of resistance to tyranny: the republic's guardian lion, the Marzocco, Donatello's *Judith* and Michelangelo's *David*.

Florence on the eve of the quattrocento, presented to the Virgin *bottom*. The Baptistery is conspicuous near the centre of the composition, with the Palazzo della Signoria behind it and the cathedral before the building of the dome.

The Pazzi chapel *left* shows the community of taste which joined rival patrons of humanist architecture in the Florence of the 1440s. The Pazzi and Medici both endowed chapels for the Franciscans of Santa Croce at this time; the Pazzi's architect, Brunelleschi, based his work on the simple harmonies of square and circle which he had already used under Medici patronage for the old sacristy of the church of San Lorenzo.

As they appear today, the towers of San Gimignano *below left* recall the kind of emulous society that combined competition in art-patronage with outbursts of political violence.

101

the art of painters – which at one level was popular art, paraded through the streets for the admiration of crowds, as well as being daubed directly onto walls – was in part a device for mass communication. The art-revolution we call the Renaissance shows how different the world looked through humanist eyes.

It was the art of sculptors which was first transformed by humanist canons of taste, partly because models of classical sculpture were relatively copious. In 1400, the Cloth Importers' Guild of Florence launched a competition for a new set of bronze doors for the greatest monument in their care: the Baptistery, which, though in fact an eighth-century edifice, purpose-built, was popularly believed to be a genuinely classical building and, in origin, a Temple of Mars. Brunelleschi and Ghiberti were the finalists and both used classical models for their startlingly realistic and dramatic trial plaques depicting the Sacrifice of Isaac. Ghiberti won the commission, perhaps because he was technically more ingenious, using less bronze and therefore cutting the costs.

The technology of bronze casting was developed by experience in

In 1447, in a rare flash of piety, Sigismondo Malatesta decided to rebuild the church of San Francesco at Rimini – the Tempio Malatestiano *below* – on humanist principles with money earned from his contracts as a mercenary. He ran out of funds, however, and, though he resorted to paying off artists with land-grants, it was never finished.

Brunelleschi's *above* **and Ghiberti's** *above far right* trial plaques for the competition for the Baptistery doors both show dramatic flair, determined realism and startling virtuosity in the handling of anatomy. Ghiberti's more classical design – the figure of Isaac owes an obvious debt to Roman models – was successful.

casting cannon: many masters of the Renaissance had sidelines in ordnance or gunnery. Ironically, the increased demand for guns starved art of a vital raw material and even led to the melting down of antique bronzes just at the time when they were most valued as models. From 1425, Ghiberti's second set of Baptistery doors genuinely marked a breakthrough in the power of the bronze relief: 'gates of paradise,' as Michelangelo called them, acquiring the realism of an extra dimension through the use of perspective. In 1440, Donatello, the most assiduous student of surviving classical art in Florence, produced his free-standing bronze David, which, under the form of a sacred subject, seemed to bring a vanished pagan world to life: secular, sensual, homoerotic

In Florentine architecture the scholarly basis of humanist influence was unsound, for neither of the most influential local models – the Baptistery and San Miniato – was genuinely classical. Nor was the 'Gothic' style, against which the architects rebelled, genuinely – as they supposed – an intrusion of 'barbarian' invaders at the time of the fall of the Roman empire. Nevertheless, Brunelleschi's first buildings in the new style – the Ospedale degli Innocenti and the Medici parish church of San Lorenzo, both complete by the end of the first quarter of the century – are unmistakably classical in inspiration. The rediscovery of Vitruvius and the examination of the ruins of the Roman Forum enabled Alberti to produce a more accurate revival of the style in the 1440s in his Tempio Malatestiano at Rimini, built for a patron so brazenly secular in his preferences that he was widely impugned as a pagan. Roman rusticated masonry which survived in aqueducts inspired the finish of palaces like Michelozzo's in Florence for the Medici. Sculptors like Donatello and painters like Masaccio, Piero della Francesca and Mantegna beautified their products with classical architectural

Donatello's David *left*, made in 1440 to stand in the atrium of the Medici palace as an earnest of the family's intention to champion the Florentine republic, represents the absorption of the lessons in classical sculpture the artist learned in Rome in the early 1430s.

A view of 'an ideal city' *below* from the ducal palace at Urbino shows clearly the classical inspiration of Renaissance painters and architects.

settings. Their work sought also to embody subtler values and aesthetic principles elicited from ancient writings about art: symmetry, *sprezzatura* – the basis of the aristocratic cult of apparently effortless superiority – and restraint of taste, the very qualities embodied in the self-image of the writer of the definitive Renaissance handbook of values, *The Book of the Courtier of Baldassare Castiglione.*

While architects and sculptors could imitate surviving relics of the ancient world, the models of painters had disappeared or remained buried under the ashes of Pompeii. The influence of humanism on painting was therefore mediated through the examples of sculpture and architecture. Though secular patronage and the vogue for profane subjects – including portraits, battle scenes, history paintings, mythological episodes and even pagan mysteries – all increased little by little, most commissions to painters were conferred by or for the church. The progress of the art was directed by changes in devotional style and clerical taste. Even Botticelli, who had developed a lucrative line in lewd goddesses painted for raffish philosophers partying in a Medici country villa, was converted to more puritanical subject-matter by the Dominican firebrand, Savonarola, who turned Florence into a 'godly republic' after the Medici Bank collapsed in 1494.

As it happened, the realism and naturalism represented by art in the classical tradition also appealed to late medieval piety. The devotion of the rosary encouraged the faithful to imagine sacred mysteries with the vividness of scenes of everyday life; similarly, the campaigns of the Franciscans to involve ordinary people ever more actively in proceedings in church encouraged the art of Giotto, in which the worshipper is drawn into a crowd of onlookers at a biblical or hagiographical event, painted around the walls of a chapel. The appeal of late medieval preachers to the raw emotions of their audience was enhanced by the availability of visual aids calculated to stir excitement and pity through their lively depictions of the humanity of the inhabitants of heaven. Giotto, whose career flourished in the first third of the fourteenth century, gave his figures a sculptural quality; 100 years later, Masaccio added realistic treatment of space.

Scientific study of perspective made this achievement possible. Brunelleschi, working on the problem of what parts of a building would be exposed or hidden from a particular viewpoint, first demonstrated linear perspective on a panel, now lost, which showed a view of the Baptistery as seen from the west doors of Florence Cathedral. He even provided a mirror so that spectators could agree that his panel and the actual view corresponded exactly. Donatello depicted perspective on carved reliefs, apparently by instinct. It was Alberti, however, who provided fellow-artists with mathematically calculated rules; his definition of a picture as 'a cross-section of the visual rays projecting to the thing observed' only made sense, however, from a single vantage-point; it was an innovation arising from the changing social context of painting, in which individual paintings were beginning to be hung on walls at eye-level instead of being normally confined to wall-paintings or vault-paintings and altarpieces.

In practice, prevailing taste demanded that perspective be used decoratively, without the limitations imposed by strict adherence to the rules. Though later critics singled out hero-artists like Giotto and Masaccio whose work seemed to represent stages in progress towards a realistic ideal, most Renaissance painting continued to reflect the riotous aesthetics of ostentatious patrons. The really popular painters, like Pisanello or Gentile da Fabriano among the contemporaries of Masaccio, or Gozzoli, Uccello, Pinturricchio and Ghirlandaio, composed their pictures like tapestry-cartoonists or manuscript illuminators, to create crowded, rich and strange effects in glowing paintings that were tinglingly expensive, sensually inviting objects, like the contents of spilled jewel-caskets.

Secular patrons, after all, were in the business of buying conspicuous display. Those who were merchants, like the Medici, were keen on value for money and money was evoked more by lavish use of gold leaf and lapis lazuli than by intellectual preferences for mathematics and monumental simplicity. The Medici Chapel painted by Gozzoli is closer in feel to a Gothic painted manuscript than to the Renaissance ideal. Medici piety shaded into self-glorification as

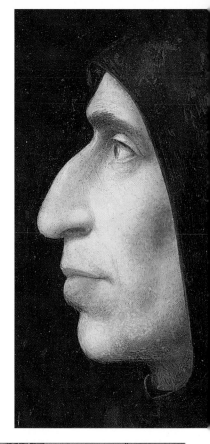

Bartolomeo della Porta's portrait *right* of Savonarola, the Dominican friar who inspired and, in effect, led the 'godly republic' established in Florence from 1494 to 1498 – characterised by puritanical sumptuary laws, 'bonfires of vanities', hellfire preaching and the propagation of an intensely personal, penitential and meditative style of devotion which anticipated aspects of the Reformation.

Savagery domesticated by wisdom: Botticelli's humanist allegory of Minerva and the Centaur of c. 1480 *below* was probably painted for Lorenzo di Pierfrancesco de' Medici, whose Platonist 'Academy' generated a demand for pagan, and sometimes erotic subjects, dignified by symbolic meaning.

Pinturrichio's characteristically lavish depiction of the coronation of Pope Pius III in 1503 *opposite page*, described by Vasari as 'Painted with the most fine and lively colours, executed with various gold ornaments and splendidly devised compartments.'

PIVS·III·SENEÑ·PII·II·NEPAÑ
M·D·III·SEPTEMBR·XXI·
APERTELECTVS·SVFFRAG·
VIII·OCTOBR·CORONATVSEST

Botticelli and Ghirlandaio, too, painted portraits of members of the family into sacred scenes. The Medici have a great reputation as vital patrons of Renaissance art, but they spent far more on jewels and antique gems, which represented sound investments, than they did on new work. As collectors of classical bric-a-brac, which lined the atrium of their palace, they were acting, in a sense, like medieval relic-collectors, amassing objects of power and influence. Yet from these antiques – including some forged by sculptors for profit – they developed an interest in the pagan world that was stimulated by humanist scholars. Venus, Cupid or the Three Graces – subjects Botticelli painted for the raffish villa society over which Lorenzo di Pierfrancesco de' Medici presided – could be enjoyed as titillating excitants or interpreted as Platonist allegories. Mythological themes were favoured because they involved drawing from the nude and also because they illustrated the types of virtue explored by the moral philosophy of the humanists. In Florence, the Renaissance was a minority movement and the fifteenth century closed with a puritanical reaction against these pagan and erotic trends. But history is influenced less by the reality of events than by the way they are perceived. Reputation made Florence the hub from which Renaissance influence radiated. By the time of Savonarola's revolution, it was already too late to check the rise of humanism.

The Renaissance could not have happened without cultural cross-fertilisation from outside Italy. Humanism borrowed from a living tradition of French Italian schools; scholarship in classical Greek benefited from the contributions of Byzantine exiles; classical texts were improved by manuscripts culled from northern libraries, like the precious haul Poggio Bracciolini found at St Gall. Florentine quattrocento painters, like their counterparts in other parts of Europe, learnt from the art of the Burgundian dominions – Flemish painting and Dijonnais sculpture. By the early sixteenth century, some of the leading figures in Christian humanism came from the Netherlands, England, Germany and Spain. Still, northern Italy, and especially Florence, became the heartland of the Renaissance from which it spread to the rest of Europe. From here architects and engineers travelled to Moscow in the 1470s and sculptors, shortly afterwards, to make the tombs of English and Spanish monarchs. Hither came Spanish and German painters to perfect their craft. There was a huge explosion of influence in the late 1530s and early 1540s, when the sonnet-form, which Petrarch had

In 1528, Diego de Siloé took over the planning of Granada Cathedral *left* and created a humanist interior, suitable for lay participation in the mass – white, light-filled, with a central altar and a sanctuary visible from all around the building.

Francis I of France, depicted on horseback *below* in a tradition derived from the equestrian statue of Marcus Aurelius (*see* page 47).

El Greco's plan of Toledo *bottom left* abstracts the exemplary Renaissance building, the Hospital de Tavera, and places it on a cloud in the foreground.

This detail of the *Three Graces right* from Botticelli's *La Primavera* betrays the interest of rich patrons such as the Medici in the pagan world of the classics.

The chateau of Chambord on the Loire, built for Francis I by Domenico Cortona *bottom*.

invented, became a favourite form of verse all over western Europe. At about the same time, Francis I of France, who had summoned Leonardo da Vinci to his court, began to amass a collection of classical sculpture; and palaces, hospitals and domestic interiors resembling those of Florence sprang up in Toledo, Cornwall, Northamptonshire and the Loire.

Techniques of study developed within the humanist tradition had a transforming effect on elite religion all over Europe. Textual scholarship, historical scrutiny and philological analysis had improved the texts and enhanced readers' understanding of classical literature; the same tools were soon being used to dig over the Fathers, the Bible and ecclesiastical tradition. In 1440 Lorenzo Valla demonstrated the fraudulent origins of the Donation of Constantine – on the basis of which rested part of the papacy's claim to temporal authority – by showing that its language was of a later vintage than its pretended date. Ambrogio Traversari had already begun to produce texts of the Fathers on the same line as humanists' editions of the classics. Scrutinised by scholarship which was philologically informed and historically sensitive, even the Bible began to look different. By the early sixteenth century, it was apparent to scholars that the traditional western text of the Bible was seriously warped by partial or inaccurate translations. In particular, there were glaring differences between the apostolic church, as depicted in the bible, the early church portrayed by the Fathers and the state to which the church had evolved.

The new aesthetic of 'Renaissance' church architecture was in part a reflection of changing secular taste – but it was also, at a deeper level, the result of an attempt to create a setting for the kind of devotion which humanism inspired and Bible-study endorsed, with open sanctuaries, brilliantly lighted and approached through wide naves and aisles. Poets who scoured the reign of Augustus for models and churchmen

107

who looked back to the time of Christ shared the same perspective and the same view. Both beheld, with a sense of renewal and a commitment to revival, the 'age of Astraea', when Virgil was said to have prophesied the imminence of the incarnation. Symbiotic fusions of Christianity with classical philosophy became popular as perhaps never before since the fourth century, when Christianity conquered the elite of the Roman empire and, in the course of the process, was re-expressed in the language of the pagan schools. 'Christian Platonism' and 'Christian stoicism' were characteristic intellectual fashions of the period and 'the philosophy of Christ', from the early sixteenth century, was a current term. The spirit of these schools infused art. Cellini's *Crucifixion* expresses serene stoicism, rather than the searing suffering depicted by earlier and later sculptors. In Michelangelo's *Captives*, the living forms seem to emerge from the rock, like Platonic universals from the coarse particularity of sublunar matter. Among the Faustian avant-garde in late fifteenth-century Florence, from where it spread all over Europe, there even began a tradition of 'Hermeticism', which tried to trump the classical antiquarianism of the Renaissance by tracing an esoteric, mystical and even magical form of gnosis beyond Greek antiquity to a bogus origin in the supposed wisdom of the ancient Egyptians.

According to a common and helpful oversimplification, humanism had to contend with a traditional, 'scholastic' curriculum that made theology the 'queen of the sciences', assigned the supreme place to logic in the search for truth and advanced by 'standing on the shoulders of giants' or climbing timidly up the rock-face of petrified traditions and fossilised authorities. In reality, most of the famous conflicts between humanism and scholasticism turn out, on close examination, cases at worst of uneasy collaboration or even stormy marriage. Bruni's controversy with Alonso de Cartagena over the translation of Aristotle was, by repute, an encounter between 'old' and 'new' learning; but it more closely resembled a dispute between scholars equally committed to using a variety of techniques to elucidate the text. Luther's quarrel with the Church was represented by some of his admirers as grounded in differences between humanist and traditionalist readings of the Bible; yet Luther's own mind had hardly adjusted to the lessons of humanism and humanists and scholiasts were numerous in all the hostile camps of the Reformation debates. While universities in the Protestant world retained barely reformed curricula, Jesuit schools in the late sixteenth century became exemplary nurseries of humanism. That great patron of printing, Cardinal Cisneros, paid fortunes to promote humanist scholarship, including critical work on the text of the Bible more rigorous in its way than that of Erasmus, but he also published copious editions of standard scholastic textbooks. The famous confrontation at Valladolid in 1550 – over the status of the indigenous subjects of Spanish imperialism in the New World – could be seen as the clash of traditional Dominican learning, with its respect for the rights of man, against new-fangled humanist attempts to apply a classical notion of slavery to hapless victims; in reality, however, the Dominican controversialist, Bartolomé de Las Casas, within a framework of traditional exposition, marshalled almost as much humanist material as his adversary and his conclusions, which set native American society in the context of a universal theory of development, showed a sensitivity to historical change which is one of the hallmarks of humanist historiography.

Humanism and scholasticism should be seen less as mutually hostile war-bands than as compatible, cross-fertilised and convergent traditions, which, between them, created the common culture of early modern Europe. The seventeenth-century thinkers in whose work that culture took shape were all influenced by both backgrounds. Descartes – pursuing the ideal of *sprezzatura* – claimed rarely to rise before twelve and more rarely still to alloy his brilliance by reading other men's work; in fact he was an assiduous reader of Thomas Aquinas and one of his proofs of the existence of God, which he claimed to think was original, bears an uncanny resemblance to the work of St Anselm. The writings of Spinoza are clogged with almost unreadable logical demonstrations which would not have been out of place in the work of a high-medieval theologian. Leibniz had so much reverence for tradition that he shelved his pioneering work on

mathematical logic because it seemed to contradict Aristotle. Newton showed himself the child of humanist tradition in his supple Latin and free mind but his work on Biblical chronology might have been wrenched by a time-warp from an earlier century.

By the time Newton was dead, the symbiosis of humanism and scholasticism had helped to form the distinctive pan-European culture of the eighteenth century. Its essential ingredients, Reason and Doubt, were evolutions from or reactions against the scholastic priorities, Logic and Authority. They were brought together in Descartes' maxim, 'I think therefore I am', which made doubt the key to the only possible certainty. Striving to escape from the suspicion that all appearances are delusive, Descartes reasoned that the reality of his mind was proved by its own self-doubts. Thought proceeding from such a conviction was bound to be subjective and political and social prescriptions developed from such a starting-point tended to be individualistic. While organic notions of society and the state never disappeared from Europe, it remains true that, by comparison with other civilisations, Europe has been the home of individualism and never more so than in the eighteenth century, which produced laissez-faire economics and the doctrine of human rights. Determinism remained attractive to

Inspired by the classics and by more recent views of the south such as this seventeenth-century view of a port *below*, in the late eighteenth century, the Grand Tour became a common educational pastime for aristocratic Englishmen.

Pinturrichio's scenes from Egyptian mythology for the Borgia appartments in the Vatican in the 1490s – like this *above* of the worship of Apis, the divine bull implicitly identified with the heraldic bull of the Borgias – show Renaissance interest in Egypt as an alternative source of wisdom to that of the classics.

The *Crucifixion left*, made by Cellini for his own tomb, was appropriated by the Medici dukes of Tuscany and presented by one of them to Philip II, who was said to have been disappointed by its stark nudity; but his objection was rather to the humanist restraint which inhibited the artist from depicting Christ's suffering intensely.

Michelangelo began to make sculptures on the theme of captives for the tomb of Pope Julius II in about 1512; but those he produced in the 1520s, such as this example *left below*, seem deliberately rough-hewn, imprisoned in the rock.

The medieval tradition of the artist as an almost priestly figure, interpreting the ways of God to man and achieving privileged access to sanctity, is represented by the illuminator William de Brailles of Oxford, in the lower right lunette of this Judgement scene of about the 1230s *below*.

constructors of world-systems: Spinoza implicitly denied free will and Leibniz eliminated it from his secret thoughts; but it became a marginalised heresy in an age which made freedom its highest value among a strictly limited range of 'self-evident truths'.

The march of freedom is illustrated in nothing so much as in the emancipation of art. Medieval artists, in the upper ranks of their profession, were by no means the humble artisans they are commonly supposed to have been: Walter de Brailles in the thirteenth century painted himself in the artist's sacral role as a communicator of heavenly truths to men. Great artists died in the odour of sanctity. By elevating art to the level of philosophy, however, and skill to a qualification for ennoblement, the Renaissance made a difference. Titian could be a Count of the Empire, Velázquez a knight of Santiago. Raphael toured Rome in a carriage attended by flunkies. El Greco moved into the former palace of a marquess. Michelangelo's godlike creativity empowered him to dictate taste to popes and inspired Vasari to sanctify artists by treating them as subjects of biography, which had formerly been the preserve of saints and heroes. By the eighteenth century, art was beyond the need of self-justification: art was 'for art's sake'. Even painters of ordinary talent could be remarkably free of patronly tyranny. Although, for reasons we shall come to in a moment, many artists working for hereditary masters in eastern European royal and aristocratic households were condemned to servile status, in no part of Europe was the cry, 'Elargissez l'art!' unheard. In the 1760s, Bernardo Bellotto, working in Poland, painted a self-advertisement in which he cuts a portly, well-dressed figure under a quotation from Horace proclaiming the absolute liberty of the artist.

Like every culture, that of the eighteenth-century European elite had its uniform art and its characteristic rituals. The artistic canon was classical. Every departure was a development or a reaction, with classical models as its starting-point; every revolution was followed by a neo-classical revival – and has continued to be so down to our own times. Baroque art represented, for instance, a revulsion from Renaissance classicism with its static restraint, its reverence for symmetry and its insistence on the closed perfection of the circle; baroque artists substituted the aesthetic of an imperfect pearl, the appeal of interesting imbalance, and the sinewy, sinuous striving of the spiral. It was a magnificent interlude, but theorists like Winckelmann – the cobbler's son who published his *History of Ancient Art* in 1763-4 – soon recalled artists to their duty.

The rituals this art illustrated and adorned served to spread classical taste and cement the solidarity of the European elite. None was more effective than travel. A broad corridor from Paris and Amsterdam to Venice and Rome became the most visited part of Europe, from where Dutch and Venetian examples of republicanism, toleration and political liberty could be spread, along with Parisian fashions in literature and Roman standards of taste. No route was more ritualised than that which turned the English elite from insularity to cosmopolitanism. 'A man who has not been in Italy,' said Dr Johnson, 'is always conscious of an inferiority from his not having seen what it is expected a man should see.' To fulfil this social qualification, tourists endured the tedium of waiting in Channel ports for suitable winds and stormy passages, sometimes of up to 36 hours. Fearful of the rumoured bad food aboard, they carried 'as many fowls, tongues, pastry and liquors as would victual a ship for a month's voyage.'

By public mails or private coach, the way led through Paris to Chalon, whence Lyon could be reached by boat. 'The one great inconvenience' was 'the want of a necessary, which may be supplied by a portable closed stool.' From there you would be carried by chair across the Var, the guides testing the shifting sands for a safe place. The Alpine passes were unfit for carriages, until the Turin carriage-road was opened in the 1780s. Meanwhile, you went up by mule and were whisked down at frightening speed by chatty porters bearing a flimsy sedan with a cord for a foot-rest. Then good roads resumed along the common tourist routes as far as Rome and on to Naples. But no traveller careful of his health would go beyond Rome in summer.

It was claimed in 1786 that English tourists spent over a million pounds a year in Paris alone. 'I would by no means be extravagant,' wrote Boswell, typically, on setting out in 1764, 'I would only travel genteelly.' 'The sum generally allowed for persons travelling with an equipage' in the 1780s was £150 a month. Bankers arranged for drafts on foreign counterparts, or issued bills of exchange which were rarely honoured until, late in the century, bankers created networks of guarantors that made these bills almost as serviceable as modern credit cards. Fleecing was a common hazard. Mr Rolle, overcharged in Lucerne in 1785 'could only revenge himself by swearing heartily in English.' A 'Dutch Bill' was typified by the mark-up of 500 per cent paid by Dr Zachary Grey for a dinner of duck and wine in Rotterdam in 1786.

Though travel *en famille* was common, the biggest class of tourists was formed by young gentlemen travelling with their tutors or 'bearleaders' to learn about art and languages. Many, however, 'acquired only the languages necessary for entertaining the fair' and a supply of condoms was an essential part of the baggage. British-made condoms were said to be so superior that Louis XV ordered his own supply. When health failed, tourists favoured English doctors, like Metcalfe of Naples, who 'would have prescribed Madeira and roast veal when his pulse beat 120 to the minute.'

Other common hazards were represented by gambling sharks, art forgers and the seductions of Catholicism, which was thought to be subversive and unpatriotic. Fox Lane in Turin in 1785 'from an infatuated complaisance ... changed his religion, or, rather for the first time adopted one.' Lady Harcourt warned her son in Rome against 'kissing the holy toe ... A great Jacobite is not far from being a very good Catholic.' Like their less aristocratic descendants, English tourists of the time had a reputation for drunken brawling: they were accused, among other things, of urinating on the senate-house of Lucca and barring the doors of the Cordeliers Church in Paris. Being still few in number – 40,000 a year, according to an estimate of the 1780s – and always well connected, they could invoke the protection of overworked diplomats. The envoy in Dresden in 1769 complained of 'an inundation of English' who 'have nearly eaten me out of house and home.'

The elite also had characteristic domestic rituals. For the guardians of high culture, critical scholarship was derived from humanist technique; scientific experiment had been learned from Aristotle and from the laborious writings of Renaissance magi. Accessible to all who could afford a little leisure was 'politeness'. The term expressed the distance by which civilisation was removed from savagery: a self-celebratory code of composure that amounted, in practice, to a long-lived obsession with etiquette, linking the world of the Duc de Saint-Simon to that of Mr Pooter, in which the gestures and actions and movements of men had the harmony and predictability of clockwork, with a regularity enhanced in beauty for being freely espoused. Painters visited rich homes to record the small triumphs of taste – tea table, Latin lesson and musical soiree.

The tic-toc of conventional behaviour had its place in a virtually identical image of an ordered universe, which almost every educated person in eighteenth-century Europe shared. In 1543 a Polish astronomer on his deathbed received the first printing of his great book on the revolutions of the heavens: but Copernicus's theories were formulated tentatively, propagated discreetly and spread slowly. The shift of focus from the earth to the sun was a strain on eyes adjusted to a self-centred galactic outlook. Heliocentrism reached the syllabus of no university except that of Salamanca, where there is no record of any student opting to study it. Still, refined and vindicated by seventeenth-century astronomers, the tradition started by Copernicus gradually re-moulded men's vision of the cosmos. It expanded the limits of the observable heavens, substituted a dynamic for a static system and wrenched the perceived universe into a new shape around the elliptical paths of the planets. In a bout of furious thinking and experimenting, beginning in the mid-1660s, Newton seemed to discover the underlying, permeating 'secret' of the universe, which had eluded the Renaissance magi. He imagined the cosmos as a mechanical contrivance – like the wind-up orreries, in brass and gleaming wood, that became popular toys for gentlemen's libraries. It was tuned by a celestial engineer and turned and stabilised by an ubiquitous force, observable in the swing of a pendulum or the fall of an apple, as well as in the motions of moons and planets.

As well as belonging to a tradition, his work was both genuinely pioneering and embedded in a broader context of English and Scottish thought of the time: empiricism – the doctrine that reality is observable and verifiable by sense-perception. The universe consisted of events 'cemented' by causation, of which Newton found a scientific description and exposed the laws. In the praise of a great poet sparing with praise, 'God said, "Let Newton be!" And all was light.' It turned out to be an act of divine self-effacement. Deism throve in the eighteenth century in Europe, partly because the mechanical universe could dispense with the clockmaker after He had given it its initial winding.

An early depiction of the solar system *below* by Kepler, before he improved on the view of Copernicus that the planets revolved in elliptical orbits around the sun. The reduction of the mysteries of planetary motion to a series of mechanical principles and equations was one of the preoccupations and triumphs of sixteenth- and seventeenth-century science.

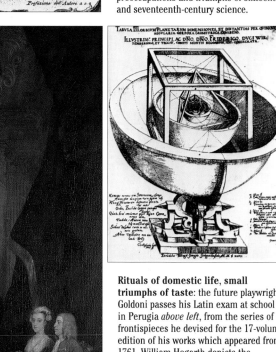

Rituals of domestic life, small triumphs of taste: the future playwright Goldoni passes his Latin exam at school in Perugia *above left*, from the series of frontispieces he devised for the 17-volume edition of his works which appeared from 1761. William Hogarth depicts the Wollaston family at tea in their classical drawing-room in 1730 *left*.

By the end of the century, Pierre-Simon Laplace, who had formulated ways of interpreting almost every known phenomenon of the physical world – broken down into the attraction and repulsion of particles – could boast that he had reduced God to an unnecessary hypothesis.

Wherever it appeared, humanism served – and, in part at least, caused – changing values. Its effects reached everywhere, but on elite self-perceptions they could vary from place to place, against the variegated backgrounds of the fragmented Christendom described in the previous chapter, and, in particular, against a growing east-west divide. From the fifteenth century, an economic fissure opened between the eastern and western lands of Latin Christendom. The line of the Elbe and Upper Danube became a cultural fault. In the west, the effects of demographic decline in the late middle ages were to diversify forms of tenure, liberate peasants and convert arable land to pasture. In the east, which gradually replaced the Mediterranean as Europe's great granary, serfdom was enforced and extended, although in parts of the Middle Mark of Brandenburg depopulation was so acute that noble proprietors took to the plough themselves. Even free towns, in what are now Poland, eastern Germany, the Czech Republic and Hungary, lost their rights of jurisdiction, on a massive scale, to aristocratic or princely litigants and usurpers. Duke Casimir of Pomerania, for instance, encountered 'ferocity like the Hussites' when he sought to enforce the taxes of Stettin in 1428: the ringleaders' bones were crushed and a castle raised to tower above the town. When the Margrave Frederick of Brandenburg came to power in 1440, he withheld the traditional vow to the saints when confirming the privileges of Berlin. In following years, he appeared in arms at the gates, seized the keys, appropriated the town hall and began to build a formidable, overawing castle. The citizens responded by undermining the foundations, breaking the doors and burning the archives. The threat of arms was enough to reduce them to submission: Frederick subjected the city to total control, appointing its aldermen, creaming its revenues and disposing at will of individual citizens' property.

The economic and social divergence of east from west seems to have been accompanied by a divergence of ethos. Hard times in the late medieval west were times of economic opportunity for those with the skill or luck to exploit them. High mortality created gaps in the elites. Government was revolutionised in the fourteenth century by the use of paper, which made the commands of princes cheaply and speedily transmissible to the furthest corners of every state: the consequent bureaucratisation added another avenue of social advancement to the traditional routes via the church, war and commerce. The magnate ranks of most western countries were almost entirely replaced with new men in the course of the fourteenth and fifteenth centuries. To suit their self-perceptions, western moralists embarked on the redefinition of nobility. 'Only virtue is true nobility,' proclaimed a Venetian patrician's coat of arms. A Parisian academic in 1306 declared that 'intellectual vigour' equipped a man best for power over others. A German mystic a few years later dismissed carnal nobility, among qualifications for office, as inferior to the 'nobility of soul'. 'Letters,' according to a Spanish humanist of the fifteenth century, ennobled a man more thoroughly than 'arms'. Gian Galeazzo Visconti, the strong-arm man who seized Milan in 1395, could be flattered by an inapposite comparison with the exemplary self-made hero of humanists, Cicero. Antonio de Ferrariis, a humanist of Otranto who defended the authenticity of the Donation of Constantine and whose very obscurity is a guarantee that he was typical, declared that neither the wealth of Croesus nor the antiquity of Priam's blood could substitute reason as the prime ingredient of nobility.

In eastern Europe, these re-evaluations were hardly heard. For Ctibor of Cimburk, Chancellor of the Kingdom of Bohemia, nobility was divinely apportioned and signified exclusively by right of blood. This was what his audience wanted to hear in Bohemia, where the traditional aristocracy had subordinated the throne, pillaged the church, burdened the peasants and emasculated the towns. East of the Bohemian forest, nobility was ancient blood, and that was that. In the neighbouring kingdom of Hungary, the similar views of István Werboczy became enshrined in what remained the standard textbook of law until the nineteenth century. Werboczy, though technically of noble birth, was really more typical of the 'novi homines' elevated by education and oratorical skill; in the 1490s he led the lower nobility in a campaign to participate in political decisions; in 1516 he became effectively the Chief Justice of the kingdom; by 1525, almost on the eve of the obliteration of the realm by Turkish conquest, he was the most powerful man in Hungary. His *Opus Tripartitum* encapsulates all the prejudices of his life: suspicion of godless magnates, contempt for bestial peasants, hatred of foreigners and heretics. His theory of a homogeneous aristocracy was a device to evade the shame of his own modest background. Only the nobles constituted the nation: their privileges were justified by their presumed descent from Huns and Scythians, whose rights in Hungary were rights of conquest. The exclusion of other classes from the political nation was likewise a consequence of disgraceful ancestry, from natural slaves whose inferiority was attested by their submission or from malefactors derogated for their crimes. Werboczy did admit that the caste could be renewed or expanded at the margins in ways that showed the influence of humanism on his thought. 'True Nobility,' he wrote, 'is acquired by the exercise of martial discipline and other virtues and gifts of mind and body.' It could be conferred by the grace of the prince or lawful adoption or begotten of a noble father out of an ignoble mother. It could arise from great possessions conquered by arms or 'acquired through learning'. But these were all mechanisms for strengthening a caste – not, as in the thought of western humanists, methods of opening up an estate.

This bifurcation of Europe had important consequences. The term 'eastern Europe' has come to have a pejorative sense in the west, denoting a laggard land of arrested social development, held back during a protracted 'feudal age' and defined not by the prevalence of orthodoxy but by an under-evolved social structure, with a servile peasantry and a tightly closed elite. In some ways, however, eastern and western Europe were brought closer together in the sixteenth and seventeenth centuries: physically closer by the improvement of communications; even, in a sense, culturally closer, because, as we shall see in the next chapter, orthodox Christianity grew more like that of the west – in the latter's Catholic and Protestant forms alike. Above all, east and west seemed to get relatively closer in the context of an enormously expanded world perspective. This started even before European maritime expansion began the piecing-together of a realistic world map. A sense of the vastness of the world began to come through first, especially in the threatened and beleaguered Christendom of the late middle ages, huddling under the menace of the Turks. The Council of Florence of 1439, for instance, had in part the character of an ecumenical conference, at which representatives of the Greek and Latin churches agreed to settle their differences in order to unite against the Turks, and in part the character of a geographical congress, in which information and speculations about the nature and extent of the world were exchanged between scholars. The optimism of the Council proved delusive – the schism remained unhealed, the advances of the Turks continued and Europe beyond the Danube and the Aegean did not feel free of Turkish pressure until the relief of Vienna in 1683, or even the Treaty of Passarowitz in 1718. While changing perceptions of the globe made people at either end of Europe feel closer to each other, a sense of having to emulate rival civilisations in a global struggle helped – without easing internal conflicts – to encourage a common self-perception.

On the eastern and northern frontiers, Europe was extended by mind-stretching experience of exploration, colonisation and the spread of the gradually emerging European culture and consciousness. When Sigmund von Herberstein visited the court of Muscovy as ambassador of the Empire in 1517, Russia was already an eye-catching giant of an empire, which during the previous century had outpaced every other state in the world in growth. As Herberstein tried to assess its true extent, its edges seemed to fade into fable; he doubted the reliability of his Russian itinerary, with its exotic description of the attributes of the River Ob – 'such as men being dumb, dying and coming to life again, the Golden Old Woman, men of monstrous shape, and fishes having the appearance of men.' By early in the second half of the century, the Volga had become a Russian river. The entire route for the products of

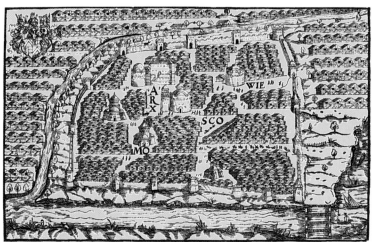

the north to the Caspian was under a single political authority. It was therefore remarkably fortuitous that in 1553, at the opposite end of the great Russian river-system, on the shores of the White Sea, by the mouth of the Northern Dvina, a 'discovery of the kingdom of Muscovy' should have been made by merchant venturers who were able to put the Volga valley in direct touch with their own native kingdom of England. Richard Chancellor was the navigator appointed to take an expedition from London to Cathay around the north of Russia by a putative route. His companion ships were lost in a storm but, according to his own account, 'Master Chancellor held on his course towards that unknown part of the world, and sailed so far, that he came at last to the place where he found no night at all, but a continual light and brightness of the sun shining clearly upon the huge and mighty sea. At length it pleased God to bring them into a certain great bay, whereinto they entered.' The inhabitants received him almost as the natives of the Bahamas treated Columbus, caught between awe and fear, prostrating themselves and kissing his feet. This was every bit as much a new discovery as that of Columbus, for it was an exploitable route, previously unknown, between mutually useful economies. The

growth of the Muscovite state progressively enhanced its importance and increased the scope of the English commerce that now began to approach Russia and Asia through the White Sea. Tsars entertained English merchants with personal embraces and dinners off gold plates, for they had opened the only outlet to the world's seas Russia would have until the eighteenth century.

It was not enough for frontier regions to be 'discovered' by the rest of Europe. To be full partakers of European identity their inhabitants had to embrace the emerging European culture. In 1650, for instance, in the jerry-built piazza in front of the royal palace in Stockholm, workmen were straining to complete the erection of a stupendous edifice in time for an imminent coronation. Vast planks of wood were hoisted aright, until they dwarfed the surrounding buildings; great expanses of canvas cloth were stretched over them and stuck down with arcane confections of resin and gum. Then the whole contraption was painted in *trompe l'oeil* to resemble stone, smothered with mock inscriptions, cofferings, medallions, Corinthian columns and fluted pilasters, and finally surmounted with 24 vast statues of the classical virtues personified, hewn of wood but again painted to look like stone. The result was a great triumphal arch of classical inspiration, which brought to this cold northern burg something of the wealth and warmth of Rome. It symbolised the policy of the young Queen of Sweden, Christina, who hoped to capture the essence of Mediterranean civilisation and transplant it, with transforming effect, into her distant kingdom. No expense was spared: the glues alone which held the arch rather precariously together cost 8,000 Swedish pounds. At the queen's *joyeuse entrée* it would accommodate the most glittering procession Stockholm had ever witnessed.

This auspicious aperture was not built to endure. But it outlasted Christina's reign. She tore through Swedish history like a ferocious sirocco, a wind from the south, revolutionising Sweden's constitution and culture before suddenly – as it seemed – changing her allegiance, embracing Catholicism and retiring to Rome to savour a civilisation and religion she esteemed more highly than those of her homeland.

Christina was not just another northern tourist seduced by the warm south. Her transformation of her country was part of a trend of her time – a tugging and wrenching at Europe's cultural frontiers northward and eastward to embrace Sweden, in her reign, and, shortly afterwards, the Russia of Peter the Great. It was an 'information revolution' – a transfer of technology as well as a transplantation of fashion and taste. Christina used her personal prestige and military clout to borrow or loot the best minds, books and techniques from countries to her south and west. The glorious art collections of the Bavarian elector and the Emperor of the Reich disappeared comprehensively on northbound barges to enrich a palace where there had formerly been only one picture. A great library was created with the same sudden voracity. The queen's self-image is best expressed in a painting in Versailles, in which she chats with Descartes and other savants of European reputation, with an armillary sphere at her feet. A similar transforming trick was effected in Sweden's hostile neighbour, Russia, with even greater urgency, on a vastly wider scale, by Peter the Great.

He was a restless, convulsively moody character – sleepless, like Justinian, jerky, like Olivares; unable to restrain his appetites or contain his energy. He kept his courtiers awake all night in joyless heavy-drinking and played humiliating pranks on bishops and ambassadors. He married a barmaid and put his heir to death. He made caprice an instrument of state. His reforms were so comprehensive – amounting to an empire-wide re-design – that they seem like his supreme act of flight from a past repudiated with a passion that transcended sanity. No project was too daunting, no detail too insignificant. He re-sited the capital, re-drafted the alphabet and re-modelled the aristocracy's facial hair. The same compulsive escapism, the same hectic evasion, inspired, perhaps, the two great journeys he made, incognito, to western Europe to learn western ways. Preachers called him the 'sculptor' and 'architect' of Russia, re-sketching and re-moulding the country in an image of his own devising, just as he did with the Peterhof Palace, for which he drew his own plans, and the palace furniture, which he carved with his own hands.

The entree of Queen Christina into Stockholm for her coronation, flanked by some of the virtues whose statues adorned her triumphal arch, engraved by Wolfgang Hartman in 1650 *above left.*

The Kremlin of Moscow in an engraving made to illustrate the 1581 edition of Sigmund von Herberstein's account of his embassies to Muscovy *left.* The walls built by Fioravanti are clearly visible and a city of wooden houses, regularly arrayed, stretches into the distance.

The mathematician and philosopher Descartes conducts a demonstration to the court of Queen Christina of Sweden, after a painting by Dumesnil of about 1700 *below.*

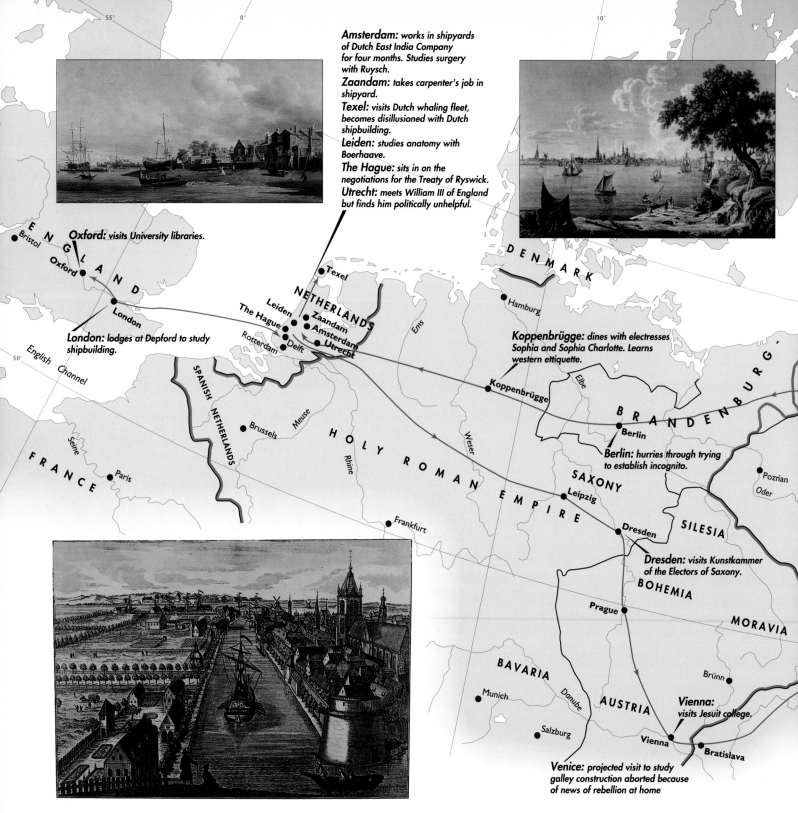

Amsterdam: works in shipyards of Dutch East India Company for four months. Studies surgery with Ruysch.

Zaandam: takes carpenter's job in shipyard.

Texel: visits Dutch whaling fleet, becomes disillusioned with Dutch shipbuilding.

Leiden: studies anatomy with Boerhaave.

The Hague: sits in on the negotiations for the Treaty of Ryswick.

Utrecht: meets William III of England but finds him politically unhelpful.

Oxford: visits University libraries.

London: lodges at Depford to study shipbuilding.

Koppenbrügge: dines with electresses Sophia and Sophia Charlotte. Learns western ettiquette.

Berlin: hurries through trying to establish incognito.

Dresden: visits Kunstkammer of the Electors of Saxony.

Vienna: visits Jesuit college.

Venice: projected visit to study galley construction aborted because of news of rebellion at home

Peter did not quite shake off the past, for all his shuddering and twitching. He behaved, from one perspective, like a traditional Russian autocrat, enforcing obedience by the arbitrary exercise of terror or conjuring it up by the magic of a tsar's mystique. But, like the institutions he promoted, the techniques he taught and the foreign experts he patronised, the self-image he worked at was western, down to the whiskers, 'clipped like a cat's' that contend for elegance, in his surviving portraits, against his blubbery lips and thyroidal eyes. His role-models were foreign. He aimed to be the 'Romulus and Numa' of his country. He appeared in engravings in Roman tradition, baton-wielding on a rearing horse, with the style of 'Imperator' transcribed in Russian characters. On his coins he wore a laurel crown and bore Augustus's title, 'Father of the Fatherland'. He seriously considered making Dutch the official language of his court. He was admired in the west: he became an honorary Danish admiral and a member of the French Academy of Sciences. But the Old Believers refused to use his

Peter the Great's reforms left the beards of the clergy and peasantry intact; the humiliation of the boyar at the barber's hands seems to have titillated the artist of this popular engraving *left*.

The Apotheosis of Tsar Peter the Great depicted by an unknown artist *top far right*.

The travels of Peter the Great *map above* took him to many of the courtly, cultural and craft centres of Europe, including Deptford *top left*, Delft *above left*, Dresden *right* and Riga *top*.

Ventspils: frustrated by bad weather from continuing by sea.

Riga: examines fortifications with an eye to future conquest.

Königsberg: interview with Elector Frederick (the future Frederick I of Prussia). Studies ballistics with von Sternfeld.

Moscow: departs 20th March 1697, returns 5th September 1698.

Cracow: visits University.

The travels of Peter the Great, 1697-98

→ route of Peter the Great

━━━ Holy Roman Empire

──── frontiers 1699

new titles and peasant-rebels regarded him as Antichrist or, at best, a changeling-emperor, satanic double of a true monarch. Thanks to his borrowings from the west, according to Voltaire, 'Russia made more progress in 50 years than any nation had made by itself in 500.' But the equivocal short-term impact is conveyed by the colourful popular print of a boyar being shorn by a demon-barber, or the report of a visitor to the new-built St Petersburg, who reported that its high society was like those of London or Paris, except that the ladies still wore cosmetic blacking on their teeth. Henceforth Russia was permanently implicated, by wars or alliances, in the politics of the world to her west. Peter the Great's daughter was the last Romanov ruler in the male line; thereafter, all the autocrats were products of the European dynastic marriage-market.

Catherine the Great, sole ruler of Russia from 1762, was an ex-Catholic and ex-Lutheran who apparently acknowledged no difference between Lutheranism and Orthodoxy except in ceremony; she was a German who had to teach herself Russian by long nights of study; she was the ornament of a European education who had been schooled in French thought by a Swedish ambassador to Prussia; and she was fully a participant in the European culture of Enlightenment, who regarded Montesquieu as the author of her 'bible' and who corresponded with Voltaire. Though Voltaire cultivated an unorthodox reputation, setting up home in Ferney so as to be easily ready to flee to Switzerland if his sovereign or his church should ever lose patience with him, he was par excellence the spokesman of the intellectual fashion of his day and the pontiff of the worship of science and reason, cults he acquired in youth during a spell of exile in England. Catherine was the remotest of his devotees, but was one of a following that spanned Europe. Voltaire corrected the King of Prussia's poetry and dined with the Marquês do Pombal. His works were read in Sicily and Transylvania, plagiarised in Vienna and translated into Swedish. The *Encyclopédie*, to which he contributed and which represented the systematic outreach of his thoughts, projected to every part of Europe Voltaire's world-view: secular, progressive (albeit never, in Voltaire's view, perfectible), informed by reason and science, a universe mirrored in the mechanical arts, to which the *Éncyclopedie* devoted vastly disproportionate space. Because Voltaire and most of his fellow-encyclopaedists regarded the Church as the great obstacle to practical reform on enlightened principles, the influence of this 'Enlightenment' can be simply measured by the incidence of anticlerical acts. Voltaire erected his own temple to 'the architect of

the universe, the great geometrician' but regarded Christianity as an 'infamous superstition to be extirpated – I do not say among the rabble, who are not worthy of being enlightened and are apt for every yoke, but among the polite and those who wish to think.' In 1759 the Jesuits were expelled from Portugal; in 1761 Tsar Peter III secularised a great portfolio of church property; between 1764 and 1773 the Jesuit Order was abolished in most of the rest of the west. In the 1780s in the Austrian empire 700 religious houses were dissolved and 38,000 religious forced into lay life. A Spanish minister proposed the forfeiture of most of the church's land. In 1790 the absolute authority of the King of Prussia over the clergy of his realm was re-codified. At the most rarefied levels of the European elite, the cult of reason was taking on the characteristics of an alternative religion, in the rites of freemasonry and the configurations of a profane hierarchy celebrated for the purity of its wisdom in Mozart's *Magic Flute*.

The Enlightenment soon came to seem streaked with shadows. In Paris in 1798 Étienne Gaspard Robert displayed a freak light-show in Paris, in which he made monstrous shapes loom at the audience from a screen or appear to flicker eerily, projected onto clouds of smoke. In other demonstrations of the wonders of electricity, the real-life precursors of Frankenstein were making corpses twitch to thrill an audience. It was not the 'sleep of reason' which produced these monsters. They were the creations of its most watchful hours – the hideous issue of scientific experimentation, the brutal images of minds tortured by 'crimes committed in the name of liberty'. The French

Revolution was both the creation of the Enlightenment and its destroyer, anticipating the relations of Frankenstein and his monster. The revolutionaries' favourite philosopher was a heretic of the Enlightenment who quarrelled with Voltaire. Rousseau was a louche, restless supertramp with a taste for low life, ugly women and gutter pleasures. He changed his formal religious affiliation twice without once appearing sincere. He betrayed all his mistresses, quarrelled with all his friends and abandoned all his children. He discarded the urbane values of restraint and classicism which united the elite of his age in favour of supposedly silvan virtues of licensed passion and contrived rusticity. The guideline of his life was addiction to his own sensibilities. In 1750, the prize-winning essay which made his name was a repudiation of one of the most sacred principles of the Enlightenment – 'that the Arts and Sciences have benefited mankind', though the fact that the topic could be set at all for a public competition shows how far disillusionment with enlightened optimism had gone. His denunciations of property and the state offered nothing in their place except an assertion of the natural goodness of man in his primitive state. His political maxims – that 'man must be forced to be free' and that the 'general will' must prevail – were means to license the tyranny of demagogy.

The rapidity with which the French Revolution was perverted was an embittering experience for the children of the Enlightenment. It opened with noble cries – for liberty, equality and fraternity, the rights of man and of the citizen, the sovereignty of the people – and ended with the sickening scream which forms the last line of the *Marseillaise*. In the revulsion of Burke and Coleridge one kind of reaction can be seen: reaching for the comforts of conservatism; in the 'black' paintings of Goya and the private darkness of Beethoven's late music, another can be sensed: retreat into hag-ridden disillusionment. In the *Critique of Pure Reason* of 1798, Kant – who became a European figure without ever leaving Königsberg – proposed a rickety, human-scale world of 'crooked timber' in place of the ruined structures of the age of reason.

The Enlightenment dissolved in blood, but, in a new sense, the Napoleonic wars welded the parts of Europe together. Unprecedented mass movements took huge conscript armies from western Europe to Moscow and from the depths of Russia to Paris. Rulers from the school of the French Revolution were imposed from Sweden to Sicily. German principalities and Ionian islands got 'Napoleonic codes', while Poland – or that part of it comprised in Napoleon's 'Grand Duchy of Warsaw' – and Spain got constitutions. Napoleon almost gave political form to the European idea by creating a Europe-wide empire. He was propelled to power in the chaos of post-revolutionary France by unrivalled military gifts, which, with the 'citizen armies' the Revolution created, gave him the chance to conquer Europe piecemeal. Only at its extremities, in Spain and Russia, did his reach become over-extended. He was an opportunist whose ambitions were unrestrained by finite goals; but he had ideals too, which overlapped with those of the Revolution he claimed to fulfil. He was child of the Enlightenment, who, like a Rousseauan hero, picked cherries with his first girlfriend. And he was a technocrat who rose to command in the artillery and won campaigns by meticulous attention to logistics. In some ways, his was an avowedly barbaric empire, descended as much from Charlemagne's as from Rome's. It was beheld from heaven, in propaganda images painted by Giroudet and Ingres, by Ossian and the Valkyrie. Its appeal was at least as much to the rising romanticism of the nineteenth century as to the fading rationalism of the eighteenth. But Napoleon's vision was of a Europe, engineered with a gunner's precision, levelled by uniform laws.

The common culture Gibbon had perceived was in flames and his serene prediction that no European people would ever again relapse into barbarism was to be repeatedly belied in the course of the next two centuries. In the nineteenth century, a European culture would still exist, but it would be of a different sort. And whereas that of Gibbon's 'great republic' had included only a small elite, huge masses of people, at ever more diverse levels of education and society, would participate henceforth: they had joined the game and would not get back into their seats. Before we turn to the Europe of the romantic era, we must look back at the woodwork from which they emerged, to see how the popular cultures of the early modern period had evolved meanwhile.

CHAPTER 7

THE FRONTIER WITHIN

Religion and popular culture

IT USED TO BE CALLED 'the Rise of the Bourgeoisie or 'the Rise of Capitalism': while people exchanged complacent admiration in the group portraits of Frans Hals, the cosy economic order painted by Gabriel Metsu and Gerard Terborch took shape. A world unlike our own – a 'medieval' world – became something recognisably akin to what we have now. In about the last 150 years, no individual had so much influence on the way this supposed transformation was commonly described than Karl Marx, an historian brilliant but unsound, who believed that all history was that of class struggles and that the slowly accumulating structures of economic change occasionally erupted in political revolutions, like lava bubbling through the crust, as the wielders of rival means of production contended for power. The eye-catching political revolutions of the early modern period – the 'general crisis' of the mid-seventeenth century, the French Revolution at the end of the eighteenth and even, in some analyses, the Protestant Reformation of the sixteenth, which could be classed as a political revolution from a secular point of view – were the birth-pangs of a new society: the emergence of capitalism, struggling blood-stained from the womb of feudalism.

Marx's predictions have proved false. The mutual embitterment of the bourgeoisie and the proletariat in modern Europe has not happened as he supposed it would: instead the two classes have collaborated in mutual enrichment and, in the process, have become more like each other in manners, values, dress and taste. Revolutions inspired by Marx have usually been successful only in conditions which defy his own predictions – where the middle class and the industrial proletariat have been small, peasantries huge and land the preponderant source of wealth. Where states have tried to apply them, Marx's economic prescriptions have been disastrous. Where the means of production

and exchange have been concentrated in the hands of the state, economic progress has been lamed or knackered. The failure of political Marxism and economic Marxism has undermined historians' faith in historical Marxism. Some adepts of the old faith remain; but most students of the past are filtering Marxist language out of their analyses.

Widely generalised changes did overcome European societies in the early modern period. Class struggles, in a sense, did attend them. But the changes are better described in a different sort of language while the class wars were fought along other lines, between other camps, than those Marx postulated. Indeed the class consciousness out of which Marxism was carved was itself a product of social change. Medieval and early modern societies were composed of 'vertical structures': interest groups, affinities and orders whose members' sense of mutual belonging depended on self-differentiation from outsiders rather than on shared rank, wealth, priorities or education. The elevated 'estates' of society, the nobility and clergy, were not classes in any sense that a modern market researcher or opinion pollster would recognise, but communities of privilege uniting some of the very rich and some of the very poor in enjoyment and defence of the fiscal immunities and legal advantages which marked them out from the rest. A prince-bishop belonged to the same estate as a penniless hedge-priest; nobility embraced a duke with an income exceeding a king's and a poor *Freiherr* or *Reichsritter* whose lance was for hire. In at least one case in seventeenth-century Ciudad Real, a noble was a boot-black – a literal prefiguration of Gilbert's 'aristocrat who cleans the boots'.

Cities formed communities of a similar kind, jealous of their jurisdiction, walled against the world and fortified in their sense of civic identity by economic 'liberties', like the rights to hold markets or fairs or to exact tolls. Within cities, the same sort of profile might be taken on

Religious divisions, 1560

- ■ date of change from Catholicism to Lutheranism
- ▲ date of change to Calvinism or Zwinglianism
- 2 delegates sent to last session of Council of Trent
- • Anabaptist minorities
- ▲ Calvinist minorities
- ᴠ Lutheran minorities
- ◑ Roman Catholic minorities
- ▪ Muslim minorities

Roman Catholic
Calvinist
Lutheran
Anglican
Hussite
Orthodox
Muslim

Scattered Jewish communities existed in the Ottoman empire, Hungary, Poland, Portugal, Bohemia and Italy.

The heroism of the commonplace: bourgeois family values are painted by Frans Hals in plain clothes and muted colours *left* as if in parody of aristocratic group portraits.

In the early stages of the Reformation, Protestant, Catholic and Orthodox versions of Christianity were thoroughly intertwined and hard to tell apart, but by the second half of the sixteenth century, an attempt can be made to map the distribution of the frontiers of the various confessions, *map this page,* as the principle became established that the religion of the state was that of the ruler.

ICELAND ■*1552*
• Reykjavik

Atlantic Ocean

SCOTLAND ▲*1560*
• Stirling
• Glasgow • Edinburgh

IRELAND
• Dublin
• York

WALES
ENGLAND *1534*
• Cambridge
• Oxford • London
• Winchester

NORWAY ■*1539*

SWEDEN ■*1527*
• Stavanger
• Bergen

FINLAND ■*1528*

North Sea

• Stockholm
• Kalmar

ESTONIA ■*1524*

LIVONI ■*152*

COURLAND *1561*

Baltic Sea

DENMARK ■*1536*
• Copenhagen
SCHLESWIG ■*1542*
HOLSTEIN
■*1526* ■*1529* ■*1531*
▲*1542*
• Emden
FRIESLAND
• Amsterdam
• Leiden • Utrecht
2
SPANISH NETHERLANDS
Flanders
CLEVES • Münster
BERG
JÜLICH
HESSE *1527*
Frankfurt *1530*
Heidelberg
PALATINATE *1544 1559*
WÜRTTEMBERG *1534*
1524
BASLE *1529*
NEUCHÂTEL *1530*
VAUD *1536*
Geneva *1536* ▲
LUCERNE
BERN *1578*
THURGAU
ZÜRICH
APPENZELL
UNTERWALDEN
SANKT GALEN ▲*1524*
URI *1524*
GRAUBÜNDEN *1525*

MECKLENBURG ■*1526 154?*
POMERANIA ■*1534*
BRUNSWICK-LÜNEBURG *1544 1559*
BRANDENBURG ■*1539*
• Wittenberg
• Berlin
• Magdeburg ■*1525*
Wittenberg ■*1524*
ELECTORATE OF SAXONY ■*1526*
DUCHY OF SAXONY ■*1539*
BOHEMIA ■*1524*
• Prague
• Nuremberg
Ansbach ■*1528*
Regensburg
BAVARIA
• Munich
MORAVIA
AUSTRIA
• Vienna
STYRIA • Graz
TYROL
CARINTHIA
CARNIOLA

Hamburg *1542* Lübeck
Westphalia

Königsberg *1523*
• Danzig
PRUSSIA *1525*
LITHUANIA

• Warsaw

POLAND
2
• Breslau ■*1524*

RUTHENIA

TRANSYLVA

HUNGARY
2
• Budapest

OTTOMAN EMPIRE

Rouen
Amiens
Rheims
Paris
Troyes
Blois
Angers • Tours
Nantes
Dijon
FRANCHE-COMTÉ
LORRAINE
POITIERS 26
Bordeaux
Gascony
León • Pamplona
Toulouse
Montpellier
Avignon
Marseilles
Aix-en-Provence
SALUZZO
Lyons
SAVOY
• Milan
MILAN
• Venice
Genoa
PARMA
Modena *1540-50*
Ferrara *1540-50*
Lucca *1541*
Florence
TUSCANY 187
Siena
PAPAL STATES
• Rome

DALMATIA 1
RAGUSA
Adriatic Sea

Corunna
GALICIA
Oporto • Braganza
León
Valladolid *1558-9*
Salamanca
Segovia
Avila • Madrid
PORTUGAL
Lisbon
Badajoz
Toledo 31
Ciudad Real
• Córdoba
Seville *1558-9*
Granada
• Málaga
GRANADA *until 1571*
• Murcia
SPAIN
Saragossa
ARAGON *until 1609*
Catalonia
• Barcelona
VALENCIA *until 1609*
• Valencia
Balearic Islands

Corsica

Sardinia

NAPLES
• Naples

Sicily

Mediterranean Sea

• Malta

WATTASIDS   ZAYYANIDS   HAFSIDS

by a number of rival 'quarters', exchanging violent sallies across internal walls, as at Pamplona, or ritualising their combats as in Siena's famous Palio. In most countries Jews formed analogous communities, also distinguished by economic and legal privileges as well as by disabilities and the despite of others. So did Protestants in early modern France and Poland. The lineages and affinities of great noble families had some of the same characteristics, often encompassing poor and remote relations as well as retainers at every level of wealth and rank, tenants, servants and other dependants, who gathered together for festivals or accounting-days and sometimes lived together in considerable numbers under a single vast roof, eating their meals in common. On a smaller scale, the 'families' – as they were usually called – or extended households of urban artisans, with generations of apprentices sharing their roofs, had the same characteristics.

This way of organising society was changed by a vast, slow process of erosion, advancing, like all such processes, by almost imperceptible stages and signified by small signs. The family was redefined as an ever smaller knot of close kin. Between the sixteenth century and the eighteenth, in aristocratic households all over Europe, family dining-rooms came to provide a privileged retreat from the communal life of the great hall. Court portraits of Philip IV of Spain and Charles I of England show us into a world more like that of a Victorian paterfamilias than of a medieval dynast. Into the courts of absolutist monarchs, provincial aristocracies were sucked, away from their estates and

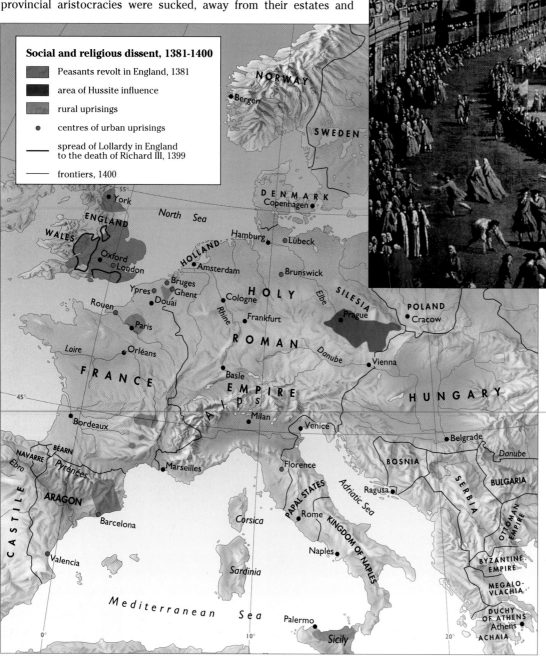

Social and religious dissent, 1381-1400

- Peasants revolt in England, 1381
- area of Hussite influence
- rural uprisings
- centres of urban uprisings
- spread of Lollardy in England to the death of Richard III, 1399
- frontiers, 1400

The Palio at Siena is an annual contest in horsemanship between the rival quarters of the city. Giuseppe Zocchi's painting of the event in 1739 *above* was commissioned in honour of the Empress Maria Theresa and her husband.

A society undergoing fragmentation can be imagined in the pews of Rycote Chapel, Oxfordshire *right*, where the space for the congregation is split into compartments by permanent structures demarcating leading families from the rest of the community.

Peasant revolt and social unrest *map left*, a phenomenon which seemed endemic in the late fourteenth century can be all-too-easily generalised. In fact they are part of a much more complex picture which embraces millenarian rebellions, local disputes and revolts against onerous forms of jursidiction and fiscal exploitation.

hereditary followings. In western Christendom, where the pace of change in these respects was faster than in the east, churches became riven by pews, dividing the space for the laity along class lines. For Shakespeare, as for Jane Austen, a man's place in society could already be defined by his income. Everywhere the string of degree of nobility was re-tuned to the clink of moneybags.

Nor, meanwhile, did vertically organised social structures immunise medieval and early modern states against social tension. There were cases all over Europe of alliances of the poor of various estates or groups against the rulers or the rich. To take cases only from one notoriously unstable century: in England in 1381, the hedge-priest John Ball ministered to rebellious peasants who hanged tax-gatherers and burned manorial court-rolls, while resentful journeymen let peasant *enragés* into London; in 1358, the city of Paris, in collective revolt against the crown, made a brief alliance with peasant *Jacques*, on the rampage in the countryside; clerics and butchers were the leaders of the rebels of Douai in 1304-5; in 1347, Cola di Rienzo, an innkeeper's son, briefly created a coalition of the poor of Rome against the pope and the patriciate, installing himself as 'tribune of the people' before he forfeited support by aping noble and even kingly ways. The abolition of rank was a demand occasionally voiced by – or, at least, ascribed to – low-born revolutionaries. In England, for instance, it cropped up in the fourteenth century in the Peasants' Revolt, in Jack Cade's rebellion in the fifteenth and among the Levellers in the seventeenth.

Still, conflicts along class lines were comparatively rare. Most revolts were not of the poor against the rich or of 'the less' against the 'great ones' but of one interest-group against another or of relatively underprivileged against relatively privileged communities. Jews, foreigners, the affinities of particular great families stranded in unpopularity by the ebb of the political tide: these were the common victims of outbreaks of mass urban violence. The bloody civil war of Flanders in the 1320s was in the tradition of the age-old conflict of nomads and sedentarists in which the rebels were 'eaters of curdled milk and cheese'. The common objects of mob violence were food-hoarders at times of famine and scapegoats at times of plague. Most European states experienced civil wars in the fourteenth and fifteenth centuries but they were usually dynastic conflicts or the blood-lettings of an endemically violent nobility, which left most ordinary people unaffected, except by the ravages of licentious soldiery. Religious conflicts usually cut across class lines, though distinctively peasant movements were also common, like the Taborites, who formed a camp of their own among the contenders in the Hussite Wars of fifteenth-century Bohemia, or the millenarian *irmandades* in Galicia shortly afterwards or the 'thieving, murdering hordes of German peasants' denounced by Luther in 1525. The so-called 'Wars of Religion' in sixteenth-century France resembled old-fashioned civil wars, in which aristocratic lineages mobilised 'vertical structures' in their power-struggles. Other sixteenth-century rebellions were of the same character or else were the protests of threatened minorities, like Moriscos in Spain and Catholics in England, or assertions of provincial identity, like those of Aragonese protesters against the infringement of provincial liberties, or the insurrections in the Netherlands against the 'tyranny' of foreign methods and officials intruded by an absent monarch. From the seventeenth century, the English Civil War used to be held up as a copy-book case of bourgeois revolution, but it seems better understood as a mixture of a traditional rebellion, a 'revolt of provinces', a struggle of 'ins' and 'outs' and a genuine war of religion.

The real 'class wars' of the period were fought between elite and popular culture and their battlefields were places of worship, as self-consciously godly minorities, clerical and urban, set out to convert

under-evangelised countrysides to a new kind of Christian awareness and to customs purged of the impurities of lingering paganism, worldliness and superstition. These campaigns were common to the whole of Christian Europe – those parts which were Orthodox, those which were Catholic and those which were Protestant. Most educated people today, challenged to name an event of transforming effect in early modern Europe, would probably name the Reformation and understand it as a great movement of secession from the Catholic Church, which permanently ended the unity of western Christendom and contributed to the ideological basis of many features of the modern world, including nationalism, individualism, toleration and even capitalism. Such a response would not be altogether wrong, but it is more helpful to see all the changes which befell early modern

In a commemorative engraving 100 years after the event *top*, the leading Protestant princes of Germany are shown presenting the Confession of Augsburg to the Emperor Charles V, amid scenes of moderate evangelical piety and the continuation in Protestant congregations of sacramental life.

The St Bartholomew's Day Massacre *above right*, painted by François Dubois, a Huguenot who fled to Geneva. In all, about 6000 Protestants were slaughtered by the Catholics, including the Protestant leader, Coligny. Catherine de'Medici's complicity is suggested by her inclusion, in front of the gate of the Louvre, inspecting corpses.

In a propaganda piece justifying the Netherlandish rebellion against the tyranny of the duke of Alba *left*, the devil crowns Alba and Cardinal Granvelle, who wields bellows in allusion to the fires of heresy. Alba holds allegorical figures of the Netherlandish provinces on a chain, while the execution of the defenders of feudal particularism, Counts Egmonts and Horn, can be seen through the arch.

The great wealth of the merchants of Amsterdam is testified to by the grandeur of their houses along the Keizersgracht and Herengracht, such as this example *right* dating from 1663, with its emblems of Africans and ropes proclaiming the sources of the owner's fortune in the slave-trade.

Christianity as underlain by a single evangelical impulse, common to Orthodoxy, Catholicism and Protestantism, of which the Protestant Reformation was only one manifestation.

In the breakers' yard of history, the Reformation has been pounded into fragments, reduced from a cosmic event to a series of local or individual experiences. What formerly seemed a world-shattering revolution has been re-classified as a 'transition' in devotional style or taste. The revolutionary changes commonly said to have flowed from it – deism, secularism and atheism; individualism and rationalism; the rise of capitalism and the decline of magic; the scientific revolution; the origins of civil liberties and shifts in the global balance of power – all appear less convincing as time goes on.

One by one, in recent years, the links by which these chains of consequence are bound have been loosened or cut by revisionist thinking and critical scholarship. The decline of Marxism has made the rise of capitalism a less attractive quarry than it once appeared to historians of the early modern era, when they were convinced that it was an event traceable to their own period, to be linked with the other revolutionary convulsions they thought they could detect. In 1904, when Max Weber formulated the link between Protestantism and capitalism, the Reformation looked like just such a revolution: sudden, sweeping, transforming. It seemed to come at the right time, ahead of the vast expansion of credit in sixteenth- and seventeenth-century Europe, before the intense and ever longer-range commercial activity of the period, the rapid urban development and the entrepreneurial culture which followed. Protestant peoples – or peoples among whom Protestants were copiously represented – had fared better in commercial empire-building than their Catholic competitors. The Dutch empire expanded at Portuguese expense. The new commercial and imperial powers of the period included England and Sweden; old ones supposedly in decline included Venice, Poland and Spain. Protestant Christendom seemed to boom while the Catholic world stagnated. The correspondences were not quite exact. Muscovy 'rose' without the benefit of Protestantism; Turkey 'declined' without the curse of Catholicism; France was a successful power, by Weber's standards, where Protestantism was first checked, then excluded. Nevertheless, the match between Protestantism on the one hand and successful commercial empire-building on the other was good enough to be suggestive. Weber believed, moreover, that he had found the key to the door which opened from Protestantism into capitalism. He felt that the 'genius', the *Geist*, of capitalism was essentially religious and that it dwelt in communities which practised a devotion of contempt for ostentatious luxury, conserving funds for saving and investment. It was proper to Protestants, whose religion elevated simplicity of life into a sign of divine election, and, by denying the efficacy of individual works of mercy, spared money for self-help.

In fact, rich Protestants were as likely to be big spenders as they were to be big savers. In the Europe of the early modern period, no country's culture was as deeply informed by self-consciously Protestant values as that of the northern Netherlands; yet Amsterdam, which was the capital of a commercial empire and a symbol of the commercial success of a Calvinist elite, was a sumptuous city of conspicuous consumption. To be sent to The Hague was exile for an Amsterdam patrician who needed to be near the Bourse and the harbour. At least a third of the city's office-holders in the late seventeenth century had pleasure-houses along the Amstel. By the late eighteenth century, owners of country houses comprised more than 80 per cent of the patriciate and the town council rarely met in July and August. Taste is the best clue to values and in all Europe, according to one of the most perceptive economic theorists of the late seventeenth century, 'you will find no private buildings so sumptuously magnificent as a great many of the merchants' and other gentlemen's houses are in Amsterdam'. There are examples still standing today on the Keizersgracht and the Herengracht. The baroque taste of Andries de Graeff rivalled Venetian palaces of the period. The simplicity and austerity commonly associated with Dutch art-patrons of the early modern period have been largely in the eyes of the beholders.

123

Many leading capitalists of early-modern Europe were neither particularly Protestant nor particularly ascetic. At first sight, the hold of Calvinist financiers on the international banking system of mid-seventeenth-century Europe looks impressive. Nominally Calvinist bankers kept the armies of the Thirty Years' War in the field – on the Catholic as well as the Protestant side. But they were, in most cases, shaky in their Calvinism or gaudy in their way of life. Hans de Witte, whose financial wizardry kept Habsburg armies supplied, had his son baptised a Catholic. François Grenus, committed no comparable defection but he supplied loans to such Catholic champions as the king of Spain and the duke of Savoy. Louis de Geer, the king of Sweden's paymaster, bought estates 'surpassing in extent the dominions of many small German princes' and affected an aristocratic title and demeanour typical of his fellow-financiers. Barthélemy d'Herwarth, Mazarin's fixer, demolished a duke's palace to rebuild it for himself on a more lavish scale. In Amsterdam, the grave of Isaac Le Maire proudly records the wounds of entrepreneurship – the loss of one-and-a-half million guilders.

If Protestantism at its most lucrative was not particularly austere, Protestantism at its most radical was actually anti-capitalist. The Fifth-Monarchy Men and Levellers, the Moravian Brethren and Shakers hardly advertised the capitalist ethic in their emphasis on equality and common goods. 'Buying and selling,' declared the Leveller Gerrard Winstanley, 'is an art whereby people endeavour to cheat one another of the land.' The Fifth Monarchists scandalised Oliver Cromwell by 'telling us that liberty and property are not the badges of the Kingdom of Christ'. Protestantism, in its more radical forms, was as likely to develop towards socialism as to justify capitalism.

The differences between the Protestants and the conventional communions tend to be exaggerated by traditional narratives, which concentrate on the heroism of individual reformers, the bitterness of the theological divisions which few people can ever really have understood or cared about, and the power-struggles between reformers and traditionalists from place to place, where the conflicts were almost invariably mixed up – like their echoes in Northern Ireland today – with other disputes that had nothing to do with religion. A few bubbles of the routine historiography need pricking: Luther, for instance, probably never nailed to the door of Wittenberg Castle Church the Ninety-Five Theses which are commonly regarded as the founding document of Protestantism. The biggest collection of saints' relics in sixteenth-century Europe belonged to Luther's patron, Frederick the Wise of

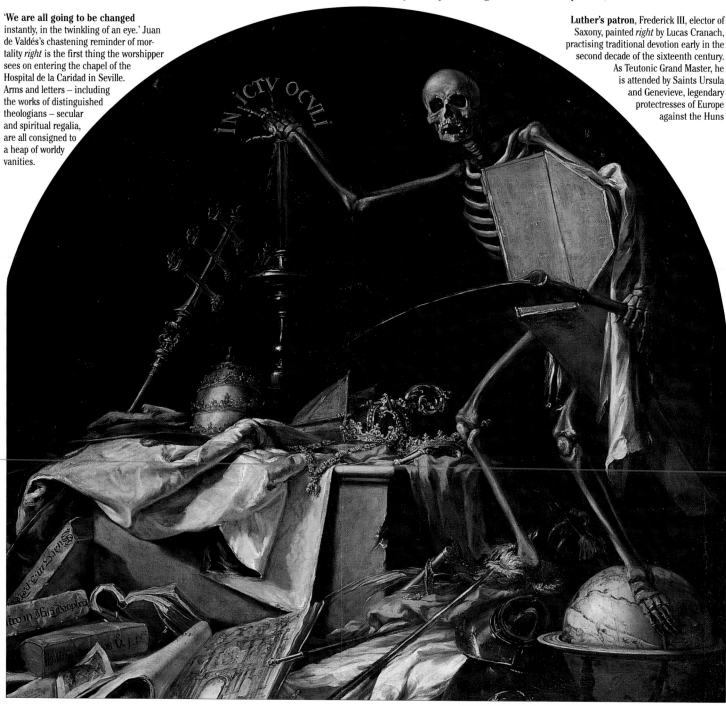

'**We are all going to be changed** instantly, in the twinkling of an eye.' Juan de Valdés's chastening reminder of mortality *right* is the first thing the worshipper sees on entering the chapel of the Hospital de la Caridad in Seville. Arms and letters – including the works of distinguished theologians – secular and spiritual regalia, are all consigned to a heap of worldy vanities.

Luther's patron, Frederick III, elector of Saxony, painted *right* by Lucas Cranach, practising traditional devotion early in the second decade of the sixteenth century. As Teutonic Grand Master, he is attended by Saints Ursula and Genevieve, legendary protectresses of Europe against the Huns

Saxony. Many highly respectable Catholic theologians in the sixteenth and seventeenth centuries believed in justification by faith alone. The theology of the mainstream sixteenth-century reformers was so traditional that a good case has been made out by a modern Catholic theologian for treating Luther as an entirely orthodox thinker. In the sixteenth century, priestly and institutional religion was by-passed more effectively by Catholic mystics than by Protestant seekers after a direct relationship with God. The real differences between Protestantism and Catholicism – as they affected ordinary people in their experience of worship and their personal encounters with God – are best evoked by the contrast between Protestant and Catholic environments.

One way of envisioning the contrast is in the iconography of Protestant propaganda – the 'Great Babylon' juxtaposed, for instance, with the 'New Jerusalem' of Henry Danvers in 1672 – another by picking out the priorities of earlier Protestant propaganda-art. In Cranach's engraving of the supposed differences between 'true and false religion', Luther preaches, attended by the Holy Spirit and the Lamb of God, while two sacraments – baptism and communion – are celebrated. In Andreas Herrneisen's panorama of the virtues of the Confession of Augsburg, the defining document of reasonable Protestantism, the same sacraments are featured along with marriage, but the emphasis is on the preaching and teaching of the word of God in temples to unintrusive fellowship and unfiltered light.

The peculiarities of Catholic tradition are also encoded in decor and design. In the chapel of the Hospital de la Caridad in Seville the trends and tenets of post-Reformation Catholicism are comprehensively packed into a tiny space. The confraternity that endowed and kept the hospital in late seventeenth-century Seville was a rich and aristocratic club with a waiting-list for membership that could run into years. But the city in which it operated was a 'Thieves' Babylon' where the anti-heroes of picaresque novels took flesh, a Golgotha where the unburied dead stank in the streets, a sin-city where the theatres were shut in expiation of the citizens' cry for penance. The members of the confraternity were obliged by their rules to carry sick paupers on their own shoulders and to tend, feed and bury them with their own fastidious hands, 'and when they arrive at the poor man, they will fall on their knees, and however wounded or disgusting he may be, they will not turn their faces.' Thus the sanctuary of the chapel is dominated by a grim and glorious altarpiece of the burial of Christ and the nave is decorated with saints who pre-figured the brothers' duties. St Elizabeth of Hungary struggles against revulsion as she picks at the lice and dabs at the sores of her patients; St John of God enacts the rule of the confraternity: 'before putting the poor, sick man to bed, wash his feet and kiss them.'

The Catholic chapel is a celebration of the saving effects of charity; the Protestant chapel, by omitting such allusions, makes an implicit statement of the sufficiency of faith. The Catholic chapel is a theatre of priestly ritual; that of the Protestants is a sheepfold for the urgings of a pastor. The Catholic chapel is a sanctuary for the enactment of a perpetual sacrifice; its Protestant counterpart a space for the commemoration of an unrepeatable event.

Our image of sixteenth-century Christendom is so dominated by our sense of these differences that we fail to see what else was going on or how the Reformation fitted into a broader picture. Competition for souls between Protestant, Catholic and Orthodox apostles was the overlap of mighty works of missionising to which each tradition allotted enormous resources in discrete spheres. They addressed unevangelised communities outside Europe, where the Catholic church won the allegiance of so many millions of souls that the secession of some European communities seemed like a little local difficulty. They assiduously cultivated the pagans who still dwelt on the fringes of their home societies and such Jews and Muslims as lived in their midst. They took the gospel to the rootless masses of new or growing towns. They invaded neglected rural solitudes. The godly elites made it their business to enhance the Christianity of their unsatisfactory co-religionists: to blow the bellows among the Laodiceans, to eradicate pre-Christian habits from their culture; to suppress non-Christian thoughts and tastes. Wherever the critical eye sought to detect them, there were practices – recreational, therapeutic, celebratory, commemorative, social and sexual – which could be condemned as survivals from a pagan past.

Rural communities still lived in worlds full of spirits and demons, where natural forces were personified and placated. St Teresa of Avila had her first vision of Christ after hearing a Franciscan preach about his order's mission to the Indies. 'There is another Indies waiting to be evangelised here in Spain,' said her celestial voice. It was a common saying of the sixteenth century that 'within Spain there are Indies and mountains of ignorance' and as the clergy made increasing demands of their flocks so the oceans seemed to narrow. 'I don't know why the fathers of the Company go to Japan and the Philippines to look for lost souls,' wrote a Jesuit correspondent in 1615, 'when we have so many here in the same condition who do not know whether they believe in God.' According to a speaker in the English House of Commons in 1628, there were places in northern England and Wales 'which were scarce in Christendom, where God was little better known than among the Indian.' The Council of Trent alerted Catholic clergy to their unfulfilled mission and to the huge gaps in evangelisation caused by the uneven distribution of the clergy. In 1553 the Jesuit Robert Claysson was outraged by the neglect of forest regions near Bordeaux 'whose inhabitants live like beasts of the field. One can find people over 50 years old and more who have never heard of mass nor heard a single word of faith.' In rural Gascony in the early seventeenth century, St Vincent de Paul organised missions among 'people, aged 60 and more, who told us freely that they had never confessed; and when we spoke to them about God, and the most holy Trinity, and the nativity, passion and death of Jesus Christ and other mysteries, it was a language they did not understand at all.' A miller in northern Italy in the early sixteenth century could formulate a remarkably

comprehensive cosmology of 'cheese and worms' from which Christian traditions about the creation of the world were entirely absent. A novel purportedly written in Rome in the 1520s could plausibly depict whole back-streets of the pope's own city as innocent of Christianity.

Missions to the ill-evangelised recesses of Christendom were matched by others to its unevangelised frontiers. Heroes in far continents have dominated the historiography, like the Jesuits who displayed the last known heart-shaped image of the world, made in 1664, to their exotic converts. On the eastern edges of European civilisation, however, the frontiers were surprisingly close to home. In Estonia and Livonia, Christianity made little progress until the Swedish conquests of 1561 and 1621 respectively; thereafter Lutheranism was

The *rificolone*, still celebrated annually by Florentine youth on the night of 7th September, involves a parade of extravagant lanterns – including, in this eighteenth-century print *far left*, glowing models of towers under siege – and culminates in a procession of decorated boats along the Arno.

Ꙋ(O)Ꙋ
La Swehta
Grahmata
Jeb
Deewa Swehtais Wahrds/
Kas
Vreekisch un pehz ta Lunga Jesus
Kristus swehtas Peedsimschanas no teem swehteem Deewa-
Zilwekeem/ Praweerscheem/ Ewangelisteem jeb Preezas-Mah-
zitajeem un Apustuleem usrak-
kihts/
Tahm latweeschahm Deewa Draudsibahm
par labbu istaisita.

RIGA/ Gedruckt bey Johann Georg Wilcken/
Königl. Buchdrucker/ M DC LXXXIX.

Title page of the Lettish Bible of 1689 *above,* produced by the German printer Georg Johann Wilcken.

Images of damnation clearly played a significant role in the popular imagination. This depiction of hell in the tradition of Hieronymus Bosch *left* shows the damned suffering a litany of nightmarish punishments. A detail of a fifteenth-century altarpiece by Hans Memling's *above left* shows sinners being scourged and burnt in hellfire.

introduced as part of an imperial programme, much like Catholicism in Mexico or Peru. The Swedes installed schools and a university and tried to communicate Christian verities in indigenous tongues. Of the Lettish Bible of 1689 only 1,500 copies could be printed owing to a shortage of paper. When the Russians took over in the early eighteenth century, they left the Swedish church intact, but it was short-staffed and despised by the German settler-aristocracy. Under both regimes, it proved easier to discharge the obligations of Christianity by hunting paganism than by kindling a new faith. In 1677 preachers were ordered to report 'household-gods, tree-borne oracles, utterers of blessings, magicians and salt blowers'. In 1693 the Swedish governor-general decreed that 'crosses, groves, bushes, trees, stones and the like be hewn down, burned with the sacrifices, purged and rooted out in every possible way, so that not the least memorial may be left which could be used for superstition.' In 1731 the preachers' conference at Reval was still agonising over the persistence of heathenism in Estonia.

Like peasants and pagans, children were part of the previously submerged world to which clerical zeal now penetrated. Protestant catechists observed the popular German maxim, 'Jung gewonet, alt getan': the Catholic equivalent was the Jesuit slogan, 'Give me the child until he is seven.' Anxiety to 'habituate' children in knowledge of the faith was a great stimulus to catechetical literature. By the last quarter of the sixteenth century there were more than 50 different catechisms in circulation in Hamburg alone. These reformers' catechisms were not a new departure but an aspect of a communications revolution already gathering pace within the Catholic Church. The late fifteenth century was the great age of 'picture catechisms' and manuals on confession, illustrated with woodcuts of the inmates of hell feeding on each other's flesh, or of the devil whisking unworthy worshippers from church. The catechism drawn up in about 1470 by the Augustinian Dietrich Coelde was a bestseller of its time, and though its emphasis on the anatomisation of sin would soon come to seem old-fashioned, it anticipated the reach of the revolution of the next century by addressing, in specially adjusted editions, young and old, clergy and laymen, beginners in piety and advanced practitioners. Many Catholic catechisms, like those of the Protestants, emphasised personal devotion, private prayer and the cultivation of an individual relationship with God as well as rote-learning of traditional formulae and the practice of traditional works of charity. Even in matters of doctrine normally thought to separate the reformed churches from Rome, Protestant and Catholic catechisms could be strikingly similar. Luther's *Short Catechism* repeatedly intones, 'We should fear God because of his threat to those who transgress his law and love him for his promise of grace to those who keep it.' This was a doctrine a Catholic could fault only by appealing to St Paul, and bemoaning pharisaic rigidity.

Alongside the catechetical offensive, the clergy's assault on unholy living was conducted without much difference between denominations. The attack was concentrated on popular fairs and festivals which combined – as Erasmus said of carnivals – 'traces of ancient paganism' with 'over-indulgence in licence'. To an Elizabethan Puritan dancing was 'a horrible vice, an introduction to whoredom, a preparative to wantonness, a provocative to uncleanness and an introit to all kinds of lewdness.' Catholic divines agreed with him. Dances were everywhere driven from church and, in some dioceses, banned or restricted outside it. Bear-baiting was denounced by the same Puritan on the ground that 'God is abused when his creatures are misused'. The seventeenth-century Russian Archpriest Avvakum, the leader of the 'Old Believers', freed a dancing bear and drove the troupe that brought him from the village. His edict 'on the righting of morals and the abolition of superstition' included dancing, fiddlers, magic, masks and minstrels in a widely spattered anathema. Bull-fighting, too, was banned or, at least, proscribed on holy days after a papal pronouncement in 1565, not because it was cruel to animals but because it was corrupting of men. The equivocal reputation of popular festivals for the subversion of society and the profanation of the sacred clung on until the late eighteenth century, at least: popular culture was at least as tenacious as elite disapproval.

Customs too entrenched to change could be sacralised. One common endeavour of Catholic and Protestant divines was the appropriation of social rituals. Marriage is the most obvious example. In the sixteenth and seventeenth centuries in most of Europe, it was revolutionised by successful campaigns to suppress clandestine marriages and to bring all sexual unions under clerical bans. Ostensibly, for instance, the Spanish Inquisition was a tribunal of faith. In practice, most of its efforts in the second half of the sixteenth century were devoted to getting laymen's sex lives under priestly control. Bigamy became one of the most frequent causes in the Inquisition's courts in the 1560s and 1570s; fornication was the tribunal's major preoccupation from the 1570s to the 1590s. Sex had never been something of which Church leaders had unequivocally approved; but they were united in thinking it did least harm when licensed by themselves. Their campaigns were motivated by charity as well as power-lust. It seemed vital, as a saintly lobbyist claimed in 1551, 'to invalidate all marriages where there is no witness' because 'an infinite number of maidens have been deceived and undone, sinning with men and trusting in the promise of marriage made to them; and some have left their parents' house and gone to their perdition.'

Good intentions, however, can be joylessly enforced and the reformation of marriage was part of a more general clerical enforcement of a monopoly of ritual. In Protestant communities, it covered rituals of misrule, sacred dramas performed by lay groups and the more overt forms of lay competition in the clergy's proper fields, like fortune-telling, folk-healing and magic. The result was one of the most beguiling ironies of the Reformation era: belief in 'the priesthood of all believers' was a powerful source of reformers' inspiration. Catholics and Protestants worked hard at devising means to involve lay people more deeply in the life of the church. Yet at the same time, vast areas of secular life were made subject to the arbitration or tyranny of a godly elite. In this connection, at least, seventeenth-century Englishmen were justified in complaining that 'new presbyter is old priest writ large'.

With the reform of customs went the subversion of local religion. Cults specific to a particular place or community were slowly, often unsuccessfully – eroded or displaced by the universal cults of the Catholic church or by Christ-centred or Bible-centred forms of devotion. Dethronement of saints and debunking of apparitions were not exclusively Protestant practices: in the campaign to make Christianity uniform, Catholics could be equally zealous in the same causes. The Fathers of Trent were anxious to keep in their kitbag the traditional spiritual paraphernalia: the invocation of saints, the veneration of relics and the sacred use of images; but they made space for Protestant criticisms of some excesses. 'All superstition,' they decreed,

shall be removed, all filthy quest for gain eliminated, and all lasciviousness avoided, so that images shall not be painted or adorned with seductive charm, or the celebration of saints and the visitation of relics be perverted by the people into boisterous festivities and drunkenness.

Local religion was the patch on Christ's seamless robe, the boil on his perfect body. This was why, for instance, in Spain generally, official attitudes to apparitions changed with the pace of reform. The devotion which apparitions attracted was concentrated, at most, within 100 kilometres of the epicentres. Whereas in the fifteenth century, local clergy and diocesan investigators were usually happy to validate the seers' claims and share the local benefits, from the early sixteenth century the posture of the authorities changed. No more visions were endorsed by the church. The same unease was directed against the deities of local religion. In Catalonia, priests struggled against local piety in a country where there were 'more advocations of the Virgin than kinds of sausage' This sort of diversity was ineradicable in most of Europe, though reformers everywhere had at least some impact on the excesses which turned patron saints or images into the tutelary gods of their dwelling-places.

In the ranks of moderate reformers, Protestant distaste for saints' cults differed, if at all, in degree, rather than kind, from that of Catholics. Like the Catholics, they had their own cults to promote: those of the

heroes of Foxe's *Book of Martyrs* or of the 'slaughtered saints' of Milton's poem, or of Luther himself, whose woodcut image was revered, according to Erasmus, in the hovel of every rebellious peasant in the 1520s. Over the following two centuries Luther was often portrayed, sometimes complete with nimbus and dove, in quasi-icons which attracted miraculous renown as incombustible, thaumaturgic or oracular. A picture of him commissioned by a Duke of Saxony in the late sixteenth-century bears an inscription which echoes the scruples of Trent: 'non cultus est, sed memoriae gratia' ('it is not worship, but for remembrance's sake').

The war of the divines against popular culture was inseparable from the struggle against popular religion; an attempt to wean lives permanently threatened by natural disaster from a religion of survival in this world to one of salvation in the next. Trials of rats and exorcisms of locusts, appeals to folk-healers and wise women, vows to saints for worldly purposes, charms to master nature and spells to conjure the occult – these were the common enemies whom the clergy of all Christian traditions strove to control or curtail. The sort of range of activities attacked is represented in a Westphalian ordinance of 1669 against

putting leaves in the water on St Matthew's eve, putting pigs' hair on the fire, binding trees on New Year's day, driving out spirits by putting St John's wort on the walls, Easter bonfires accompanied by all sorts of songs that take the name of the Lord in vain while a great deal of devilry goes on, soaking meat in water tied up with bread, butter, lard and the like, hanging up St John's wreaths or crowns, making sacrifices.

The frontier between religion and superstition was, of course,

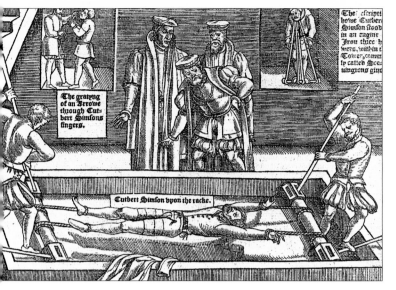

A witch burns in the market-place on Guernsey *above left*. The persecution of witchcraft was one aspect of the desire to root out threateningly entrenched popular beliefs which united both Catholics and Protestants.

'A true description' of the racking of Cuthbert Simson in the Tower of London. *above*. Foxe's *Book of Martyrs*, which includes the account of Simson's torture, was a rich vein of colourful propaganda for the Protestant cause.

Martha Veit in the role of Mary *left* in the Oberammergau Passion Play of 1922, manages to convey the humanity and vulnerability of a baroque Virgin, evoking the period of the vow in which the tradition originated.

Goya's earliest witchcraft scenes date from his period under the patronage of the duke and duchess of Osuna in the 1790s, when the perversions of the French Revolution had alerted the painter to the dark recesses of popular culture unpenetrated by the Enlightenment. This coven *below* was part of the disturbingly horrific decoration of the dining-room of his own house – an oddity of taste the Osuna couple seem to have helped to inspire.

undefined, and Protestants and Catholics may have differed about where to draw it but their common ground, in this as in so many contexts, was more substantial and, in the long-term perspective, seems more significant than the grounds of difference.

Only a Protestant, for instance, could dismiss the rite of mass as magical, but Catholic reformers were equally keen to purge it of mumbo-jumbo and to purify congregations' understanding of its significance. Eucharistic processions were restricted by repeated decrees in German synods in the fifteenth and sixteenth centuries; bans were issued on traditional ceremonies abusing the host as a talismanic object to influence the weather or other forces of nature. Catholics were more tolerant than Protestants of hopes invested in relics or holy water or blessed candles or incense as aids in healing or props to prayer but Catholic reformers were also alert to the threat of impropriety which such practices carried. By the end of the sixteenth century in Salzburg, traditionally-minded laymen had to plead with the clergy to get their blessed bread and salt for the Sunday table. The efficacy of 'sacramentals' – objects of power hallowed by blessing or by use in church – was denied altogether by Protestants; but in Catholic circles their number and nature were progressively limited and controlled. Catholic and Protestant divines were as one in outlawing parish wakes and the traditionally light-hearted vowed vigils which so often degenerated into lewdness: these activities largely disappeared from early-modern Europe. Catholics and Protestants agreed, on the whole, about the necessity of persecuting witchcraft, though they could get involved in characteristic disputes over means. In Germany in 1529, for instance, the Catholic bailiff of Urach proposed to counter the alleged malevolence with 'Easter candles, baptismal water, stoles, albs etc as though they were about to baptise the witches' souls once more,' whereas the Protestant-inclined priest recommended that 'it would be better to drop the witches in the water in which the sheep had been washed.' In the seventeenth century, Catholic scrutineers were prominent in the re-classification of witchcraft as a psychological delusion; but all kinds of Christian communities remained subject, with diminishing frequency, to the fear of it, and inclined to persecute it.

Like the Christian missions to the wider world, the evangelisation of Europe encountered mixed success. Where Protestantism was triumphant, it co-existed with survivals from before the Reformation: with the need for saints and angels, sometimes supplied by images of Luther; with an antiquated popular theology that went on stressing the necessity of good works; in parts of England, with demand for prayers for the dead; in parts of Norway, with magical awe of the eucharist; in parts of the Calvinist Low Countries with an indelible intellectual attachment to free will; in Lutheran congregations, with the *Kyrie* in Greek. Similarly, the reformed Catholicism of the 'Counter-Reformation' could not eliminate pre-Tridentine Catholicism altogether – in some places, hardly at all. The bull-fights persisted in Spain. Many of the ceremonies enacted today in expiation of parish and municipal vows,

from Oberammergau to Barcelona, originated in the seventeenth century. Even exorcisms of locusts turned up again in a Jesuit mission in twentieth-century Africa.

Without looking so far afield, the observer must be astonished at how many irrational bumps in the spiritual landscape survived the epoch of reform. In Catalonia, religion 'stayed where it had always been – in the community, rather than the church'. Everywhere, devotion ticked away to the traditional rhythms of the countryside, with feasts and fasts adjusted to the oscillations of dearth and glut. The god of rural Christians still looked like a demiurge, personifying a Nature who was not always benign. In southern Germany in the late eighteenth century, the Blessed Sacrament was still being used to ward off fire and flood; magic was exorcised by sprinklings of water blessed on certain holy days and bewitched cows were fumigated with holy smoke. The last witch burned in Switzerland was the victim of Protestants in 1781; Catholics burned the last in Poland in 1793. When the Quaker anthropologist William Christian studied the religion of a Cantabrian valley in the 1960s, he found priests still struggling to mop up the excesses of local religion left undisturbed in the aftermath of Trent. There is still a circle of ladies in Écija who put the image of their patron, Saint Pancras, in the fridge when he disappoints their hopes of a win in the lottery. They mean it, no doubt, as a joke; but pre-Reformation rites of misrule were also celebrated in jest and the best jokes, to be funny, must have a grain of truth.

As well as the mission to the pagans of new worlds and the under-evangelised Christians of an old one, the churches of early modern Europe faced the responsibility of communicating the gospel to unassimilated outsiders at home. These fell into three categories: Jews, Muslims and adherents of pre-Reformation heresies. By the time of the Reformation expulsions had winnowed the Jews of western Europe and shifted their settlement eastward, into the central and eastern Mediterranean, Poland and the region of the lower Danube. Missions were rarely mounted among them in any systematic way. Mass conversions could be achieved only by persecution, which was widely applied; by bribery – which proved useful in Venice where Jews were relatively numerous and where 5,000 were said to have converted in 1724 for 100 scudi each; and by encouraging movements of desertion of their own traditions within Jewish communities.

A spectacular example was that associated with Jacob Frank in eighteenth-century Poland. Even before he was exiled in 1756 as a breaker of the peace, Frank had a dubious reputation. Despite self-avowed ignorance, he became the seer of a sect of worshippers of Shabbetai Zevi, a self-proclaimed 'Messiah' who had defected to Islam in 1666. Frank was a lithe chameleon, who professed Islam in Turkey and Christianity in Poland, where the cult he founded was accused of conducting orgiastic revels with select female novices. His triumphant return in 1759 was marked by a successful disputation with the rabbis of L'viv and a mass baptism of Jewish citizens. After confessing to having impersonated the Messiah he was exiled again to a luxurious retirement near Frankfurt, where he was maintained, by the subscriptions of thousands of devotees, with an income reputedly greater than that of the Polish state. His guard of 1000 hussars wore diamond-studded uniforms and he went to mass in a gilded coach. Outside such unrepresentative episodes, Christian missions among Jews had little success until the nineteenth century, when social emancipation eased Jews out of their ghettos and into ways of life and thought, both Christian and secular, of the societies which surrounded them.

Until the Turkish empire receded in the nineteenth century, the only pockets of Islam in Christian Europe were in Spain and the Russian empire. The Russian conquest of Khazan in 1552 was followed by intensive evangelisation of limited success and a much longer era of persecution; by the mid-eighteenth century the Mongols were no longer considered a political threat and Catherine II began a policy of favouring the preservation of Islam. In early sixteenth-century Spain the mission to the conquered Moors of Granada was something of a dress-rehearsal for the evangelisation of the New World. It had some exemplary features. By the master-mind of its earliest phase, Archbishop Hernando de Talavera, it was conceived as a slow and careful enterprise, typical of the culturally transforming ambitions of the clergy. He would nurture Christianity by changing the dress and language of the converts, who would be spared from the scrutiny of the Inquisition for 40 years. In practice, evangelical impatience wrecked the effort. 'Conversions' were imposed by force and rebellions provoked. Acculturation was rendered impossible by the ghetto-like structures of 'Moorish' communities – not only in Granada but in other areas where Moorish populations were concentrated, in Valencia and Murcia. In 1578, the Granadine communities were split up and spread around the kingdom by a policy of forcible

deportations. In 1609, most of the remaining populations were expelled.

The only large and concentrated heretical churches to survive the middle ages in the west were those of the Hussites in Bohemia and the Waldenses of the Alps. Both in their different ways were swamped by the eddies of the Reformation. Hussites was a catch-all name for followers of doctrines of Jan Hus, the Czech advocate of an invisible 'church of the predestined' who had been burned at the Council of Constance. They included bourgeois congregations, whose worst excesses were communion in both kinds or vernacular services, and menacing practitioners of peasant communism. When Luther read the works of Hus in 1519, he declared that all his doctrines had been anticipated by the earlier reformer. From 1521 he called Hus a saint. Yet a drift of moderate Hussites back to the fold of Rome was already under way. The election of a Habsburg as king of Bohemia in 1526 stimulated it. The establishment of a Jesuit College in Prague in 1547 speeded it. In 1564 it was confirmed by the pope's decision to concede the Hussites' main demand – admission of the laity to the use of the chalice in the eucharist. Meanwhile, overtly Protestant evangelisation was not permitted in Bohemia but the more radical Hussites, especially among the pious movement known as the Unity of Brethren, were in touch with German reformers and influenced by them. Thus between the twin fires of reformist Protestantism and resurgent Catholicism the Hussite tradition melted away.

The nature of the Waldensian heresy is much harder to pin down. Unlike the Hussites, the Waldenses had no coherent body of writings in which their beliefs were defined and differentiated from mainstream Christian tradition. They had their own collective Christian life in parallel with that of the Church, which they never utterly repudiated. The ministry of their preachers or *barbes* was preferred to, but not exclusive of, that of Catholic priests; their morality was particularly tough – or, at least, expressed with particular toughness – but not fundamentally different from that of the rest of western Christendom. Riddled with contradictions, none of the surviving evidence from before the sixteenth century discloses a belief-system which is unequivocally heretical. The Waldenses were distinguished only by their sense of their own distinctiveness and by the harassment, occasionally overflowing into active persecution, with which the Church responded.

This was enough for reformers in Geneva, not far from the Waldenses' valleys, to see them as kindred spirits, potential allies and conscripts to the cause. In Provence, a group similar to the Waldenses initiated contacts with Protestants in the 1530s and received Calvinist writings and preachers with apparent enthusiasm. The Alpine communities have traditionally been seen as similar converts to Protestantism in a rapid mission, launched at their own invitation, at about the same time. In reality, the process was much slower and patchier. Missionary pastors from Geneva began to appear as permanent residents of the valleys in the 1550s; former *barbes* participated in Calvinist synods in the 1560s. In some ways the missionaries themselves were converted at least to Waldensian 'style'; the pithy, jokey preaching of the tradition of the *barbes* persisted in the communities converted to Protestantism. Here, as in much of Europe, 'reformed' religion was really syncretic – a blend of the reformers' doctrines with many of the habits and much of the language of pre-Reformation Christianity.

The evangelical vocations of Protestants, Catholics and Orthodox were most severely tested in the relatively few places where they were trying to convert one another. By repute, the most teeming of these arenas was Poland. In 1838 Count Valerian Krasinski dedicated a history of the Reformation in his native Poland 'to the Protestants of the British Empire and of the United States of America'. He set himself the task of explaining to his co-religionists how, after a promising start, Protestantism had withered in his country. His implicit agenda was even more ambitious. The Protestant in him was fascinated by a tale of subverted Providence, the patriot by a spectacle of national decline; the historian in him wanted to explain both. He beheld the Poland of his day, divided, crushed and oppressed and recalled the Poland of the middle ages, strong, conquering and unconquerable. The defeat of the Reformation was, for Krasinski, the cause of the decline. 'No country in the world affords,' he thought, 'a more striking illustration of the blessings which a political community derives

The burning of Jan Hus, after trial at the Council of Constance, in spite of a safe-conduct, is depicted here with deadpan horror in the fifteenth-century chronicle of Ulrich Richtental *top*. The incident became a *locus classicus* of foreign and Catholic perfidy for Protestant reformers and Czech nationalists while Luther declared that Hus had anticipated his own doctrines perfectly.

'Communicating the gospel to unassimilated outsiders at home.' Sedilia in the mausoleum of Ferdinand and Isabella of Spain *above* are decorated with scenes of the conquest of the last Muslim stronghold in Spain and of the beginnings of the conversion of its inhabitants.

The contrast between 'true' and 'false' religion was made intelligible to a popular market in a woodcut by Lucas Cranach *left*. Luther's preaching and the ministry of baptism and eucharist engage the attention of pious crowds, while away from them scenes of deception, corruption and irreverence in the Church take place, including, in the right foreground, the sale of indulgences.

from the introduction of a scriptural religion, and of the calamities which are entailed by its extinction.' Catholicism was 'the incubus which paralysed the energies of the nation'.

It was not altogether a contemptible theory: similar views have been popular among historians of the decline of Spain, and the power of Protestantism to enhance the liberties of a polity, the achievements of a culture and the performance of an economy is an old theme of Protestant historiography. In the case of Poland, the chronology did not fit: one of the country's most glorious periods, measured by military effectiveness, followed the triumph of Catholicism and during the seventeenth century Polish power was in some ways as remarkable for its durability as for its decline. Yet Krasinski's version of events was typical of its time and influential until ours.

For him, Protestantism and Catholicism seemed like contenders in a cosmic struggle; to us, they look like fighters on the same side, prone to squabble among themselves. In Poland, as in most of western Christendom, they were phases of a single movement – an evangelical movement, aiming to heighten the volume and clarity with which the good news was broadcast. The peculiarity of Poland was that it was a marchland of the Latin west, and the competition of Rome and Reform was complicated in some parts of the kingdom by the presence of a third force: evangelically committed Orthodoxy.

The first big breakthrough of resurgent Catholicism in the Polish dominions came at the expense of Orthodoxy, not Protestantism. In 1596, Catholics and Orthodox met to counter the Protestant threat together, but the Synod of Brest ended in mutual excommunications and squabbles over property. Nonetheless, the adhesion of a large Uniate communion to Roman allegiance was the biggest single coup for Catholicism in Poland since the conversion of the kingdom in 987. The unrepentant Orthodox fought back and in the early seventeenth century seemed in some instances more susceptible to Protestant than Catholic overtures. Cyril Lucaris, who became Patriarch of Constantinople in 1621, broke out of his 'bewitchment' by reading the 'writings of the Evangelical Doctors. ... I left the Fathers, and took for my guide Scripture and the Analogy of Faith alone. .... I can no longer endure to hear men say that the comments of human tradition are of equal weight with Holy Scripture'

Increasingly, however, competition with Catholics and Protestants sharpened Orthodox self-assertion in Poland. In 1632, the Mohlya Academy was founded as a centre of Orthodox teaching; in 1633 the Orthodox hierarchy – in effective abeyance since the Synod of Brest – was re-instated; by the mid-century, Orthodox reconversions from Protestantism matched or exceeded those made by the Catholics in the Ruthenian and Ukrainian provinces. Over a longer period, however, the general outcome favoured Catholicism where the contest was three-cornered. Noble families lost by Orthodoxy to Calvinism in the sixteenth century tended to become Catholic in the seventeenth.

Because of the three-way competition, southern and eastern Poland was a particularly interesting zone of missionary competition; it was also highly exceptional. The fervour the missionaries of different branches of the Church turned outward on the wider world or inward on their own flocks was sparingly expended on rivalry on each others' frontiers. Usually, where territory was in dispute and souls where wavering – in the Low Countries and across Germany, in the eastern Alps and along the Danube – the limits of the Reformation were set by persecutions, expulsions and war. The spiritual Reconquista achieved by the Counter-Reformation and especially by its conquistador-vanguard, the Jesuits, worked best in under-evangelised terrain, as in Ireland, or where a non-Protestant 'third force' could be galvanised on its behalf, as in Poland.

The missionary impulse inside Europe, despite its limitations, was not without effects. There was no revolution in the spirituality of ordinary men, but there was a genuine transformation in the language and imagery – the total communication – of the Christian faith. For Protestant divines, vernacular services and the promotion of the Bible in translation were ways of helping the laity to a more active involvement in their faith; for Catholics the same purposes came to be represented by frequent communion and – for the particular involvement of women – the extension of the cults of Mary. 'You seem to think Christ was drunk,'

132

Luther thundered against sophisticated doctrines of the eucharist, 'having imbibed too much at supper, and wearied his disciples with meaningless words!' This daring joke had a scandalous whiff of blasphemy about it when it was uttered. But it had the great virtue of treating Christ's humanity as literal and of picturing him, if only for our reproof, in the flesh of characteristically human weakness. Veronese, who introduced ribald scenes into his version of the *Last Supper*, was obliged to re-label it *Feast in the House of Levi*. Yet by the end of the sixteenth century, Caravaggio was able to depict the same event as an episode of tavern low-life, without irreverence. Mathias Grünewald locked away his drawing of Christ as a coarse and low-browed picaroon; but after more than a century Murillo could paint the Christ-child as a naughty boy without fear of correction. As a result of the churches' early modern mission to bring Christianity to the people, sacred subjects were hallowed precisely by their relevance to the lives of ordinary people. On the ascent to heaven, Martha had caught up with Mary.

The Reformation is often understood as a movement to purge the sacred world of profanities; to some of its critics, it was almost the opposite: a step on the road to a secular society, a transference of sacred responsibilities into profane hands. The total effect of the changes made by early modern developments in Christianity seems rather to have been to re-define the relationship between the holy and the secular – to re-knit the two kinds of stitching in a new pattern. What Catholics could do with uninhibited freedom in the visual arts, Protestant propagandists could do in hymns: bringing the denizens of heaven down from the clouds as companions for us in our sufferings, sharers in our woes. The cults of a human Christ – wounded or dead – and of suffering saints, writhing in martyrdom, are most vivid in the tearful and bloody representations of baroque art. But in Protestant hymnody some of the images are just as clear, just as poignant, and just as powerful in bringing heaven home to earth. The vulnerability of a baby asleep on the hay was perfectly captured by Luther. The love gaping from Christ's wounded heart is as touching in Moravian hymns as in the visions described by St Margaret Mary Alacocque and depicted on Catholic altars. Contemplation of a sanguinary *Ecce Homo* can only be helped by Bach's setting of *O Sacred Head*.

Cultural conquests usually happen reciprocally. Hard as early modern European elites wrenched at popular culture, the images of collective memory and imagination survived to become influential in their turn. The romantic movement, which supplied the common culture of Europe in the nineteenth century, was not just a reaction against informally deified reason and classicism: it was also a re-blending of popular sensibilities into the values and tastes of educated people. Its poetry was 'the language of ordinary men'; its visual aesthetics were drawn from the grandeur of rustic habitats; its religion was the 'enthusiasm' which had been a dirty word in eighteenth-century salons and consistories but which had inspired peasant 'Pietism' in Halle and drawn thousands to Methodist meetings in the open air of rural England. The music of romanticism ransacked traditional airs for its melodies; its theatre and opera borrowed from the charivari of street theatre and roving mummers. Its prophet was Herder, who identified the moral power of the 'true poetry' of 'those whom we call savages'. Its philosopher was Rousseau, who taught the superiority of untutored passions over contrived refinement. Its slogan was devised by that indefatigable collector of folk-tales, Jakob Grimm: 'Das Volk dichtet.' Its *reductio ad absurdum* included the late eighteenth-century portraits of society ladies in peasant dress and the garden-designs in which nature took its revenge: no art was more expressive of reason's power to re-fashion the environment, but none was more vulnerable to re-invasion by romance. The phoney folk-poems forged by exploiters of the fashion for '*Reliques of Ancient Poesy*' represent the same trend – though the most notorious example, that of James Macpherson, who claimed to have discovered the epics of Ossian in 1760, was an informed imposture, crafted in part out of a pastiche of genuine Gaelic ballads. 'The people' had arrived in European history as a creative force and as a re-moulder of its masters in its own image. The century of romanticism would also be a century of awakening democracy, socialism, industrialisation, 'total' war and of the 'masses backed', by far-seeing members of the elite, 'against the classes'.

In the eighteenth century, many towns in Poland remained predominantly Protestant. Baroque shrines, such as the church of Swieta Lipka near Ketrzyn in Poland *above left*, mobilised Catholic pilgrims and advertised the glories of Catholicism as part of the religious orders' campaign of evangelisation.

Eighteenth-century idealisation of the shepherd-life generated much charming nonsense: theatrical and operatic idylls, the romantic preference of Gibbon for the history of 'shepherd-peoples' and the huge numbers of paintings of society ladies in pastoral disguise, such as Joseph Wright's portrait of Anna Ashton, Mrs Thomas Chase *left*.

The early Methodist habit of meeting in the open air accorded with an eighteenth-century spiritual idealisation of nature, and symbolised the exclusive attitude of the Anglican establishment. John Wesley, the founder of the Methodist movement, preaches from his father's tomb *above*.

Goya's scenes of popular culture painted in the 1790s included witchcraft, bullfighting, banditry, festivals, prison- and mad-house-life and, here *below*, a performance of strolling players before a vulgar audience. Harlequin juggles with wine-glasses, suggesting the fragility and hazards of the love-triangle depicted by the performers in what the billboard announces as an 'Allegory in the manner of Menander'.

Snowstorm: steamboat off a harbour mouth J.M.W. Turner 1842

CLIMACTERIC

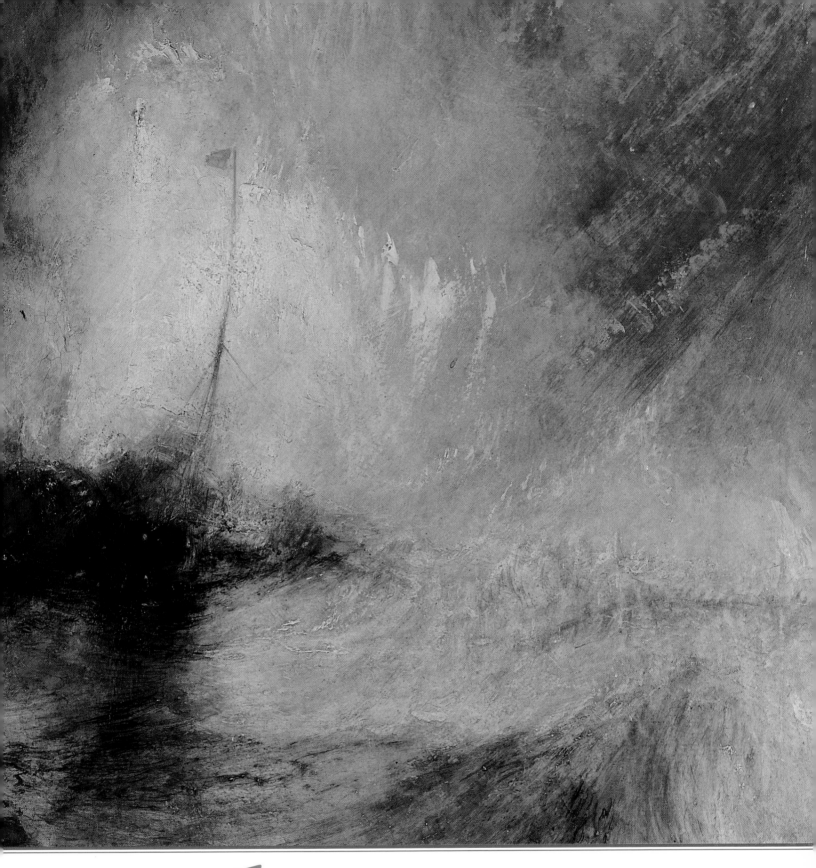

and SURVIVAL

1815–2000

CHAPTER 8

A PLACE IN THE WORLD
The European miracle

THE EMBASSY WHICH ARRIVED OFF CANTON in June 1793 lacked nothing that might embellish its dignity and emphasise its prestige. George III had elevated its leader to the peerage for the occasion and equipped him with a retinue 84 strong. His gifts for the Chinese court, worth over £15,000, included a letter to the emperor in a box made of gold and all the most new-fangled hardware of early British industrialisation: a planetarium, globes, mathematical instruments, chronometers of apparently magical accuracy, a telescope, instruments for chemical and electrical experiments, plate glass, Wedgwood ware, Sheffield plate and samples of textiles woven on power looms.

The Chinese were not wholly contemptuous of these efforts. Indeed, restrainedly pleased at the arrival of this 'first tributary mission' from Britain, the emperor ordered that on account of the envoys' long journey they should be accorded a better welcome than corresponding missions from Burma and Annam. He did not endorse, however, the high value the British put on themselves: Lord Macartney's refusal to knock his head on the ground in greeting to the emperor was indulged as a piece of barbarian bad manners, but all the ambassador's diplomatic overtures were rejected. The British were told that they were incapable of 'acquiring the rudiments of our civilisation', that they possessed nothing China needed and that their representatives could not be accommodated at the imperial court. 'It is your bounden duty,' the emperor concluded in his reply to George III, 'reverently to appreciate my feelings and to obey these instructions henceforth for all time'.

The Chinese attitude has generally been regarded as arrogant, unrealistic and hidebound by outmoded traditions. In fact, it reflected the world balance of power. During the eighteenth century, despite the long reach of some European empires, China's was by almost every standard still the fastest-growing in the world. European outposts of, as yet, unpredictable importance had been founded in Australia and the American far west, but at the time of Macartney's embassy Britain and France had recently lost most of their American colonies while the other European seaborne empires – those of Spain, Portugal, the Netherlands, Denmark and Sweden – all seemed to be stagnant or declining. Napoleon's opinion that 'it is in the east that great reputations are made' was based not only on his reading of the history of earlier would-be world-conquerors but also on a realistic appraisal of the opportunities of his day.

Although some of Macartney's 'tribute' showed how fast Europe was catching up and, in some respects, taking the lead in industrial production, China still had a more mature industrial economy by most standards – including size of firms, numbers employed, rates of output and degree of geographical specialisation – than any potential rival in the west. According to eye-witnesses a porcelain centre in Kiangsu province 'made the ground shake with the noise of tens of thousands of pestles – the heavens are alight with the glare from the furnaces, so that one cannot sleep at night'; there were ironworks in Szechuan that employed two or three thousand men; in Kwangtung water-driven hammers pounded incense 'without any expenditure of muscular effort'; in Kiangsi similar machines for husking rice were lined up by the hundred; in Fukien water-driven paper-makers hummed 'like the whir of wings'. China still enjoyed her centuries-old advantage over Europe in terms of trade: indeed, this remained the case until the 1860s.

A Chinese tapestry depicting Macartney's visit *far right* portrays the fabulous gifts which the emissary brought with him to impress the Chinese emperor, including, to the right, a huge globe needing more than a dozen men to carry it.

Napoleon's oriental route to 'a great reputation': the Battle of the Pyramids, 1798 *top*, engraved on wood for the popular series of nostalgic imperial images produced by the Epinal Press in the reign of Louis-Philippe.

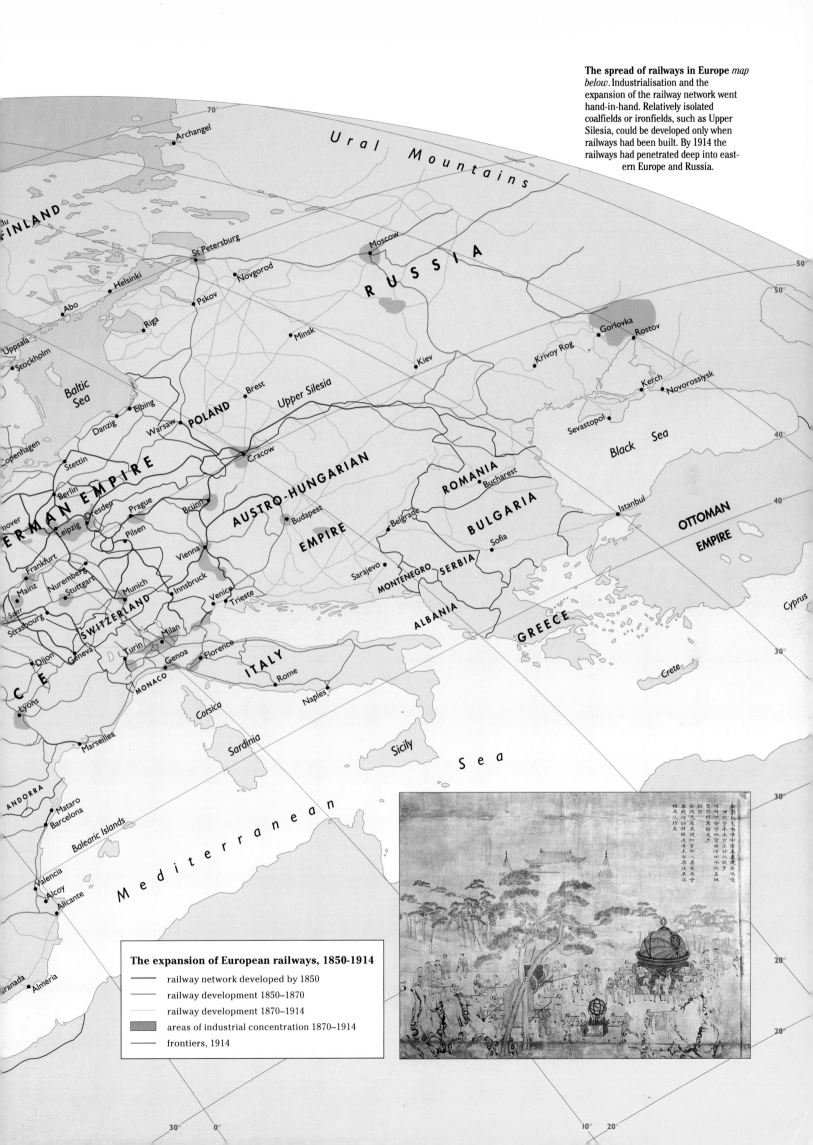

The spread of railways in Europe *map below*. Industrialisation and the expansion of the railway network went hand-in-hand. Relatively isolated coalfields or ironfields, such as Upper Silesia, could be developed only when railways had been built. By 1914 the railways had penetrated deep into eastern Europe and Russia.

The expansion of European railways, 1850-1914

— railway network developed by 1850
— railway development 1850–1870
— railway development 1870–1914
▓ areas of industrial concentration 1870–1914
— frontiers, 1914

At the start of the nineteenth century, Blake could still draw Europe as a Grace among equals in the dance of the continents. Over the century as a whole, however, Europe's place in the world was transformed by unprecedented demographic, industrial and technological strides. The result was a period of European world-hegemony in which European powers directly ruled much of the world and European political influence and 'business-imperialism' combined to guide or control much of the rest. It was, by the standards of world history, a brief phenomenon: by the end of the century Japan and the United States had overtaken most European countries in industrial prowess and in their capacity for war. After half a century more, European empires would collapse as spectacularly as they had arisen. Still, the nineteenth remains a century of 'European miracle': the startling culmination of long, faltering commercial 'out-thrust', imperial initiatives and scientific progress in the early modern period.

At the beginning of the process, neither Europe as a whole nor any part of it had obvious advantages: an Atlantic-side position, however, proved to be of crucial importance. In the age of sail, maritime route-finding depended on access to favourable winds and currents. Navigators from the Indian Ocean and western Pacific

would not have found conditions particularly propitious for long-range navigation outside the zone of monsoons, even had they wished to do so. The only navigable route eastwards across the Pacific was an effective dead-end until trading-places developed on the west coast of America in colonial times. The ways out of the Indian Ocean to the south were laborious and dangerous and led, as far as was known, only to unrewarding destinations. The Atlantic, by contrast, was a highway to the rest of the world. Its wind-systems provided potential links with the Pacific and Indian Oceans, as well as routes between the Old and New Worlds.

Above all, the Atlantic led towards the exploitable seaborne empires of the early modern period. It is easy to over-estimate the contribution these made to the European miracle. On the whole, overseas colonies demanded laborious investment and paid modest returns. They drained manpower from the home country without normally adding much to long-term demand: on the contrary, in the early modern period it was a common experience for mother-countries to find that their colonies developed regional economies, 'creole mentalities' and independence movements. The biggest, most precocious and, in terms of cash yield, richest of the empires – that of Spain – never stimulated much of a domestic commercial or industrial revolution. Yet gradually and in less obvious ways, overseas imperialism did contribute to the making of European world hegemony. In the late seventeenth century, the Dutch in the spice islands of what was to become Indonesia switched the focus of their efforts from trade and piracy to the direct control and manipulation of production. This change of policy imposed the expensive travail of territorial conquest and the ruinous burden of extensive garrisons but it enriched Amsterdam and helped to shift the terms of trade between Europe and Asia in the former's favour. In the late eighteenth and early nineteenth centuries, the industrialisation of Britain kept rough pace with the de-industrialisation of India at British bayonet-point. Domination of

Forming the colophon of J.G. Stedman's account of his experience during the horrific war against rebellious Black slaves in Surinam in the 1790s, Blake's engravings of the dance of the continents showed Europe supported by Africa and America *left*.

The power of opium: the drug outweighs the scruple and the merchant towers over the producer in a nineteenth-century Indian painting on mica *right*. Organised production and trade on a massive scale enabled the British to reverse the secular balance of trade with China.

At first welcomed in the east as traders, the Dutch were increasingly, as the seventeenth century went on, resisted as conquerors, a development illustrated by the fortifications of the Javanese royal stronghold at Palembang *below*.

India acquired even more significance in the nineteenth century when Indian land was turned over to the production of tea and opium, with which China's trade balance was destroyed, and ultimately to the farming of quinine in industrial quantities, which immunised European armies against the worst effects of warfare in tropical environments.

Then there were the food products of the colonies which nourished Europe's demographic upsurge. The real treasure of the New World is sometimes said today to have been the indigenous food crops – above all, maize and potatoes – the sustaining stodge which revolutionised Old World diets. In Europe, which had privileged access to New World agronomy, maize was unsuitable for the climate of much of the best land, and unpalatable to the people of much of the rest. It had a restricted but vital importance in the Balkans, where it made life possible at relatively high altitudes in the eighteenth century, nourishing effectively autonomous communities beyond the grasp of Ottoman tax-gatherers and the reach of Ottoman administrators, weaning the future political independence of Greece, Serbia and Romania from their mountain cradles. Thus in this corner of Europe, a resource from the cornucopia of European overseas expansion really can be shown to

have made a direct contribution to the adjustment of the frontier with Islam in Christendom's favour.

In nutritional value, maize is exceeded by the potato. Both crops have a significantly higher yield of calories than all other staples except rice – which is roughly equivalent – but the potato, unlike maize, supplies unaided all the nutrients man needs. Thanks to the adaptation of this Andean tuber, the influence of New World crops on regional agronomies of the Old World was probably highest in northern Europe, where the potato attained a mastery maize could never achieve anywhere outside the New World. Potatoes supplanted rye as the food base of a vast swathe of mankind from Ireland across the northern European plain to Russia. It was spread by war, for peasants, eluding requisition with the aid of a crop that could be left concealed in the ground, survived on potatoes when other food was in short supply.

Essayed with success in the Basque country and Ireland, the potato began its war-linked career of conquest in Belgium in the 1680s under the impact of Louis XIV's drive for a rational French frontier. The troubles of the next century sowed it in Germany and Poland and the Napoleonic wars took it to Russia, where it conquered a territory Napoleon was unable to subjugate with the

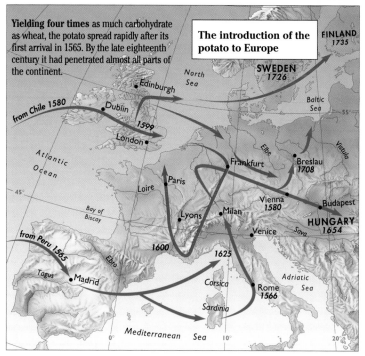

The introduction of the potato to Europe

FINLAND 1735

SWEDEN 1726

North Sea

Baltic Sea

from Chile 1580

Edinburgh

Dublin

1599

London

Atlantic Ocean

Elbe

Breslau 1708

Vistula

Frankfurt

Paris

Loire

Vienna 1580

Budapest

Bay of Biscay

Lyons

Milan

HUNGARY 1654

Sava

from Peru 1565

1600

Venice

1625

Ebro

Tagus

Madrid

Corsica

Adriatic Sea

Rome 1566

Sardinia

Mediterranean   Sea

entire Grande Armée. The acreage planted with potatoes increased with every European war down to and including the Second World War. On its way, it was helped by the patronage of savants and monarchs. Catherine the Great promoted it in 1765. In the 1780s, when the peasants of Austrian Galicia refused to eat this suspicious newcomer, Joseph II had it planted by soldiers, who then, by contrived negligence, left the potatoes unguarded at night. The peasants stole them and so acquired the taste. Marie Antoinette – unfairly cast as a promoter of cake for the masses – advertised the merits of the same vegetable by wearing potato flowers in her dress. It fed some of the industrialising, urbanising surplus populations of the nineteenth and twentieth centuries in Germany and Russia. In Ireland, its failure in 1845-6 released emigrant labour for the British and North American industrial revolutions. It can therefore be said to have helped to make possible the new means of production which gave the nineteenth-century west an advantage in competition with the rest of the world. Alongside the potato, traditional food-sources were produced with revolutionary efficiency in nineteenth-century Europe. Winter roots like turnips and beetroot or soil-nourishing crops like clover and alfalfa reduced the amount of land lying fallow at any one time and fed increasing numbers of livestock.

In part, the new methods were responses to already-discernible increases in population caused by declining death-rates – and some increase in birth-rates – in the relatively peaceful and orderly

Europe of the eighteenth century. This world-changing phenomenon has been explained in various ways, all of them more or less unsatisfactory. The postponement of the victory of death, the drawing of its sting, probably owed less to human efforts than to the vagaries of epidemiology: the rapid, ill-documented and unpredictable evolution of the micro-organisms that carried fatal disease. The mass pestilences that attacked Europe in the eighteenth and nineteenth centuries seem in general to have been less virulent than those which struck in the 'age of plague' from the fourteenth to the seventeenth century.

The doom-fraught theories of Thomas Malthus were therefore of their time – a voice crying for the want of a wilderness, an earnest, rational clergyman peering with anxious charity into a grave new world of over-population tempered by disaster. Most of Malthus's fellow-intellectuals – the Board of Agriculture in Britain, the 'physiocrats' in France, the Royal Economic Societies in Spain – were convinced that population growth could be sustained by 'progress' and, in particular, that agricultural 'improvement' could enhance the nutrition of individuals while generating a surplus to feed many more mouths. These optimistic opinions were justified in the event. In the course of the nineteenth century, most European countries roughly doubled their populations. That of Russia increased four times over. At the same time, enough surplus population was generated to populate 'new Europes' in the

An Irish peasant hut during the Potato Famine of 1845 *below left*. An air of rustic simplicity jars with the grim ugliness of starvation in this powerful engraving.

An image of warfare *below*: Cholera 'Tramples the victor and the vanquish'd both.'

Agustín de Betancourt, the engineer who helped establish scientific training in his native Spain, was honoured all over Europe by the organisations which promoted 'useful knowledge', including Britain's Board of Agriculture, who conferred on him the diploma reproduced *above*.

temperate parts of the Americas, Australia, New Zealand and South
Africa. Over the eighteenth and nineteenth centuries as a whole,
despite the big rises in population in some parts of Asia, Europe's
relative share of the world's human resources rose dramatically,
from around a fifth to over a quarter.

Even so, Europe never had enough manpower to dominate the
world. The shortfall was made up with the resources of industrial
technology, harnessing the power of steam to make the labour of
workers more effective and improving the precision, adaptability
and reliability of European armies in hostile environments. The
industrial 'revolution' gave the civilisation which sponsored it a
decisive advantage over others. Europe's head start, though
closely followed by North America and East Asia, helped shape
what remains, on the map, one of the most conspicuous features of
the modern world: a zone of fairly densely clustered industrial
cities from Belfast and Bilbao to Rostov and St Petersburg. By the
end of the nineteenth century, industrialisation, though it had
started at the western end of the continent, was a genuinely
pan-European feature: by 1890, twenty per cent of Austrians were
factory workers; the first electric underground railway was in
Hungary in 1896; the biggest factories in Europe were undertakings
of 'state capitalism' in Russia. Even today, in the last decade of our
millennium, when the world has had time to catch up and the
technology of the industrial revolution is itself out of date, the
legacy of early industrialisation gives the European economy a
distinctive profile, with an industrial zone more concentrated than
in North America, more extensive than in Japan.

Flattering reasons are sometimes cited for the priority of
Europe's, and in particular Britain's, industrialisation on the
assumption that industrialised societies are better, more
'progressive' than those which leave industry in the hands of
traditional artisanates. In the nineteenth century in Europe, even
socialists, who deplored the supposed effects of industrialisation
on workers' lives, revelled in the march of history towards an
inevitable climax. Nowadays, when we are still clearing up the
detritus of the industrial revolution, the progressivist fallacy is

Rus in urbe: Bath Road, Bedford Park,
London *above right*. This development,
designed by Norman Shaw from 1875
onwards, was the earliest attempt to
simulate a rural idyll for the urban middle
class: 'a garden suburb' of semi-detached
brick houses in tree-lined avenues.

Factories erupted in rural solitudes.
The Lendersdorf steel works *above*, which
is seen here in a painting by Karl Schütz
of the 1830s, appeared suddenly near
Düren, west of Cologne, to supply the new-
born railways on what became one of the
most heavily industrialised economic
corridors of Europe.

Population growth in Europe *maps right*
closely followed the contours of the spread
of the Industrial Revolution. In 1820,
Europe's principal centres of population
were the industrialised regions of the
United Kingdom and a few major cities
and ports (London, Paris, St. Petersburg,
Liverpool, Bordeaux, Hamburg,
Marseilles). By 1900 population density
had increased throughout most of Europe,
but remained concentrated in the industrial regions of Britain, Belgium, France,
Italy and Germany.

more easily eluded. The people responsible for the domestication of steam power are no longer likely to be credited with superiority of intellect, morals or imagination over the rest of mankind. Nor is there any demonstrable correlation between industrialisation and an identifiable set of social values.

Britain was in some respects well suited to be a 'steam intellect' society, where invention could be mothered by taste rather than necessity, but the values of the elite in most of the country remained profoundly rural throughout the industrial revolution; for captains of industry, industrial wealth was typically a means to the creation of a rural idyll; their managers, who could not afford country estates, simulated the longed-for way of life in garden suburbs. The industrial revolution was not strictly a British, but a regional phenomenon; the south of the country actually experienced a de-industrialisation, like India's in miniature, as its traditional industries were replaced by the new mechanised versions taking shape in the Midlands and the north. Britain was briefly 'the workshop of the world' but remained the world's insurer and rentier for much longer.

Industrialisation in nineteenth-century France, formerly condemned as backward by native historians in the grip of an inferiority complex as they looked across the Channel, has now been elevated to its due rank among the steam-clouded olympians. Here too the industrialists often reflected the values of the society around them in evincing scorn for the enterprise that made them rich. In 1836, a member of a great textiles dynasty of the north went on a pilgrimage 'to obtain illumination from the Holy Ghost so that we should never undertake anything in business above our strength, lest we should be troubled by hazardous speculations'. When François Wendel died in 1825, he left a fortune of four million francs from his iron works but claimed to regret this diversion from his envisioned destiny as a soldier or sailor – he ended up 'against my will, iron master and owner of several firms which have prospered despite and against all'. An 'enterprise culture' did come to exist in nineteenth-century Europe, but it seems from the chronology to have been the child, rather than the begetter,

European population growth, 1820 – c.1900

1820		c.1900	
0–20	60–80	0–20	100–200
20–40	80–100	20–50	Over 200
40–60	over 100	50–100	

inhabitants per square mile   inhabitants per square mile

c. 1900

NORWAY SWEDEN St Petersburg

Atlantic Ocean

North Sea

DENMARK Baltic Sea

Hamburg

UNITED KINGDOM Belfast Liverpool London HOLLAND BELGIUM

GERMAN EMPIRE RUSSIA

FRANCE Paris

SWITZ. AUSTRO-HUNGARIAN EMPIRE

Bay of Biscay Bordeaux

Bilbao Marseilles

PORTUGAL SPAIN

ITALY MONTE-NEGRO Adriatic Sea

ROMANIA SERBIA BULGARIA Blac

OTTOMAN EMPIR

Mediterranean Sea

GREECE Aegean Sea

NORWAY SWEDEN St Petersburg

North Sea DENMARK

Baltic Sea

Hamburg

GERMAN CONFEDERATION RUSSIA

UNITED NETHERLANDS

SWITZ. HABSBURG EMPIRE

ITALY MONTE-NEGRO Adriatic Sea OTTOMAN Black Sea

EMPIRE Aegean Sea

Sea

of industrialisation – another mass product, factory-produced and widely circulated. In Russia, the shaky foundations of industrialisation owed virtually nothing to entrepreneurialism. In the 1860s the government invested nearly three times as much in the railways as private sources of finance. The metallurgical industry of the Urals was government-owned and relied at first on serf labour.

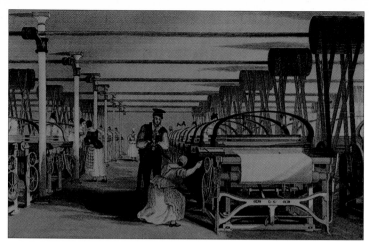

The philosophies which seem best to characterise the industrial phase of western history – utilitarianism, pragmatism, Marxism – were among its results, not its causes, and their opposition is profound to the disembodied rationalism, disinterested science and disinterred classicism which ruled western intellects on industrialisation's eve. Mr Gadgrind's curriculum of facts was as far from the humanist tradition as you could get. Individualism – admittedly – is a good ethos for an industrialising society and may have helped to impel mechanisation by raising labour costs in Britain, say, or Belgium. In Japan, conversely, individualism has never been a prominent part of prevailing values but the country was as avid as any in embracing industrialisation. If propitious social values and intellectual trends were sufficient conditions of industrial advance, Egypt, where Islamic apologists had written capitalism into the prevailing scheme by the late eighteenth century, might almost have been expected to rival Britain as the 'first industrial nation'. Nor can Europe's supposedly 'scientific culture' be shown to have bred industrialisation. The inventors of the late eighteenth-century processes which made the nineteenth-century revolution possible – of coke smelting, mechanised spinning, steam-pumping and the steam-driven loom – were all heroes of 'self-help', self-taught artisans and engineers with little or no scientific formation. It would be truer to say that European science was hijacked for the aims of industry – bought by money for 'useful research', diverted by dogmas of social responsibility – than that it had an inbuilt practical vocation.

An engine of the industrial revolution: the steam loom *top left*, developed at the end of the eighteenth century, increased the speed of power-driven machinery and helped establish firmly the factory system of weaving in Europe.

While de Louthenbourg's view of Coalbrookdale *above* – the pioneering smelting-works of the Darby family – of 1801 has a demonically heroic quality, outlined against noxious flames, William Ibbitt's mid-nineteenth-century views of Sheffield have a tranquil, pastoral character, uneasily suited to the panorama of smoking factory chimneys *above left*. In 1872, Kurt Ekwall opted for faintly crusading realism in depicting the lives of construction workers in a shanty town outside Berlin *left*.

Rather than speculating further about the causes of industrialisation, it may be more fruitful to try briefly to evoke it through its effects. The spread of industrial revolution has been measured in various ways: by planting pinheads in the map to show the proliferation of steam-powered factories or railway termini; by counting profits and collating statistics of output; by chronicling the characteristic diseases and disorders that bred in the fearsome early-industrial slums of Europe, over-crowded and under-sanitised; by enumerating the saints of 'the gospel of work' who created wealth through enterprise or invention and spread it through philanthropy or enlightened self-interest; or by echoing the volume of the cries of the urban slum-dwellers, deracinated and re-located in ruthless environments, like the Manchester of Engels or Zola's mines.

Or one can track the effects of industrialisation in landscapes and townscapes or see the process unfold, through the eyes of artists who beheld it directly. Late-eighteenth century painters all shared what might be called a Cyclopean vision of industrial work: a single-eyed and romantic image of Vulcan's forge, like Durameau's Roman salt-petre factory of the 1760s or de Louthenbourg's view of Coalbrookdale in 1801, in which the mephitic blaze of the furnaces seems to have been re-sanctified in a pastoral setting. Near the latter painting in the Science Museum in London hang others which document later phases. To William Ibbitt in the mid-nineteenth century, Sheffield seemed like a utopian city, merging into the surrounding hills; the uniform, gentle light was unsullied by the smoke of 50 factory chimneys that rose in parallel with church spires; mines and railways in the painting juxtapose a re-forged land-scape with a great piazza of sidings and sheds. In the foreground, workers relax, children play and a bourgeois family surveys the city with pride. By contrast, the vastly increased scale and pace of indus-trialisation in the second half of the century is reflected in Lowry's nameless town of 1922, from where every hint of nature is excluded, except in the patches of bleak sky visible between smoggy blots.

No individual better exemplifies the nineteenth-century cult of the engineer as hero than Gustave Eiffel, who specialised in monumental projects calculated to extend the limits of the possible, like the bridge over the Douro at Oporto *above*.

The Templeton carpet factory, Glasgow, 1889 *left*, designed by William Leiper, looks more like a civic 'palace' in the Venetian gothic style romanticised by Ruskin's mid-century work *The Stones of Venice*.

Bourneville *right*, built from 1893 by the chocolate-manufacturing Cadbury brothers, primarily to house their workers, was erected to a picturesque aesthetic, with a variety of simple, vernacular designs built into the natural contours of the site.

Little matchstick-people with pale, featureless faces move mechanically in gas-light and grimy shadows. A spectral cathedral seems to vanish into the background, like the wraith of spiritual values.

The industrial era is also recalled by the survival of the new kinds of public space it erected on cast-iron arches: its sinuous bridges and its crystal palaces – the covered markets, railway stations, winter gardens, shopping arcades – were its equivalents of the aqueducts and agoras of antiquity. The implicit messages of its most solid monuments, the great factories, can be read where they still stand. The best examples still visible today are often in uncharacteristically rural settings. Just outside a country town in Oxfordshire, one of the 'cathedrals of industry' – Bliss Valley Tweed Mill of 1872 – has recently been converted into luxury flats. It was made to resemble a grand château in a parkland setting, with a balustraded parapet and corner towers crowned by urns. In the central dome and elegant tapering chimneystack, a church or abbey is vaguely suggested. In a rural setting on the Marne, the Menier factory still looks much as in engravings of the 1860s: the main building is an iron-framed palace incongruously perched on the weir which gave it power, decorated with the fussy geometry of the mansions and civic monuments of the northern European tradition.

Sometimes the factories' messages to onlookers are made explicit in contemporary accounts of these unprecedented buildings. The notions that informed them were captured, for instance, in a newspaper's praise of the factories of Sabadell, outside Barcelona, in 1855: the nobility of work, the power-hunger of a meritocratic bourgeoisie, the puritanical morals of bosses' paternalism.

And these factories, grand and elegant ... are sumptuous palaces which ought to inspire their owners and all the people with pride ... These palaces house no pharaohs, no orgies, but are a means of life for hundreds of families. These palaces are not there to inspire vanity or arrogance, but love of work and respect for effort and for merit.

Description of life in the textile mills of the time reeked, on the contrary, of the 'sweat of the common man'. But the praise offered here was not disingenuous. Factory builders sensed a genuine contrast between the common good served by their edifices and the vainglory of those which past ages had produced on a similar scale. Theirs were the first palaces of production in a history of palaces of consumption. Barcelona's Casarramona factory of 1911, now a police barracks, expresses this ethos perfectly: two fairytale campaniles preside over a battlemented skyline, below which huge windows in ranks of slim bays flood the interior with light from large interior spaces. Churches, castles, palaces and artists' studios are all archly quoted or brazenly trumped. Templeton's carpet factory of 1889 still stands on Glasgow Green, a Venetian palazzo built in brick to be 'the finest thing outside Italy' and enriched with

turquoise mosaics and twirling pilasters, guelfic battlements and spiralling towers.

Outside the model-factories and the model-towns built by some philanthropic industrialists for their workers, in the streets and slums created by the concentration of labour, the effort to erect a romantic environment for the industrial society – to rebuild Jerusalem among 'dark, satanic mills' – was a horrible failure. In most places where it happened, industrialisation was nasty, brutish and quick and threw up gimcrack cities which were fearsome incubators of disease and disorder. Manchester in the 1830s and 1840s and Barcelona in the 1850s and 1860s are the best-known cases, because of the large number of enquiries and reports they attracted from philanthropic reformers. In Barcelona the physician Jaume Salarich was commissioned to survey working-class health by well-intentioned proprietors, in imitation of Edwin Chadwick's *Sanitary Condition of the Labouring Population* of 1842, based chiefly on the author's work in Manchester. His clinical picture of the effects of breathing in the atmosphere of the textile mills – profuse sweat, languor, gastric trouble, respiratory difficulties, laboured movements, poor circulation, mental torpor, nervous prostration, pulmonary corrosion and poisoning from noxious machine oils and dyes – is amply confirmed by surviving personal testimony. When he got home from such a workplace, the mechanic might find the conditions deplored in Manchester in 1832 by the cotton-workers' doctor, Philip Kay: 'an air of discomfort, if not

loathsome wretchedness, ... dilapidated, badly drained, damp'; or he might even be confined to one of the cellar-dwellings described by Chadwick, swilling with filth from the street and sopping with wetness from underground, while disease got trapped in the bad ventilation. The new concept of 'public health' was the goad reformers used to get cities rebuilt. When Charles Creighton published his *History of Epidemics in Britain* in 1894, he was disinclined to share the self-congratulation of his fellow-medics on the progress of their battle against disease; he regarded the elimination of typhus from British cities, for instance, as in part a statistical illusion caused by the re-classification of cases as 'typhoid'; but he acknowledged the importance of the re-housing of the working class 'in regular streets opening on wide thoroughfares' and the provision of sewerage and clean water.

Reformers stressed the effects of an industrial environment on workers' morale even more than their material plight. Philip Kay watched the tenants of such vile housing 'denying themselves the comforts of life in order that they might wallow in the unrestrained licence of animal appetite'. Jaume Balmes, the great ethical critic of Barcelona's industrial revolution, thought the workers of that city were worse off than the slaves of antiquity, who had at least some protection from the economic lurches and fluctuations that could turn poverty into destitution overnight. One of the most effective strictures on urban overcrowding was – in the words of a London physician in 1858 – that 'it almost necessarily involves such negation

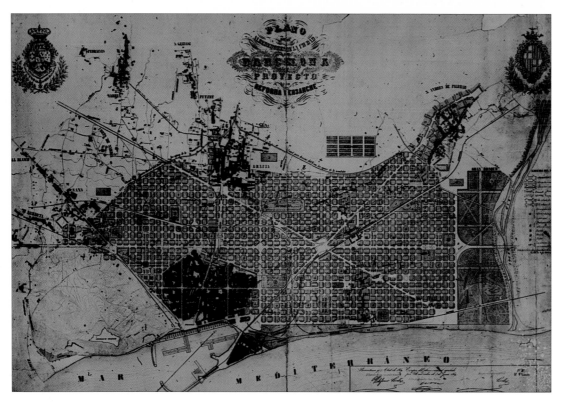

of all delicacy, such unclean confusion of bodies and bodily functions, such mutual exposure of animal and sexual nakedness, as is rather bestial than human.' As if this were not enough, Marx, who slept with his housemaid, claimed that ruthless bosses threatened workers with sexual exploitation.

The moral dangers were not confined to the workers. In Barcelona, a newspaper which urged workers to see their masters as divine instruments for their sustenance also warned owners that 'the mechanics in your factories are made of the same clay of which you are formed ... and must not be confused with the machines you have in your workshops.' This mixture – a conscience tempered by pragmatism – was typical of the Catholic response to industrialisation in countries where the church moulded the moral consensus. Moral restraint, Christian philanthropy and 'enlightened self-interest' blunted the fangs of industrial capitalism and helped to ensure that in the long run the proletariat benefited from the wealth which industries created. Marx's warnings that the workers would be driven to revolution by impoverishment went unfulfilled because it was heeded in time. They soon had more than chains to lose – a genuine stake in the societies of which they formed part. Prominent among Creighton's reasons for the decline of disease were cheap food and good wages. The rise of town planning in the second half of the nineteenth century was in part the embodiment of a romantic aesthetic of light and air, in part the triumph of an originally classical prejudice in favour of rational layouts and grid plans. But it also served to illustrate the 'improving' power of industrial capitalism: the light and air made practical contributions to public health; the uniformity of the grid plan spoke to the depths of social egalitarianism.

And so one can judge industrialisation by the reaction against it: not only that of the reformers who tried to civilise its effects, or of the Luddites who smashed its machinery in defence of their jobs, or of the political movements, which are the subject of the next chapter, and which tried to exploit or deflect it in the interests of the people or the state, but also that of the romantics who tried to escape from it. Ironically, these included some of its beneficiaries. G. Poldi-Pezzoli, one of the fathers of industrial Milan, had a 'Dante room' in his house, where he would retreat among his collection of medieval art. The sublime architect Antoni Gaudi professed to hate the machine age and created fantasy-buildings in which the Barcelonese bourgeoisie could be secluded from its effects, but,

until his religiously inspired retirement from the world, he relied on the patronage of captains of industry. The most extravagantly escapist country-house of Victorian England, Cragside in Northumbria, where every detail embodied the craftsmanlike revulsion from industrial uniformity proclaimed by Ruskin and William Morris, was built for the country's biggest arms manufacturer: it was also the first house in England to be lit by electric light. In Holstein, Theodor Storm wrote rustic lyrics from the safety of his Aktentisch. Ironically, the machine-age helped to fortify

the sentimental hold of romanticism on the nineteenth-century elite, partly by providing a foil and partly by enabling romantic fantasies to be lived in comfort.

Finally, one can try to interrogate the ghosts of the pre-industrial past, to conjure the 'world we have lost': the ways of life and social structures eroded or destroyed by the new organisational imperatives of factory-based production. The nearest thing to a factory in pre-industrial Britain was the perhaps fictional — certainly romanticised — 'great household and family' of Jack of Newbury, who was supposed to have employed 600 people on 200 looms in a single building in the reign of Henry VIII. But the terms applied by the poet who recorded it in 1619 reflect the model on which industry was commonly organised – the 'household and family' in which master and apprentices worked together, with a shared life in a homely setting. In the opinion of the historian who has made a famous study of it, the scale and intimacy of the pre-industrial era are so lost to us in the 'developed' world today that we know them only from prompts to 'folk-memory', like Grimm's Fairy Tales and the cartoon-films of Walt Disney. The vanishing world of artisans and guildsmen was buried in the seismic upheavals which raised factories over old cities like smoking volcanoes and flattened the 'vertical' structures of traditional society. Instead of identifying with communities that encompassed people at all levels of rank and prosperity – neighbourhoods, cities, provinces, sects, orders, lineages, clans, capacious 'households' – people uprooted and re-grouped in industrial centres came to place themselves in society in horizontally ordered tiers, defined by wealth or 'class'. Now that the industrial revolution is over, people seem uncomfortable with this legacy. 'Class' is disappearing from our active vocabulary and historians are being asked to write a new kind of social history, in which people are placed in the intricate, overlapping contexts of the company they keep.

Despite differences of pace, texture and density in the spread of railways and mechanised production, the common experience of industrialisation restored a kind of uniformity to European society in place of the contrast between the societies of east and west that had grown up over the preceding period. The status of the servile peasantries of the east, whose freedom to move, trade and marry was limited by hereditary subjection to a lord, was improved in the late eighteenth century by the sort of enlightened despotism satirised in *The Marriage of Figaro*. The Napoleonic wars shifted the frontier of 'eastern' Europe further east by forcing the emancipation of the peasants of Prussia. In the Habsburg empire, serfdom was eroded bit by bit – often at the insistence of lords who expected that a laissez-faire peasantry would be economically efficient. Claimed at bill- and sickle-point by peasants in Galicia, freedom and land were finally granted to the former serfs throughout the monarchy in 1853-4; the government was winded by the revolutions of 1848 and anxious to buy off peasant power but the most pressing argument for reform was the need to free labour for railway construction.

Russia was left as the great anomaly, the last empire of serfdom. In the early part of the century, in consequence, Russian peasants were a favourite subject of picturesque costume-artists in search of exotic contrasts. In 1847, Baron von Haxthausen published an account of his travels in Russia in which he predicted that Russian society would never conform to a European model. Though there were Slavophiles who revelled in the exceptional nature of the country's peculiar institution, the prejudices of the imperial court and ministerial bureaucracy, imported from western Europe, were embarrassed by the oddity. Alexander I had wanted to abolish serfdom until fear of the French Revolution turned him into a reactionary; Nicholas I acknowledged the intellectual case for such a measure, but postponed it in anxiety at the unpredictability of the consequences. Increasing peasant violence in the 1840s and the shock of defeat in the Crimean War in 1855 helped concentrate minds in favour of reform. Relentless in the background, however, when emancipation was proclaimed in 1861, was the pressure of a

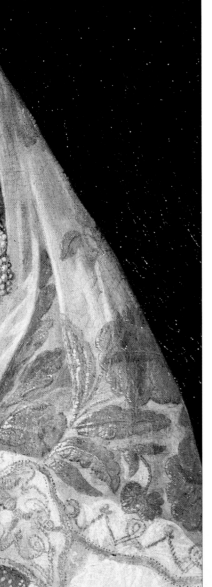

Industrialisation by forced labour: the earliest phase of Russian industrialisation depended on serf labour. When construction of the Trans-Siberian railway began in the 1890s *top*, convict gangs under armed guard played the same sort of role.

The use of sticks as tools – though not widely attested among apes – was a traditionally cited piece of evidence on behalf of the view that humankind should be understood to include a range of primates. The Punch cartoonist's satire *above* was misdirected: Darwin's theory of the descent of man explained how different species could evolve from common ancestors.

Peasants in traditional dress became icons of exoticism for western travellers in Russia, like this peasant woman from Toropec in an anonymous painting of 1825 *left*.

European model of economic change: recognition that Russia had to enter the railway age and that the manpower of the empire had to be reorganised for industrialisation.

Ironically, the most spectacular effects of European industrialisation were felt outside Europe. Empowered by industrial technology, white imperialism was certainly hard to resist, whether by weight of numbers, extreme fanaticism or sophisticated statecraft. The helplessness of the Chinese empire in the opium war; the havoc wrought by a single gunboat on the road to Mandalay; the hecatomb of dervishes at Omdurman all demonstrated that bloodily enough. The crucial inventions were those which conferred a battlefield advantage, like the steel rifle and the maxim gun, or which speeded communications, like the steam-powered vessels able to cross seas against the winds and penetrate rivers with impunity, or which made hostile environments tolerable, like tropical kit and quinine pills. Even where no enemy had to be overcome, the possibilities of imperial exploitation were transformed by the application of industrial technology: Russia's extra-European empire, for instance, in Siberia had effectively been conquered by the end of the seventeenth century but remained a sparsely populated territory where, for much of the nineteenth century, emigration was officially discouraged. In 1891, however, construction of the Trans-Siberian Railway began and by the end of the decade 800,000 settlers had poured into the country.

Old empires – especially of the Dutch in the East Indies and the Portuguese in Africa – were rejuvenated by modern technology, while new ones were created in the last quarter of the century as European powers scrambled for Africa and began to carve up what remained of south-east Asia and the Pacific. Germany, Italy and even Belgium, whose predecessor-states had no possessions outside Europe, acquired them virtually ready-made by strokes on a map in collusion with other Europeans and without reference to the inhabitants of the territories concerned. Even European peoples who continued to have no extra-European empires participated in imperialism vicariously by supplying manpower to the colonies of other states; those of south-east Europe, alternatively, registered their own local victories against the non-European world. Greek independence in 1830 was, in a sense, a triumph of European sentiment, in which allies and volunteers from all over the continent collaborated in a sort of last crusade to expel the Turks from a numinous corner of Europe's cultural heartland. Without the united backing of the powers, Romania achieved the same status by 1861 and Serbia by 1878, while Bulgaria, though still technically subject to Turkish suzerainty, functioned effectively as a sovereign state hostile to the Ottoman empire from the 1880s.

All European peoples could share in the collective feeling of superiority over the rest of the world conferred by the unstoppable imperialism of the great powers. For not only did the imperial experience give Europe a new place in the world, it also gave Europeans, in their own minds, a privileged rank in the order of mankind. European thought of the nineteenth century abounds in naked racism, but apparently disinterested science contributed to the same end. The most conspicuous achievement of nineteenth-century European science – Darwin's theory of evolution – was in this, as in every other respect, thoroughly typical of its time.

Almost nothing commonly believed about Darwin is strictly true. The theory of evolution – that all species descend from, at most, a few common, rudimentary ancestors – was already well established before he contributed to its refinement. His great addendum, the doctrine of natural selection or of 'the survival of the fittest', was never meant to be an all-encompassing explanation of how evolution works. It was disregarded by some of his closest supporters. Thomas Huxley, for instance, who was justly acknowledged as a mouthpiece of Darwinism and who preferred an ape to a bishop as a remote progenitor, never believed in natural selection. Darwin himself was barely faithful to it, at times preferring 'sexual selection' – the elimination of unfavoured types

151

in the joust for mates – as the 'main agent' of evolutionary change. Theories of evolution were in the air of his day – like Mr Casaubon's 'key to all mythologies' and Mr Lydgate's search for 'the common basis of all living tissues'. Other researchers were on the track of natural selection or had foreshadowed the idea when Darwin published. He was important less as an original thinker than as a cogent publicist and, above all, an accumulator of evidence powerful and copious enough to convince the world.

The image projected by his friends and family, of Darwin as the embodiment of Victorian philanthropy and natural charity, was a propaganda device, a campaign promise of a candidate for hero-worship, honoured in the breach. Despite his great wealth, he was prudent with it to the point of miserliness. His treatment of Alfred Russel Wallace, the poor scholar who shared with Darwin initial credit for unveiling the principle of natural selection, was shabby and evasive: while making a calculated display of generously conceded co-equality with a fellow-discoverer, Darwin withheld scientific information and withdrew an offer of employment. His attitude to St George Mivart, the Catholic evolutionist who deserted the Darwinians' anti-clerical crusade, was small-minded and vindictive: he incited hostile reviewers and blackballed Mivart from his club.

Nor was Darwin's science more politically dispassionate, more socially disinterested, than any other. It was a product of its circumstances and served the interests of a particular race and class. There was no clear dividing line between 'scientific' and 'social' Darwinism. The founder of both doctrines was a child of an inbred family and compounded the tradition by marrying a cousin. He was tortured by ill health, often in pain, given to bouts of vomiting which lasted for weeks and troubled by anxiety over the weakness and vulnerability of his own children. His interest in scientific breeding and the survival of the fittest had an obvious resonance in his own predicament. His conviction of the unity of creation was, in part, the result of social observation: contempt for the savages of Tierra del Fuego, encountered on the *Beagle*, persuaded him that unaccommodated man was 'just a bare, forked

animal'. The official artist of the *Beagle* drew the natives with depressing realism: shaggy and simian-featured, knock-kneed and woebegone, the epitome of ignoble savagery.

As his work proceeded, Darwin grew increasingly committed to the search for a theory which would explain the evolution of social structures, manners, morals and the properties of the soul – including conscience and shame, the human fruits of the apple-trees of Eden. 'Oh, you materialist!' he reproached himself: partly because, having lost his faith in an accession of bitterness when a loved daughter died, he wanted to eliminate Providence from history as from creation; partly too because of the influence of a model before his eyes, of a competitive world and an emulous society, selecting ranks and races just as the brutal, beautiful justice of nature selected species.

Reflecting on his notes from aboard the *Beagle* in 1839, Darwin made the parallel explicit. 'When two races of men meet, they act precisely like two species of animals. They fight, eat each other … But then comes the more deadly struggle, namely which have the best fitted organization or instincts (i.e. intellect in man) to gain the day.' Blacks, he speculated, would have evolved into a distinct species had imperialism not ended their isolation. As it was, they were doomed to extinction.

He repeated almost exactly the same views at intervals until 1881, the year before his death. Though Darwin took no lead in applying the theory of natural selection to the justification of racism and imperialism, he concurred in the efforts of the many contemporaries who did. The British, who succeeded in an amazing variety of environments, seemed chosen by Nature and tried in the struggle, as the Jews had once seemed chosen by God and tested in faith. It was therefore fitting that despite his apostasy Darwin should be buried in Westminster Abbey, the pantheon of specimens of British superiority.

In the same year as Darwin, the Comte de Gobineau died. Relying more on what was then beginning to be called anthropology than on biology, de Gobineau had worked out a ranking of human races in which Aryans came out on top and Blacks at the bottom. Two years later Gregor Mendel, the Austrian monk whose experiments with peas established the foundation of the science of genetics, died. The implications of his work were not followed up until the end of the century, but, when drawn, they helped to complete a trend to which Darwin and Gobineau had contributed: among the results, the most socially influential was the scientific basis on which, in combination with the effects of Darwinism, racism could seem to rest.

Genetics provided an explanation of how one man could be, inherently and necessarily, inferior to another by virtue of race alone. The anthropology of scholars in the tradition of Gobineau supplied what passed for evidence. Darwin helped provide a

'Mother's little helper' *far left*: George Kilburne's presents an idealised image of womanhood and girlhood far removed from the domestic pressures of common life.

'A piece of commonplace vice': domestic felicity tumbles like the children's house of cards *right* as a betrayed husband crumples the evidence of his wife's infidelity. Her future, indicated by the open door, leads in the other parts of Augustus Egg's triptych of 1858 to what a contemporary critic called a 'sink of misery and loathsomeness.'

'Is man no more than this?' Darwin found 'Man in his savage state' on Tierra del Fuego *below left* 'a foul, naked, snuf-fling thing with no inkling of loveliness, no spark of the divine.' As well as alerting him to man's essentially bestial nature, the Fuegians suggested to Darwin a model of natural adaptation: they seemed to have evolved resistance to the cold of their habitat.

justification for the subjection of naturally inferior races to those better adapted. In partial consequence, the first half of the twentieth century was an age of empires at ease with themselves, where critics of imperialism could be made to seem sentimental or unscientific, in a world sliced by the sword and stacked in order of race.

No previous age had been able to formulate racist doctrines so completely or so convincingly. Early modern empires had been erected with much less comprehensive theories – of the rights of tutelage of developed cultures, or the limits of the protection of natural law; the appropriation of untenanted territory, or the fiction of purchase from unsophisticated occupants; the imperfection of the sovereignty of pagans or Aristotle's doctrine of the 'natural slavery' of conquered men. Now, just when white power was at its most penetrative and most pervasive, scientific theory helped to ram it home. Imperialists from the white west could confront the rest of the world in confidence.

It might be objected that racism, in one form or another, is ancient and ubiquitous: it is said that most human languages have no term for 'human being' except that which particularly denotes the members of the tribe or group; identity has always been nourished by hatred for outsiders; contempt is a common mechanism of defence against the stranger. What the nineteenth century called 'race' had been covered in earlier periods by the discourse of 'lineage' or 'purity of blood'. Still, the assumptions of modern imperialism were uniquely arrogant. They can be glimpsed in stark relief in the pages of children's literature, in the treatment of the image of the white child in Black worlds. Paternalism was an old device of empire and sixteenth-century Spanish theorists, adapting a metaphor of Aristotle's, had likened the development of human societies to the ages of man: 'primitive' societies were immature and could be guided to adulthood under the guardianship of responsible elders, who might be missionaries, settlers or colonial administrators appointed by the Spanish crown. In nineteenth- and twentieth-century works, the paternalism could be exercised by white child-heroes, so hopeless seemed the arrested development of the societies to which authors transferred

them. Juvenile literature represented empires as the playgrounds of boyish virtues. The schoolboy protagonist of G.A. Henty's novel of the Ashanti War learned that Blacks can never be fit for self-rule. Tchaikovsky made a middle-class Muscovite girl princess in that exotic land of primary produce, the Kingdom of Sweets.

It was a distant projection of a re-evaluation of childhood that was going on at home. Together with a corresponding revolution in the perception of women, this was the last feature of the new pan-European society moulded by the effects of industrialisation. The exploitation of children's and women's labour was one of the scandals of the early phases, when mining was recklessly intensified and factories were greedy for labour. The net effect of mechanisation, however, was to liberate marginally efficient groups from economic demands. Abstracted from the world of work, womanhood was placed on a pedestal and childhood was treated as a distinct rank in society – almost as a sub-species of mankind. Both women and children were deified by artists and advertisers and confined to their special shrines in the home. These were uniquely European cults, barely intelligible in cultures where women and children were still men's partners in production. The status looked enviable from a distance or in the icons of delicately nurtured femininity or cherubic childhood in which European art abounded. But it had its disadvantages. Societies which freed children from the slavery of the work-place tried to incarcerate them in schools. Sweeps did not naturally get transformed into water-babies and the romantic ideal of childhood tended to be coerced rather than coaxed into being. Brilliantly captured by Henrik Ibsen in 1879 in his most famous play, women were cast in a role and, in some respects, with rights like those of honorary children. For them the fall from the pedestal could be bruising. Like the adulteress depicted by Egg in three terrible stages of decline and destitution, like La Traviata and Manon, the fallen woman become the favourite anti-heroine of the age. The *Doll's House* and the *Secret Garden* proved, in practice, to be oppressive pens from which the women and children of twentieth-century Europe would have to struggle to escape.

153

CHAPTER 9

THE ARENA OF STATES

European political culture in the nineteenth century

IN PARIS, PEOPLE WERE 'talking of nothing but the porpoise' seen swimming upstream between the Pont Neuf and the Pont des Arts. Compared with a portentous freak like that, Napoleon's victories in Austria in the winter of 1805 seemed merely routine. Yet the campaign, which culminated at Austerlitz on 2nd December, on a field of freezing slush, was one of the most ingeniously planned and perfectly executed in the history of warfare. 'Using our legs more than our bayonets', the French had surrounded and captured an Austrian army of 27,000 men on the upper Danube in October. Now, with the vast manpower of their Russian allies to draw on, the Austrians expected revenge: they had Napoleon trapped, as they thought, far from base, at the end of perilously extended lines of supply, outnumbered in the clutches of a Moravian winter.

In reality, it was all a carefully contrived counter-trap. The scale of the French victory at Austerlitz left the Habsburg dynasty at Napoleon's mercy. He could have dismembered their empire; but he had begun to do that already, after a rather chancier victory in 1800. Now, as well as sheering off its seaward provinces, he changed its name. The Habsburg emperor had already begun to call himself 'Austrian Imperial Majesty' in an attempt to associate imperial style with his hereditary lands in Austria rather than his elective office as Holy Roman Emperor; by August, 1806, when Napoleon's bullying of Prussia had made the outcome of Austerlitz seem irreversible, the name of the Holy Roman Empire, which Napoleon had declared himself 'unable to recognise', was abolished and its few remaining institutions dissolved. Europe's last title with

universalist pretensions was extinguished. All that was left was a naked state-system.

'Symbolic moments' are usually euphemisms for events of no importance. In practice, the change seemed to make little difference. An anachronism had been correctly labelled, a fossil embedded a little more deeply in the rock. The Hungarian chancellery demanded and received assurances that the change of style made no legal difference to the relationships between the dominions the monarchy comprised. The disappearance of the old imperial style did not signify the Habsburgs' withdrawal from their traditional role as self-appointed figureheads of German national identity and it did not predetermine – though it may ultimately have eased – the eventual surrender of their pretensions to German leadership. Nor did it mark any sort of transition from a 'Europe of empires' to a 'Europe of nation-states'. Lucien, Napoleon's only clever brother, had told him that by making himself 'Emperor of the French' Napoleon had committed a vulgar error, because there were two emperors in Europe already. He might have said three, since the Ottoman sultan, like the Habsburg monarch and the Tsar, sat on a trunk-full of ill-assorted European lands. Most other fully sovereign European states were still multiple monarchies with no definable national character: only Portugal, which no one but the Portuguese thought a model, was altogether homogeneous. But if the vanishing of the Holy Roman Empire changed almost nothing, it confirmed the way almost everything was going. In the nineteenth-century arena of states, no form of political legitimacy would be beyond challenge.

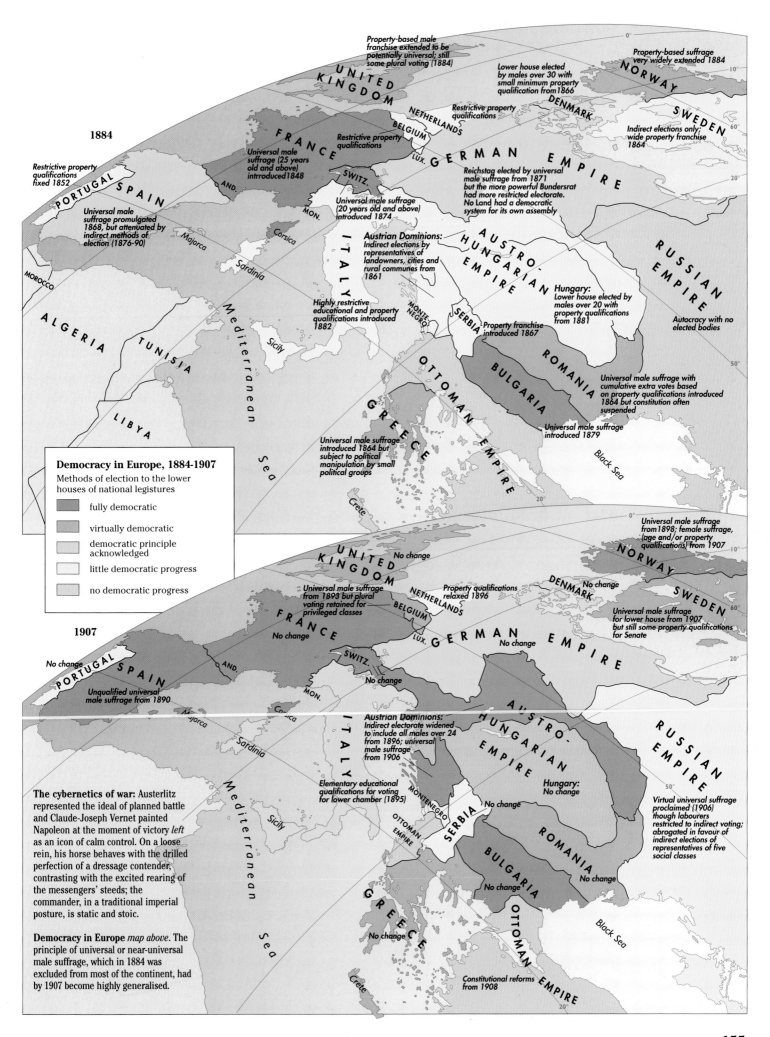

Europe has inherited two claims to a distinctive political culture from the nineteenth century: first, it is said that modern Europe has been the particular home-continent of the 'nation-state' – a type of polity of equivocal merit, which was blamed as a cause of wars when it was flourishing, and for which many European politicians have developed a curious nostalgia now that it is threatened with demise. Secondly, Europeans tend to congratulate themselves on the grounds that European countries have a peculiarly democratic vocation, acquired in the course of conflicts between the subject and the state.

Neither claim is admissible. Europe's state-system was similar to that of south-east Asia, where, indeed, nation-states – in as much as such things have ever existed at all – can claim to have had a much longer history. Those of the Khmer and Vietnamese are more ancient than any in Europe; those of the Thai and the Burmese have at least as marked a national character. Nation-states created in Europe have tended to be erected on the basis of bogus identities or unworkable boundaries: 'the pretence,' for instance, 'that Spain is one country'; the strenuous efforts of historians to concoct a 'national' Belgian past; the shuttlecock histories of border-communities like the Alsatians or Ruthenians; the 'ethnic cleansings' and re-drawings of frontiers that have made Malcolm Bradbury's fictional Balkan state, re-carved until it occupied none of its historic territory, seem plausible. Nationalism contributed little to the making of European states except false hopes and unconvincing descriptions.

As for democracy as we know it today – as a system of representative government elected by universal or near-universal suffrage – it was really an American invention. Attempts to trace it from the ancient Greek system of the same name or from the French Revolution are equally, delusively romantic. Nor has it ever spread far or lasted long in Europe. The political history of Europe in the nineteenth century is a story of 'mouldering edifices' where nationalism was held at bay and democracy deferred. The rhetoric of where power belonged changed much faster than the realities of where power actually lay.

Nationalism was most conspicuous in its failures and frustrations. Though validated – in some of its advocates' claims – by history and science, it was more often couched in mystical and romantic language apparently ill adapted to practical ends. Infected by the romantic yearning for the unattainable, nationalism was doomed to self-frustration. Indeed, like the passion of the lover on Keats's urn, it would in many cases have been killed by consummation. German nationalism throve on unfulfilled *grossdeutsch* ambitions; that of the Serbs was nourished by inexhaustible grievances; even in the land of Chauvin, nationalism would surely have been weakened by the attainment of secure frontiers. In the twentieth century it has been common for European nations who have achieved statehood to resign it to federations and super-states. Even the most impassioned nationalists disagree about what a nation is and no two analysts' lists of the nations of Europe have ever quite matched.

Because nationalism was a state of romantic yearning rather than a coherent political programme, music expressed it better than words and *Ma Vlast* or *Finlandia* have outlasted their era as no nationalist literature has done. Nationalism belonged to the values of 'sensation, not thought' proclaimed by romantic poets and its rhetoric resembled, at its worst, flights of mystical rapture. 'The voice of God' told Mazzini that the 'Nation' – capital letters were characteristic of the rhetoric of nationalism, with its great debt to thoughts formulated in German – supplied the individual with a context for moral perfection. In the eighteenth century such Finnish nationalists as there were tended to stake their claims on the myth of Finnish descent from a lost tribe of Israel. Now the romantic nationalist A. I. Ardwisson appealed to 'ties of mind and soul mightier and firmer than every external bond'. German romantic philosophers, inspired by Plato's theory of forms, tended to reify terms undiscriminatingly at the best of times: in the minds

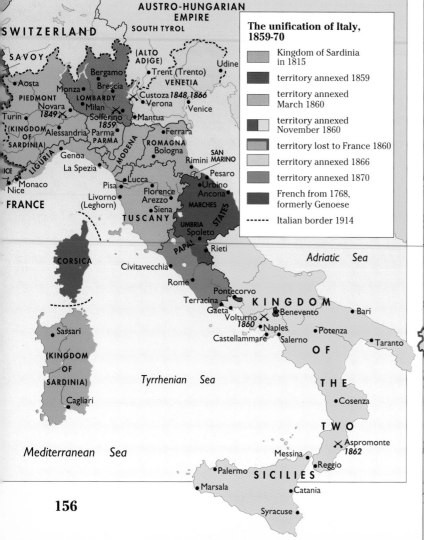

The unification of Italy, 1859–70

- Kingdom of Sardinia in 1815
- territory annexed 1859
- territory annexed March 1860
- territory annexed November 1860
- territory lost to France 1860
- territory annexed 1866
- territory annexed 1870
- French from 1768, formerly Genoese
- - - - Italian border 1914

of Fichte and Hegel the *Völk* became an ideal, a transcendent reality, autochthonous and immutable. 'To have character and be German,' according to Fichte, was 'undoubtedly the same thing.' Hegel saw Germany as charged by the force of history with the leadership of a world naturally composed of nations. No good reasons underpinned these convictions: it was purely a matter of intellectual fashion.

Powerful emotions were enfeebled by such metaphysical maunderings. Poland's was a tragic case. Partition of the old Polish kingdom among more powerful neighbours left Poles in three states and the desire for national liberation and reunification could never be effectively mobilised. Every failure postponed the desired end, while radicalised Polish nationalists turned to fight 'for your freedom and ours' in other people's revolutions. Basque nationalism, which grew up late but in a virulently racist form – represented by the slogan, 'Let your daughters marry none but Basques!' – became mired in self-regarding nostalgia and did not succeed in communicating with a mass electorate until well into the twentieth century. Most other nationalist movements hesitated to seek separation from super-states. Slovenes in 1848 and Czechs in 1867 called for autonomy within the Habsburg monarchy. Until the twentieth century Irish nationalism was a movement seeking not independence but a fair share, in 'dominion status', of the pickings of the British empire. The cry of Catalans was for 'Spain with Justice' and 'the Spain of All of Us'. Such modest demands tended to be rewarded with even more modest concessions.

Some new nation-states, however, did step into the arena, while older powers, like Britain and Spain, which were not really nation-states, pretended to be so. Some multiple monarchies, meanwhile, tried to stir themselves into spurious consistency by policies of internal colonisation which were usually oppressive of minorities: 'Russification', for instance, or 'Magyarisation', or, in the United Kingdom, Highland clearances and the implantation into every Irish parish of 'an agent of civilisation' in the shape of an Anglican clergyman. The two most conspicuous newcomers, Germany and Italy, though often cited as evidence of the creative power of triumphant nationalism, were really examples of one of the oldest methods of *Staatsbildung*: conquest outwards from a small core.

Italy was half-formed by Piedmontese conquests in 1859-61. Cavour, the mastermind of the diplomatic programme which made this feat possible, never wanted more than the choicest pickings of the peninsula in his state. For the sake of the French alliance that was essential to his policy, he even alienated Italian-speaking territory in Nice and Savoy, which by truly nationalist standards ought to have been integral to any genuinely Italian kingdom. He affected to believe that Sicilians spoke Arabic and feared – as some northern Italians still fear – that the backward and impoverished south would drag and drain his dynamic creation. Union was forced on him – and, in a sense, on the country, in defiance of the particularist trend of the revolutionary movements of the first half of the century – by two determinants: the unstoppable impetus of Garibaldi's campaigns and Cavour's own need to forestall any genuinely popular movement.

The so-called unification of Germany had a dual character. In part it was an expansion of Prussia, in part, the consolidation, under new leadership, of an existing state, like the American civil war and the Meiji revolution in Japan, both of which happened at about the same time. There were irredentist conquests at the edges – of Schleswig and Holstein from Denmark in 1864, of Alsace and most of Lorraine from France in 1870 – but not much of the new Reich had been absent from the old one. Indeed, considered from one point of view, the 'unification' was a partition of Germany: just as Cavour had laboured to keep the new Italy within dimensions he could control, so Bismarck, the Prussian chief minister, planned a division of Germany which would guarantee Prussian dominance of half of it. The basis of his plans was an expansion of Prussia proportionate to 'the supply of Junker officers'. A fairy-tale realm,

The unification of Germany, 1815-71

■ Prussia in 1815

□ acquired by Prussia 1815-66

— boundary of German Confederation 1815

---- boundary of North German Confederation 1866

▨ imperial territory of Alsace-Lorraine 1871

• free city

— boundary of German empire 1871

Contrasting images of the *Risorgimento*: Garibaldi is shown *top* among the people and the land, receiving looks and gestures of adoration and acclaim, waving an unambiguously pan-Italian symbol, dynamically active in the dashing, pistol-packed role of a romantic *banditto*. Cavour *above* is alone, aloof, inert, restrained, emotionless and unattended by symbols except of loyal service to the Piedmontese monarchy.

The unification of Germany and Italy *maps left* centred on the expansionist tendencies of Prussia and Piedmont respectively, to give political reality to what had hitherto been geographical terms or romantic nationalist aspirations.

A palace for a Swan King *above left*: Ludwig II's mountain retreat in medieval pastiche, planned in 1868 to be 'in the genuine style of the old German knights' castles ... with reminiscences of Tannhäuser and Lohengrin'. The king's susceptibility to *romantisch* notions of German tradition helps to explain how Bavaria, despite its cultural peculiarities, could be brought to immerse its independence in the Reich.

The humiliation of France: Kaiser Wilhelm III is shown *above* riding down the Champs-Elysées on a representation of Napoleon III as a pig, accompanied by Bismarck.

The Balkans, 1878-1913 *map left*. In the late nineteenth century, surgery by nationalist movements and Great Power diplomacy had amputated the limbs of 'the sick man of Europe', as former Balkan provinces one by one broke away from the Ottoman empire, beginning with Greece in 1830. The result was an unstable and strife-ridden region.

The Greek perception of the struggle for independence was projected in the popular art of late nineteenth-century Greece as a continuation of a crusade of reconquest waged since the middle ages, evoked in Theophilos Khatzimakhail's painting of the defence of Byzantium *right* by the last emperor, Constantine XI Paleologos.

like Ludwig II's 'swan-kingdom' of Bavaria, Catholic and extravagant, hardly belonged in the chillingly efficient state Bismarck envisaged. His plan was for two Germanies, one Habsburg-ruled in the south, one Prussian-ruled in the north. It was only the unpredictable invincibility of the Prussian army that enabled him to enlarge the Prussian sphere beyond his expectations. Even then, the hereditary German lands of the Habsburgs remained outside the new Reich. Neither the new Italy nor the new Germany was a triumph of nationalism, except by accident.

Alongside these cases of state-building by conquest and agglutination there were other new states which flaked off the facades of mouldering edifices or emerged from their cracks. In a formal sense, the Netherlands was the newest of the multiple kingdoms of Europe, created by the Congress of Vienna in 1815; but it was only a re-working of an ancient formula for forcing the inveterately particularist communities of one corner of the continent to cohere. The Valois dukes of Burgundy had tried it in the late middle ages and Habsburgs repeated the attempt in the early modern period. After their failure, Vermeer included in his *Art of Painting* a map which is a flashback to a supposed golden age of Netherlandish unity, while Clio in the middle ground dons a come-hither look. It is not surprising that the project should have failed again, as the edifice mouldered almost into dust and the new realm split into three – Belgium, Luxembourg and the Netherlands – all of which aspired to be nation-states, but only the last of which had any plausible claim to be so considered: Luxembourg, which even today has only 300,000 inhabitants, had its nationalist 'school' of romantic poets. The enforced union of Sweden and Norway in 1814-15 was gerry-built in a similar way: less a mouldering edifice than a botched re-joining of buildings long detached by slippage. A flexible constitutional relationship maintained the waning connection for the rest of the century.

The Magyars, meanwhile, were one of the best-defined national communities in Europe, with a distinctive historical pedigree and a language intelligible to nobody else; yet the Hungary which emerged from the division of the Habsburg monarchy in 1867 was no nation-state either but the result of the partition of an empire between its German and Magyar elites. The Ottoman retreat from the Balkans left some rather more coherent nation-states behind, or states, at least, with strong national myths; but even these had a less marked national character than is commonly supposed. The Greeks, who achieved statehood in 1830, had a remarkably uniform set of notions of themselves, as well as a unique script which could serve as badge of identity; Rigas Velestinlis, however, the hero who launched their independence movement in 1797, was a Vlach and most of the native participants saw it as a crusade rather than as a *risorgimento*: their propaganda-art was full of images of the defence of Constantinople against Mehmet the Conqueror. Until the archipelago was handed over to Greece in 1864, *enosis* – union with Greece – in the Ionian islands under British administration was demanded by island-godfathers of Italian descent.

Europe's other post-Ottoman states all emerged very late in the century or – in the case of Albania – only in the twentieth and in every instance their national self-perceptions were blurred by ambiguities. The Montenegrins had a long history of autonomy but were divided between those who pursued a cult of distinct nationhood and those who considered themselves Serbs. Serbia was founded on a strong notion of national identity but its rulers almost always wanted it to be an empire reminiscent of the 'Great Serbia' of Stefan Dusan rather than a nation-state. Bulgarian sentiment, not embodied in an autonomous state until 1878, was muddled by the myth of descent from the medieval Bulgar empire and compromised, from 1885, by the incorporation of a Rumelian minority, some of whom clung to a sense of community of their

own. Even Romanians, whose history and language combined to make them think of themselves as a nation, were unsure of their national affinities: the banner of the 'nationalist' revolutionaries in 1848 was emblazoned with the slogan 'Liberty, Equality and Fraternity' in Cyrillic characters.

Without bringing fulfilment to big communities, nationalism threatened minorities with destruction or repression. Some of them, like the Finns in the Russian empire or the Slav peoples locked into the Habsburg system, could respond with counter-nationalisms of their own. The Jews were not so lucky. The triumph of enlightened principles in the French Revolution and their spread in consequence of the Napoleonic wars extended to Jews the 'rights of man' and led to the general relaxation of the civil disabilities and fiscal disadvantages under which they laboured. Notable exceptions were the Iberian peninsula, where, except in Gibraltar, they were still not allowed, and the Russian empire, where they were restricted to a pale of settlement and excluded from most schools and livelihoods. The process of emancipation was matched from within Jewry by efforts to discard the traditional exclusiveness of ghetto and tribe in favour of self-assimilation into secular society. The transition was fraught with dangers of loss of identity and even of faith. By the time of his death in 1786, Moses Mendelssohn, generally regarded as the first great figure in the movement, had become the progenitor of a Christian dynasty. Heinrich Heine filled his poetry with Jewish self-awareness but regarded Christian baptism as 'a ticket into European culture'. Part of self-emancipation was the adoption of the dress and manners of host-societies and conformity to their ways of life. A 'Reform' movement, generally held to have originated in Seesen, near Hildesheim, in 1810, brought these new ways into the synagogue, introducing organ music, singing in melodic unison and sermons. Some congregations even switched the sabbath to Sunday and one of the acknowledged leaders of the movement, Samuel Holdheim, was willing to abandon circumcision.

When the biggest synagogue in the world opened in Berlin in 1866, in the presence of Bismarck, the Chief Rabbi preached in German of his hopes for the coming of a 'common Messiah' to unite all nations of men as brethren. In a period when other people's nationalism always threatened to overflow into anti-semitism, which the Jews' remarkable demographic vitality seemed to incite, this was perhaps the best he could do. The alternative was attempted immersion in the nationalism of host-peoples, which never seemed to work. In the prayerbook of French Jews in the 1890s, France was praised as the country 'preferred by God' and the French, in the submission of the country's chief rabbi in 1891, were exalted as 'the chosen race of modern times'. Dreyfus was led into exile shouting 'Long live France!' Joseph Moses Levy, who owned the *Daily Telegraph*, sought – in Marx's jibe – 'to be numbered among the Anglo-Saxon race'. The young Walter Rathenau believed that Germany's Jews could help her to world supremacy. In fledgling Romania, Sir Moses Montefiore was threatened by the press with a street-lynching when he went to plead for the rights of Jews, but the period's most heartfelt celebration of Romanian nationhood in song was composed in Yiddish.

Advanced, in some ways, by the end of the century in the creation of nation-states, south-east Europe was also precocious – by the standards of most of the rest – in democracy. Though France, Switzerland and – with less consistency – Spain were western beacons of universal male suffrage, the most conspicuous concentration of states with democratic franchise in the last quarter of the century was in the former Ottoman dominions. In Greece, Bulgaria and Romania the right to vote was more widely spread than in Britain or Scandinavia. The dawn of European democracy – it is almost fair to say – came up in the east. Of course, effective democracy is not just a matter of the breadth of the franchise. Mass electorates were everywhere subject to manipulation by small political groups. In Romania, the constitution was often suspended or inert; in Britain, the biggest single

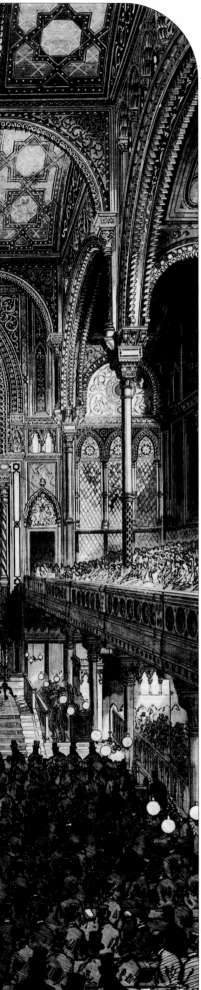

'**Throw open your gates,** that the King of Glory may come in': the opening in 1866 of the new synagogue of Berlin in the Oranienburger Strasse *left*, in the presence of Bismarck, when the Chief Rabbi preached a sermon 'contrasting the present happier condition of his people with their persecutions in the middle ages'.

A Chartist procession at Blackfriars Bridge in 1848 *below*. The Chartist movement, campaigning for universal male suffrage, was by now past its peak, yet its character as the first working-class movement truly national in scope can still be discerned in this engraving. The marchers' banners echo this, bearing slogans such as 'The Voice of the People'.

extension of the franchise – in 1884-5 – was accompanied by a redistribution of seats designed to preserve the existing parties' shares of power. Constitutional reform never prised open the 'half-closed world' of the political caste and its adopted recruits. 'Parliamentary dictatorship' in Greece subverted the democratic constitution by *rousfeti* – judiciously placed patronage, – vote-rigging and tactics of intimidation for which the government empressed brigands. Even in France, Napoleon III – whose demotic style included rank offences against aristocratic propriety, like smoking on horseback – was the first great master of that dictator's art, the cynically manipulated plebiscite. When universal suffrage was introduced into the German Reich, its application was limited to the toothless chamber of the legislature.

There was therefore no 'march of progress' towards practical democracy: on the contrary, democracy remained marginal and malleable throughout the century. There was, however, a remarkable and general change in the way it was perceived – progress, of a sort, towards its legitimation as a form of government in the eyes of the elite. At the beginning of the period, it would have been hard to find a respectable spokesman for the system Burke called 'the most shameless in the world': even advocates of popular sovereignty avoided a term which Plato and Homer had seemed to condemn and Aristotle damned with faint praise. Kant, who can fairly be credited with democratic instincts, was inclined to repudiate them, branding democracy in 1795 as inherently despotic, because 'the "whole people" who carry their measures ... are really only a majority.' Radical movements were more concerned with curbing executive power or installing the rule of law or achieving constitutional guarantees of the subject's basic freedoms than with empowering the crowd. Even a nominally democratic campaign, like that of the English Chartists, could easily get deflected into what was called 'the Trade of Agitation': the merchandising, as we should say now, of 'Chartist ink' or stickers printed with the slogan 'The Charter and No Surrender', or the promotion of 'Orator' Hunt's breakfast food, supposedly for the good of the working classes' health. By the 1840s Chartism was more concerned with cheap housing projects than with franchise reform; in 1848, its last great mass demonstration was rained off.

In partial consequence, the first half of the century was a period of democratic retreat in Europe, as constitutions, conceded to enlarge political nations in the crises of the Napoleonic wars, were abrogated or attenuated. Europe's republics, casualties of the same wars, were not restored. Embryonic working-class organisations

were aborted, radical presses censored, demonstrators shot. In Britain, the Reform Act of 1832, often miscast as a piece of proto-democratic progress, actually disenfranchised such working-class voters as there were. The drift towards a less hostile perception of democracy was only gradually stimulated by the example of the United States.

The first influential apologist for the American model was Karl Postl, who in 1828 published a recommendation of a system which 'unites the population for the common good'. He became an American citizen, planter and slave-owner. In 1831 Tocqueville visited America and saw a future which seemed to work: democracy, he found, restrained the egotism unleashed by individual liberty. At about the same time, Sandor Bölöni, 'the Columbus of democracy', returned to his native Hungary full of praise for 'the young giant of human rights and freedom'. After the failure of the Hungarian revolution of 1848, Kossuth took refuge in America, where he discovered that 'Democracy is the Spirit of our Age.'

Meanwhile, in Europe, democracy seemed ever less threatening as the numbers of voters qualified by property grew with the momentum of industrialising economies. To a surprising degree, not only did democracy lack popular initiative but also, apparently, popular effects. Mass electorates began to look assimilable without revolutionary consequences. Elite groups were made aware of the possible advantages of alliances with portions of the people: landowners with peasants in defence of agriculture, manufacturers with workers in favour of cheap food, aristocrats and workers against bourgeois bosses. In 1878 Pope Leo XIII pronounced democracy 'not necessarily culpable'. The map (see page 155) shows how suddenly the citadels of privileged voting capitulated in the last few years of the century and the first few years of the next. This was not one of history's many unpredictable lurches, but the effect of the long accumulation of pressure.

Most of the pressure was from above. Until the rise of women's suffrage movements, it is impossible to show that any mass extension of the right to vote was ardently sought by those to whom it was granted. Democracy came as the late fruit of a ripening elite consensus. Its background was a Europe-wide conflict over how the relationship between the state and the people should be understood. Three traditional images had been current: those of lord and vassal, of sovereign and subject, of state and citizen. Against a rearguard action by *anciens régimes*, the last came, gradually, narrowly and precariously, to prevail; but the beauty of democracy was that it served the ends of contenders of contrasting views. For what was at stake in practice was the power of the state over individuals. From an individualist viewpoint, democracy could be made to seem favourable, because it was a system of government based on the principle that the state had no sovereign except the people and no rights except those which its people confided to it. At the same time, for those distrustful of liberty, democracy provided a justification for a repressive state: individual rights could be subordinated to the 'collective' or 'general' will; minorities could be ignored under the tyrannies of majorities; traditional elites could manipulate the voters. In the twentieth century, totalitarian and authoritarian regimes would be brazen in proclaiming themselves 'democratic' and would sometimes even be installed by genuinely popular votes.

More significant, therefore, than the advances of democracy were the debates over the limits of the power of governments: whether they were 'absolute' – free, in the strict sense, of laws or of any other discipline arising outside institutions they controlled – or bound by customs, traditions, conventions, constitutions and 'fundamental' statutes, which could not be altered except by consensus. In practice, these were not quite mutually exclusive notions, since the power to make and unmake law is a defining property of a state and naked despotism can always be thinly veiled with the specious decency of a plebiscite or similar constitutional device. Nevertheless, all the constitutional strife of the century was fought across the ideological gulf between those who saw no

The antithesis of revolution: John Phillip's painting of Lord Palmerston addressing the House of Commons in 1860 *above right* seems to epitomise a political process characterised by reasoned debate and growing by slow accretion, far-removed from the perceived violence of Continental development.

The leader of Hungary's revolution of 1848, Lajos Kossuth, is depicted *above*, sheltered by his 'fast friends', England and America, from whom he may have found his democratic inspiration and where he spent the later years of his life agitating for Hungarian independence, following his expulsion from Hungary in 1849.

Democracy in action was a social rather than a strictly political phenomenon. Walter Hargreaves's 1862 painting of *Hammersmith Bridge on Boat Race Day right* captures the spirit of popular involvement in the annual aquatic contest between teams from the two great seminaries of the British ruling class, the Universities of Oxford and Cambridge.

possible justice unless the citizens' rights were enshrined, and those who saw no stability in society unless the subject were left at the mercy of the state.

In November, 1848, Macaulay sat in his study congratulating himself on living in a country which had escaped the revolutionary convulsions of continental neighbours 'impatient to demolish and unable to construct'. Since he belonged, in his own estimation, to 'the greatest and most highly civilised people that ever the world saw', he might have accepted British superiority as unnecessary of explanation; instead, he stopped to enquire rationally why he had been spared the sight of 'the pavement of London piled up in barricades, the houses dented with bullets, the gutters foaming with blood'. His answer, crudely summarised, was that Britain had pre-enacted the struggles of her neighbours between constitutionalism and absolutism, and settled them, a century and a half before, in favour of 'the popular element in the English polity'. The English revolution had established that 'kings reigned by a right in no respect differing from the right by which freeholders chose knights of the shire or from the right by which Judges granted writs of *habeas corpus*'. He perceived, in short, that the European revolutionaries of his day were trying to implement what had become an English shibboleth: that the rights of governments were limited by the law and conferred by merely human grace. He was no democrat. He was haunted by nightmares of a Europe engulfed, like the declining Roman empire, in a new barbarism, inflicted by under-civilised masses. At the same time, however, he was confident of the progress of history and the long-term perfectibility of man.

The clash of political visions inside European elites was the echo of a mightier clash of rival philosophies of man. Was he ape or angel? Was he the image of God or the heir of Adam? Would the goodness inside him emerge in freedom or was it corroded with evil which had to be controlled? Among the philosophers Peacock gathered at

Headlong Hall in his novel of 1816, 'Mr Forster, the perfectibilian', continued to expect 'gradual advancement towards a state of unlimited perfection', while 'Mr Escot, the deteriorationist', foresaw, with gloomy satisfaction, 'that the whole species must at length be exterminated by its own imbecility and vileness.' In France, a practical form of the same sort of difference was represented by the contrast between men of the same generation, the idealist Louis Blanc and the cynic, three years his senior, Alphonse Karr. Blanc thought social reform was simple: state socialism would eliminate competition, the root of all wickedness, and release man's natural goodness. Karr, who coined the phrase, 'plus ça change le plus c'est la même chose', looked for no improvement in society and therefore mistrusted every intervention by the state.

Some perfectibilians proposed policies which could be repressive in the short term because, though they might be out-and-out utopians, like Karl Marx and Herbert Spencer in their different ways, they also expected things to get worse before they got better: Marx believed the classless society would have to be preceded and provoked by a spell of misery and a bout of bloodshed, Spencer that the way to the perfect society would be picked across the ruins of those unfitted to survive. In the tradition of Rousseau, impatient perfectibilians might be willing to inflict on god-like man a period of dictatorship to 'force him to be free'. Victor Hugo, the poet of the Paris sewers, wrote novels in praise of reformed criminals and prostitutes, but he was susceptible to the Bonapartist myth of the 'Great Man'. No philosopher of the nineteenth century had a more exalted view of mankind (or, at least, of the male half of it) than Auguste Comte, the originator of positivism, who aspired to found a religion of humanity: but after the French revolution of 1848 he proposed that as 'servants of humanity' he and his disciples should be confided with 'the general direction of this world'. Of course, however well or ill disposed towards one's fellow man, one still had a range of political options to choose from: racism and social Darwinism were founded on essentially perfectibilian assumptions, but both assumed that people could be improved only by discarding undesirable types. Stragglers or *Untermenschen* would have to be abandoned at the wayside of the march of progress. In the circumstances of the nineteenth century, however, it was possible to subscribe to these ferocious ends and still be a faithful advocate of economic liberalism and of constitutionalism in politics.

Two kinds of politics therefore collided in nineteenth-century Europe: the politics of hope and the politics of fear. The conflicts of these rival sources of inspiration were paralleled in the contrasting ways fathers had of regulating that microcosm of society: the family. Dialogue between Mr Midshipman Easy and his father caricatured a great debate. In Russian families the traditional relationship of fathers and sons was repressive: children were seen as 'enemies' and sometimes the generation gap did work a form of revenge that seemed to justify repression. Before serfdom was abolished the children of noble households were often the allies of the domestic serfs with whom they naturally spent most of their time at home and took their part in the 'little wars' of family life. The young Wrangel, who distinguished himself as a general in the Crimean War, pledged that when he and his sister grew up 'all our serfs will be freed and we shall never treat them or our children unjustly'. Commonly, however, repression worked its intended effects and the maxim 'teach them and beat them' was passed on from generation to generation, based on the kind of pessimism about human nature which commonly sustains authoritarian thought. 'Punish with real severity,' advised a French theorist of 1890, on the grounds that children had no instinct beyond the fear of suffering. Optimistic parents, who invested love in their children, produced revolutionaries. Bakunin's father 'lavished on his children a wise and far-seeing affection, unalterably indulgent and kind'. Women revolutionaries – according to an authoritative study – were not separated from their mothers by a generation gap but united with them by support and encouragement. Lenin and his siblings were his father's 'constant' chess partners.

'A torrent for justice': Giuseppe Pelizza's vision of the purposeful, unstoppable march of the working class *above* 'expresses the extremes of grandeur and grind at the heart of socialism'.

The revolutionary intellectual: bookish, frowning, domed, Victor Hugo is caricatured *right* by Honoré Daumier in 1849 as a typical intellectual subversive of his time. He re-created the teeming life of the Paris poor most vividly in *Les Miserables*. In the scene shown *left*, young revolutionaries distribute swords and pistols to a ragged crowd of malcontents.

A wizard visits a peasant wedding in Russia *left*. In societies such as this, superstition and fear could act as the allies of autocracy and repression, inhabiting and shaping a world far removed from the well-springs of enlightened liberalism.

The Holy Alliance of 1815 and the similar organisations which succeeded it throughout the century – the union of Munchengratz of 1833 and the 'League of Three Kaisers' – represented the politics of fear. The founder of the Holy Alliance, Tsar Alexander I, was that most dangerous type of reactionary, a disillusioned liberal. Its propaganda was full of what Castlereagh called 'mystical nonsense' about the divine obligations of rulers and the pursuit of the ideal of a united Christendom. Eventually, all European states except Britain, the Papal States and the Ottoman empire subscribed to its charter: nothing thought to be meaningful ever commands such wide assent. The real purpose of the alliance, however, was to make the European trauma of 1792-1815 unrepeatable by sanct-ifying existing frontiers and outlawing constitutional reform within them. Instead of a crime to be excused, intervention to repress each other's revolutions became an obligation of reactionary governments. The system worked well and revolutionaries only achieved freedom to act in the relatively short periods when the reactionary powers fell out among themselves. The Warsaw Pact re-embodied the essential character of the alliance in the second half of the twentieth century, with the difference that the cant of Christian unity was replaced by the cant of international socialism.

The politics of hope were represented in an extreme form by socialism. In Milan in 1899, Giuseppe Pelizza, a convert from a guilt-ridden bourgeois background, began his vast symbolic painting on the subject. The scene depicted in *Il Quarto Stato* was a vast crowd of workers, advancing, the artist said, 'like a torrent, overthrowing every obstacle in its path, thirsty for justice'. Their march is certainly relentless, their solidarity intimidating; but, except for a Madonna-like woman in the foreground – who seems bent on a personal project, appealing to one of the rugged leaders at the head of the march – they are individually characterless,

165

The novelist Émile Zola *left* surrounded by images of the intellectual fashions of his day: Oriental art, symbolism, a print of Manet's *Olympia* and avant-garde writing.

'Awaiting admission to the casual ward': Sir Luke Fildes's portrayal of the misery of urban life *right*, as the huddled poor queue in the cold for shelter, is an eloquent testimony to the deprivation which, given the right catalyst and leadership, could give rise to radical working-class movements.

To the victors the spoils: German troops crown themselves with laurels plucked in the Tuileries gardens at the capture of Paris in 1871 *far right*.

moving like the parts of a gigantic automaton, with a mechanical rhythm, slow and pounding.

No work of art could better express the extremes of grandeur and grind which are at the heart of socialism: noble humanity, mobilised by dreary determinism. In the history of socialism, the humanity and nobility came first. They were expressed in the ideals of equality and fraternity, proclaimed by utopians of the enlightenment and applied in the practices of sharing and co-operating attempted in early socialist communities, like the 'Icarian' utopias devised by Étienne Cabet. Icarus was brought down to earth by Louis Blanc and Karl Marx, who both died in the early 1880s: the former convinced most socialists that their ideals could be entrusted to the state, to be imposed on society; the latter gave them a conviction of the historic inevitability of their triumph in a cycle of class conflicts, in which workers – degraded and inflamed by employers' exploitation – would establish a decisive advantage as labour wrested control of economic power from capital. Early socialist experiments had been peaceful, with no land to conquer except in the open spaces of the wilderness, no human adversaries except selfishness and greed. Transformed by language of conflict and coercion, socialism became an ideology of violence, to be resisted uncompromisingly by those who valued property above fraternity and liberty above equality.

The very conviction of ultimate victory helped socialist leaders in Europe restrain their hands. In most European countries they built up mass organisations for political and industrial action in the very late nineteenth and early twentieth centuries, generally without risking premature revolutionary attempts. Urban violence was understandably common in the growing towns of nineteenth-century Europe but riots, communal action and rushes to the barricades should not necessarily be taken as evidence of the early politicisation of the masses: most manifestations of the kind had a distinctly old-fashioned air and look, to objective scrutiny, like traditional urban disturbances. There were places where 'class consciousness', accompanied in some cases by a sense of identity based on the 'neighbourhood', replaced traditional loyalties. Radicals and politically militant trade unionists had a sea to swim in, but they often foundered. Working-class consciousness was often expressed in a learned language of classical allusions, like the French working men's refusal in 1886 to be 'helots in a nation of sybarites' or was left to the formulations of alienated bourgeois like Marx and Engels.

No thriving city was more prone to street revolution than nineteenth-century Barcelona, but the workers, hard to organise, were, once organised, even harder to control: there is no convincing evidence that the masses were effectively politicised until well into the twentieth century – they did not vote *en masse* until 1929, though enfranchised originally in 1861 and permanently from 1890. When they took to the streets, they had a habit of disappointing agitators by exposing some non-ideological cause. In the slums and factories, conditions did exist for their radicalisation: in 1852 a young Carmelite visited a factory at lunchtime to find the workers all listening in silence to young children reading aloud from 'highly coloured political journals which generally spread subversive doctrines, mocked holy things, ... spoke ill of the proprietors and government and preached socialism and communism'. On the whole, however, what little is known about the motivation of the working-class movement in industrialising cities – not the mob rule of hot summers with which, in Barcelona, it is often confused – seems more practical than theoretical, more economic than political, more capricious than consistent. By practical political analysts, workers' parties could be ignored everywhere in Europe until the 1890s at the earliest and even then those with mass appeal tended to be pragmatic rather than ideologically committed: the Secretary-General of the supposedly revolutionary French anarcho-syndicalist organisation in the early

years of the new century claimed to read Alexandre Dumas in preference to Kropotkin and Bakunin.

Peasants, of course, were even harder to politicise than workers, once their masters had bought them off by suppressing serfdom and distributing smallholdings. There were no peasant parties until the twentieth century, perhaps because so large and numerous a class could not feel threatened until the industrial revolution was well advanced. So much of the peasantry, as the century wore on, consisted of new landowners or their early descendants and, in eastern Europe, of former serfs suddenly transformed into proprietors. This is the kind of elevation calculated to breed conservatism. The stereotype represented by the peasant characters in Zola's novel, *Earth*, was of the peasant as the embodiment of the values of feudalism and principles of *laissez-faire* capitalism, greedy for land and cut-throat at market. In consequence, revolutionaries ignored or defied them. Marx compared the political inertia of French peasants to potatoes in sacks. Russian social democrats saw kulaks as class enemies – a 'rural bourgeoisie'.

Once the passions of 1848 were spent, the fear of a revolution of the masses was therefore greater than the real threat. Most violent changes of government remained, in late nineteenth-century Europe, firmly in the hands of elite factions. The potential evils of an ill-controlled outbreak were revealed in one terrible brief spell, in the insurrection of the Paris commune from March to May, 1871. This bloody uprising of 'red republicanism' was reported in the press all over Europe with the same sort of comfortable terror in which a modern horror-film audience wallows. The inception of the rebellion was ascribed to an international conspiracy and its objects declared to be the abolition of property, family, religion and morals. It is true that some of the proceedings seemed to justify such fears. There were a few unknown working-men on the committees which formed the government of the commune, though most of them were journalists and other intellectuals with established public profiles and radical reputations. 'Revolutionary justice' re-created the atmosphere of the Jacobin terror: official religious ceremonies were curtailed; rents were suspended; and, in the extremities of revolutionary finance, rich businesses and individuals suffered expropriation.

In reality, however, the rebellion was the result of peculiar circumstances and the work of a broad coalition. Like so many revolutions, it was a response to the miseries of war and the frustrations of defeat. The victors of the Franco-Prussian war had stripped the leaves in the Tuileries to wind wreaths around their *pickelhauben* and 'danced for joy on the heights of Montmorency and Sannois' to see Paris in flames. The balloons which had floated the liberal republican leaders to secure seats of temporary government on the Loire and, later, in Bordeaux, had left the capital to the *enragés*. The 'red republicans' were, in any case, only a minority among the insurrectionists. They were outnumbered by opponents of the peace, who wanted to fight on to avenge the national humiliation; civic enthusiasts who wanted to assert the pre-eminence of Paris as 'the head and heart of a Democratic Republic' or safeguard the privileges of the capital in a new constitution; and moderate republicans who suspected the nearest thing France had to a legitimate government – the National Assembly – of collusion with Bonapartists and Bourbons. But in a city under siege, amid the ferment of revolution, politics get polarised and the extremists, who are most committed, always come to the fore. When the blood was mopped up and the flames had died down, Paris was still the cynosure of Europe, held up by

Strauss in *Die Fledermaus* of 1874 as the source of flashy fashion – though now, perhaps, challenged by Berlin for the long-arrogated role of 'capital of civilisation'.

As the fangs dropped out of the maw of revolution, as economic 'improvement' helped to make progressive fallacies plausible, so the politics of optimism gained ground. Extended franchises late in the century were a sign we have already noticed. More surprising was the triumph of *aggiornamento* in the Church. The politics of hope seemed to defy the doctrine of original sin and to challenge clerical interests. Anti-clericalism was the defining feature of liberalism – an attempt, as Jules Ferry expressed it, 'to organise mankind without God'. If liberalism was identified with anti-clericalism, socialism seemed implicitly atheist, denying the role of providence in history and wresting the individual's responsibility for charity into the hands of the state. There was, however, less peril for the church in an entente with these enemies than in dependence on nationalist allies, who exploited clerical conservatism in the interests of their own agenda. Protestations of Catholic faith were useless from those who wanted, like Jules Le Maitre, to 'make a religion of the fatherland'. The gospel had, in practice, more in common with the political vision of liberals and socialists.

Leo XIII came to the pontiff's throne in 1874 with prestige immensely enhanced by his predecessor's defiance of the world: Pius IX had refused to submit to force or defer to change; he had condemned almost every social and political innovation of his day; and had retreated from the armies of a secular Italian state into a virtual bunker in the Vatican. As a result, he had seemed to demonstrate a godly vocation unprofaned by compromise. His

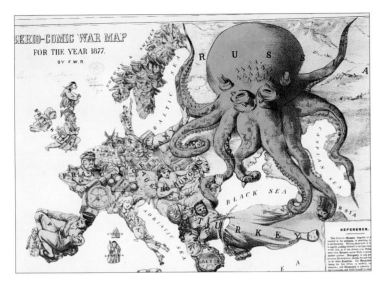

fellow-bishops had rewarded him by proclaiming papal infallibility. Leo exploited this unique advantage to manoeuvre the church into a position from which it could work with governments to minimise the damage inflicted by the changes Pius had condemned; he seems also to have realised that the vast Catholic laity was the Church's most valuable ally in striving to influence policy in an increasingly democratic age. He could not approve of republicanism, but made it possible for the clergy to co-operate with republican regimes. He could not deny the validity of slavery in past centuries when the Church had allowed it, but he proscribed it for the future. He could not countenance the subversion of a social hierarchy in which the Church had a strong vested interest, but he did authorise trades unions and encourage Catholics to found their own. He could not denounce property – the Church had too much of it for that – but he could remind socialists that Christians, too, were called to social responsibility. He could not endorse socialism but he could condemn naked individualism. Leo's was a church of practical charity without moral cowardice. After his death, the political fashion changed in Rome, and there were always clergy committed to the politics of fear – some of them, in the twentieth century, prepared to collaborate with repression and authoritarianism on the political right. *Aggiornamento*, however, was an inextinguishable light. The tradition launched by Leo XIII has prevailed in the long run: the Church has gone on adjusting to changes in the world without compromising its custodianship of eternal verities.

Elites who felt ever more secure from revolution were increasingly inclined to make war on each other. In 1870, under the threat of Prussian militarism, a French cartoonist published a map of Europe in

The National Guard was the armed force of 'red republicanism' in the Paris of the Commune in 1871. The Barricades *below left* became a symbol of the red republican strategy of uncompromising resistance against the German invasion and a device to wrest control of the city from the national government. The Paris Commune under siege was nourished by bizarre expedients, including the sacrifice of the elephant in the Jardin des Plantes *below*.

A 'Serio-Comic' map for the year 1877 *above*: one of a series depicting political developments in Europe. Russia is portrayed as a menacing octopus: having seized a recumbent Turkey, she is stretching forward to take hold of Poland. A belligerent Hungary is restrained from attacking Russia by a soothing courtesan-like Austria, while Britain watches all with furled umbrella.

which each country was represented by a personification of its national vices. Spain is laid-back and smoking; Turkey is a opium-greedy houri; Turkey-in-Europe is bursting out of Turkey's stomach in monstrous birth-pangs; and Prussia is death's-headed and groping for conquests. Yet, despite the occasional re-structurings of frontiers and the waves of constitutional fashion that sometimes threatened to erode and re-mould the natures of states, this was still the familiar Europe of the cosy family-conflicts of dynastic politics, in which patrician statesmen met to retune the 'balance of power'. Only civil wars were caused by ideological conflicts. The international warfare of the age of Metternich and Palmerston would have been equally intelligible to Richelieu and Olivares. The raw ingredients of power, however, were new, and as they changed so did the distribution of power. Most continental states maintained massive conscript-armies, who – especially after 1870, when short-term service became the almost universal fashion – had to make up in technology what they lacked in professional aptitude for battle. Ever more efficient means of mobilising them were called on, especially in the second half of the century when railways linked the front lines to the muster-points all over Europe. Ever more accurate and long-range weapons were required to compensate for soldiers' inexpertness in firing them.

These were signs that, more than on manpower or even, for real security, on morale, the ability to wage war depended on industrial muscle. Coal was the fuel of the industrial revolution and iron its housing; therefore Britain, which was relatively best-off in the key commodities, was able to maintain the status of a great power throughout the period without mobilising large numbers of troops except in emergencies. Germany's coal and iron reserves were of inferior quality and not systematically exploited until the last third of the century. Russia had vast reservoirs of manpower and had emerged as a pre-industrial super-power during the Napoleonic wars, but for most of the rest of the century industrial under-development kept her hobbled. France lost out in both respects: for most of the century her population was virtually static and she had too little exploitable coal and iron to make up for it. The memory of Napoleonic glory continued to dazzle the French and menace their neighbours but the dazzle was superficial and the menace illusory.

Still, until the end of the century in the arena of states there were enough powers, sufficiently evenly matched, to keep the peace for most of the time. Though revolutions and civil wars were pretexts for intervening powers to hold their armies combat-trained or for volunteers to step in where their rulers feared to tread, for nearly 50 years after the defeat of Napoleon no major international conflict flared. When in 1854, in defence of the balance of power, France, England and Piedmont joined to defend the Ottoman empire against Russia, the war was kept on the edge of Europe, confined to 'a corner of a corner' in Crimea. The wars fought to create the Kingdom of Italy and the German Reich were swift and contained, though the last of them, the Franco-Prussian war of 1870-71, introduced a chilling new awareness of the horrors of total war waged with the technical resources of the industrial revolution. Emile Zola chronicled them in a novel of *vérité humaine*, depicting 'battlefields without chauvinism' and 'the real sufferings of the soldier'. His most vivid material, supplied by a field surgeon, depicted horrible hospital scenes and sickening evocations of decaying dead, gangrenous wounded and frenzied amputations. Already celebrated for the realism of his description of suppurating cheese, Zola was unbeatable in communicating the disasters of war.

However, like all European wars for nearly a century after Waterloo, the Franco-Prussian conflict had the merit of being quickly over. The edifices of Europe were able to moulder in relative quiescence. On their peace Europe's world hegemony was founded and by that peace revolution was deferred. By the end of the century, the fear of revolution had so far abated, and the habit of short wars had become so familiar, that neither the delicacy of the peace nor the danger of war excited due alarm. 'Peace Congresses'

were the playgrounds of cranks and idealists more marginalised even than nuclear-disarmers during the Cold War. Alfred Nobel, the guilt-racked, lonely weapons-magnate, morbidly cynical, who took refuge in extravagant and alarming projects for world peace, was typical. War would 'stop short, instantly,' he promised during a congress in Paris in 1890, if it were made 'as death-dealing to the civilian population at home as to the troops at the front.' The best hope he could see for peace was spreading the fear of germ-warfare.

That balance of power, moreover, on which the peace depended, was beginning to list. The kind of fitness for hegemony which France and, briefly, Russia evinced at the start of the century was beginning to be displayed by Germany at its end. Partly, this was a consequence of the long process, begun by Castlereagh at the Congress of Vienna in 1815, of 'strengthening the centre of Europe against the ends': the assumption that such an adjustment was necessary made other powers indulgent of Germany's growing power. On the other hand, the decisive difference was made by the uneven distribution of industrialisation. Bismarck had promised solutions of 'blood and iron': the real difference was made by coal and iron. By the end of the century, Germany produced vastly more coal, iron and steel than all the other powers of the continent combined. The fact – little noticed outside Germany – that Russia, with her crushingly big population, was just beginning to show signs of being able to catch up, made a trial of strength seem urgent. The arena of well-raked sand was ready for the gladiators.

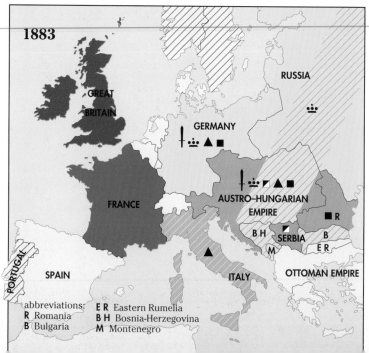

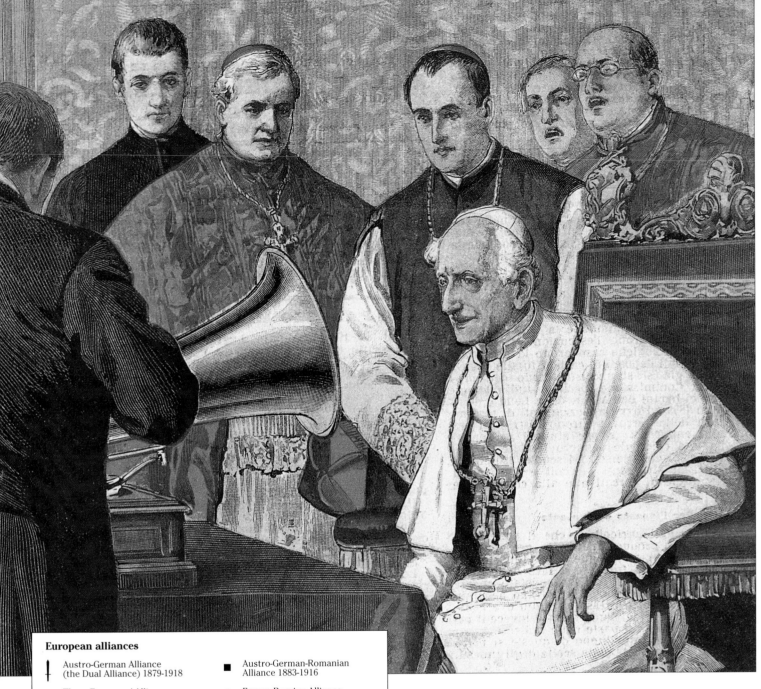

European alliances

Austro-German Alliance (the Dual Alliance) 1879-1918	Austro-German-Romanian Alliance 1883-1916
Three Emperors' Alliance 1881-95	Franco-Russian Alliance 1894-1917
Austro-Serbian Alliance 1881-95	Russo-Bulgarian military convention 1902-13
Triple Alliance 1882-1915	Stripes, similar and identical colours indicate an entente or community of interests

The technology of mass destruction: Krupp's 50-ton steel cannon displayed at the Paris exhibition in 1867 *left*.

Alliance-systems in Europe, *maps below*. From 1871 until 1914 a flexible system of multi-faceted diplomatic alignments and alliances ensured peaceful adjustment of rivalries.

Aggiornamento **in action**: Pope Leo XIII contibutes to the church's reconciliation with the modern world by recording the apostolic blessing on a gramophone in 1903 *above*.

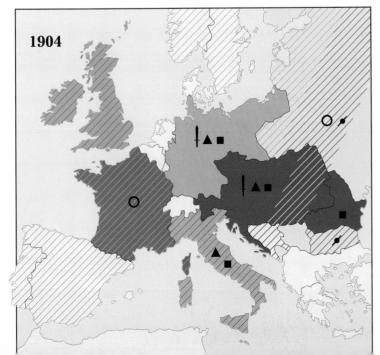

1904

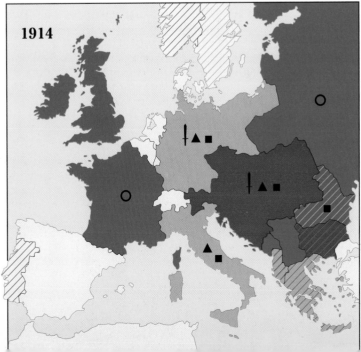

1914

CHAPTER 10

EUROPE'S CIVIL WARS
The forfeiture of world hegemony

ITLER WOULD BE PLEASED with much of what we have done since his death. Within a few years of his suicide in a bunker under the ruins of the Reich, historians, unapproving but awed, were already talking about 'the age of Hitler'. So much of the way Europe looks and is developing would meet with his approval. 'The road,' as he forecast, 'is taking the place of the railway.' Blood sports are on the way to being banned, as he wished. Hitler also predicted that 'the future of energy belongs to winds and tides', that the world of the future would be vegetarian and that what he called 'the disgusting habit' of smoking could be eliminated by campaigns 'to re-educate the young'. All these prophecies have begun to look convincing. He anticipated some of

the ecological shibboleths of our time by condemning the man who 'exploits the ground beneath his feet without ever asking if he is thus disposing of products indispensable to the life of other parts of the ecological system'. Exponents of the 'selfish gene' have seemed to vindicate his 'divine commandment, thou shalt preserve the species.' Panic-perceptions of rising crime rates are inducing neo-fascists to revive his cruel prescriptions for 'a society in a state of legitimate defence', entitled 'to wipe out recidivists' and 'to maintain social cohesion by force'. The objects of his two great hatreds – Jews and Bolsheviks – have virtually disappeared from parts of Europe where they were numerous in his day; and, though it has not come about as he would have wished, a vision of a

'When I meet children, I think of them as my own. They all belong to me.' The remark was recorded in 1941, but Hitler's sympathy with children had been part of his propaganda image at least since the mid-1930s, when this photograph *left* was released to the press.

Europe after the First World War *map right*. The peace treaties of 1919 created as many problems as they tried to solve. Some were settled by plebiscites under League of Nations auspices; others were the subject of unilateral action. The new-found autonomy of nations such as Ukraine and Belorussia proved short-lived; they would re-appear as independent states only in the 1990s. Conversely, the new creations of Czechoslovakia and Yugoslavia achieved an illusory permanence which foundered by 1993. Then, as now, purely European co-operation settled finally only minor issues, such as the status of the Aland islands, the Dardanelles and Alexandretta.

politically united Europe under German leadership is beginning to take flesh.

Happily, of course, the features of modern Europe which would appall Hitler outweigh those which would please him. He would deplore the enrichment of European peoples by settlement from outside. The triumphs – at the level, at least, of lip-service – of democracy and capitalism would outrage his tastes and defy his predictions. He would despise our efforts to keep human and civil rights from being crushed by the state. The 'ceremonies of thanksgiving to Fascism and Socialism', which he expected 'for having preserved Europe from Christianity', have not materialised in a continent where religion has revived. Nevertheless, the extent to which we have realised aspects of Hitler's vision is surprising and disturbing. It helps to suggest that, extreme and extraordinary as he was, he was a representative figure of modern European history – not, as we should prefer to think, an aberration whose career temporarily warped that history out of course.

In the very violence of his hatreds he was typical of his time. Since toleration in religion had come to prevail in the eighteenth century, it had been possible for Europeans to think of Europe inclusively, differentiating themselves collectively from those outside without making their sense of European identity depend on the exclusion of any of their fellow-inhabitants. Thereafter, no ideology of hatred was strong enough to capture any state for long until the twentieth century. The concept of Europe inherited from the Enlightenment was then imperilled by the rise to power of parties dedicated to the extirpation of whole races and classes. All the humane values that had become identified with what people called 'European civilisation' were abjured by the communists and fascists who challenged each other for supremacy and dragged old-fashioned democrats, liberals and conservatives into their wars.

Mikhail Tukhaveski, best of the generals of the first Red Army, threatened 'to make the world drunk ... to enter chaos and not to return until we have reduced civilisation to ruin.' His programme for the future of the revolution included the burning of all books, 'so that we could bathe in the fresh spring of ignorance', and the transformation of Moscow into 'the centre of the world of the barbarians'. 'If Lenin,' he declared, 'is able to de-westernize Russia, I will follow him. But he must raze all to the ground and deliberately

National conflicts and frontier disputes, 1919-36

—— frontier of German empire in 1914

—— frontier of Austro-Hungarian empire in 1914

—— frontier of Russian empire in 1914

—— post-settlement frontiers

new states

■ conferences

▲ plebiscites held

areas of dispute

areas temporarily autonomous or independent

areas under armed occupation

areas under League of Nations High Commissioners

1 plebiscite Feb. 1920: divided between Denmark and Germany

2 occupied by France 1923-5

3 to Belgium 1919

4 to Belgium 1919

5 evacuated 1930, remilitarised 1936

6 League of Nations Mandate, by plebiscite to Germany 1935

7 to France 1919

8 divided between Germany and Poland by plebiscite Mar. 1921

9 allied occupation 1920-3, annexed by Lithuania 1923, autonomous 1924

10 plebiscite July 1920: to Germany

11 to Poland Dec. 1918

12 partitioned between Czechoslovakia and Poland 1920

13 to Hungary 1921

14 annexed by Poland 1920; to Poland by plebiscite 1922

15 to Greece from Bulgaria 1919

16 demilitarised 1924, remilitarised 1936

17 Greek-Bulgarian conflict 1925

18 independent, in personal union with Denmark 1918

hurl us back into barbarism.' The repudiation of European ideals was less explicit at the corresponding extreme on the right, but the latent savagery was at least as horrible and quite as silly. Just as Tukhachevski dreamed of 'returning to our Slav gods', so the Nazis fantasised about restoring ancient folk-paganism and turned *Heimschutz* – the preservation of the purity of the German heritage – into a mystic quest, leading through stone circles to the castle of Wewelsburg, where, Himmler believed, the ley-lines met at the centre of Germany and the world.

Futurism was the art and literature which both political extremes had in common: from the time of Marinetti's first Futurist Manifesto in 1909, war, chaos and destruction were glorified and tradition vilified in favour of the aesthetics of machines, the morals of might and the syntax of babble. Marinetti's highest beauty was the 'speeding automobile' – a taste he shared with Hitler, whose love of fine cars was his only departure from personal austerity. The 'lines of force' which his lectures inspired Russian artists to paint symbolised the politics of coercion. The movement he founded was endorsed by the fascists in Italy and for a while – until the collapse of the Left Front of the Arts in the mid-1920s – by communist revolutionaries in Russia.

In a series of 'civil wars' between the extremisms of left and right, European powers bludgeoned the strength out of one another and unfitted themselves for world supremacy. Even before the First World War there were signs that Europe's hegemony might be not be very durable. In white men's wars, the Americans blew away, with humiliating ease, most of what was left of Spain's empire in the Pacific and the New World, while the Boers came embarrassingly close to beating the British. More surprisingly for minds sunk in nineteenth-century racism, in 1896 a black emperor in Abyssinia crushed Italian would-be conquerors and became a participant on almost equal terms in the partition of Africa. In 1904 Japanese forces reversed Russian expansion in Asia and in India 'remote villagers,' it was said, 'talked over the victories of Japan as they sat in their circles and passed round the hookah at night.' The apprehension caused in Europe was not, however, commensurate with the excitement in Asia. Kaiser Wilhelm II was the most powerful of those who became anxious about the 'yellow peril' but they were outnumbered by Japan's friends and admirers. By most of the European intelligentsia, the Japanese, with their industrial precocity, techncial proficiency and military efficiency, had already been classified as honorary Europeans – the 'British' or 'Prussians of the East'. Their compliment to European industrial culture had been returned when Europeans copied their art. In 1876 Madame Monet was painted in a kimono. By the 1890s Japanese prints were a major source of models for artists of the French avant-garde.

Nor was one world war enough by itself to break the mastery of European imperialists. The First World War did, however, mark the beginning of a new, more nicely tilted relationship between Europe and the rest of the world. It started as a tourney between *anciens régimes*, the last turn of the gladiators in the old arena of states. Like all Europe's earlier wars since the middle ages, it was advocated with the rhetoric of chivalry, idealism and crusade but it was really only a heightened form of *Staatspolitik* – a 'continuation of politics by other means'. For Germany, it was an embodiment of two priorities of foreign policy: a pre-emptive strike against the menace of an industrialising Russia; and an attempt to break out into a world of far-flung opportunities from the narrow seas in which the British navy seemed able to confine her. For Britain it was an exercise in a historic strategy of pinning a world-imperial rival down in a continental war. For France, it was revenge for Sedan and the humiliations of 1871; for Austria-Hungary, an act of desperate impatience with Serbian subversion – an opting for 'an end with terror rather than terror without end'. For Italy the war was an ambitious essay in frontier-snatching; for Turkey, twitching insecurely in Russia's shadow, it was a miscalculated gamble on German strength. For all the major belligerents, it went wrong. On Germany's western front, armies got stuck in the mud in

unflankably long trenches from the Channel to the Alps. In the east, they collided blunderingly in the vastness of the terrain. The elites who started the war could not control its course or its costs.

A generation of the natural leaders of the old societies was immolated: that in itself was enough to ensure disruptive discontinuities in the development of Europe. The dead left gaps which societies were convulsed to fit – replacing the dead with the young or the old, men with women, aristocracies with meritocracies. The material impact of the First World War is eye-catching because it can be computed in digits which take up a lot of a line: perhaps 10,000,000 killed in action, 30,000,000 casualties in all, 9,000,000 tons of shipping sunk, for instance. The political consequences are conspicuous because they can translate into colours on a map: twelve new sovereign, or virtually sovereign, states in Europe or on its borders; frontiers re-shuffled between a dozen more; super-states demolished; overseas colonies swivelled and swapped. The war ended by provoking political revolution or transformation everywhere. The Russian, German, Austro-Hungarian and Turkish empires were pruned, pollarded or felled and even the United Kingdom lost a limb. Above all – from the perspective of European history as a whole – the war was a collective humiliation for Europe in the eyes of the world, for the bloody stalemate was ended by American intervention and the United States was revealed as the world's major power. 'Just wait for the next European war,' threatened E.M. Forster's character, the amiable Doctor Aziz in 1924, looking forward to dismantling western dominance and dismembering its empires.

At a deeper level, under the political change and the social dislocation, the war bred psychological trauma. A novelist from a neutral country who took part as a volunteer saw – in the flesh, it

'**Tomorrow belongs to me**': a German propaganda poster of 1935 *above* promotes the Nazi ideal of youth, uniformed and striding confidently towards an Aryan future.

John Singer Sargent never escaped the reputation for superficiality imposed on him by his skill as a fashionable portrait artist. But his war paintings, with their bloody colours and carefully posed realism, were the counterparts in flat art of the poetry of the trenches: raw experience made bearable by artifice. In *Gassed*, the victims of mustard gas stumble, linked by the comradeship of disablement, at the dressing station of Le-Bac-de Sud on the Doullens-Arras road *right*.

The garment, the tilt of the head, the curve of the back, the tent-like hem, the posture and sense of movement are all borrowed by Monet from *ukiyo-e* engravings in his painting of his wife in 1876 *above right*. The 1870s were the decisive decade in the western reception of Japanese artistic influence – part of an orientalising trend which has grown stronger in European taste and thought ever since.

seemed – mankind herded towards Armageddon by apocalyptic horsemen. In this respect, as in so many others, Hitler's experience was typical: 'It was with feelings of pure idealism,' he said, 'that I set out for the front in 1914. Then I saw men falling around me in thousands. Thus I learned that life is a cruel struggle... The individual can disappear, provided there are other men to replace him.' Sigmund Freud, who before the war had identified the sex urge as the motor of human conduct, revised his opinion to add the death-wish, Thanatos, alongside Eros, as co-ruler of the mind. Oswald Spengler was the most eloquent spokesmen of war-induced pessimism, prophesying 'the decline of the west', proposing, indeed, tangled downward spirals of senescence and decay for all civilisations.

There were, of course, still optimists left. Some thought the First World War would 'end all wars' and that the west would climb back out of its trench. The wreckage of the pre-war world looked well, at first, to those who had enjoyed little stake in its lost era of splendour: the poor, the previously suppressed nations, the hitherto unenfranchised, the political radicals and extremists. Spengler's great rival among popular world-historians, H.G. Wells, published the *Outline of History* in praise of progress in 1920. He was ill qualified, by today's standards, to be a wholly progressive figure, for he was sexually predatory and tyrannically opinionated. He was, however, the seducer or spokesman of those emancipated by the effects of the conflict. In spite of him, in what Keynes called 'the dead season of our fortunes', pessimism prevailed. With recession and slump, it spread. By the end of the 1920s, the world was singing *Twentieth-century Blues* and the decline of the west was actively anticipated or believed to have begun.

Shell-shock was the *mal de siècle* of the post-war years. The strain was tightened, the effects heightened by the self-awareness which the growth of psychology and, especially, of psychoanalysis encouraged. Freud was, in a sense, both the model and mentor of the age. In an experiment conducted on himself in Vienna in 1896, he exposed his own Oedipus complex. The therapeutic effect seemed to be confirmed in a series of patients, who rose from his couch – or that of his mentor, Josef Breuer – and walked more freely than before. Women who only a few years previously would have been dismissed as hysterical malingerers became case studies from whose example everyone could learn. Freud generalised, from the evidence of a few burgesses of pre-war Viennna, to illuminate the human condition in general. Every child experienced, before puberty, the same phases of sexual development and repressed similar fantasies or experiences. Hypnosis, or, as Freud preferred, the mnemonic effects, in a stirred subconscious, of the free association of images and memories, could retrieve repressed feelings and ease their nervous symptoms. Introspection became a rite in the modern west, defining this culture, as self-mutilation or dance or codes of gesture might define another. Repression became the modern demon and the analyst an exorcist.

This is not to say that the neuroses of twentieth-century westerners were unreal – only that psychology enhanced awareness of them and therefore, paradoxically, while contributing to their treatment increased their effects. The survivors of the unprecedented slaughter of the First World War returned with mental scars which, if communicated, could change sensibilities and pass on, in chat or silence, art or verse, the effects of the war to future generations, even when harvests were back to normal and cities rebuilt.

It is conventional but wise to look for the evidence in the poetry written on the western front. There in the trenches poets lived a conducive life of leisure and peril, trapped, with no view any way but upwards, between earth and sky. For literature, which usually does well out of war, this scoured and blasted landscape was a productive environment. Romanticism, the ruling passion of European civilisation in the nineteenth century, is commonly said to have been the first victim. Among the English poets, for instance, contrasts are drawn between two kinds of voice. Romanticism survived only in the heroic rhetoric of those who never saw the war, like Thomas Hardy, and the poignant mawkishness of Rupert Brooke, who died before joining combat. The frank anguish of real experience, by contrast, is detected by readers of Isaac Rosenberg, say, or Wilfred Owen. Hardy's trumpets are silenced by the 'monstrous anger' of Owen's guns; the scent of Rupert Brooke's remembered flowers is smothered among the front-liners by the urgent stench of gas or the pungent excretions of fear.

Yet all the poets drew screens of romance and rhetoric across the horrors of the war and Wilfred Owen himself was as evasive of the truth, as repressive of his own memories, as any child of a Viennese *Konditorei*. The very act of turning vicious memories into poetry clogged and padded them with softening wads of literary artifice. Associations with the sentiments, lovely or mawkish, evoked by most of earlier poetic tradition, tugged writers and readers away. Everyone who tried to write about the war with frank realism found that language filtered reality out. A typical hero, back among the comforts of Blighty, could not communicate anything that mattered: the people he found there – only 70 miles, less than a day's journey, from his 'stinking world of sticky, trickling earth' – had understandings grounded in an unoverlapping universe of experience; his was unfathomable and came to seem unmentionable in their company. Philip Gibbs and Robert Graves both found that they 'didn't want to tell' what it was like at the front. In consequence, the societies of home were exposed to the nightmares and unvoiced horrors of repressive returnees. In Galtier-Boissiere's disturbing painting of a Parisian victory parade, the figures under the bunting and triumphal arch are all maimed.

In a world grown accustomed to the wisdom of Freud, unspoken neuroses were the worst. The horrors of those who fought the war were answered by the guilt of those who missed it. Christopher Isherwood's generation, 'suffering from a feeling of shame that we hadn't taken part', went on fighting 'a subliminally persistent war'. French memories were nourished and transmitted by similar means. French psychiatrists turned *en masse* to blame the war for conditions familiar for years. French law developed the fiction of 'tacit consent' to cuckoldry of those absent at the front. In 1920, France's post-war president retired to a mental home. Churchmen blamed the high incidence of mental illness on the revival of the tango in hedonistic clubs.

Nervous disorders naturally found their way onto canvas and collage as well as into print. Though governments had patronised conventional war artists, the characteristic art of the First World War was Dada: externalised disillusionment and contempt for order and tradition embodied in the deliberately meaningless name. After the war, in Germany, Kurt Schwitters scraped art-works together from the detritus of a broken world – bits of smashed machines, fragments of demolished constructions. The visionary painter Max Ernst exposed post-war nightmares in weird, sickening dreams of evil, sometimes pieced, like Schwitters's work, from scraps of ephemera, or itchingly textured by rubbing the paper over wires or sacking or unplaned planks. The jangle of nerves could be 'heard' in music on the twelve-note system developed by Schoenberg in the early 1920s.

Combatants with shaken nerves went home to political landscapes jolted and jarred into new shapes, as if by a giant's hand. Considered from one point of view, it had been an American war of liberation in Europe – the revenge of the millions of migrants who had left the old empires to take refuge in the New World. When intervention came from across the Atlantic, it was not on behalf of Britain and France, but for America's own objectives: crushing German militarism, freeing the seas, weakening European overseas imperialism, dissolving America's debts and 'making the world safe for democracy'. Before the war, after a generation of intensive industrialisation, the United States was already beginning to look like more than a great power – a super-power, capable of taking on all the rest. The only curb on her might was the massive indebtedness of her economy, chiefly to British investors. The experience of the war reversed that relationship and proved that American might could slice Europe to its liking.

The result was reflected in receding images on the walls of the Hall of Mirrors at Versailles. At the end of the war Austria-Hungary

Max Halberstadt's photograph of Freud in 1921 *top left* captures the image the master wanted to project: inscrutable himself, because half in shadow, but penetrating with an intense gaze deep into the psyche of the beholder.

America's entry into the First World War was made on the basis of exact calculations of national interest, but it was advertised, like the war-mongering of the original combatants, as a struggle for the defence of civilisation. Official propaganda adopted the Franco-British image of the barbaric 'Hun' who glowers in the background of this poster *centre left*.

The art of disordered nerves. Kurt Schwitters, *Merzbild*, 1930 *left*. 'Merz', invented in 1920, was Schwitters's version of Dada. The term was meaningless, the works were collages or painted constructions, from wood, paper, scrap metal and bits of fabric, characterised by the 'itchingly grainy' textures obtained by filing, rubbing and scraping.

'Images multiplying in a hall of mirrors': Sir William Orpen's painting *right* brilliantly captures the scene at the signing of the Treaty of Versailles on 28th June 1919, with recessive reflections wobbling in the delusively warped glass.

177

was, like most of the belligerents, impoverished and selectively starved, but – uniquely among armies east of the Rhine – hers were undefeated. They occupied more territory than in 1914. Except for the Czechs and the Serb minority in Croatia and Bosnia, none of the national communities of Austria-Hungary repudiated the house of Habsburg while the prospect of a surviving monarchy lasted. Yet the empire fragmented at the rhythm of a typewriter in Washington, issuing 'notes' and 'points' that dictated the future. First, in the summer of 1918, came President Wilson's avowal that 'Czecho-Slovakia' was an independent, co-belligerent nation – a fateful step that condemned both the Austrian and Hungarian halves of the Habsburg world to dismemberment. There would, Wilson also declared, be a re-unified and independent Polish state with access to the sea, implicitly without Habsburg tutelage; and 'the justice of the national aspirations of the Jugo-Slavs for freedom' was to be 'recognised in the fullest manner'. Austria-Hungary was not even to be represented at the peace conference. Like Berkeley's tree, it was destroyed by being overlooked. Meanwhile, at the edges of the Russian empire, the distribution of the fragments separated by war and revolution was again determined from outside: 'national aspirations' were fulfilled only with great-power sponsorship. Thus Finland, Estonia, Latvia, Lithuania and Poland survived as independent states, while Ukraine, Georgia, Armenia and Belarus did not. Only Romania and Poland succeeded in getting more than President Wilson wanted for them – both at Ruthenian and Ukrainian expense.

As embodiments of nationalist ideals, all the post-war states were flawed. The ragged hemming of their frontiers had to be unpicked and re-stitched in an 'age of plebiscites' during the 1920s, supported by civil wars, ethnic massacres and mass exchanges of populations across hostile frontiers. Most of the plebiscites left almost as many people resentful as content. The results included cross-national hybrids comparable to those produced by the Napoleonic Wars. 'Czecho-Slovakia' and the 'Kingdom of Serbs, Croats and Slovenes' would be hardly more viable in the long term than the 1815 Kingdom

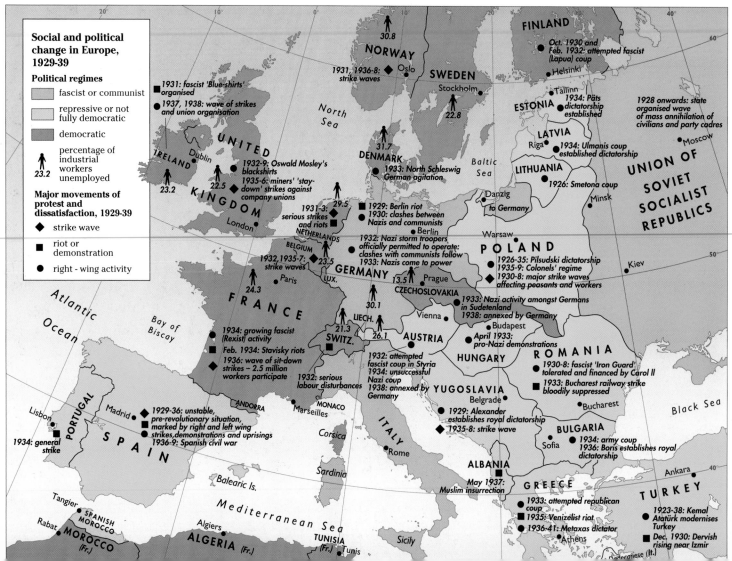

Social and political change in Europe, 1929-39

Political regimes

- fascist or communist
- repressive or not fully democratic
- democratic

23.2 percentage of industrial workers unemployed

Major movements of protest and dissatisfaction, 1929-39

- ◆ strike wave
- ■ riot or demonstration
- ● right - wing activity

NORWAY 30.8

1931, 1936-8: strike waves ◆ Oslo

FINLAND

Oct. 1930 and Feb. 1932: attempted fascist (Lapua) coup

Helsinki

SWEDEN Stockholm 22.8

ESTONIA Tallinn
1934: Päts dictatorship established

LATVIA Riga
1934: Ulmanis coup established dictatorship

1928 onwards: state organised wave of mass annihilation of civilians and party cadres

Moscow

UNION OF SOVIET SOCIALIST REPUBLICS

1931: fascist 'Blue-shirts' organised
1937, 1938: wave of strikes and union organisation

IRELAND Dublin 23.2

UNITED KINGDOM 22.5

1932-9: Oswald Mosley's blackshirts
1935-6: miners' 'stay-down' strikes against company unions

London

North Sea

DENMARK 31.7
1933: North Schleswig German agitation

Baltic Sea

LITHUANIA
1926: Smetona coup

Danzig to Germany

Minsk

1931-3: serious strikes and riots 29.5

NETHERLANDS

1929: Berlin riot ■
1930: clashes between Nazis and communists
Berlin ●

Warsaw

POLAND

1926-35: Pilsudski dictatorship ●
1935-9: Colonels' regime ●
1930-8: major strike waves ◆ affecting peasants and workers

Kiev 50

BELGIUM 23.5
1932, 1935-7: strike waves ◆

1932: Nazi storm troopers officially permitted to operate: clashes with communists follow
1933: Nazis come to power ●

GERMANY

Prague 13.5

1933: Nazi activity amongst Germans in Sudetenland ●
1938: annexed by Germany

24.3

Paris ●

FRANCE

LUX.

CZECHOSLOVAKIA

30.1

Vienna ●

Budapest ●

1934: growing fascist (Rexist) activity ●
Feb. 1934: Stavisky riots ■
1936: wave of sit-down strikes – 2.5 million workers participate ◆

LIECH.
21.3
SWITZ. 26.1

1932: attempted fascist coup in Styria
1934: unsuccessful Nazi coup
1938: annexed by Germany

AUSTRIA

HUNGARY

April 1933: pro-Nazi demonstrations ●

ROMANIA

1930-8: fascist 'Iron Guard' ● tolerated and financed by Carol II
1933: Bucharest railway strike ■ bloodily suppressed

Bucharest ●

Atlantic Ocean

Bay of Biscay

1932: serious labour disturbances

MONACO
ANDORRA Marseilles

1929: Alexander establishes royal dictatorship ●
1935-8: strike wave ◆

Belgrade ●

YUGOSLAVIA

BULGARIA

Black Sea

Lisbon ●
Madrid ●

1929-36: unstable, pre-revolutionary situation, marked by right and left wing strikes, demonstrations and uprisings ◆
1936-9: Spanish civil war

PORTUGAL

1934: general strike ◆

SPAIN

Corsica

ITALY

Rome ●

Sardinia

1934: army coup ●
1936: Boris establishes royal dictatorship

Sofia ●

Ankara

ALBANIA

May 1937: Muslim insurrection ■

GREECE

TURKEY

1923-38: Kemal Atatürk modernises Turkey ●

Balearic Is.

Tangier ●
SPANISH MOROCCO
Rabat ●
MOROCCO
(Fr.)

Algiers ●

Mediterranean Sea

Sicily

1933: attempted republican coup ●
1935: Venizelist riot ■
1936-41: Metaxas dictator ●

Athens ●

Dec. 1930: Dervish rising near Izmir ■

Dodecanese (It.)

ALGERIA (Fr.)

TUNISIA (Fr.) Tunis ●

of the Netherlands or the union of Sweden and Norway. Ukraine was, in effect, partitioned between powerful neighbours and Hungary so diminished by the pickings of the victors and beneficiaries of the war that all her neighbours were left with significant Magyar minorities. Lithuania ended up without its historic capital. The 'Irish Free State' was rent by war between rival nationalist parties, who differed chiefly in the degree of their rejection of the British Empire, and shorn of six counties in the north-east where a plebiscite favoured continued adherence to the United Kingdom. Greece deported millions of Turks and conquered millions of Slavs, becoming – in combination with her pre-war gains in the region – an indelibly Balkan power. The most dangerous hostages to fortune were the many millions of dispersed Germans who became minorities in despised states, vengefully nursing the myth that everyone's national destiny had been fulfilled except their own.

Even more ominously, national hatreds were now transcended by ideological defiance. In the years before the war, shaking off the complacency described in the previous chapter, European elites talked themselves into expecting a showdown with the working class. In 1902 Ramon Casas, the pet painter of the Barcelona bourgeoisie, exhibited a scene of heroic workers scattered or trampled by the hooves of police mounts. Galsworthy's play *Strife* was performed in 1909. The assumption that society was divided by antagonistic class differences was almost universal. An experienced employer of dockers in Marseilles told an inquiry in 1901 that 'a wave threatens to submerge us'. In Britain, the appeal of Fabianism – a campaign to introduce socialism gradually – was as much to bourgeois fear as to bourgeois conscience: Fabius, after all, had 'saved the state by delay'. On the eve of war in 1914, Sir Edward Grey predicted, 'There will be socialist governments everywhere after this.' Meanwhile, in parts of Europe, workers' demonstrations could kindle such fear that, for instance, on a Sunday in 1905, Russian troops opened fire on petitioners to the Tsar from a trade union which banned socialists from membership. The screams of the victims were echoed in the elation of the middle-class

demonstrators who followed, painted by Ilya Repin in their feather-trimmed hats, fur muffs and stiff collars, or in the 'red laughter' of the skeletons in a commemorative design by Boris Kustodiev.

Even so, until the effects of war bit deep into industrial prosperity, socialism in Europe remained manageable by the elite. The only revolutions where socialist rhetoric seemed to have any part in mobilising masses were the vast but remote peasant rebellions in Mexico and China. When socialist revolution did reach Europe, it continued to defy Marx's own predictions. The misery which provoked it was brought on not by the excesses of capitalism but by the unmerciful demands of war – though theorists claimed these were the same thing. It was supposed to flow from vast, impersonal historic forces, yet it was acclaimed as the achievement of heroes: profane tsars, Lenin and Stalin, of contrasting charisma – the first the restless, active genie immortalised in Eisenstein's jerky cinematography, the second substantial and still, controlling by chill calm from vast, sedately posed posters.

Like so many great formative movements in European history, the revolutions started in the east and spread west. The first – and, for a long time, the only – success was hardly the victory of masses of workers. The Bolshevik 'uprising' was a well-planned and initially bloodless coup, engineered in November 1917 by Lenin and Trotsky, with the balletic precision captured in Kliment Redko's commemorative painting. During 1918, the threat of the transfer of Bolshevism to Finland was settled in the civil war and 'white terror' in which General Mannerheim smashed the 'Red Guard' – a rare case of democracy restored by repression. A year after the Bolshevik coup in Russia, Germany – or, at least, Berlin – had its 'November revolution', crushed by conservatives and Social Democrats in collusion, while the fledgling Nazi party was forming in Munich. As the communists died in Berlin, Béla Kun arrived in Budapest from Moscow to proclaim a Bolshevik republic, which Romanian invaders overthrew and native militarists mopped up bloodily. In 1920 fascist streetfighters helped break up soviets proclaimed in north Italian factories. In 1923 a Russian-backed insurgency was destroyed in

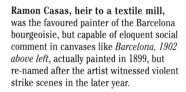

Ramon Casas, heir to a textile mill, was the favoured painter of the Barcelona bourgeoisie, but capable of eloquent social comment in canvases like *Barcelona, 1902 above left*, actually painted in 1899, but re-named after the artist witnessed violent strike scenes in the later year.

Social and political change in Europe, 1928 to 1939 *map left*. Protest movements of the left and right arose in almost every country in Europe in response to political dislocation following the First World War and the economic slump of the 1930s, severely testing the social and political fabric. In countries where democratic traditions and institutions were weak – and this included most of Europe – some form of dictatorship resulted or was confirmed.

Boris Kustodiev's *Bolshevik,* **1920** *right,* was a re-working of a scene he originally painted in 1906, when the place of the colossal worker bestriding the cityscape had been occupied by a scythe-wielding skeleton in allusion to the events of 'Bloody Sunday', 1905.

the militant peasant democracy of Bulgaria.

The revolutions showed most promise in unevenly industrialised environments and tended to get checked or domesticated wherever industrialisation was most mature. In England and France, for instance, the progress of democratic socialism seemed to make revolution unnecessary, though most French socialist groups voted to join the Comintern in 1920. Indeed, everywhere west of the Russias, in the first round of Europe's 'civil wars' from 1917 to the early 1920s revolutionaries were defeated and socialist compromisers seduced by embourgeoisement. Militant socialism, however, retained or gained impetus for every subsequent stage of the conflict – the street fighting of the 1920s and 1930s, the Spanish Civil War, the Second World War, until its energies drained slowly away in the re-channelled hostilities of the Cold War.

People judge ideologies in power by their performance and ideologies in opposition by their promises. The appeal of fascism and communism was in proportion to the failure of capitalism to deliver justly distributed prosperity through the lurches of hardship and slump, inflation and depression, which disfigured the 1920s and 1930s. The cartoons of George Grosz – caricaturist of the crude egotism and coarse manners of profiteers – are mirrors of the critique of capitalism. They grew more savage as he got older. Even in his relatively gentle satirical phase, represented in *The Glutton* of 1923, tellingly political messages were coded into the picture: the big ring and smoking-jacket cut were the marks of the plutocrat, the bulky claws were the rough hands of the parvenu – helping to suggest a terrible isomorphism between the devourer and his prey. The rose, which was part of the luxury of the table-setting, also made two subtler points: its fragility contrasted with the eater's own crushing massiveness and it completed the range of submissive nature spread on the table before him. The globules of sweat shaken from the eater's head were drops of irony: he was consuming the products of the sweat of the workers.

The fighting spirit of those who stayed or became loyal to Moscow in Europe's civil wars could be illustrated from literally millions of individual stories. They include 'Clydebuilt men' – honest workers who rose through the hierarchy of their trades unions without ever losing their painfully sharp self-perceptions as the victims of class war – and wine-bar traitors: journalists and politicians employed by Moscow as 'agents of influence', blinded by KGB bribes to the deficiencies of societies other than their own. Conspicuous at one extreme are the elegant double-agents who gave the most precious British secrets to the Russians. Anthony Blunt, 'Surveyor' or keeper of the royal collection of paintings, demonstrated that a courtier's qualities were ideal for a spy: the mask of deference, the command of insincerity, the guarded tongue. He was a conspirator in a toffs' treason, with fellow-Oxbridge men who, at one level, merely transferred their allegiance from one power-establishment to another. His colleague, Guy Burgess, wore his old Etonian tie in exile in Moscow. On the other hand, they were genuinely victims of the climate of their times, revolted by the apparently fossilised inequalities and inefficiencies of pre-war capitalism. Blunt evoked disgust when he defended his record with the claim that he had preferred conscience to country: in the context of the Cambridge of the 1930s, where youthful idealism had every stimulus and few restraints, the apology rings true. The real mystery is how such a fastidious aesthete, who was an authority on the Italian baroque, can have aligned himself with the patrons of socialist realism.

No western communist, perhaps, has a more legendary status than 'Dolores' Ibarruri, a loud international voice of Moscow's for most of the century. In contrast to the willowy Blunt, she was cut out to be a figurehead. Her lumpy figure might have been carved from hardwood. In her early forties, her bulging breasts excited republican soldiers' passion. Her staring eyes held audiences spellbound. Even her characteristic posture – leaning forward to declaim, with out-thrust head – might have been designed to adorn a prow. She joined the Spanish communist party at its foundation

Critiques of capitalism in images of womanhood: 'La Pasionaria' *centre left*, in the uniform of the regiment of which she was honorary colonel-in-chief during the Spanish Civil War represents sex sacrificed for military efficiency. Capitalism is equated with prostitution in George Grosz's café nude of 1923 *above left*.

The spy as aesthete: Sir Anthony Blunt, the crypto-communist traitor who was Surveyor of the Queen's Pictures, photographed in 1962 *below left*. The appearance is complete: languid but erect, patrician pose, impeccable courtier's attire, passionless mask, gestureless stance, partly concealed hands.

Photographed from the Eiffel Tower, with the Palais de Chaillot in the distance, a panoramic view across the plaza of the International Exposition, Paris, 1937, where the Nazi and Soviet pavilions faced each other, echoing each other's architecture *below*.

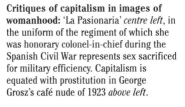

and died, at the age of 93, in 1989, when it was crumbling as fast as the Berlin Wall. It brought her fame and failure, prominence but not power.

This daughter of a well-paid miner came to communism, tainted by the piety and prosperity of her pithead childhood, when she married an impecunious revolutionary. She hated her husband but became wedded to his politics – perhaps in penance for her hatred. She was a frustrated priestess who served the party with the passion of a vocation transferred. Moscow became her Rome, Stalin her pope: inside the communist there was always a catholic trying to get out. During the Spanish Civil War, the 'priest-eater' of right-wing propaganda protected nuns and ransacked religious imagery for her famous speeches. Her real name was Isadora. 'Dolores', like the highly exploitable pen-name of 'La Pasionaria', was a nickname that evoked the sorrows of Holy Week.

She was the naughty Lola of the Left, practising what she claimed was politically correct sex with a lover 20 years her junior. Her choice, however, with his mudless boots and silk pyjamas, suggested some fatal tendency towards bourgeois deviation: she later came to see him as a traitor to the cause. She was a feminist who was good at knitting and who patched the holes in the commissar's jacket. Her revolutionary credentials were combined with old-fashioned values: she was flattered by a gift of perfume and she hated women to smoke. She reminded some fellow-communists of a medieval queen, others of a sixteenth-century saint. She was Stalin's dupe, but the authoress of her own personality cult. 'You have such a famous mother,' she told her children, 'why must you behave so badly?' She stormed through the conflicts of militant socialism and snored through its senescence – noisily asleep, a returnee from exile in her eighties, on the back benches of Spain's Chamber of Deputies.

During its period of vigour, socialism, like any growing creed, was vulnerable to fracture by heretics and schismatics. The triumph of one of the most militant fragments in the Russian revolution exacerbated enmities within the left, from where the sects would wage civil wars of their own while contending with external enemies. 'Aren't we all socialists?' George Orwell naively asked during the gun-battles of rival revolutionaries in Barcelona in 1937: this was like asking, 'Aren't we all Christians?' at the massacre of St Bartholomew. Whether fascism was a splinter of socialism, or an independently evolved doctrine, or just a slick name for unprincipled opportunism, has been a matter of passionate debate. From the perspective of the future, the differences between all forms of violent political extremism will blur. The politics of twentieth-century Europe were horseshoe-shaped and the extremists at both ends seemed close enough to touch. In practice, individuals moved between fascism and militant socialism as if by connecting channels. Mussolini was a socialist youth leader before he became a fascist duce. At least until Hitler's hijack and purge, many Nazis tried to make the party conform to its name: the German National Socialist Workers' Party. Britain's failed 'Man of Destiny', Oswald Mosley, was a socialist cabinet minister before he took to the streets. Tukhachevski extolled 'the carnival of death' and fought for the Bolsheviks because he hated Jews – 'dogs who sow fleas in every land' and who had 'infected Russia with the pest of civilisation and the morality of capitalism'.

The heritage of futurism clad regimes of the extreme left and right in the same dreary livery of state-sponsored art: crushingly monumental architecture, boringly heroic figures, the bleak aesthetics of the factory and the machine. Across the plaza at the Paris Exposition of 1937 Nazi and Soviet pavilions exchanged identical stylistic reverberations. In Salazar's Portugal, the beautiful old university buildings of Coimbra were all but obscured with the unyielding blocks of authoritarian taste. The buildings with which Stalin planned to dwarf the Kremlin – the Palace of the Soviets and the Commissariat of Heavy Industry – were so vast that the work never got beyond the foundations. Yet not even authoritarian aesthetics quite crushed the inventiveness out of art. Mussolini never really succeeded in making the trains run on time but he did build one of the world's most impressive railway stations at Milan, in an original style, evocative of an imaginary, pre-Roman civilisation: this was a fit setting for Carlo Carra's late futurist

painting, celebrating the explosive, almost procreative power of the high-speed train of the day. In a more restrained style, the tomb Franco carved out of a mountainside with slave labour is genuinely awesome and, to an objective eye, beautiful.

Fascism's doctrine of the omnipotence of the state was shared with the dominant tendency in socialism. Its celebration of the sanctity of violence resembled the militancy of two strands in the ragged fabric of the far left: the anarchist tendency proscribed by Marx; and the zealots of perpetual revolution, who had Lenin's comrade and rival, Leon Trotsky, as their patriarch. The military model followed by fascists for the organisation of society is, in one perspective, a model of fraternal community-life. 'Revolutionary discipline' was also demanded by Lenin. In the 1930s, the economic programme of fascism, summarised in Hitler's slogan, 'Arbeit, Freiheit und Brot', included planned re-inflation and wealth-distribution through public works – which was or became the orthodoxy of social democracy. For all these reasons, fascism is classifiable as a variant of socialism, adapted to the needs of a variegated electorate. Fascists mobilised small property-owners from the petty bourgeoisie, as well as workers, by advocating policies which could be crudely reduced to 'socialism without expropriation'.

The 'civil wars' of Atlantic civilisation were not just confrontations of left and right; nor simply struggles of the traditional mixed societies – with their irrationally evolved institutions, conservative habits and liberal orthodoxies – fending off the attacks of radicals on either flank. The killing grounds were crossed with old enmities which the new lines of battle overlay. Among them were those of liberals for clericalists; local and regional majorities for their ethnic or racial victims; nationalists and imperialists for liberals and separatists; and neighbouring nations for each other. Age-old violence went on under the shell of pan-European conflict. Secular hatred took on the language but rarely the forms of class war.

'Work, Freedom and Bread': the Nazi propaganda poster for the 1932 Reichstag elections *left* appealed to a German electorate battered by depression and political instability. It was sinisterly echoed in the slogan on the gate of the concentration camp at Auschwitz: 'Arbeit macht frei' (work makes you free).

The photographs of 'Robert Capa' – the *nom de guerre* of a consortium of socialist photographers – helped keep an inspiring image of Spanish republican resistance before the eyes of the world during the Spanish Civil War. The defiant anti-fascist salute of the Italian volunteer made one of their most famous and most characteristic compositions *above*.

Subtle Dreyfusard propaganda, 1895 *right*: the disgraced Jew is shown dignified and erect, while his sword is broken by a figure of almost simian ungainliness: ill-controlled, stooping, frenzied and contorted by a bestial crouch.

The Valley of the Fallen: Franco's mausoleum and monument to the 'ethic of victory' *far right*, which he pursued in defiance of reconciliation for more than a generation after the civil war, took 20 years to build. The basilica, hewn from a mountainside to a depth of 250 metres, is one of the most beautiful surviving examples of the monumental 'dictator's art' which was erected over much of Europe in the twentieth century, but its brutal grandeur was achieved by forced labour.

Between 1936 and 1939, for instance, young poets deferred their bicycle races through English suburbs to 'explode like bombs' in a Spanish war, because they oversimplified it as a theatre of the fight between right and left. Most ended disillusioned, because the war was really fought between broad coalitions pursuing introspectively Spanish agenda. The 'national' coalition included virtual fascists, but partnered them with an uncomfortable wagon-full of fellow-travellers: traditional Catholics, fighting to save nuns from rape and churches from incineration; old-fashioned liberal centralists, who were equally numerous on the other side; romantic reactionaries who, in armed thousands, yearned to restore a long-excluded line of the former royal dynasty; constitutional monarchists who wanted to get back to the cosy, remunerative parliamentary system of the previous generation; worshippers of 'the sacred unity of Spain', who thought they were fighting to hold the country together; *hispanizadores* who wanted to purge supposedly Spanish virtues of foreign pollutants. On the other side, along with all the mutually warring sects of the left, were conservative republicans, who included Catholics as well as secularists; anti-clericals of the liberal tradition; admirers of French and English standards of democracy; and right-wing regionalists, who, recognising the nationalists as the greater threat, supported the republicans as the lesser evil.

Similarly in France the Second World War masked a civil war in which old enemies bared their knives. Here, however, the traditional divisions more closely matched those of left and right. Swathes of French society had never accepted ungrudgingly the republic that had been created after the last crushing defeat by Germany in 1871. Clericalists regarded the republic as an affair of freemasons; for royalists it was a thing of bad taste, symbolised by the frightful hat knocked from a president's head by a baron at the races in 1899. Bonapartists and other authoritarians deplored successive governments' spineless record in foreign affairs. The symbolic 'Marianne', nubile bearer of the *tricolore* at the barricades of the revolutions of the nineteenth century, was 'the slut' in an aggressively nationalistic paper.

The acquiescence of a large part of this powerful lobby was secured through the glory and patronage accruing from an unwieldy empire in Africa and Indo-China. But disloyalty to the republic was too tightly entwined with some groups' hatred for others to be easily unravelled. The scale and tenacity of the hatred were brought home by the Dreyfus scandal of 1894-1906 – a slow agony of national humiliation, mutually inflicted by rival interests in pursuit or defence of incompatible ideals of France. Dreyfus was a staff officer of creditable record, but a double outsider: an Alsatian of German antecedents, when Germany was the national enemy; and a Jew at a time when anti-Semitism was inflamed against France's fastest-growing minority. Intelligence officers colluded with a real spy – who was also an aristocrat from a traditional army family – to indict the innocent Dreyfus for espionage. When a brother-officer, outraged by the injustice, leaked the decisive evidence, officialdom, denying its crime, refused even to admit its mistake. Lobbyists for justice were persecuted in their turn. The verdict was shored up with fabricated evidence, justice denied by delay. Dreyfus was returned for re-trial, white and crushed, after three years' penal exile on Devil's Island. His sentence was lightened before he was pardoned; he was pardoned before he was officially exonerated. Meanwhile, the conspiracy against him had come to be seen by republicans as a reactionary plot against the constitution. The anti-dreyfusards saw the Dreyfus lobby as an unpatriotic gang. The issue was not, a propagandist said, 'whether a wretched individual is guilty or innocent – it is whether the Jews and Protestants are or are not the masters of the country'.

The civil war narrowly escaped in 1899 broke out in 1940, when

the anti-dreyfusards emerged from the tumbledown woodwork of fallen France, some of them openly gloating. The name 'Republic' was excised from that of the French 'State'. A government of old soldiers and Nazi sympathisers in Vichy 'collaborated' with the Germans against their fellow-citizens; Jews and leftists were slaughtered and enslaved; Germany preyed on the economy, looted works of art and 'exported' hundreds of thousands of Frenchmen as labour. Feeble at first, the 'Resistance' was transformed by the German invasion of Russia in June 1941. This released communists, previously quiescent on orders from Moscow, into the woods. The resisters were now a coalition reminiscent, in its breadth and its fragility, of those of the Spanish Civil War, encompassing communists and Catholics. From 1943, the fascist *milice* fought a ruthless war in the wastes against the *maquis*. The Germans fled in 1944, leaving Frenchmen at each others' throats. More, perhaps, than by any other single influence, peace and democracy were restored by women's suffrage: the votes of widows and spinsters gave power to the Catholic centre and an opportunity to policies of reconciliation. Meanwhile, France was reduced to prostration, derided or pitied by the young Leon Brittan for 'clapped-out Citroens and filthy loos'.

Even when Hitler was beaten and dead, protracted conflict threatened from three sources: continuing civil wars in 'liberated' countries; Russian desire for security or power on her western borders; and the internationalist idealism of militant socialists – exploited but not really supported from Moscow – who wanted to take advantage of a 'revolutionary situation' across the continent. Depending on his point of view, the onlooker could be disgusted by Stalin's greed or astonished at his moderation: the Soviet Union re-absorbed Ukraine, Estonia, Latvia and Lithuania but did not resume efforts to annex Finland; of the nominally allied countries, Stalin occupied Poland but withdrew from Czechoslovakia and Yugoslavia; he garrisoned the territory of hostile belligerents in Romania, Bulgaria, Hungary and eastern Germany, but co-operated with the other allied powers in the administration of Austria and Berlin. In practice, American decision-makers seem to have been willing to allow him more liberties than he took. In March 1946, Churchill announced the descent of an 'iron curtain' across Europe, but it was still perforated by chinks and draughts.

The struggle became focussed on Greece, where Stalin had promised Britain 'ninety per cent predominance' and where Britain was determined to exact her rights: there was no 'east-west' confrontation, only a civil war settled by British intervention, in which the left was disarmed and destroyed. In the rest of Europe, over the next few years, economic necessity imposed a fragile equilibrium. Economic aid was the best means of seducing former enemies into dependence. By the time the 'Marshall Plan' was introduced in 1948 to fund European re-construction from America and create 'social and political conditions in which free institutions can exist', most of the central and eastern countries were already tied to the Soviet market by reparations-debts or the want of

The timelessness of war: Greek government forces set out on a mountain patrol against Communist guerrillas in 1948 *far right above*, while a local villager ignores yet another intrusion by the authorities.

'Two peoples, two countries, two leaders': this 1949 cover-page from a German right-wing magazine *above right* plays on the nationalist slogan 'Ein Reich, ein Volk, ein Führer' to express disquiet at the division of Germany. The leaders of the two German states are superimposed on the Habsburg double-headed eagle, clutching the emblems of their servility to different masters: the communist hammer and sickle and the capitalist dollar.

The defeat of Germany, 1942 to 1945, *map right*. As the German *Wehrmacht* was rolled back and overwhelmed by the strain of fighting on two fronts, the pattern of Allied advances cut deep into the German *Heimat*.

French partisans, having received arms by parachute-drop, at a farmhouse near Châteaudun in mid-August 1944, await orders to move on against the fleeing Germans *below*.

alternatives. All of them, by choice or putsch, became 'people's republics' and Soviet satellite-states – even Czechoslovakia, which was close to the west and had a long democratic tradition. Russian fear of prosperity bought with dollars showed in the attempt to force East German currency on West Berlin in 1948-9: the American response included the 'Berlin airlift' to break the blockade and the formation of the North Atlantic alliance to oppose 'the Kremlin's intimidation'. Like so many others, Europe's civil wars had resulted in partition between armed camps: a ring of American client-states, of varying degrees of unruliness; a heavily-fenced Soviet empire.

International politics were immobilised by the 'balance of terror'. The explosive properties of nuclear fission had been noticed by British experimenters before the First World War. The prospect was popularised by H.G. Wells in a futuristic novel about the emergence of a utopian world from the ashes of civilisation, incinerated by atomic war. When Frederic Jolilot, the Curies' son-in-law, received his Nobel Prize for work on nuclear energy in 1935, he warned that an atomic chain-reaction could destroy the world. By 1939, the technical obstacles to the manufacture of the imagined bomb were nearly overcome but war, which ought logically to have speeded the research, stymied it in Europe. British science was distracted by the more immediate demands of the war effort. The French team under Jolilot, which was closest to completion when war broke out, was dispersed by the Nazi conquest. In Germany, Werner Heisenberg headed a team with the talent to make the bomb in an empire which controlled significant sources of the vital raw materials – German uranium and Norwegian heavy water. But he was unwilling or unable to put a bomb in Hitler's hands. When Germany fell, her bomb project was found to have made no progress.

Thus the first bombs were built in America by an odd-ball collection of talent, in which decisive contributions were made by J. Robert Oppenheimer, a left-wing mystic with a genius for scientific administration, and Leo Szilard, an intuitive physicist of

sententious habits who had been inspired by H.G. Wells. Had America kept her monopoly of the weapon, she would have been permanently secure in the role of world-arbiter for which her size and wealth equipped her and which her decisive intervention in the world war had confirmed. She felt obliged, however, to share her secrets with her British allies, to whose collaboration American success was indebted; probably in part as a result of the treason of the spy-ring in the British foreign service, a Russian 'A-bomb' appeared in 1949. As Russia's great strength was in manpower, the new technology of war did not favour her: outside her sphere of influence, Europe could enjoy, under the shadow of the bomb, a security unthinkable without such protection. On the other hand, nuclear equivalency with the United States – extended within a few years by further technical innovations to the level of 'mutually assured destruction' – guaranteed Russia's free hand in the territories she had already conquered or coerced. Yugoslavia broke free of Russian hegemony before the completion of the Soviet bomb. Afterwards, most of the other eastern European 'satellite states' tried a similar manoeuvre and failed.

The bomb was no protection, however, against the corrosion of the Soviet system from within. Better than in statistics contorted by propaganda, Soviet climacteric and decline can be followed in the work of painters. The rigours of Stalinism are filtered out of Yuri Pimenov's painting of *New Moscow* of 1937. The picture is so idealised that the beholder suspects some daring satirical intention. The thinly applied paint and streaky brushwork create an impression of soft-focus, making hard-core propaganda palatable. The broad street, with its smart cars and gay buses, is observed through a flapper in the foreground – bobbed hair, modern dress – emancipatedly driving an open-topped tourer. The vague, vertical buildings, towering out of the canvas in the background, make it look more like New York than New Moscow. In the next few years, war gutted the subtlety out of Soviet image-projection. Images of rural Russia abounded in the war years and after as the regime

The changing self-image of Soviet Russia: a rare flourish of freedom and gaiety under Stalin *top right* in Yuri Pimenov's *New Moscow*; a nationalistic rehabilitation of Holy Mother Russia *bottom right* in Mikhail Savitsky's *Partisan Madonna* (1967) ; an embittered vision of a returnee from the Afghan War by Boris Ugarov (1985) *far right above* .

The power of the atom unleashed. The first underwater atom bomb explosion by the Americans at Bikini on 25th July 1946 *centre right* produces the mushroom cloud which has become the symbol of the nuclear instruments of mass destruction.

Capitalist Manna from heaven: the Allied airlift to West Berlin in action *left*, relieving the blockade which had threatened to strangle this democratic enclave within the Soviet empire.

rediscovered the heroism of Holy Russia and the ennobling effects of staggered economic progress. The theme remained dominant, the mood retrospective, right through the 1960s, typified by Mikhail Savitsky's *The Partisan Madonna* of 1967 – still nurturing hope in fortitude, apparently unaware that the Second World War was over. By the time of the next war, the feeling had changed. Boris Ugarov's *The Return* of 1985 captures the disillusionment of failed intervention in Afghanistan, 'Russia's Vietnam'. Sombre figures exchange a despairing embrace in an apocalyptic landscape of ruins and ice.

The huge post-war Russian penumbra in eastern and central Europe can be understood in two ways. First, as an unsurprising empire – typical of the entire recorded history of the region – which reflected Russia's natural endowments for hegemony: huge population, untold resources and an unassailable heartland. Such an empire had been foreseeable for centuries and might have taken shape more than 100 years earlier, after the Napoleonic wars, when the opportunity of 1945 was startlingly prefigured. On the other hand, with equal conviction, it could be claimed that Soviet power was a jerrybuilt edifice, ramshackle and extemporised, incapable of containing for long – much less eliminating for ever – the inveterate national and religious identities of the subject peoples. Its collapse was predicted almost from the start and it could be said that what was surprising was not its sudden demise but its long survival.

1989, the bicentennial year of the French revolution, was decisive in dismantling it. In June, in Poland, the communist party was swamped in the first free elections since before the war, while in Hungary the martyrs of resistance to Soviet domination were re-habilitated. In October, the communist party in Moscow formally resigned its 'leading role'. In November, the Berlin Wall – the concrete successor of the 'iron curtain' – began to come down; by 22nd December, when Romania's dictator was slaughtered after

An empire founders: the closure of the imperial artery of the Suez canal after its nationalisation by Nasser and the subsequent debacle of Franco-British intervention is highlighted by a blockade of sunken shipping on the canal *left*. The failure of the Suez campagn was, arguably, the *coup de grace to* the British self-image of an unshakable imperial power.

Bucharest, 6th December 1989 *right*. A communist flag is burned by some of the demonstrators who felled the Ceaucescu regime: a gesture repeated all over Europe's disintegrating eastern bloc.

The multi-cultural cocktail, even in the early days of 'New Commonwealth' immigration, contained an illiberal dosage of suspicion and outright hostility to the newcomers. The frosty welcome accorded this new arrival *far right* did not differ substantially from that faced by Jews and Irish in previous centuries.

crowds had rushed his palace, changes of leadership had occurred in almost all the Soviet Union's former satellites. At the time, the change was attributed variously to the economic deficiencies of state socialism and the cumulative toil of the democratic 'dissidents'.

Neither analysis was completely right. The Soviet empire was, in a sense, the victim of its own economic success. Until the 1970s communism looked like 'the future which works'. Russia had escaped the slump of the early 1930s and, despite the vulnerability of a command economy to policy-makers' mistakes, had found the means to score daunting technical successes after the war, symbolised by a terrible nuclear arsenal and the spectacle of the sputniks. In 1960, a Cuban cartoonist drew a Russian spaceship scattering stardust while an earthbound priest told a stupefied catechumen, 'The Russians can't get to heaven.' Throughout eastern Europe – as in the right-wing dictatorships which survived from the pre-war period at the other end of the continent, in the Iberian peninsula – prosperity created bourgeoisies which the regimes tried unsuccessfully to buy off. Russian surpluses, especially in energy, subsidised most of the satellites without impoverishing the home economy. The era of economic success seems, in retrospect, to have ended with the world economic crisis of 1973, when rising oil prices convulsed the energy market and contributed to unprecedented inflation.

Against the form-book, capitalism now began to 'work' better. The western world began a collective revulsion against the economics of intervention, which had prevailed since the slump. This was a phase of the predictable cycles of the history of economic policy. When the enemy is recession, the experts reach for the economic pump; when it is inflation, classical economics are revived. As a gap in economic performance opened, satellites slipped out of economic dependence on Moscow and into heavy indebtedness to western bankers. The American administration of Ronald Reagan boldly accelerated the arms race in an attempt to outstrip Russian paying-power. Meanwhile, even the cheap end of Russia's military-industrial complex became an unbearable burden and proved, when Afghanistan appeared unconquerable, to be bad value at the price.

In 1985, the Soviet Union floated off the shoals and into the wake of the west, piloted by a leadership which, through a mixture of

corruption and pragmatism, had ceased to believe the traditional socialist rhetoric. Some of the revolutions of 1989 were manipulated from Moscow, the last leverings of a doomed supremacy. The outgoing East German dictator blamed the Kremlin for his fall; in Prague, the Soviet secret police engineered the outbreak of demonstrations fatal to the communists. The conspirators who took over Romania were recently back from Russia.

Moscow's was a rational but, in the circumstances, an over-ambitious ploy. The back fires lit from the Kremlin became part of a more general conflagration. Dissidents were on hand to take over the revolutions they had not started. Most of the new governments of the early 1990s were clericalist or nationalist in different degrees. The satellite states zoomed out of orbit; communist parties all over Europe – including the Soviet Union – were dissolved or re-christened. The two communist super-states – the Soviet Union and the Yugoslav Federation – collapsed like marble edifices, cracked along the veins.

In some ways, post-Soviet Europe resembled that of the Treaty of Versailles, with images multiplying in a Hall of Mirrors. As in 1919, the super-states were broken up and the frustrated nations restored to independence – including some, like Slovenia and Croatia, Slovakia and Ukraine, that had missed their turn in the share-out of sovereignty that followed the First World War. Eastern Europe seemed to have gone straight from the world of Marx to that of the Marx brothers, with bewildering new states bubbling like Duck Soup.

When Reagan called the Soviet world an 'empire' – which by any reasaonable test it was — he associated his anti-Soviet policy with a long tradition of American anti-imperialism. The desire to dismantle European empires was one of the oldest and most constant objectives of the foreign policy of the United States. Within Europe, a start had been made as a result of American intervention in the First World War. When the Second left European imperial powers prostrated and dependent on American patronage, the retreat of European powers from the rest of the world began in earnest. It started in Asia, where Japanese aggression in the Second World War exposed the weakness of the British, French and Dutch as an earlier version of the same phenomenon had of the Russians. In 1956, the American government signalled time for a general debacle:

when Egypt nationalised the Suez Canal Company, American disapproval of Anglo-French military intervention left the imperial powers to 'choke on their rage'. Between then and the end of 1960 'winds of change' blew European empires out of most of Africa.

Meanwhile, the population boom in colonial and ex-colonial territories reversed the long demographic trend which, in the eighteenth and nineteenth centuries, had made Europe a relatively populous continent. The ecology of imperialism, filling vacant niches in the ecosystems of conquered lands, had covered underpopulated places with the descendants of European migrants. Now the balance of numbers was being redressed and the flow of migrants reversed.

In what might have been a prophetic instance, the direction of prevailing migration had been inverted, even before decolonisation, between Ireland and mainland Britain. The settlement of English and Scotch at the expense of Irish victims in the seventeenth century was exceeded, in numerical terms, by the transfer of Irish labour in the opposite direction in the nineteenth. Like their more recent Pakistani successors, permanently uprooted Irish nourished their 'myths of return', poignant in songs like *Come Back to Erin*. Religion and nostalgia fortified them against assimilation by mainland societies. Thanks to dogged distinctiveness, they became a recognisable type in the human zoo of music-hall humour, docketed as safely stupid. When immigrants from the 'New Commonwealth' arrived to join them, landladies added 'No Coloureds' signs in their windows to those which read 'Irish not Required'. This was the price of identity preserved.

After decolonisation, this sort of contraflow between metropolis and empire would become normal. As birth rates in the former imperial powers dropped below reproduction rates, labour from the colonies was welcomed to take up the slack. It happened quickly, in pace with the dismembering of the empires. The first 500 Jamaicans arrived in Britain in fog on an old troop carrier in 1948, astounded at the sight of smoking chimneys and of white men doing menial work. There were 200,000 Algerians in France in 1958, four times as many 20 years later. In Britain immigration levels reached five figures annually from the West Indies in 1954, India in 1955, Pakistan in 1957. Between 1945 and 1971, when controls were tightened, the numbers of the identifiably 'Asian' minority in

England increased a hundredfold and was more conspicuous for being largely concentrated in a few urban areas. In the retina of white fear, 'English culture' would be 'swamped' and Britain would house 'a coffee-coloured society' by the year 2000. There are now four million Muslims in France, more than two million in Britain and a legislator of the party in government has declared 'a threat to the British way of life'. Inter-racial violence is common in France and Germany. By the end of the 1980s in the Netherlands, in the effort to accommodate nearly 800,000 Indonesians, Surinamese, Moluccans and Antilleans, the multicultural consensus for which the country was renowned was being denounced as a myth.

For migrants seeking a new home, there is a lot of pull in old colonial bonds. When Ronnie Knox-Mawer returned from a magistracy in a South Sea island, and was seconded to a new branch of the British judiciary, he found his former Indian clerk installed ahead of him as his boss. In Salamanca in 1969, refugees from Nguema astonished a little girl who thought they must be 'made of chocolate'. In the 1980s uncensused Guinean and Angolan street-vendors hawked beads to the milk-white tourists of the Algarve – the truck of the early colonial era, travelling in reverse; and the Inner London Education Authority acquired an adviser on Bengali education. There are 40 hours of broadcasts a week in Gujerati in Leicester, scores of Vietnamese restaurants in Paris, dozens of Javanese eating-haunts in Amsterdam. In Moscow, migrants from Chechenia are blamed for the ravages of criminal syndicates.

Imperial retreat and counter-colonisation did not, however, affect only the former imperial powers. European countries that had missed the eras of overseas empire-building were implicated by association or caught up in what might be called the psycho-geographical effects: the feeling that former imperial neighbours had withdrawn to join them in a European redoubt; the relative shrinking of Europe on a world map that came to be re-drawn on new projections, with perspectives centred in other parts of the world; the growing sense of European solidarity and potential identity in a world suddenly full of competitors; and the fear, which grew towards the end of the century, that 'the north' of the world would be swamped by people from 'the south', as the Roman empire was by the barbarians. Reduced to a small corner of a hostile world, Europeans began to huddle together for comfort and defence.

CHAPTER 11

HOW MANY EUROPES NOW?
Convergence and divergence in Europe today

I
N THE SUMMER OF 1789, a few days before a mob stormed the Bastille – in an event commemorated ever since as marking the beginning of the French Revolution – a prodigiously fat inmate was removed to the safety of a lunatic asylum at Charenton. He subsequently insisted that he had persuaded the crowd to assault the gaol by haranguing them on behalf of liberty and humanity from the window of the sumptuous room, which, as a prisoner of aristocratic birth, it was his privilege to occupy. Yet in marked contrast to the enlightened idealism he claimed to profess, he had a record of pernicious behaviour unsurpassed in the annals of eighteenth-century libertinism. He was the Marquis de Sade, who gave his name to perverse and morbid sexual cruelty. His offences included ejaculating over a crucifix, torturing and imprisoning prostitutes, whom he also poisoned with laxatives and supposed aphrodisiacs, and – so he claimed – 'proving that God does not exist' by inserting consecrated hosts in the rectums of his buggery victims.

Although the marquis masqueraded as 'Citizen Sade' and became a leading revolutionary propagandist in his section of Paris, his private correspondence exposes his revolutionary enthusiasm as a sham; but his contradictions were of his time and ours. His characteristics were crude distortions of enlightened and revolutionary ideals: his libertinism was a distortion of liberty, his egotism a warped version of

individualism, his violence and cruelty a caricature of the vicious fervour of Jacobin justice. As if in parody of Rousseau, he thought no instincts could be immoral because all are natural; and as if in parody of Laplace, he thought no passions could be condemned because all are governed by the motions of chemical forces in the body. The unresolved quest of his brief career as a revolutionary spokesman was to combine the extreme individualism to which he was inclined with the social responsibility demanded by the Revolution.

European political tradition since the Enlightenment seems to have shown that liberty, equality and fraternity – with that other enlightened aim, validated by another revolution, the pursuit of happiness – are incompatible goals. Equality is impossible without sacrifices of the fruits of liberty 'from each according to his abilities'; the communitarian solidarity which fraternity implies is unattainable except at the cost of some of the individual's freedom to seek his own ends. The marquis illustrated the dilemma in an extreme form, since, in his own opinion, his happiness depended on the suffering of others, but the problem of forging a cohesive society out of self-consciously free individuals has dominated the political history of Europe since his day. The Revolution bequeathed linked curses to European history: it made almost all subsequent revolutions violent; it encouraged the illusion that equality and fraternity were compatible

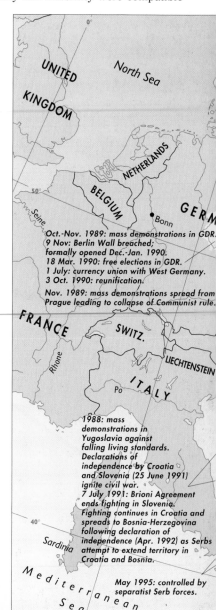

Faut-il brûler de Sade? The Marquis de Sade's two trials for imprisoning, torturing and poisoning prostitutes inspired demonic and prurient lampoons *left*.

Evidence of the memorability of the French Revolution's most famous slogan greeted President de Gaulle *above right* on a visit to Poland under a communist regime whose repressive nature seemed to demonstrate the tension between liberty, equality and fraternity.

The collapse of communism 1989-94 *map right*. It began in Poland, where democrats won an election rigged against them by a communist rearguard: protests swept across eastern Europe and one by one the socialist dominoes tumbled. Hampered in their response by long schooling in the arts of repression and unquestioning obedience, the communist rulers could find no imaginative response to the phenomenon of people's power. In November 1989 the Berlin Wall was breached. By the end of the year all the former Soviet satellites save Albania had eschewed their former ideology. In August 1991 a botched coup by hardliners in Moscow against the reforms of Soviet president Gorbachev led to the dissolution of the communist party in the country which had seen its first spectacular success 74 years before: the Soviet Union broke up into its constituent republics, today independent states. In most countries the communists, excluded from government and the difficult choices of reform, retired to the luxury of sniping from the side-lines. By 1994 their perseverance had paid its dividends and, in a variety of forms – social democrats, nationalists or unreconstructed communists – they were in governing coalitions across a wide range of eastern Europe and the former Soviet Union.

Map labels:
UNITED KINGDOM
North Sea
NETHERLANDS
BELGIUM
Bonn
GERM
Seine
FRANCE
SWITZ.
Rhone
LIECHTENSTEIN
ITALY
Po
Sardinia
Mediterranean Sea
Sicily

Oct.-Nov. 1989: mass demonstrations in GDR.
9 Nov: Berlin Wall breached; formally opened Dec.-Jan. 1990.
18 Mar. 1990: free elections in GDR.
1 July: currency union with West Germany.
3 Oct. 1990: reunification.

Nov. 1989: mass demonstrations spread from Prague leading to collapse of Communist rule.

1988: mass demonstrations in Yugoslavia against falling living standards. Declarations of independence by Croatia and Slovenia (25 June 1991) ignite civil war. 7 July 1991: Brioni Agreement ends fighting in Slovenia. Fighting continues in Croatia and spreads to Bosnia-Herzegovina following declaration of independence (Apr. 1992) as Serbs attempt to extend territory in Croatia and Bosnia.

May 1995: controlled by separatist Serb forces.

with liberty; and it sanctified crimes committed in liberty's name.

Heroic solutions have been sought in vain to the problems of reconciling the contradictory elements in the Revolution's legacy. For a long time, socialism looked the most promising of such solutions, but it had serious defects: for the taste of most democratic electorates, it stressed equality and fraternity too much at the expense of liberty; and where it was tried, it seemed generally to be economically inefficient – distorting markets and seizing up economies for want of the lubricant of profit. In practice, socialism fathered over-powerful states and top-heavy bureaucracies, as oppressive in their way as any institutions of power yet developed within capitalism. Socialism would be compatible – even conterminous – with individualism if it were enough to say that 'man is by nature a political and social animal': the claims of some social theorists who maintain that self-fulfilment can be found only in social relationships would then be validated. Really, however, our gregarious instincts do not extend very far: to a spouse, a family, a tribe or its modern equivalents – neighbourhood, if we are not too snobbish, street or village; but wider loyalties, to communities too big for us to get to know personally, can only be built up beyond the range of instinct. Sometimes, as in loyalties to nation and 'race', the results of well-propagated zeal can be appalling.

A widely-espoused alternative solution, some way short of socialism, has been to combine liberal law-and-order policies with a welfare state and a mixed economy, regulated and 'planned'. For a while in the mid-twentieth century, this looked like becoming the common model for European states, at least between the Iron Curtain and the Pyrenees. Its failure, however, was soon apparent. It created 'Scandisclerosis' and the 'suicidal utopia' of Sweden in the 1960s and 1970s, which seemed to show that social engineering, however benevolent, could not deliver personal happiness. Its endurance depended on waning faith in the

The collapse of communism, 1989-95

- Soviet Union to 1991
- Yugoslavia to 1991
- Czechoslovakia to 1993
- frontiers, 1993
- disputed area subject to military action, May 1995
- united with the Federal Rep. of Germany, 1990
- independent, 1991
- independent, 1992
- independent, 1993
- other formerly communist states 1994
- de facto independent states in 1994 on former USSR territory, internationally unrecognised

SWEDEN

Tallinn

ESTONIA
Nov. 1988: Estonian Supreme Soviet adopts right to veto all Union laws.
Mar. 1990 Congress of Estonia formed and independence declared.
Sept. 1991: independence recognised by USSR.

DENMARK

Baltic Sea

Riga

LATVIA
1989: mass anti-Communist demonstrations.
Jan. 1990: free elections.
Sept. 1991: independence recognised by USSR.

RUSSIAN FEDERATION

LITHUANIA
1989: mass anti-Communist demonstrations.
Mar. 1990: independence declared.
Sept. 1991: independence recognised by USSR.

Moscow

RUSSIAN FED.

Vilnius

Elbe
Berlin

1945-90: under four-power military control.

POLAND
Warsaw

Minsk

BELARUS
June 1989: Popular Front founded.
Aug. 1991: independence declared.
Dec. 1991: founder member of CIS.

June 1991: Boris Yeltsin directly elected President of Russian Federation.
14 Dec. 1991: Commonwealth of Independent States (CIS) established.
25 Dec. 1991: USSR dissolved.
Oct. 1993: crisis between Yeltsin and parliament; fighting in Moscow.
Dec. 1993: first free parliamentary elections.

ANY

Prague

June 1989: partially free elections.
Sept. 1989: Solidarity-led government takes office.
Jan. 1990: Communist party dissolves itself.
Oct. 1991: free elections under new constitution.

CZECH REPUBLIC

June 1992: Slovak nationalists win elections in Slovakia.
1 Jan. 1993: Slovak independence.

SLOVAKIA
Bratislava

AUSTRIA

R. Dniester

Kiev

U K R A I N E

Don

1 Dec. 1991: referendum vote for independence.
Dec. 1991: founder member of CIS.

KAZAKHSTAN

Dec. 1991: Joins CIS.

Budapest

HUNGARY

SLOVENIA
Zagreb

Oct. 1989: Communist rule ends peacefully,
Apr./May 1990: free elections.

MOLDAVIA

TRANSNISTRIAN REPUBLIC

Volga

June 1989: Popular Front (founded May 1989) wins 75% of votes in election.
27 Aug. 1991: independence declared.

C R O A T I A

ROMANIA

BOSNIA HERZEGOVINA
Sarajevo

Belgrade

Bucharest

Dec. 1989: mass demonstrations lead to armed uprisings and overthrow of Ceaușescu regime.
May 1990: free elections.
Nov. 1991: new constitution approved.

May 1995: part of Chechenia secured by Russian forces.

Caspian Sea

CHECHENIA
Grozny

YUGOSLAVIA

BULGARIA
Sofia

Black Sea

ABKHAZIA

GEORGIA

ALBANIA
Tirana

Skopje
MACEDONIA

Nov. 1989: Dictator Zhivkov removed from office.
June 1990: free elections.

AZERBAIJAN
NAGORNO-KARABAKH

ARMENIA

Dec. 1991: Joins CIS.

May 1995: Area controlled by Armenian forces.

8 Apr. 1993: admitted to UN.
Dec. 1993: independence recognised by European Union.

Mar. 1991: free elections follow restoration of contact with West in 1989.

T U R K E Y

viability of economic 'public sectors'. Apart from a flurry of nationalisation – brief and soon reversed – by the French government elected in 1981, the Swedish 'Meidner Plan' of the 1970s, an abortive scheme to transfer shares from private hands to a 'wage-earners' fund', was the last European initiative in the extension of public ownership of industry. Socialist parties in other European democracies in the 1980s seemed to race to shed nationalisation and to make peace with 'market forces'. In Spain and Greece they achieved enduring rapports with bourgeois electors.

In varying ways all over twentieth-century Europe, social policy has constituted a tradition of experiment in attempting to balance the growth in demand for freedom with the need for regulation of increasingly complex and unwieldy societies. Even where there was no ideological incentive to adopt it, planning – which meant, in effect, a huge surrender of individual liberty to public power and an extension of state interference into the nooks and crannies of private life – seemed an irresistible panacea in Europe's era of 'emergency repairs' after the end of the Second World War. The assumption was universal that governments, with the help of international agencies established by the victorious allies, would be responsible for getting devastated economies back to work. The example of the United States, where federal initiatives were credited with having dispelled the slump of the early 1930s, was encouraging. The influence of the economic thought of J.M. Keynes, who had been arguing for years for 'the end of laissez-faire', was important; with some governments, decisive. The war had accustomed the citizens of belligerent countries to taking orders from their governments. Production was commanded, consumption rationed. Peace eased but did not end these conditions: rationing was actually stricter in some countries after the war than during it.

Planning failed, not only because human beings are instinctively liberty-loving but also because its assumptions were naive. Societies and economies are chaotic systems, in which vast effects issue from undetectably small causes and the planners' models are streaked and split under bombardment by unpredictable particles. Four- and five-year plans were produced almost everywhere at some time up to the 1970s and almost everywhere discarded. The perfectly planned urban projects of the 1960s, which represented the fulfilment of the ideals of rationalist architects – creating aesthetically functional, socially egalitarian, technically proficient environments – proved practically uninhabitable and began to be pulled down after a generation or so. At about the same time, in the 1980s, the mixed economies and command economies favoured in the post-War era were dismantled, de-regulated and restored to private enterprise. In 1989, the illusion of state 'management' was exposed by the bewilderment of the arch-controllers, the communist parties of eastern Europe, as the countries they ruled slipped out of their control. Their successor-regimes joined the privatisers. By 1995 private enterprise was responsible for more than 50 per cent of output even in the former communist states, with only two exceptions.

As well as planning, the Second World War also encouraged fraternity – the collective spirit of the battlefield and the air-raid shelter, the 'Strength through Joy' holiday installations and the 'Land Army'. 'Home fronts' exposed to bombing raids or to the intrusion of foreign forces of occupation were socially levelling environments; traditional distance between the ranks of society was crushed out of social landscapes by the camaraderie of battles in which everybody had a part. Regimentation and collectivism lingered in some of the tastes formed in the war years – for holiday camps, for instance, community singing and old combatants' reunions. The perpetuation of societies of solidarity, however, was never likely. Wartime fraternity was an emergency response, bound to vanish with the emergency or to disappear into the 'generation gap' which opened up in belligerent countries in the 1950s and 1960s. As young people grew up without shared memories of war-time, they picked up the threads of some longer strands – libertarian, existentialist, anarchist, or, for the less reflective, simply selfish – which the war had tucked out of sight. Existentialism was particularly powerful in generating cults of self-indulgence, for it offered the 'void with full powers' praised by Camus in the visitor's book of a notorious exhibit-less exhibition staged by Yves Klein in Paris in 1958.

Youth could afford to defy parents and buy self-indulgence because

The sleek hair, opulent brows and lips and sensual, fleshy nose and ears belong to the prophet of the 'end of laissez-faire', John Maynard Keynes, who made a fortune from stock-market speculations, photographed here by Gordon Anthony in the late 1930s *above left*.

Exposure to the notoriously bracing sea-air of Butlin's holiday camp at Skegness in 1957 *left*. Knobbly knees contests became the representative self-caricature of a tradition of working-class holiday fun which seemed to derive from the kind of entertainment extemporised in air-raid shelters: cheap frivolity, cheerful indignity, collective self-amusement.

Stirrings of market forces: free enterprise is made to look seedy and furtive in Moscow's black market during the declining years of communism *above*.

State interference in the crannies of private life: the British government not only imposed wartime rationing but also presumed to advise housewives to practise additional austerity when shopping, representing the Squander Bug as a Nazi agent *above right*. Propaganda from the Scottish Office invited the victory-minded to abandon their holidays to the common good by helping food production *right*.

of the speed and spread of post-war economic recovery, especially thanks to copious infusions of American aid and to the obsession of governments with full employment as the key to social and political stability. The prosperous youth of western Europe spent its money in ways calculated to offend its elders and express its independence – on fashions, for instance, that were first extrovert, then psychedelic. The growth of the generation gap was measurable in the 1960s when pop groups discarded their uniforms and grew their hair, and when the effects of sexual permissiveness began to be reflected in health statistics, with 'epidemics' of sexually transmitted disease and cervical cancer.

Remarkably, the gap opened almost as wide in communist eastern Europe – or, at least, in parts of it – as in the capitalist west, despite the facts that the east refused American aid, paid its youth cautiously low wages, created oppressive educational monopolies and invested heavily in security forces. The failed revolutions which marked the coming-of-age of post-war youth in 1968 came nearest to success in Paris and Prague. Student-revolutionaries on one side of the Iron Curtain denounced 'the crisis of capitalism' while those on the other called for a post-communist 'spring' or 'thaw': this made them look like mutually opposed movements, but both were inspired by revulsion against an older generation and both shared the libertarian yearnings expressed in 'protest' music and 'counter-culture' music and cinema.

The trends of the next generation, when voters swung right, hair got shorter, fashion re-buttoned and 'moral majorities' found voice, were widely perceived as a reaction against 'sixties permissiveness'. In reality, they represented the continuation in maturity of the projects of the young people of the earlier decade. The demands for personal

freedom, sexual liberation and existential self-fulfilment when one is young transform themselves naturally, when one acquires economic responsibility and family obligations, into policies of economic laissez-faire and 'less government'. To 'roll back the frontiers of the state' became the common project of those who rose to power in Europe in the 1980s 'from the Atlantic to the Urals'.

Thus despite all the evidence of trends towards collectivism earlier in the century, Europe's common culture has wrenched itself back to its individualist and libertarian traditions. To a startling degree, for most Europeans in the last two centuries liberty has regularly proved more attractive than equality and fraternity. Equality has been diluted as 'equality of opportunity' or 'equality before the law'; despite the rise of democracy, it has never meant equality of power for all citizens. For fraternity, nationalism was the nineteenth century's usual substitute; state welfare, increasingly, took its place in the twentieth. Now even welfare is fashionably rejected or questioned as an outmoded programme: an expensive way of anchoring allegiance to society and of alienating private responsibilities to the state. From one point of view, the history of the twentieth century could be summarised thus: two great political movements have put society or the state ahead of the individual in their scale of values; both have been defeated — fascism in 1945, communism in 1989 – and, though both have more potential for revival than is commonly credited, capitalism is riding the continent bareback, free of stirrups and bridle, as the end of the century approaches. In Britain, parvenu entrepreneurs exploit de-regulation to loot former public utilities for monstrous emoluments, like incarnations of Francis Bacon's prophetic screaming businessmen.

The Soviet Union brooked no deviation from its brand of Marxism-Leninism among the satellite powers of the Warsaw Pact. When, in 1968, the Czech leadership sought to introduce a reformed socialism, the comparative freedom of the 'Prague Spring' which followed soon ran up against Moscow's intolerance. On the night of 20-21 August 1968, 27 divisions of Warsaw Pact troops crossed into Czechoslovakia to suppress the faint stirrings of free expression. Here protestors bearing the Czech flag march on Prague's City Hall in a vain lament for the Spring which the city would not see again for 22 years *left*.

The students' crusade: much of Europe experienced serious unrest among its student populations in 1968-70, most seriously in France in 1968. Here *right* students face Paris riot police in a movement which had taken on the hallmarks of an insurrection against the established authorities. The Paris *événements* saw a coincidence of student unrest and industrial strife which at one point seemed likely to bring down the Gaullist government.

In the 1960s, Europe finally broke free from the grey-hand of post-war austerity in an explosion of youth-centred culture and concerns. The resulting upsurge of unconventional protest, passion, music and fashion shocked as many as it delighted and later gave rise to a nostalgia for the 'swinging sixties' at odds with the desire to break with the past which inspired teenagers of the time *below*.

Since it is precisely in major utilities, like communications, power and water, that most small investors have their holdings, the abuses of a handful of controllers at shareholders' expense make a mockery of the 'people's capitalism' which politicians of the right had hoped to create through privatisation programmes. In post-communist Russia, part of the coercive power of the party has descended to mafias. Lovers of liberty, in this context, should be less pleased at its achievements than apprehensive of its survival. In much of former communist Europe, copy-book conditions exist for a fascist revanche, where communism is remembered with detestation and capitalism experienced with disappointment. Even socialism is a corpse suitable for resurrection, perhaps in an altered state.

One of the drawbacks of freedom is that free choices are regularly made for the worst, ever since the setting of an unfortunate precedent in Eden. To expect people to improve under its influence is to demand unrealistic standards from freedom and, ultimately, to undermine its appeal. Something similar could be said of the other victims of late twentieth-century disillusionment: prosperity, democracy and education. Freedom, however, is uniquely intractable to political moulding, because in the recent past it has come to be influenced far more by technological progress than by political decisions.

The object of technology, in a sense, is freedom. By replacing or extending the power of brain and muscle it liberates people to do what they want instead of what they must. No statute or constitutional amendment has done more in the twentieth century for the freedom of ordinary people in the western world than inventions – to take a couple at random – like the internal combustion engine and the mass-producible

Life in the slow lane: the automobile promised unprecedented freedom of movement for all, but when cars became widespread, the result in urban areas such as London was often not movement but traffic jams *left*, noise and pollution.

contraceptive. Yet neither has been unequivocally beneficent. The motor car rolled into the world, puffing and chuckling like a creepy fictional fat boy, just ahead of the present century. It began as a rich man's toy but gradually became accessible to people at almost every level of society in the more affluent parts of the world. While conferring the unheard-of freedom to go where one liked when one felt like it, the car created aggressive drivers, demanded ugly roads, and polluted the world with its noxious fumes and stertorous noise. Contraceptives, meanwhile, are often credited with liberating women for employment: but the enhanced freedom to choose sexual partners on an unprecedented scale fulfilled a more basic human craving. The effect has been equivocal on the spread and multiplication of morbid conditions, both physical and psychological. And rather than just facilitating 'family planning', the pill probably also contributed to the erosion of monogamy and the unforeseeable consequences, which await western countries in the next century, of families on new patterns, composed, in a majority of cases, of step-relations and 'single parents' instead of the traditional 'nucleus'. When information microtechnology becomes as widespread as cars and pills, the consequences will be just as liberating in their way, and just as morally equivocal.

Technological change seems likely to take over from unaided human wickedness as the focus of fears of barbarism. The first indictments were uttered under the mushroom-cloud, for weapons of mass destruction threaten civilisation more radically than any brutality of manners. Technology too powerful for existing political controls can zap and click familiar forms of brutalisation across breakneck networks. Satellite-borne pornography outflanks the efforts of legislators. As the end of this millennium approaches, artificial intelligence researchers are poised to become the Frankensteins of the next; what Hitler could not achieve by exterminating those he deemed under-races, eugenics engineers threaten by genetic manipulation. The complexities of defining life, the deftness with which it can be prolonged or terminated, have transferred a terrifying power over it into the hands of medical technicians. Embryos, for extermination and experiment, are the 'persecuted minority' of a new form of inhumanity.

In a fashion eerily reminiscent of de Sade's idea of liberty, sexual liberation has been a harbinger of the triumph of individualism in late twentieth-century Europe. As in one of Balthus's sexually provocative paintings, light has broken painfully into the bedrooms of the west. One of de Sade's recent apologists was Simone de Beauvoir, who, condemned by existentialism to be destitute of objective values, saw free love as a good example of responsible moral action. Though philosophical and psychological fashions have eroded sexual inhibitions, sexual jealousy remains as characteristic of human beings as ever. In consequence, increased freedom to choose and change sexual partners destroys some of the collective loyalties on which European societies have traditionally relied for cohesion. Small communities – parish, school, club and mess – can be ripped apart by sexual rivalry. Families periodically rescrambled by sexual betrayal or ennui are now typical of almost every European culture on a scale unprecedented in Europe and unparalleled in most of the rest of the world.

It is hard to imagine the modern revolution in sexual habits without psycho-analysis, existentialism and sophisticated contraceptive technology, but a longer intellectual pedigree is obvious in the terms in which people justify capricious changes of partner. Loyalty to the family or responsibility to a wider community is, they claim, transcended by the right to pursue personal happiness or 'fulfilment' in freedom. Even within the ever smaller and more unstable nuclear families of Europe now, individualism still seems to have a dissecting effect on the household, at least in the richer and more technically advanced parts of the continent, as family-members forego collective activities, eating individual meals out of microwaves and withdrawing each into his own computer-screen or television.

Individual gratification – or, to use a widely-favoured euphemism 'fulfilment' – has largely replaced broader codes of conduct and established an almost tyrannical monopoly over most people's decision-making: whether to marry, whether to divorce, whether to procreate, how to occupy one's time, how to vote. The Marquis de Sade is out of the asylum and back on the streets. Nevertheless, there are unmistakable signs that collectivism will return on the rebound, that individualism will be swamped by an undamming of community values and that the politics of social responsibility will again make libertarianism a marginal creed. State-control in big units will be sanctified by environmentalism, the ideology of a kind of post-socialist leftism, which denounces profit-grabbing and exploitation: no longer in the name of the 'human race' extolled in the party songs and newspaper-names of discredited communism, but in favour of Nature herself.

One of the most formidable arguments in the long run for Europe-wide political unification emphasises the need to tackle problems of environmental pollution, which do not respect traditional borders, on the widest possible basis. Governments must protect the natural world from over-exploitation for short-term gain. In any case, the triumph of laissez-faire economics will be reversed when electorates realise that, in an economic world dominated by huge near-monopolies and international corporations, the rational self-interest of individual producers and consumers can no longer work to balance the system. Keynes was too precipitate with his prediction of the demise of classical economics: but the same prediction can be convincingly re-formulated for a slightly remoter time.

Even if socialism remains defunct for a while, there is a still-vital ideological tradition impelling Europe back to community values. Christianity has ways of making liberty and fraternity work together in a tradition which has maintained since apostolic times that to 'love the brotherhood' is 'to pass from death to life'. Emphasis on the individual worth of every soul makes Christianity a profoundly individualist creed. Sanctification of the integrity of conscience commits Christianity, properly understood, to political liberalism. Emphasis on the personal duty of almsgiving – at least in the Catholic and Orthodox versions of Christianity – limits the scope and need of state welfare. More generally, Christian other-worldliness ought to usher the believers' thoughts away from the triviality of political solutions in 'kingdoms of this world'. Yet the reader of the New Testament has ever before his eyes the model of a church where goods were held in common, and the Old Testament is full of stories of an ancient search for a way of making this world conform to divine prescriptions about 'justice'. The Christian individual is imperfect outside the society of the church or, in traditional Christian language, when severed from 'the body of Christ'. On the eve of the Second World War, T.S. Eliot summarised 'social Christianity' in words which still fairly characterise Christian critiques of the excesses of individualism:

The realisation of a Christian society must lead us inevitably to face such problems as the hypertrophy of the motive of Profit into a social ideal, the distinction between the use of natural resources and their exploitation, the use of labour and its exploitation, the advantages unfairly accruing to the trader in contrast to the primary producer, the misdirection of the financial machine, the iniquity of usury, and other features of a commercialised society which must be scrutinised on Christian principles. ... A great deal of the machinery of modern life is merely a sanction for un-Christian aims.

It is a widespread but false assumption that European society is irretrievably plunged in a secularist sea-change. Most people who think about it still accept the myth that Europe once had an 'age of faith' and assume that, after the Enlightenment and industrialisation had devastated Europe's native Christianity, materialism and consumerism began clearing away its remains. Yet nowhere in Europe does there exist a people who were once spiritual and have become secular. On the contrary, because their human components are inherently worldly, societies tend normally to be secular. On the bedrock of worldliness spirituality beats, generation by generation, like a restless ocean, sometimes crashing with a re-shaping force, at others retreating to distant sandbanks.

Charity collectors for the NSPCC *above*: the attraction of individual giving to a collective cause has remained potent, buttressing a sense of community.

Hope without power: the crucified Christ renounces power in suffering: the candle flame and clasped hands of the pastor signify hope *right*. The banner cackhandedly draped at the east end of the Protestant Church of St Nicholas, Leipzig, calls for democracy and freedom, without force.

Of course, religious revival in twentieth-century Europe has not been exclusively Christian: Islam and Oriental religions have had a small but conspicuous stake, as have some new cults which seem marginal, at best, to all traditional religions. Nor can the revival easily be measured in terms of increased observance in mainstream churches, where numbers of adherents have gone up and down in patches, at different rates over different spells of time in different places. Much of the revival has to be accounted for by the heightened religious consciousness or sense of transcendence claimed in opinion soundings by people who never go to church: sometimes it takes recognisable forms – pantheism, nature mysticism, deism or fideism; sometimes it is unformulated except as 'belief in God' or adherence to the teachings – or some of them – of a particular master or text; often it takes the form of a relationship with the transcendent which is purely personal, perhaps unshared and generally unritualised. This is indeed the religion of individualists and it is impossible to link it with the progress of the 'social gospel'.

On the other hand, it is also clear that mainstream churches, with their particular commitments to social ideals, or implicit endorsements of them, have grown and are growing overall, both in numbers of worshippers and in social and political influence. Like so much of the culture of contemporary Europe, the trend in religion can be traced back to Europe's 'civil wars': confrontation with anti-religious ruling ideologies at the high tide of fascism and communism turned Christianity into an opposition movement in much of the continent. In more recent times, Protestant pastors were among the revolutionaries who unseated communism in Hungary and East Germany; Catholic bishops helped to perform the same role in Poland, Hungary and what was then Czechoslovakia. The endurance of Orthodoxy under communism played a less active but perhaps no less vital part in other east European countries. For a while, after the Second Vatican Council, which met for the first time in 1962, the Church was the most left-wing organisation tolerated in Franco's Spain.

The Council showed that, even in the Catholic tradition, with its strong hieratic and authoritarian tendencies, Christianity could offer a model of a society of liberty and fraternity. It affirmed liberty by proclaiming anew the primacy of conscience and acknowledging, in line with a tradition the Catholic Church seemed almost to have forgotten, that some sort of revelation of God is accessible to individuals who seek him directly, outside the church. At the same time, the council rebuilt solidarity in bold ways, strengthening the sense of a common mission shared between pope and bishops, clergy and laity. The Church was unerring when the 'whole body of the faithful, from the bishops to the last member of the laity shows universal agreement in faith and morals'. The *Missa nunctiva* – the new text of the mass which emerged from the council – dismantled some hieratic formulae. The altar was shifted away from the east wall of churches so that the priest faced the congregation. The worshipper made his confession to 'brothers and sisters' as well as to the priest. The kiss of peace emphasised the status of the community. The priest invited the congregation to pray for the acceptance of 'this sacrifice, mine and yours.' The emphasis the Council placed on congregations as communities and on the participation of laypeople in the life of the church was echoed in other communions. The eucharist – the rite which defines the congregation as a community 'sharing in one bread' – grew in popularity in many Protestant congregations; in orthodox celebrations, liturgical reforms were introduced which – albeit more weakly – reflected those of the Council. The Anglican church created new structures of power-sharing between clergy and laity and many Anglican congregations discarded their own prayer-books in favour of the Roman rite.

Politically, the most powerful consequence of these changes has been to create a constituency for what is loosely called 'Christian socialism'. The sentiments a young Fiat worker expressed in the early 1980s – 'the farther you are to the left, the more you are Christian' – have become unshocking, even commonplace. The soi-disant Christian Socialist movement began in the mid-nineteenth century among English reformers of working-class sanitary conditions and Sisters of Charity exercising a practical mission among the poor of Paris.

The development of the European Union from 1957

The European Economic Community (EEC), from 1994 the European Union (EU)

- EEC members 1957
- joined January 1973
- joined January 1981
- joined January 1986
- admitted October 1990
- joined January 1995
- applied by May 1995 for EU membership

The European Free Trade Association (EFTA)

— EFTA members late 1972

UKRAINE

MOLDOVA

RUSSIAN FEDERATION

GEORGIA

Black Sea

ARMENIA

BULGARIA

TURKEY

SYRIA

IRAQ

Crete   CYPRUS

JORDAN

Jean Monnet *above left*, one of the architects of European integration, signs its first blueprint, the Schuman Plan, in 1951.

Neutral colours, traditional typography, faintly blushing rose: British socialism doffs some of its wolf's clothing for the Labour Party Conference of 1989 *above*.

The development of the European Union, *map left*. 'The Six' who were the founder members of the European Economic Community in 1957 had become 'The Fifteen' by 1995, while the organisation itself had transmuted into the European Union. Within the Union, arguments about its future abounded: whether to concentrate on enlargement or on deepening the ties of integration for those already members. Outside it, the countries of eastern Europe clamoured for membership, while Norway, uniquely, rejected membership a second time in a referendum in November 1994.

Pope John XXIII *below*, who convoked the Second Vatican Council in 1962, inaugurating reforms which brought vital modernity to the Catholic church.

Monsignor Affré, Archbishop of Paris, responded to the 1848 revolution – in which he was martyred in crossfire at the barricades – by changing the prayer 'God save the King' to 'God save the people'. Despite these inauspicious beginnings, Christian socialism has somehow survived more than a century of ridicule and contempt to fill the gap left by the collapse of communism and the discomfiture of secular socialism. In revulsion from the sometimes rampant individualism of the 1980s, churches can urge collective goals. John XXIII, who summoned the Second Vatican Council, adumbrated in his encyclical *Mater et Magistra* of 1961 a vision of the state enhancing freedom by assuming social responsibilities and 'enabling the individual to exercise personal rights.' He was prepared to license state intervention in health care, education, housing, work and the provision of activities in leisure, drawing on a tradition of Catholic social theory which has been immensely powerful: some of the buzz-words of current political discourse in Europe – including 'subsidiarity' and 'common good' – are drawn from it. Catholic social theory has been reinforced by the Protestant 'social gospel' which draws directly on biblical evidence of the apostolic life to inspire social prescriptions. That scourge of international capital, the Transnational Information Exchange, grew up in the 1970s partly out of the 'Participation in Development' programme of the World Council of Churches. The secular socialist parties which are fading from power in the closing years of the century are in danger of conversion to or replacement by Christian Socialism.

The most striking example is in Britain, where the Labour Party, according to its most electorally successful leader, always 'owed more to Methodism than to Marx'. When the self-avowed Christian Socialist Tony Blair took over the leadership of the party in the 1990s he wrote the remnants of secular socialism out of the constitution. In Spain in the 1980s, a socialist government climbed down from a century of anti-clericalism to subsidise church schools. For socialist parties, use of the Christian Socialist label is limited or precluded by the need to appeal to multi-cultural constituencies and to include the secular socialist rump; but members of Christian Socialist movements, societies and tendencies occupy rising positions in all western Europe's major parties of the left, except perhaps the waning Italian PSI. 'Christian socialism' may be a little less disastrous than secular socialism because of its debt to a tradition which hallows the individual

199

person; but there is no likelihood that in government it will be less expensive, less inefficient or less susceptible to bureaucratic hypertrophy.

As community values resume their place in European society, the question arises of how the political map of Europe will continue to change: whether European peoples will have a common political future and, if so, whether it will take the form of common institutions. The future shape and strength of political frontiers depends on how people's allegiance gets re-distributed around the different potential foci of identity available to them: whether to a pan-European ideal, such as engaged the sympathies of the eighteenth-century elite; or to a Europe-wide super-state; or to the traditional *patries*, the nation-states or so-called nation-states; or to historic communities which have not necessarily been embodied in states in the recent past; or to regions in which various such communities might be grouped by free association across traditional borders; or to local particularisms smaller in scale than any of these. Or, to put what is really a complex and interlocking array of possibilities in terms of a stark dilemma, whether the future of Europe will be integration or fragmentation: 'Balkanisation' or 'Helveticisation'.

The chance to build loyalties across traditional frontiers arose from the ruins of Europe's civil wars. The devastation of 1945 constituted a vast admonition against conflict and a summons to collaboration. The collapse of the world empires of European states threw them back on each other. It took this crisis to give Europe's sagging identity some institutional vertebrae. European institutions were unnecessary while Europe's elites were swathed in the comfort of a collective sense of superiority and protected from the competition of other continents by colonial supremacy and an industrial lead. The first creative steps in erecting supra-national structures are usually credited to Jean Monnet, a former cognac-salesman who had worked wonders in co-ordinating Anglo-French supply policy during the world war. He proposed a 'High Authority' for coal and steel to overtrump Franco-German rivalry. Thus at the start of the process of European integration, European identity was squeezed out like Polyfilla to smudge over the cracks between enemies. The European Coal and Steel Community was formed, with six countries participating, on 18th April 1951.

From the start, it showed all the promise and all the limitations which have continued to characterise it. Member states would not surrender 'an iota of sovereignty'. The High Authority gave way to a Council of Ministers which was in practice an international rather than a supra-national body. A common approach to defence proved unattainable. The Messina Declaration of June 1955 proclaimed 'work for … a united Europe, by the development of common institutions, the progressive fusion of national economies, the creation of a common market and the progressive harmonisation of social policies' but the Treaty of Rome, which launched the drive – sometimes more of a drag – towards the common market in 1957 postponed almost everything to a remote future. The major achievement of the early years was the formulation of a common agricultural policy in 1964 – in reality a conservative measure, devised to protect uneconomically small farmers, which tended to impede further progress.

"It's disgraceful, Mme. Thatcher! Who do you think you are – you're behaving like a Frenchman!"

'Madame Non': Cummings's cartoon *above* captures Margaret Thatcher's role as the legatee of de Gaulle's vision of a Europe des patries. The flying croissant, baguette and Turkish coffee-pot are teasing details of the subtly xenophobic iconography of which the *Daily Express* caricaturist was a master.

Ain Temouchent, 10th December 1960: de Gaulle turns failure in Algeria into a propaganda coup *left*. Lyrics by the English satirical duo, Michael Flanders and Donald Swan, summed up the situation. 'Sing a Marseillaise. Algérie n'est pas française!'

Yugoslavia unravels: in summer 1991, bitter fighting tore the newly independent Republic of Croatia apart, as Serb separatists fought for autonomy or their own independence to unite with their ethnic brothers in Serbia proper and Bosnia. Serb militias, aided by elements of the former Yugoslav army, swept through the western Slavonian plain and the craggy country around Knin, threatening the capital Zagreb with capture. Here an injured Croatian soldier is carried away from a tank during the siege of Slavonski Brod in Slavonia *right*.

Efforts in the 1960s to press towards a 'United States of Europe' were frustrated by the strong chauvinistic susceptibilities of the French leader General de Gaulle, then slowed in the 1970s and 80s by the enlargement of the European Economic Community to include twelve member states by 1985. De Gaulle was a Samson in Dagon's temple, struggling to push apart the 'twin pillars of the Atlantic alliance' and expel the Philistine. In a sense, he was himself a product of the Atlantic system he detested. In the darkest hour of the Second World War, when his country was overrun with shattering ease, he was transformed by British patronage from a general of small importance to the unchallengeable leader of 'Free France'. American power restored him to his homeland as a liberator. Free French units led the allies into reconquered Paris in 1944. American support, however, fell short of keeping a Chauvin in the Elysée Palace. When de Gaulle was summoned by acclaim to almost dictatorial powers in France in 1958, it was as a phoenix, rekindled from rejection – like his old comrade and rival, Churchill, in 1940 – by a crisis so terrible that it had daunted or discredited every other contender: Algeria, the colony in which France had invested most effort and emotion, was about to fall to independence-fighters. In the meantime, the United States had incurred de Gaulle's hatred by expropriating the French empire in Indo-China, undermining it at Suez and eroding its credibility and diplomatic support. The purity of the French language was being polluted by Americanisms, the influence of French culture drowned by the loud voice of 'le monde anglo-saxon'.

He feared that national sovereignty would be undermined and the divisions between eastern and western Europe would be perpetuated if the currently fashionable European ideal was fulfilled: a closely integrated western Europe as a 'pillar of the Atlantic alliance' was advocated in Washington and endorsed by America's clients and courtiers in Europe. De Gaulle proposed a vague – and perhaps purely tactical – alternative: a *Europe des patries* 'from the Atlantic to the Urals'. While the Soviet empire remained strong, this looked like a pipe-dream drawn by Magritte.

In the 1980s de Gaulle's role in pouring cold water on Euro-fever was taken up by the redoubtable British Prime Minister Margaret Thatcher, whose soubriquet of 'Madame Non' was an echo of de Gaulle's diplomatic language. Her stress on the spread of parliamentary democracy and economic liberalism as preconditions of progress in European integration came to seem prophetic as Europe became increasingly 'homogeneised' and European institutions 'converged' – not as a result of the efforts of the European Economic Community but because of two waves of political and economic re-alignment: first, in southern Europe from 1974 to 1978, when Greece, Portugal and Spain all abandoned authoritarian systems of government; and once more in 1989-92, when most of eastern Europe followed suit.

Europe today is being ground between two vast, slow and apparently contradictory changes: an integrative process, which tends to extend the limits of Europe and the reach of European institutions; and a fissiparous process, which threatens empires and federations with break-up and other states with erosion by devolution. Under the shell of integration and homogeneisation, the old historic communities – out of which the familiar Europe of nation-states and modern empires was formed – are being re-fertilised. Some have attained devolution or autonomy; others are calling or fighting for it. The re-fashionings of the Soviet Union and the Yugoslav federation are only the most conspicuous and violent examples of a Europe-wide phenomenon of self-discovery by resurgent peoples. Seen from a distance – or even from the height of some seats of European government – the nation-state is still the cultural unit of which Europe is composed. Yet even after generations of attempts to 'purify' some states by deporting or exterminating minorities in their millions, most so-called 'national' frontiers enclose a variety of highly self-aware historic communities. In some ways, Europe's complexion resembles South Africa's in the last years of apartheid: a well-stirred tribal mixture, imperfectly divisible into maddeningly complex Bantustans. Future constitutional problems for European states could be as daunting as those of South Africa. Most states within the European Union have too many devolutionary problems inside their own borders to contemplate their neighbours

with equanimity. Spain could not welcome an independent Scotland into the Union for fear of Basque and Catalan separatism. France could not safely give the Corsicans more autonomy than Italy allows the Tyrolese. In eastern Europe, ethnicities are so dangerously mixed that concessions can provoke civil wars.

The re-drawing of frontiers from above in 1918 and 1945 was no precedent for today's shake-up from the roots, which shows that historic identities incubate under centralising despotisms and thrive even during federative processes like that which is transforming the European Union today. When the states of the former European Community committed themselves to union at Maastricht in January, 1992, the world assumed that eastern and western Europe were destined for divergent futures: fission in the east, fusion in the west. In fact, a devolutionary virus is destroying the immune systems of political units all over the continent, from the Faroes to the Caucasus.

Alternative models of the way long-suppressed identities emerge in favourable political conditions are suggested by the examples of Spain and Yugoslavia. Both have had strong, centrally placed and hegemonic peoples – the Castilians in Spain, the Serbs in Yugoslavia – whom their neighbours credit with imperial ambitions. Both areas had long histories of Muslim rule which in the Yugoslav case left Muslim enclaves in Bosnia and Kossovo. Between them, Spain and Yugoslavia illustrate the means by which most European states have come into being: violent engorgement, dynastic manipulation and international fiat. They adopted distinct policies to preserve unity: centralisation in Spain, which after two and a half centuries of experiment left peripheral identities strengthened; federalism in Yugoslavia, which meant that the aspirations of historic communities were neither suppressed nor satisfied. In both states, the old structures were incapable of withstanding the impact of democracy.

In 1975-8 in Spain, the urgency of recognising the rights of communities with glaringly idiosyncratic cultures and autonomous

Another Flanders and Swan lyric apostrophised the Irish: 'They blow up policemen – or so I have heard – and blame it on Cromwell and William III.' The image of 'King Billy', whose victories over James II in the seventeenth century marked the definitive establishment of the Protestant Ascendancy in Ireland, continued, from elaborate graffiti, to direct Loyalist resistance during the troubles of 1969-95 *above*.

The fortunes of war: a market in Tuzla in central Bosnia, an area which formed part of the heart of the territory the Muslim government's army managed to cling onto after war erupted in 1992. The glamour of pre-war advertising contrasts with the squalid reality of making ends meet in a war-zone which gave the world the term 'ethnic cleansing' *left*.

A Chechen fighter at prayer in the ruins of Grozny, shortly before the capital fell to Russian invaders in 1995. During nearly 300 years of intermittent resistance, and especially in the Murid war, the cause of Chechen independence from Russia has become sanctified by the traditions of *jihad, right*.

traditions – the Catalans, Basques and Galicians – led to a formula referred to as 'coffeee all round'. This meant that devolutionary concessions to the Catalans, Basques and Galicians were matched by similar concessions to every other area in the country, regardless of their sense of regional identity. Seventeen 'autonomous regions' were proclaimed. The process has had two extraordinary effects: first, traditions and even languages have been invented or exhumed for peoples of formerly vestigial identity, such as the Asturians and Canarians. Secondly, the chances of creating regional super-states have been frustrated: Valencia and the Balearic Islands could not be subsumed in a 'Great Catalonia' or Navarre in the Basque country, any more than the diversity of Spain could be permanently contained in a centralised structure. The region remains an 'unamalgamated bundle' of acutely self-conscious peoples and 'most of its problems in the last 500 years,' it has fairly been said, 'derive from the pretence that Spain is one country.'

In Yugoslavia, where the coming of democracy was late, sudden and ill prepared, the situation was exacerbated by the deep historic enmity of some communities for others and by the willingness of the federal army to fight for unity. Communities naturally well adapted to collaboration with each other, such as the Slovenes and Croats, were the most willing to exchange mutual recognition of independence, whereas Serbs were disposed to fight, not merely to protect enclaves of compatriots in other republics, but also to enforce unity across barriers of reciprocal hatred with the Croats and Kossovans. Communities such as Macedonia and Bosnia-Herzegovina, initially willing to find solutions within a federal framework, lost patience with the more militant ethnicities and turned to cultivation of their own identities and institutions. Meanwhile, groups which rejected a Yugoslav label reached for Europeanism as a source of fellow-feeling. Beethhoven's *Ode to Joy*, the European Union's anthem, was played at the proclamation of Slovenian independence. The prominence of mediation by the European Union in the Yugoslav-Croatian war and the Bosnian civil war demonstrated their perceived status as European conflicts. This has not prevented Bosnia-Herzegovina from being effectively partitioned between Croats, Serbs and Muslims. In the dark days of the Second World War, the intellectuals of Travnik used to meet in Lufti's Bar to console themselves that 'everything now will once again be as it used to be and by God's will always was.' Not this time round. After the ethnic cleansers, 'Lufti's Bar will not be opening again.'

Most other European states could be fed through the shredder almost as easily. The United Kingdom – a self-styled model of political stability – lasted little more than 100 years before the detachment of most of Ireland. Nearly 300 years after the loss of its status as a kingdom, Scotland keeps its peculiar, privileged profile with its own legal system and disproportionate representation in the common legislature. Even Wales, which was 'shired' to make it administratively uniform with its neighbour as long ago as 1536, is treated as a discrete case with a government department of its own. Northern Ireland is about to have its parliament restored; meanwhile, though it clings to the kingdom with an intensity unreciprocated on the mainland, it is the most ill-matched piece in the United Kingdom's jigsaw. Huge cultural differences distinguish these regions from England. Scots can take more pride in a Scottish victory at Wembley than in a British victory at Waterloo. The calls for independence or devolution characteristic of these historic 'nations' are beginning to be echoed in regions of England which are re-asserting or inventing identities of their own. Talk of a 'north-south' divide corresponds not only to present economic realities but also to cultural divergences which seep into such commonplaces as the fat-content of traditional foods (higher in the north than the south) and the rules of rugby football. 'Wessex nationalists' and 'Mercian nationalists', now treated as jokes, could come into their own if the United Kingdom catches Europe's devolutionary virus.

Europe's largest state is also the most vulnerable. The Russian Federation has had to fight a war in 1995 to keep the Chechens in. The

The fruits of conflict: in the buffer zone between Greek and Turkish Cyprus, the United Nations monitoring force provides protection for old women who pick the grapefruit *left*. Cyprus provided another example of 'ethnic cleansing', as populations were moved across a hypothetical dividing line to create two ethnically homogeneous statelets, following the Turkish army's invasion of the island in 1973.

The politics of subsidiarity: Umberto Bossi, leader of one of Europe's most powerful regionalist parties, the Italian Lega Nord, is caricatured in chain mail *right* in allusion to the party's shadowy medieval ancestor, the Lombard League, which defended the sovereignty of city-states against the Emperor Frederick Barbarossa in the late twelfth and thirteenth centuries.

The French National Front on the march at its annual demonstration in Paris in 1988 *below*. Drawing its strength from economic deprivation and resentment at the size of the Muslim immigrant communities in France, the xenophobia of Jean-Marie Le Pen's political party grew in the 1990s, infecting the main stream of French political life and penetrating middle-class salons during the presidential election campaign of 1995, when the party achieved over 15% of the vote.

Chechens represent the most tenacious case of nationalism among the ethnic minorities of the federation: their struggle against Russian control was almost continuous from the 1780s until the Second World War, when they were among the peoples carried off en masse from homelands in the Caucasus and lower Volga regions by Stalin's policy of forced migration; their repatriation a few years later left them determined never to face another such catastrophe again. There are many other peoples in the vast penumbra of Russian domination who are almost as likely to develop secessionist ambitions. Most of the Chechens' neighbours to the north and along the federation's frontier with Kazakhstan share their strong sense of Islamic identity. Tatarstan and Bashkortostan have secured privileged status inside the federation without quenching demands from within for greater autonomy or absolute independence. Between the Volga and the Urals are the lands of peoples who have been kept inside the Russian fold only with difficulty: the Chuvash, for instance, have nourished memories of a long-lost state ascribed to their ancestors; the Udmurt, Mari and Komi have all been susceptible at times to the lure of pan-Finnic nationalism. Although in recent times, all these peoples have seemed willing to collaborate with Russians in a large multi-national state, they are potential separatist fodder. The Russians' huge numbers, daunting to their partners in the federation and to their neighbours in the former Soviet Union and Empire, are also bound to militate against progress towards a Europe 'to the Urals'. Some member-communities of the European Union are already uneasy at German preponderance, by virtue of numbers and wealth. To admit to the European Union another vast nation, nearly twice as numerous as the Germans, would call for more courage than the existing members are likely to summon in the foreseeable future.

Almost all the states beyond the western fringe of the Russian federation have significant – in the Estonian, Latvian, Moldovan and Belarusian cases, perilously huge – Russian minorities. In Ukraine where ethnic Russians are concentrated so as to encourage powerful secessionist movements, the unity of the state is also threatened by similar but smaller-scale concentrations of Poles, Romanians and Hungarians. Ukrainians divide themselves into sub-groups with strong communal identities, such as Podillians, Polishchuks and Volhynians and though none of these has evinced strong fissile tendencies so far, Ukrainian identity is actively rejected by many, perhaps most, of those who consider themselves Ruthenians and who number nearly a million in the region of Uzhorod. The ragged overlapping of ethnic minorities is particularly untidy around the borders of Hungary, where huge Magyar communities remain locked outside their home country by frontiers imposed in the aftermath of the First World War. The 600,000 Magyars of Slovakia have been promised autonomy; but there are a million of them in Romania who have so far been denied it. There is hardly a frontier between the Adriatic and the Black Sea that is unsmudged by ethnic spillage.

It is a grim fact that most of the progress made since the First World War in the stabilisation of European frontiers has been achieved by war and 'ethnic cleansing' – the massacre or forced migration of minority populations. There is no Jewish problem in Poland any more because Hitler exterminated most of the Jews and the communists mopped up or drove out most of those who survived. There is no German problem in Transylvania, Russia or Yugoslavia because – after the counter-holocaust of revenge that followed the Second World War – there are no Germans left; and in the Czech Republic the horrible memory of the Sudeten question survives only as a dispute over reparation claims by the descendants of expelled Germans. There are no longer significant numbers of Turks in Greece or Greeks in Turkey. In Cyprus, the partition that brought uneasy peace was drawn between refugees. The vicious solution currently being applied in Bosnia and on the Croatian-Yugoslav border is another round of the same long process. It is hard to hope convincingly that it will be the last.

Even where frontiers seem stable, many European countries will find it hard to stay united. Belgium is a dumbbell which could snap in the middle, as has already happened to the former Czechoslovakia. In a sad prefiguration, the library of the University of Louvain has been split between remote campuses to provide separate sites for Flemings and Walloons. The French are re-examining 'the identity of France' with great ingenuity, but the Breton homeland of that quintessentially Gallic spirit, Astérix, is French only in the weakest of senses, as are Corsica, the Basque and Catalan lands and, to a lesser extent, Alsace. Italian unity is threatened – in a state with as many cheeses as France – by regionalist feeling in the north powerful enough to sweep a regional party into central government as the second-largest group in the governing coalition in 1994. Except during spasms of German nationalism, Austrians' loyalty to their *Länder* has always been fiercer than to the state. German unity has been enormously strengthened by the huge internal migrations that broke down regionalist feeling after the Second World War. But after a while migrants become naturalised in their regions, turning into passionate advocates of their adopted identities; the federal structure ensures that the regions all have substantial cultural budgets which are available for fomenting such susceptibilities if required.

Identity is a many-layered cake. A single individual can properly feel both Hungarian and Jewish, Bulgarian and Slav, Catalan and Spanish. A Tatar can feel loyalty to the Russian federation, or a Russian to the Lithuanian state, without sacrifice of cultural allegiance to his particular home-community. A Welshman may feel Welsh in conversation with an Englishman and British in an encounter with a Frenchman. A single individual may feel simultaneously Montenegrin, Serbian, Yugoslav and Slav. In today's conditions of inter-regional economic competition, it is possible to envisage the development of new tiers of fellow-feeling among communities with no previous shared political structures. To these levels of identity a further, European layer can be added as, for some Europeans, it already has been. But if every possible level of identity is represented by institutions, the cost will be enormous and the inefficiencies of government will multiply as the various tiers tilt at each other and the rival agencies obstruct. Nor would it do to force the pace of European identity-formation by creating institutions across the European Union for which public opinion is not yet ready: identity-creation is necessarily a slow business, and identities are more likely to endure if they have grown up gradually. The *locus classicus* is presented by Switzerland: a country of cantons riven by mountain-particularism and cultural diversity which has nevertheless grown into a nation. That kind of transmutative magic cannot be worked quickly or without conflict. The road to Switzerland – so to speak – leads through Bosnia and the Swiss have only established their current set of uniform notions of themselves after centuries of slow-outgrowth punctuated by civil wars. A real European Union may only be attainable by the same means,

Europäischer Rat Essen 1994

The Austrian Freedom Party's leader, Jorg Haidar *left* at a political rally. In Austria, as elsewhere in Europe, opportunistic ultra-right wing parties upset cosy political consensus and coalitions, tapping into a feeling that the established order had failed to deliver prosperity or, worse, had sold national birthrights to foreigners and immigrants.

Europe's political classes largely professed loyalty to the idea of a European Union with increased powers, but they were out of step with popular sentiment. Nowhere more than in France was the fight to ratify the Maastricht Treaty more bitterly contested, as evidenced by these placards *right* from the 1993 referendum campaign.

Beneath the show of unity displayed by European Union leaders at the European Summit in Essen in 1994 *bottom*, deep tensions mounted over Europe's future: France and Germany pushed in concert for closer integration; others, including Britain and Denmark, remained sceptical; the majority went with whichever tendency prevailed.

over the same sort of length of time.

If history is anything to go by (and it probably is not), a strong and widespread sense of European identity is not necessarily favourable to European integration. It has never restrained Europeans from fighting each other in the past. Even if political unification were achieved, it would only mean that future wars would qualify more precisely to be called 'civil'. If progress towards integration comes, it will probably be in one of two forms: a continuation of the old European state-system, with a light confederative dressing, in which most of the existing states of Europe survive, scotched but not killed; or a federal Europe, with a strong 'High Authority', embracing tiers of smaller units which include old states, regional agglomerations and a large number of autonomous historic communities. Whatever political solutions are adopted, the success of Europe, in a world of emulous regions and increasing economic inequalities, depends on whether the torturous process of economic integration can be developed within the states of the European Union and extended to other parts of the imperfect continent. Meanwhile – though small as continents go – Europe has all the characteristics of a giant: poor articulation, lumbering gait, limited intelligence and enormous reserves of strength.

PICTURE CREDITS

We have pleasure in acknowledging the following museums and picture agencies. The abbreviations indicate *t* top, *b* bottom, *l* left, *r* right, *c* centre.

CHAPTER ONE
AKG, London 11*t*, 18*tr*, (National Museum, Athens) 22-3*tc*; Ronald Sheridan/ Ancient Art and Architecture Collection 14, 16*t*, 17*t* & *b*, 18*bl*, 20*bl*, 21, 22*tl*, 22-3*bc*, 23*tr*; C M Dixon 13*bl*; E T Archive 9, 13*t* & *c*, (National Museum, Copenhagen) 18-19; Janet & Colin Bord/Fortean Picture Library 12; Scala 10; Werner Forman Archive 18*tl*, 20*tl* & (National Museum, Copenhagen) *tr*.

CHAPTER TWO
AKG, London 40*t*; Archivo Fotografico, Madrid 29*tc* & *tr*; Archivo Oronoz, Madrid 29*tl*, 30-1*bc*; C M Dixon 25, 34*tr*, 34-5*b*, 40-1*c*; E T Archive (Archaeological Museum, Sofia) 26*t* & (Historical Museum, Sofia) *b*, (National Historical Museum, Bucharest) 27, (Archaeological Museum, Madrid) 28; Werner Forman Archive (National Museum, Copenhagen) 36*tl*, (Heritage Museum, St Petersburg) 38*tr*, *b* & 39; Michael Holford 40-1*b*, 41*t*; MAS, Ampliaciones y Reproducciones 30*t*, 31*c* & *r*; Musée Gallo-Romaine/ Christian Thioc 35; Photo RMN 37*tr* & (G Blot) *l* & *br*; Scala 36-7*c*, 38*tl*.

CHAPTER THREE
AKG, London 46; Archivo Oronoz, Madrid 55*tr*; Bibliothèque Nationale, Paris 54-5; British Museum 55*br*; J Alan Cash 44*tl*, 45*t*; Collection Speciale de l'Abbaye Sainte Croix de Poiters 58*lc*; C M Dixon 52*t*; E T Archive (Cathedral Treasury, Aachen) 47*tl*, 50*bl*, *c* & *br*, 51, 55*cl*, (Archaeological Museum, Madrid) 57, 58*cr* & *r*, 59*l*; Werner Forman Archive 48*t* & *b*, 59*r*; Sonia Halliday Photographs 44*r*, 58*tl*; Michael Holford 47*c*, 50*tr*; National Gallery, London 56; New York Public Library 42; Romisch-Germanisches Museum, Cologne 45*b*; Scala 53*b*, 56-7.

CHAPTER FOUR
Archaeological Museum, Prague 71*t*; AKG, London 65*tl*; Archivo Fotografico, Madrid 62*l*, 62-3, 67*lc* & *bl*, 74*l*; Arxiumas 74-5*bc*; Bildarchiv Foto, Marburg 64*rc*, 74-5*tc*; E T Archive 63, 64*b*, 70*tr*, 70-1*b*; Werner Forman Archive 68*br*, 68-9*t*, 69*bl*, 70*tl*, 71*b*; Hirmer Fotoarchiv, Munich 65*tr*; Michael Holford 61*b*; Metropolitan Museum, New York 65*br*; Photo RMN/H Lewandowski 68*c*; Trustees of the National Museums of Scotland 61*t*.

CHAPTER FIVE
AKG, London 91; Archivo Fotografico, Madrid 79, 82, 84*tr* & *c*, 82; Bridgeman Art Library (Giraudon) 96; British Library 90; E T Archive (Oldsaksammling, Oslo) 80*lc* & *r*, (Staats Archiv, Hamburg) 83*t*, (Sucevita Monastery, Romania) 88, (Sir John Soane's Museum) 89, (Palazzo Pubblico, Siena) 92-3, (Bibliothèque Nationale, Paris) 93*t*, (National Gallery) 94-5*t*, (University Library Heidelberg) 97*tr*, (Museo de Arte Antiga, Lisbon) 97*bl*; Fratelli Alinari 93*b*, 97*tl*; Robert Harding 84*tl*; Michael Holford 80*b*, 81, 94*b*, 95; National Museum of Finland 87*t*; Scala 84-5; Victoria & Albert Museum, London 84*bl*; Viking Ship Museum, Roskilde, Sweden/ Ole Malling 80*tr*; Hackenberg-Zefa 83*b*.

CHAPTER SIX
AKG, London 111*c*; Archivo Fotografico, Madrid 106*t* & *b*, 109*tc*; Bridgeman Art Library (John Van Haeften Gallery, London) 108-9*b*, 110-11*b*, (Giraudon) 116-17*b*; E T Archive 99, (Uffizi Gallery, Florence) 104*b*, (Musée Conde, Chantilly) 107*tl* & (Uffizi Gallery, Florence) *r*, 112*c*, 112-13*b*, (Tate Gallery) 114*tl*, *tr*, *cl* & *b*, (Historical Museum, Moscow) 115*tr*, *b*, (Musée de Versailles) 116*t*; Fitzwilliam Museum, University of Cambridge 109*b*; Michael Holford 107*b*; Kungl Biblioteket, Stockholm 112*t*; Scala 100-1, 102-3, 104-5*t*, 105, 109*t* & *bc*, 116*br*, 116-17*t*; Reg Wilson 116*bl*.

CHAPTER SEVEN
AKG, London 122*t*, (Statens Museum for Kunst, Copenhagen) 125, 126-7*b*, (Museum Pomorskie, Danzig) 127*t*, 128*t*, (H Traut) 129*c*, 130-1*b*, (Prado, Madrid) 133*b*; Archivo Fotografico, Madrid 124; The Bridgeman Art Library (National Gallery, London) 118, (University of Liverpool Art Gallery and College) 132*b*; Edifice/Lewis 123*b*; E T Archive (Monte dei Paschi Bank, Siena) 120-1*t*, (Museum of Fine Arts, Lausanne) 123*t*, (Peter Jackson Collection) 129*t*, (University Library, Prague) 131*t*, (Royal Chapel, Granada, Spain) 131*c*, (City Temple, London) 132-3*t*; Gemeente Musea, Delft 122*b*; Robert Harding 132*t*; A F Kersting 121*b*; Scala (Museo di Firenze com'era, Florence) 126*t*, (Prado, Madrid) 128-9*b*.

CHAPTER EIGHT
Jean-Loup Charmet, Paris 136; AKG London 142, 144-5*b*; Arcaid (Farrell Grehan) 146 inset, (Lucinda Lahrton) 146*l*, (Dennis Gilbert) 147, (Kurwenal/Prisma) 149; Arxiu Fotografic 148*t*; Bridgeman Art Library (Christopher Wood Gallery, London) 152*t*; E T Archive (National Maritime Museum, London) 137, 138*b*, (Victoria & Albert Museum, London) 139, 141*t*, 141*b*, 143, 144*t*, (Science Museum, London) 145*t*, (Russian Historical Museum, Moscow) 150-1*t*, 152*b*; The Mansell Collection 140, 150-1*t*, 151*c*; National Trust Photographic Library/ Andreas von Einsiedel 148*b*; The Science Museum, Science & Society Picture Library 144*c*; Tate Gallery Publications 153.

CHAPTER NINE
AKG London 158*l*, (Bibliothèque Nationale, Paris) 165*c*, 168; The Bridgeman Art Library (Chateau de Versailles, France) 154, (House of Commons, Westminster, London) 162-3*t*, (Tretyakof Gallery, Moscow) 164-5*b*, (Royal Holloway & Bedford New College, Surrey) 166-7; British Library 169*t*; Michael Clogs 159; E T Archive (Risorgimento Museum, Turin) 157, 158*r*, 160-1, (Tate Gallery) 162-3*b*, (Villa Reale, Milan) 164-5*t*, (Musée d'Orsay, Paris) 166*l*, 167*r*, (Bibliothèque Nationale, Paris) 169*b*, 171; The Mansell Collection 157*t*, 161, 162*c*, 164*c*, 170.

CHAPTER TEN
AKG 176*b*, 182*bl*; Archivo Fotografico, Madrid 178, 183*r*; The Bridgeman Art Library (Lauros-Giraudon) 175*t*; E T Archive 174, 174-5*b*, 176*c*, 177, 180*t*, 182-3*bc*, 184*t*; Mary Evans/Sigmund Freud 176*t*; Hulton Deutsch 180*b*, 184*b*, 185*t*, 188*l*, 189*r*; David King Collection 179; Magnum Photos (Ferdinando Scianna) 180*c*, (Robert Capa) 182*t*; Range/Bettmann 186, (UPI) 187*cl*; Scala 187*bl*; Sygma (Keystone) 172, (B Bisson) 188-9*tc*; CAP Viollet 180-1*b*.

CHAPTER ELEVEN
E T Archive 193*c* & *b*; Mary Evans Picture Library 190; Gamma 192-3*t*, 197*r*, 201, 206-7*t*, (Merillon-Simon) 206-7*b*; Hulton Deutsch 192*tl* & *b*; Cummings/Express Newspapers plc/The Centre for the Study of Cartoons & Caricature, University of Kent, Canterbury 200*tr*; Magnum 191, 195*t*, (Eric Lessing) 199*b*, (Nicolas Tikhomiroff) 200*b*; Network (Don Miller) 196, (Jonathan Olley) 197*l*, (John Sturrock) 199*tr*, (Homer Sykes) 202*tr*, (Jenny Mathews) 202*b*, Nikolai Ignatiev) 203, (Mike Abrahams) 204*t*, (Grazia Neri) 205; Pictorial Press Limited 195*b*; Sygma (Prache-Lewin) 194, (Keystone) 198-9*b*, (A Nogues) 204-5*b*, (Bernard Bisson) 207*tr*.

SECTION OPENERS
E T Archive (National Museum, Belgrade) 6-7; The Royal Collection © Her Majesty the Queen 76-7; E T Archive (Tate Gallery) 134-5.

END PAPERS
Imperial War Museum, London.

SELECTED FURTHER READING

GENERAL

Europe as a concept is tracked in D. Hay, *Europe: The Emergence of an Idea* (1957). Heroic surveys of European history as a whole include H.A.L. Fisher, *A History of Europe*, 2 vols (1952), W.G. East, *An Historical Geography of Europe* (1956), M.M. Postan, ed., *Cambridge Economic History of Europe*, 7 vols (1966-78), M. Mollat, *Europe and the Sea* (1993) and N. Davies, *The Oxford History of Europe* (1995). The guide which follows is meant to help readers pursue topics raised in the text chapter by chapter.

CHAPTER ONE

The best general introduction is B. Cunliffe, ed., *The Oxford Illustrated Prehistory of Europe* (1994). On ice age chronology, environment and settlement, see A. Sutcliffe, *On the Track of Ice Age Mammals* (1986) and A. Morrison and C. Bonsall, 'The Early Post-Glacial Settlement of Scotland: A Review' in C. Bonsall, ed., *The Mesolithic in Europe* (1985), pp.134-42. The references to Mesolithic dogs are based on L. Larsson, 'Dogs in Fraction: Symbols in Action' in P.M. Vermeesch and P. Van Peer, ed.s, *Contributions to the Mesolithic in Europe* (1990), pp.153-60. G.N. Bailey, 'Shell Middens as Indicators of Postglacial Economies' in P. Mellars, ed., *The Postglacial Settlement of Europe* (1978), pp.37-63 raises an important subject. On the migrationist fallacy, the work of Colin Renfrew is fundamental. See especially *Problems in European Prehistory* (1979) and *Before Civilisation* (1973). The examples reviewed above are covered in R.J. Harrison, *The Beaker Folk: Copper Archaeology in Western Europe* (1980) and, for the Indo-Europeans, C. Renfrew, *Archaeology and Language* (1987), though the latter should be studied in conjunction with the arguments of critics in 'Archaeology and Indo-European Languages', *Antiquity*, lxii (1988), pp.563-95 and J.P. Mallory, *In Search of the Indo-Europeans* (1989). J.D. Evans, *Prehistoric Antiquities of the Maltese Islands* (1971) is essential; the details about houses come from C.Malone, S. Stoddart and D. Trump, 'A House for the Temple-builders', *Antiquity*, lxii (1988), pp.297-301. On the Balkan civilisation see 'Varna and the Social Context of Early Metallurgy' in C. Renfrew, *Problems*, pp.377-84; the art of Varna is is thoroughly studied in the Paris exhibition catalogue, *Le premier or de l'humanité en Bulgarie: 5e millennaire* (1989). J. Chapman, *The Vinča Culture*, 2 vols (1981) confirms the processual approach recommended by Renfrew. M. Gimbutas, *Bronze Age Cultures in Central and Eastern Europe* (1965) is helpful on the cultures of the steppes; for wagons see S. Piggott, *The Earliest Wheeled Transport, from the Atlantic Coast to the Caspian Sea* (1984). P.V. Glob, *The Mound People* (1974) is a good introduction to bronze-age Scandinavia. Among many important works on the megalithic cultures, C. Renfrew, ed., *The Megalithic Monuments of Western Europe* (1983), A. Burl, *Megalithic Brittany* (1985), D.V. Clarke, T.G. Cowie and A. Foxton, *Symbols of Power at the Time of Stonehenge* (1985) and C.L.N. Ruggles and A.W.R. Whittle, ed.s, *Astronomy and Society in Britain during the Period 4000-1500 BC* (1981) can be particularly recommended. On the emergence and fate of Aegean civilisation, the most authoritative work is now O. Dickinson, *The Aegean Bronze Age* (1994).

CHAPTER TWO

On Greek colonisation and its domestic background, see *Cambridge Ancient History, iii, part III: The Expansion of the Greek World*, ed.s J. Boardman and N.G. Hammond (1982) and J. Boardman, *The Greeks Overseas* (1988). O. Murray, *Early Greece* (1980) is the best introduction to its subject.

I have relied on R.F. Hoddinott, *The Thracians* (1986) and J. Wilkes, *The Illyrians* (1992). On Trajan's column, see P. MacKendrick, *The Dacian Stones Speak* (1975). On Iberian civilisation generally, see R. Harrison, *Spain at the Dawn of History* (1988). On Pozo Moro, see M. Almagro Gorbea, 'Pozo Moro,' *Madride Mitteilungen*, xxiv (1983), pp.177-293 and T. Chapa Burnet, *La escultura ibérica zoomorfa* (Madrid, 1985). The stories from Herodotus are in *Histories*, I, p.163 and IV, p.152. On Tartessos, see J. Maluquer de Motes, *La civilización de Tartessos* (1985) and on mining, B. Rothenburg and A. Blanco-Frejeiro, *Ancient Mining and Metallurgy in South-West Spain* (1981). The standard work on Numancia and its contexts is still volumes iii-iv of A. Schulten, *Fontes Hispaniae Antiquae* (1935-7). For Tiermes, see T. Ortega, 'Tiermes: ciudad rupestre celtíbero-romana,' *Celtiberia*, xxviii (1964). The best introductions to the Celts are provided by B. Cunliffe, *The Celtic World* (1979) and the Venice exhibition catalogue edited by V. Kruta, S. Moscati et al., *The Celts* (1991). The Germans are covered by M. Todd, *The Early Germans* (1992). On Scythians and Sarmatians, see T. Talbot-Rice, *The Scythians* (1957), E.D. Phillips, *The Royal Hordes* (1965), T. Sulimirski, *The Sarmatians* (1976) and R. Rolle, *Die Welt der Skythen* (1980).

Classical Greece is the subject of a brilliant conspectus by S. Hornblower, *The Greek World, 479-323 BC* (1991). The anecdote about W.H.C. Guthrie is from his *History of Greek Philosophy*, 6 vols (1962-81), vi: *Aristotle; An Encounter* (1981). On Greek democracy M.H. Hansen, *The Athenian Democracy* (1991) is the standard work, but M.I. Finley, *Democracy: Ancient and Modern* (1985) is of particular interest and enduring topicality. Popular morality in the period is brilliantly reconstructed in K. Dover, *Greek Popular Morality in the Time of Plato and Aristotle* (1974). See also the same author's *Perceptions of the Ancient Greeks* (1992). On the importance of Greece, M.I. Finley, *The Legacy of Greece: A New Appraisal* (1981) is a master work now under attack. O. Taplin, *Greek Fire* (1989) is a sparkling introduction.

CHAPTER THREE

On Greek geography, E.H. Bunbury, *A History of Ancient Geography* (1883) or J.O. Thomson, *History of Ancient Geography* (1948) are still valuable introductions. The *Geography* of Strabo is best consulted in the edition of H.L. Jones, 8 vols (1954). G. Anjac, *Strabon et les sciences du monde* (1966) sets it in context. Dark age Verona is explored in the collection *Verona in età gotica e langobarda* (1982). See B. Ward-Perkins, *From Classical Antiquity to the Middle Ages: Urban Public Building in Northern and Central Italy* (1984) on the transformation of ancient cities. On Roman imperialism, F. Millar et al., *The Roman Empire and its Neighbours* (1981) and S.L. Dyson, *The Creation of the Roman Frontier* (1985) are particularly good. The standard guide to Italica is M. García y Bellido, *Colonia Aelia Augusta Italica* (1960); see also A.M. Canto, 'Die Vetus Urbs von Italica,' *Madride Mitteilungen*, xxvi (1985), pp.137-48. J. Alarcão and R. Étienne, ed.s, *Fouilles de Conimbriga*, 7 vols (1977-9) deals with the Portuguese site. R. Duncan-Jones, *The Economy of the Roman Empire* (1982) approaches its subject from a quantitative and macro-economic perspective, while the more locally sensitive essays of C.R. Whittaker are collected under the title, *City and Trade in the Roman Empire* (1993). A.H.M. Jones, *The Later Roman Empire 284-602*, 2 vols (1986) is a faithful companion and P. Brown, *The World of Late Antiquity* (1989) a brilliant conspectus. On paganism and Christianity in the fourth century, see R. Lane Fox, *Pagans and Christians* (1988) and R. Browning, *The Emperor Julian* (1975). W.H.C. Frend, *The Rise of Christianity* (1984) and J. Herrin, *The Formation of Christendom* (1989) cover the whole period to about 600. E. Kitzinger, *Early Medieval Art in the British Museum and British Library* (1983) greatly exceeds the promise of its title. J. Stevenson, *The Catacombs* (1978) is a good guide.

On political and intellectual history, it is invidious to select, but I found useful D. Bowden, *The Age of Constantine and Julian* (1978), J. Matthews, *Western Aristocracies and Imperial Court* (1975), T.D. Barnes, *The New Empire of Diocletian and Constantine* (1982) and *Constantine and Eusebius* (1981), N.B. McLynn, *Ambrose of Milan: Church and Court in a Christian Capital*, R. McMullen, *Constantine* (1987) and M. Grant, *The Emperor Constantine* (1993). Of the work of Ammianus Marcellinus, *The Later Roman Empire*, ed. W. Hamilton and A. Wallace-Hadrill (1986) is an excellent selection. E.A. Thompson, *A History of Attila and the Huns* (1948) is a study of social development, while J.O. Maenchen-Helfen, *The World of the Huns* (1973) attempts to reconstruct a culture. On the Visigoths, see Thompson's *The Visigoths in the time of Ulfila* (1966) and 'The Visigoths from Fritigern to Euric', *Historia*, xii (1963), pp.105-26. They have been copiously studied in their Spanish phase – most comprehensively in L.A. García-Moreno, *Historia de la España visigoda* (1989). Ravenna is evoked in the illustrated works of G. Bonfini – most generally in *Ravenna: arte e storia* (1978). R. Browning, *Justinian and Theodora* (1987) is arresting and scholarly. On Franks, Anglo-Saxons and Lombards respectively, E. James, *The Franks* (1988), H. Mayr-Harting, *The Coming of Christianity to Anglo-Saxon England* (1991) and C. Wickham, *Early Medieval Italy* (1981) have a contagious feel for the cultures they describe. J. Wallace-Hadrill, *The Barbarian West* (1973) is a succinct survey of Germanic kingdoms. On Isidore and Sisebut, see J. Fontaine, *Isidore de Séville et la culture classique dans l'Espagne wisigothique*, 3 vols (1959-84). Though there are more recent editions of *The Rule of St Benedict*, I rely on J. McCann's (1952).

CHAPTER FOUR

The historiography of the period to the ninth century has been dominated in recent times by H. Pirenne, *Mohammed and Charlemagne* (1954). On Bede, see P. Hunter Blair, *The World of Bede* (1990). C.H. Talbot, ed., *The Anglo-Saxon Missionaries in Germany* (1954) gives sources in translation. Two of the most

SELECTED FURTHER READING

helpful studies of Charlemagne are short pamphlets: F.L. Ganshof, *The Imperial Coronation of Charlemagne* (1971) and P.D. King, *Charlemagne* (1986). F. Heer, *Charlemagne and his World* (1975) can also be recommended. The magnificent Aachen exhibition catalogue, W. Braunfels, ed., *Karl der Grosse: Werke und Wirkung* (1965) is a wonderful quarry.

For Ottonian Saxony see K. Leyser, *Rule and Conflict in an Early Medieval Society* (1979); on the Ottonians generally, his *Medieval Germany and its Neighbours* (1982), pp.1-189. H. Mayr-Harting, *Ottonian Book Illumination: An Historical Study*, 2 vols (1991) is full of insights.

On eastern Europe, see D. Obolensky's *The Byzantine Commonwealth* (1971) and on Christian Spain, R. Collins, *Early Medieval Spain* (1983). On Muslim Spain, E. Lévi-Provençal, *España musulmana hasta la caída del califato* (1967) is unsurpassed on its period, after which see M.J. Viguera, *Los reinos de taifas* (1994) or her more concise and more general *Los reinos de taifas y las invasiones magrebíes* (1992), followed by L. P. Harvey, *Islamic Spain* (1250-1500). H.R. Ellis Davidson, *The Viking Road to Byzantium* (1962) is helpful on the Rus and G. Vernadsky and M. Karpovich, *Kievan Russia* (1948) on what followed. See P. Foote and D. Wilson, *The Viking Achievement* (1984) and G. Jones, *The Vikings* (1968) on the Vikings in general. Ibn Fadlan, *Voyage chez les bulgares de la Volga* is available in an edition by M. Canard (1988). S. Runciman, *The Eastern Schism* (1955) is concise and robust. On heresies, R.I. Moore, *The Birth of Popular Heresy* (1975) and M. Lambert, *Medieval Heresy* (1992) are suggestive and efficient. On the Gregorian Reformation, the relevant papers in K.J. Leyser, *Communications and Power in Medieval Europe* (1994) are the best place to start. On the romanesque, see G. Zarnecki, *Romanesque Art* (1971) and J. Beckwith, *Early Medieval Art* (1969). On medieval geography, though originally written nearly sixty years ago, H.T. Kimble, *Geography in the Middle Ages* (1968) is still the best general introduction.

CHAPTER FIVE

K. Leyser's lecture, *The Ascent of Latin Europe* (1986) introduces the subject. Written in the fifties, R.W. Southern, *The Making of the Middle Ages* (1993) is the best survey of the Latin west. R. Bartlett, *The Making of Europe* (1993) is a splendid account of its eastward expansion. A. Murray, *Reason and Society in the Middle Ages* (1978) is original and indispensable.

On Abbot Suger, see E. Panovsky, ed., *Abbot Suger on the Abbey of St Denis* and M. Bur, *Suger* (1991). R. Bechmann, *Les Racines des Cathédrales* (1984) is an important work of historical ecology. In paragraphs borrowed from F. Fernández-Armesto, *Millennium: A History of our last Thousand Years* (1995), I have relied heavily on R. Bartlett, *Gerald of Wales* (1982). The renaissance of Matthias Corvinus can be approached through R. Feuer-Tóth, *Art and Humanism in Hungary in the Age of Matthias Corvinus* (1990).

The resumption of European expansion from the thirteenth century can be followed in P. Chaunu, *L'expansion européenne du XIIe au XVe siècle* (1969); G. Scammell, *The World Encompassed* (1984); F. Fernández-Armesto, *Before Columbus* (1987) and J.R.S. Phillips, *The Medieval Expansion of Europe* (1988). An outstanding book on the eastern front is E. Christiansen, *The Northern Crusades* (1980). P. Dollinger, *La Hanse* (1964) is still the standard work on the Hanse. D. Waley, *The Italian City-Republics* (1988) is a concise introduction to a subject on which a magnum opus by P.J. Jones is imminent. On urban history generally, see D. Abulafia et al., ed.s, *Church and City 1000-1500* (1992). L. Benevolo, *The City* (1983) is a valuable general urban history which concentrates on the European middle ages.

My paragraphs on classical traditions in art are indebted to W. Oakeshott, *Classical Inspiration in Medieval Art* (1959) and those on Andalusia to L. Bolens, *Agronomes andalous au moyen âge* (1987). The two volumes of the *Cambridge Medieval History*, iv parts I and II, edited by J.M. Hussey (1982) are standard on medieval Byzantium. G. Buckler's *Anna Comnena* (1968) is, I believe, still the leading work on that blue stocking. For the background of the Mongol invaders, R. Grousset, *The Empire of the Steppes* (1979) is a lasting source of entertainment and instruction. The relevant period of Russian history should be approached through J. Fennell, *The Crisis of Medieval Russia* (1983) and the subsequent history through his *Emergence of Muscovy* (1968) and R.O. Conway, *The Formation of Muscovy* (1987).

On the late medieval Balkans, see G.C. Soulis, *The Serbs and Byzantium during the Reign of Tsar Stephen Dušan and his Successors* (1984), E. Dimitrova's British Library booklet, *The Gospels of Ivan Alexander* (1994) and the papers of D.S. Angelov collected in *Les Balkans au moyen âge* (1978). N. Malcolm, *A Short History of Bosnia* (1994), though covering the whole subject, is particularly valuable on this period. The Hundred Years' War has found a fine historian in J.P.C. Sumption, *The Hundred Years' War*, 1 vol so far (1990-in progress).

On Aventinus, see G. Strauss, *Historian in an Age of Crisis* (1963) and on late medieval Germany, F. Du Bellay, *Germany in the Later Middle Ages* (1983). The best work on Frederick II is D. Abulafia, *Frederick II* (1992), though the great study by F. Kantorowicz, *Kaiser Friedrich der Zweite*, 2 vols (1927) remains an essential guide to the sources. On the eschatological imperial tradition, see M. Reeves, *The Influence of Prophecy in the Later Middle Ages* and the wide-ranging A. Milhou, *Colón y su mentalidad mesiánica* (1984). N.Cohn, *The Pursuit of the Millennium* (1970) is justly admired on popular millenarianism.

Changes in kingship and government in the late fourteenth and fifteenth centuries are best approached through particular studies. E.H. Kantorowicz, *The King's Two Bodies* (1957) and M. Bloch, *Les rois thaumaturges* (1961) are classic guides to important themes. My account is indebted to M.G.A. Vale, *Charles VII* (1974). On the Wilton Diptych, see the National Gallery exhibition catalogue, D. Gordon, *Making and Meaning: the Wilton Diptych* (1993), which also provides an excellent introduction and guide to further reading on Richard II. My account of chivalric imagery borrows from P. Binski, *The Painted Chamber at Westminster* (1986). *Philip the Good* (1970) is one of an impressive series of volumes R. Vaughan devoted to the Valois Dukes of Burgundy. On chivalry generally, M. Keen, *Chivalry* (1984) is the outstanding work. For the details on p.96, I am indebted to P. Liss, *Isabel the Queen* (1994).

The paragraphs on the maritime dimensions of chivalry are based on two papers by me: 'The Sea and Chivalry in Medieval Spain' in J.B. Hattendorf, ed., *Maritime History in the Age of Discovery: An Introduction* (1995) and 'Inglaterra y el Atlántico en la baja edad media' in *Canarias e Inglaterra*, ed. A. Béthencourt y Massieu (forthcoming).

CHAPTER SIX

On Cassini, see M. Pelletier and J.F. Carrez, *La Carte de Cassini* (1990). On the transmission of classical learning, N. Wilson and L. Reynolds, *Scribes and Scholars* (1974), R. Bolgar, *Classical Influences on European Culture* (1976), R.W. Southern, *Medieval Humanism and other Studies* (1969), P.O. Kristeller, *Renaissance Thought and its Sources* (1979) and J.G. Pococke, *The Machiavellian Moment* (1979). H. Baron, *Cicero and the Roman Civic Spirit in the Renaissance* (1938) should be mentioned for its seminal importance. P. Burke, *Culture and Society in Renaissance Italy* (1986) makes a rich backdrop. On Florence, see G. Holmes, *The Florentine Enlightenment* (1992), R. Goldthwaite, *The Building of Renaissance Florence* (1980), and Baron's essays, *In Search of Florentine Civic Humanism* (1988). E.H. Gombrich, 'The Early Medici as Patrons of Art' in E.F. Jacob, ed., *Italian Renaissance Studies* (1960) is the key work on patronage. *Filippo Brunelleschi: la sua opera e il suo tempo*, 2 vols (1980) is a collection full of helpful papers. Astraea is studied in some of the essays in F. Yates, *Astraea* (1993) while the fundamental work on Hermetic studies is her *Giordano Bruno and the Hermetic Tradition in the Renaissance* (1991). R.J.W. Evans, *Rudolf II* (1973) is an outstanding study of an esoteric court. Except on Cisneros, for studies of the thinkers in the tradition scanned on p.108 above, readers are spoiled for choice. Introductory recommendations can be made: J. McConica, *Erasmus* (1991) and L. Halkin, *Erasmus* (1993), which, despite thorough mastery of the sources, is a shade uncritical of its subject; H.R. Wagner, *The Life and Writings of Bartolomé de Las Casas* (1967); T. Sorrell, *Descartes* (1987); R. Scruton, *Spinoza* (1989); G. McDonald Ross, *Leibniz* (1984); R. Westfall, *The Life of Isaac Newton* (1993).

The same is true of artists mentioned on p.109. See H. Hibbard, *Michelangelo* (1985); the Venice catalogue, *Titian*, ed. F. Valcanover et al. (1990); J. Beck, *Raphael* (1994); J. Brown, *Velázquez: Painter and Courtier* (1986). I know no work on El Greco that is really satisfactory, and the catalogue by H.E. Wethey is now very out of date; but X. de Salas and F. Marías, ed.s, *El Greco y el arte de su tiempo* (1992) approaches the essence of the artist's inspiration through his annotations to Vasari. On baroque art, F. Haskell, *Patrons and Painters* (1980) and A. Blunt, *Baroque and Rococo Architecture* (1982) are influential. G. Bazin, *Baroque and Rococo* (1964) is efficient. My account of the Grand Tour is based on J. Black, *The British Abroad* (1992).

For origins of developments described in eastern Europe, see F. Carsten, *The Origins of Prussia* (1954), G. Barraclough and F. Graus, *Eastern and Western Europe in the Middle Ages* (1970) and P. Longworth, *The Making of Eastern Europe* (1992). Werboczy is studied in context in J.M. Bak, *Königtum und Stände in Ungarn in 14-15 Jahrhundert* (1973). A concise introduction to nobility generally is J. Powis, *Aristocracy* (1984). On the retreat of the Turks, see J.W. Stoye, *The Siege of Vienna* (1964) and contributions by V.J. Parry and A.N. Kurat in M.A. Cook, ed., *A History of the Ottoman Empire to 1730* (1976). G. Masson, *Queen Christina* (1968) retains value and I have borowed from the National Museum catalogue, *Queen Christina of Sweden* (1966). The reign of Peter the Great is covered in C.S. Leonard, *Reform and Regicide* (1993) and that of Catherine in I. de Madariaga, *Catherine the Great: A Short History* (1990). The outstanding work on the French Revolution is S. Schama, *Citizens* (1989). Origins of romanticism are described in K. Clark, *The Romantic Rebellion* (1993) and reflections added in a monograph by J.C. Isbell, *The Birth of European Romanticism: Truth and Propaganda in De Stäel's de l'Allemagne* (1994). The leading study of Napoleonic imperialism is G. Ellis, *The Napoleonic Empire* (1991).

CHAPTER SEVEN

M. Mollat and P. Wolff, *The Popular Revolutions of the Late Middle Ages* (1973), despite dated perspectives, is useful. On some of the movements mentioned see H. Kaminsky, 'The Religion of Hussite Tabor' in M. Reichigl, ed., *The Czechoslovak Contribution to World History* (1964), pp.210-33, and *A History of the Hussite Revolution* (1967); F.M. Bartos, *The Hussite Revolution, 1424-37* (1986); G. Parker, *The Dutch Revolt* (1977); J. Morrill, *The Revolt of the Provinces* (1980) and his essays, *The Nature of the English Revolution* (1993), as well as the work of C. Russell on the origins of the British civil wars, especially *The Fall of the British Monarchies* (1991).

The interpretation of the Reformation is based on F. Fernández-Armesto and D. Wilson, *Reformation* (forthcoming, 1996). Especially valuable are J. Bossy, *Christianity in the West,1400-1700* (1985), J. Delumeau, *Le Catholicisme entre Luther et Voltaire* (1971), P. Burke, *Popular Culture in Early Modern Europe* (1994) and O. Chadwick, *The Popes and European Revolution* (1981). My discussion of Weber is indebted to H. R. Trevor-Roper, *Religion, the Reformation and Social Change* (1967), pp.1-45. A satisfying outline of the period is by J.H. Elliott, *Europe Divided* (1968). On the Netherlands see S. Schama, *The Embarrassment of Riches: An Interpretation of Dutch Culture in the Golden Age* (1978) and J. Israel, *The Dutch Republic* (1995).

The best survey of the Reformation is E. Cameron, *The European Reformation* (1991). The quibble about Luther's theses comes from E. Iserloh, *The Theses were not Posted: Luther between Reform and Reformation* (1968). On Catholic justification by faith, see D. Fenlon, *Heresy and obedience in Tridentine Italy* (1972). A fine work on the Catholic Reformation, though not one entirely followed above, is A.D. Wright, *The Counter-Reformation* (1982). The focus on Spain above can be developed by consulting W.A. Christian, Jr, *Local Religion in Sixteenth-Century Spain* (1981) and H. Kamen, *The Phoenix and the Flame* (1993). The description of the Hospital of Charity is indebted to J. Brown, *Ideas and Images in Seventeenth- Century Spanish Painting* (1978), pp.128-45. The reference to C. Ginzburg, *The Cheese and the Worms: The Cosmos of a Sixteenth-Century Miller* (1992) is easily recognisable. The novel mentioned on p.126 is F. Delicado's *La lozana andaluza*. On Swedish evangelisation and other subjects, I am indebted to W. Ward, *The Protestant Evangelical Awakening* (1991). On catechisms, I rely chiefly on G. Strauss, *Luther's House of Learning* (1978) and the Spanish Inquisition, mainly on B. Bennassar, *L'Inquisition espagnole* (1979). Marriage is now a subject with a large literature: M. Ingram, *Church Courts, Sex and Marriage in England* (1987) is an exemplary and representative work. My information on the cult of Luther comes from R.W. Scribner's invaluable collection, *Popular Culture and Popular Movements in Reformation Germany* (1987).

For Shabbetai Zevi, see G. Scholem, *Sabbatai Sevi: The Mystical Messiah* (1973). On Granada, see M. Ladero Quesada's masterly *Granada después de la conquista* (1988) and, for a more general perspective, his *Granada: historia de un país islámico* (1989). My account of the Waldenses is based on E. Cameron, *The Reformation of the Heretics* (1984) and of Poland on N. Davies, *God's Playground*, 2 vols (1981). Krasinski, as far as I know, can be approached only through his own *History of the Reformation in Poland*, 2 vols (1838-9).

CHAPTER EIGHT

On the Macartney embassy, R.A. Bickers, ed., *Ritual and Diplomacy: The Macartney Mission to China 1792-4* (1993) is useful. On Chinese industry in the eighteenth century, see M. Elvin, *The Pattern of the Chinese Past* (1973). On the development of the Dutch seaborne Empire, see A. Reid, *Southeast Asia in the Age of Commerce*, 2 vols (1988-93) as well as C. Boxer, *The Dutch Seaborne Empire* (1990). D. Brading, *The First America* (1992) introduces the concept of Creole mentalities. H. Hobhouse, *Seeds of Change* (1992) deals well with quinine in the context of world-wide exchanges. A.W. Crosby's *Ecological Imperialism* (1993) is outstanding. Additionally on the potato, W. MacNeill's contribution to the Smithsonian catalogue, *Seeds of Change*, ed. H.J. Viola and C. Margolis (1991) is important. On the rural economy of the Habsburg dominions, as on Austro-Hungarian history generally, C.A. Macartney, *The Habsburg Empire* (1968) is the best guide. Agustín de Béthencourt's life is admirably covered in context by A. Rumeu de Armas, *Ciencia y tecnología en la España ilustrada* (1980).

F. Braudel, *Civilization and Capitalism*, 3 vols (1985), iii, *The Perspective of the World* helps set the problem of 'the rise of Europe' in global context. E. Jones, *The European Miracle* (1981) is highly suggestive as an introductory essay. My account here is based on *Millennium*. A fine work on technology in colonial expansion is D. Headrick, *Tools of Empire* (1986). On this subject, G. Parker, *The Military Revolution* (1989) is indispensable. The history of European industrialisation is being radically revised. See P. O'Brien, ed., *The Industrial Revolution* (1994). Details on France come from T. Zeldin, *A History of French Passions, 1848-1945* (1993) – rich in insights into French history throughout the period. The paragraphs on factories are adopted from *Millennium* and those on

Barcelona from F. Fernández-Armesto, *Barcelona* (1992). On housing and planning in England, I have relied on J. Burnett, *A Social History of Housing 1815-1970* (1970). The paragraphs on Darwin are lightly adapted from *Millennium*. The leading study of Darwin is A. Desmond and J. Moore, *Darwin* (1991). For an introduction to childhood, see L. de Mause, ed., *The History of Childhood* (1976).

CHAPTER NINE

The interpretation above is based on C. Manceron, *Austerlitz* (1966). On Napoleonic warfare, D.G. Chandler, *The Campaigns of Napoleon* is an exemplary guide. On Austria-Hungary, C.A. Macartney, *The Habsburg Empire* (1968) is essential. T. Nipperdey, *Deutsche Geschichte 1800-66* (1993) and *1866-1918*, 2 vols (1991) provides an exhaustive guide to German history. Volumes in the *Oxford History of Modern Europe* are among the best on the nineteenth century histories of particular states, especially R. Carr, *Spain 1808-1975* (1982) and H. Seton-Watson, *The Russian Empire* (1988). The low countries are dealt with in F.E. Huggett, *Modern Belgium* (1969) and A.R. Zolberg, 'The making of Flemings and Walloons, 1830-1914', *Journal of Interdisciplinary History*, v (1974). On Italy, D. Mack Smith, *The Making of Italy, 1796-1866* (1968) and, for the subsequent period, M. Clark, *Modern Italy 1871-1982* (1984) provide helpful introductions. On Greece, R. Clogg, *A Concise History of Greece* (1992) and – more directly on the period – J. Campbell and P. Sherrard, *Modern Greece* (1968) are excellent surveys. On Ireland, R. Foster, *Modern Ireland* (1989) is the most admirable study of its subject. On Poland, the second volume of N. Davies, *God's Playground* generously covers the period; on the rest of eastern Europe, see Longworth, *The Making of Eastern Europe*. The Scandinavian countries can be approached through T.K. Derry, *A History of Modern Norway* (1973) and W. Glyn Jones, *Denmark: A Modern History* (1986). The best political history of nineteenth century Europe is probably now R. Gildea, *Barricades and Borders: Europe 1800-1914* (1985).

F. Fernández-Armesto, ed., *The Times Guide to the Peoples of Europe* (1994) helps to make sense of the background to nationalism. M. Hurst, ed., *States, Countries, Provinces* (1986) is suggestive. See also M. Biddiss, 'Nationalism and the Moulding of Modern Europe', *History*, lxxix (1994), pp.412-32. On Jews, S. Almog, *Nationalism and Antisemitism in modern Europe* (1990) provides a short overview.

The details on Chartists come from P.A. Pickering, 'Chartism and the "Trade of Agitation" in Early Victorian Britain', *History*, lxxvi (1991), pp.221-36. A. Arblaster, *Democracy* (1994) is an introduction to the concept. On Leo XIII, I found L.P. Wallace, *Leo XIII and the Rise of Socialism* (1966) interesting. Vast studies of Hugo and Comte can be found in A. Decaux, *Victor Hugo* (1984) and M. Pickering, *Auguste Comte: An intellectual biography*, 1 vol so far (1993). A lecture delivered in 1946, L.P. Namier, *The Revolution of the Intellectuals* (1992), continues to dominate the historiography of 1848. On socialism, see J. Droz, *Histoire générale du socialisme* (1972). Peasant history is introduced by W. Rosener and T.M. Barker, *The Peasantry of Europe* (1994).

CHAPTER TEN

The concept of civil war derives from E. Nolte, *Der Europaische Burgerkrieg 1917-45* (1989). The biography with the most convincing picture of Hitler is N. Stone, *Hitler* (1980). My quotations are from *Hitler's Table Talk*, ed. H.R. Trevor-Roper (1973). On Tukhachevski, see V. Alexandrov, *The Tukhachevsky Affair* (1963). My introduction to this figure was provided by J.F.C. Fuller, *The Decisive Battles of the Western World*, 2 vols (1970), ii, pp.405-28. On aspects of fringe Nazism, see A. Bramwell, *Blood and Soil* (1985) and, for some of their origins, P. Weinding, *Health, Race and German Politics between National Unification and Nazism* (1989).

Futurism is studied in P. Hulten, ed., *Futurism and Futurisms* (1987). On Japanese influence on art, I rely chiefly on S. Wichmann, *Japonisme* (1981).

L. Albertini, *The Origins of the War of 1914*, 3 vols (1952) is still the most comprehensive work on the combatants' motives, but see also A.J.P. Taylor, *How Wars Begin* (1980) and M. Howard, *The Causes of Wars* (1984). Among many excellent accounts of the war, M. Gilbert, *The First World War* (1995) provides a good and meticulous narrative. The account above of post-war 'nervous disorders' is adapted from *Millennium*. On Freud, see also R. Wollheim, *Freud* (1991) and on war poetry, P. Fussell, *The Great War and Modern Memory* (1977).

On the Russian revolution and the early history of Soviet Russia, the work of E. H. Carr is summarised in *The Russian Revolution from Lenin to Stalin* (1980), which can be set alongside S. Fitzpatrick, *The Russian Revolution*, 1917-32 (1982). I. Golomshtok, *Totalitarian Art* (1990) is an outstanding study of its subject, ranging beyond Europe.

E. Wiskemann, *Europe of the Dictators* (1985), first published in the sixties, surveys the inter-war scene. Valuable contributions on particular areas include: C.L. Mowat, *Britain between the Wars* (1968) – another enduring work; D. and M. Johnson, *The Age of Illusion: Art and Politics in France 1918-40* (1987); J. Willett, *The Weimar Years: A Culture Cut Short* (1986); H. Seton-Watson, *Eastern Europe between the Wars* (1986). Of the Spanish Civil War, H. Thomas,

SELECTED FURTHER READING

The Spanish Civil War (1986) is the fullest single volume account. P. Preston's monumental *Franco* (1994) is indispensable, but J.P. Fusi, *Franco* (1987) remains valuable. The account of *La Pasionaria* above is taken from *Millennium*. On the circle of Anthony Blunt, A. Boyle, *The Climate of Treason* (1979) is revealing. The paragraphs above on the relationship of fascism and socialism are adapted from *Millennium*. See also K.E. Popper, *The Open Society and its Enemies* (1947), S.J. Woolf, *Fascism in Europe* (1981) and P.M. Hayes, *Fascism* (1973). N. O'Sullivan, *Fascism* (1983) is succinct and sees fascism in a broad time frame. On Mussolini, C. Hibbert, *Mussolini* (1973) makes delightful reading, while D. Mack Smith, *Mussolini* (1993) is enjoyable, authoritative and convincing. On the Dreyfus affair, see P. Bionbain, ed., *La France de l'affaire Dreyfus* (1994) and J. Bredin, *The Affair: The Case of Alfred Dreyfus* (1986).

The French experience in the Second World War can be approached through J. Lacouture, *De Gaulle*, 3 vols (1970), which is also helpful for topics covered in chapter 11 above. For narratives of the war, J. Keegan, ed., *The Times Atlas of the Second World War* (1989) and J. Keegan, *The Second World War* (1990) are particularly useful.

H. Thomas, *Armed Truce: The Beginnings of the Cold War* (1986) is the best introduction to the post-war international scene. P. Duignan and L.H. Gann, *The Rebirth of the West: The Americanisation of the Democratic World* (1992) is an engaging exploration of post-war culture. R. Rhodes, *The Making of the Atomic Bomb* (1986) is the most comprehensive study of its subject, but for the specifically European background, see S.R. Weart, *Scientists in Power* (1979) and T. Powers, *Heisenberg's War* (1993). The fall of the Soviet Empire has already generated a huge bibliography, among which T. Garton-Ash, *We, the People* (1990) and I. Banac, ed., *Eastern Europe in Revolution* (1992) have helped set the terms of debate. My allusion to Duck Soup is owed to the excellent summary P. Longworth provided in *The Making of Eastern Europe*. The remarks on counter-colonisation towards the end of the chapter are taken from *Millennium* and were influenced by E. King, ed., *Mass Migrations in Europe: The Legacy and the Future* (1993). On Suez, see K. Kyle, *Suez* (1991) and, from the French side, C. Pineau, *1956: Suez* (1976).

CHAPTER ELEVEN

Good biographers seem attracted to the Marquis de Sade: I found R. del Quiaro, *The Marquis de Sade* (1994) perceptive. F. Hayek, *The Fatal Conceit: The Errors of Socialism*, ed. W.W. Bartley (1988) is the essential critique of socialism. See also W. Brus and K. Laski, *From Marx to Market* (1989). R. Skidlesky, *John Maynard Keynes*, 2 vols (1992, in progress) is the standard life.

On existentialism, A. Fontana and J.A. Kotarba, ed.s, *The Existentialist Self in Society* (1984) provide selected readings and M. Warnock, *Existentialism* (1979) a sensible introduction. The sixties from a British perspective appear in B. Masters, *The Swinging Sixties* (1985) and an idea of fashion from N. Drake, ed., *The Sixties: A Decade in Vogue* (1988). The great book by D. Worster, *Nature's Economy* (1994) should be the starting point for any study of the history of ecological ideas; A. Bramwell, *Ecology in the Twentieth Century: A History* (1989) is good on the period it covers.

A.M. Pazos, ed., *Un siglo de catolicismo social en Europa* (1993) and P. Misner, *Social Catholicism in Europe* (1991) deal with the background from which the Christian socialist tradition emerged. The anecdote on p.198 is from J. Barkan, *Visions of Emancipation: The Italian Worker's Movement since 1945* (1984), p.197.

On the revival of regional feeling and of historic communities, see *The Times Guide to the Peoples of Europe* (1994) and R. Acuña, *Las tribus de Europa* (1993). On European integration, see B.F. Nelsen and C.G. Stubbs, *The European Union: Readings on the Theory and Practice of European Integration* (1994), F. Duchêne, *Jean Monnet* (1994) and D.W.P. Lewis, *The Road to Europe* (1993).

INDEX